MW01140399

Modernity at the Edge of Empire

Modernity at the Edge of Empire

State, Individual, and Nation in the
Northern Peruvian Andes, 1885–1935

David Nugent

STANFORD UNIVERSITY PRESS

STANFORD, CALIFORNIA

Stanford University Press
Stanford, California
© 1997 by the Board of Trustees of the
Leland Stanford Junior University

Printed in the United States of America

CIP data are at the end of the book

Last figure below indicates year of this printing:
05 04 03 02 01 00 99 98 97

To Victor Santillán Gutierrez,

Ricardo Feijóo Reina, and all the others

who risked so much to make a reality

of el pueblo

Preface

This study is the product of many years of research and reflection, in both Peru and the United States. In the long course of completing the work I have accumulated a great many debts, personal and professional. It is impossible to thank everyone who has helped me along the way, but numerous are those who have encouraged me to develop and refine my ideas, and who have provided much-needed criticism as I attempted to work through my material. In particular, I want to thank Sr. Victor Santillán Gutierrez, whose experiences as one of the original organizers for the APRA in Chachapoyas in the late 1920s and 1930s added a unique perspective to the book. Despite his advancing age Sr. Santillán tirelessly spent day after day with me over a period of years, drawing on his keen intellect and his vast store of knowledge to explain fine points of the history of Chachapoyas, to provide crucial background about key individuals long since dead, and to alert me to the significance of developments that would otherwise have remained obscure. It is no exaggeration to say that this study would not have been possible without Sr. Santillán's cooperation. I am equally indebted to Dr. Carlos Torres Mas, friend and *compadre*, and director of the *Instituto Nacional de Cultura* for the department of Amazonas. From virtually my first day in Chachapoyas in December 1982, Dr. Torres put all the resources of the institute at my disposal. During my numerous stays in Chachapoyas he was instrumental in solving the many mundane and not so mundane personal and professional problems that inevitably arise during fieldwork. In particular, however, I wish to thank him for his assistance during my two extended periods of fieldwork (December 1982–November 1983; December 1984–December 1986). It was during these periods that Dr. Torres helped me gain access to the archives that have acted as the basis of the present study: the *Archivo Prefectural de Amazonas* (whose documents have since become housed in the archive of the *Subprefectura de la Provincia de Chachapoyas*), the *Archivo de la Municipalidad de la Provincia de Chachapoyas*, the *Registro de Propiedades Inmuebles*, and the birth and baptismal records of the Catholic Church. More recently, Dr. Torres was instrumental in arranging access to yet another key archive, the *Archivo Notarial del Sr. Notario Público de Chachapoyas, Don Roberto Trigoso y Santillán.* Without the friendship and assistance of Dr. Torres, I would have been unable to complete the present work.

In addition to these two Chachapoyanos, a host of others were instrumental in bringing this study to a successful conclusion: Gabriel Aguilar Gallardo, and the entire Aguilar Gallardo family; Juana de Añazco; Asunta Burga Mas; Susana Caro; Victor Castilla Pizarro; Carlos Echaiz; Isabel Monzante de Villacrez; Padre Reategui; Padre Rodriguéz; Máximo Rodriguéz Culqui; Mariano Rubio Pizarro; Gilberto Tenorio Ruiz; Celso Torrejón; Zoila Torrejón Monteza de Zúbiate; Antonio Valdez Vasquez; and Nelly Zubiate Torrejón de Torres. My dear friend Roberto Lazo Quepuy, and the members of his extended family, although not Chachapoyanos, endured much hardship with me, and provided friendship and support that made my stays in Peru more like family gatherings than research trips. The same is true of Yolanda Díaz Mas, who cared for me as a mother would a son.

In addition to singling out these individuals, I would like to express my profound gratitude to all the people of Chachapoyas, who received me into their homes with graciousness and generosity, and endured endless hours of odd questions with uncommon patience and good humor.

I have been fortunate to receive very generous financial support for the present study. The research phase of the project was supported by grants from the Henry L. and Grace Doherty Charitable Foundation; Sigma Xi, the Scientific Research Society; the MacArthur Foundation Program in International Peace, Conflict, and Security, Doctoral Dissertation Award; the Fulbright-Hays Doctoral Dissertation Abroad Program; the National Endowment for the Humanities; and the Colby College Social Science Grants Committee. The writing phase of the project was supported by grants from the Wenner-Gren Foundation for Anthropological Research and the Program in Agrarian Studes at Yale University. I gratefully acknowledge the very generous financial and institutional support made available to me by all these institutions.

Papers in which ideas from the present work were first introduced to professional audiences were presented at the Program in Agrarian Studies, Yale University (in April 1993); as part of Yale University's Council on Latin American Studies Colloquium Series (in April 1993); at "Ethnicity and the Making of Nations in Latin America," a symposium held at the New School for Social Research (in May 1994) and sponsored by the Janey Program in Latin American Studies; and as part of "Labor, Citizenship, and the Concept of Rights," a panel held at the annual meeting of the Social Science History Association (in November 1993). I would like to thank the organizers of these symposia for inviting me to present the results of my research, and the participants for their probing comments and insightful criticisms.

I am also indebted to the following individuals, who read part of or the entire manuscript, or who commented on ideas in progress in ways that were important to the final product: Catherine Besteman, Tom Biolsi (who read the entire manuscript, and some chapters more than once), Christine Bowditch, Emília Viotti da Costa, Akhil Gupta, Angelique Haugerud, Constantine Hriskos, Deborah Kaspin, William W. Kelly, Catherine LeGrand, Mary Beth Mills, Stacey Pigg, Sonya O. Rose, James C. Scott, Gerald Sider, and Joan Vincent. I would also like to thank two anonymous reviewers for Stanford University Press, who read the manuscript with great care and provided invaluable criticism and commentary. Finally, I would like to express my gratitude to Muriel Bell, senior editor at Stanford University Press, who gave me crucial assistance throughout the entire process of bringing the book project to a close.

I am beholden in a very different way to Weisu Zhu Nugent. Throughout the two long years during which this book was written she accomplished what few other people could have. With very little at her disposal she managed virtually all aspects of a quite complex household with such competence and skill that she was able to create the warmest of living environments for the entire family. Without her calm support and her consistent care I could never have brought this project to a successful conclusion.

D.N.

Contents

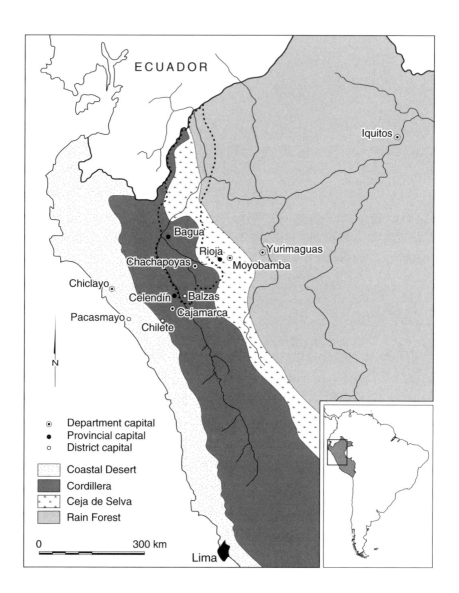

Map 1. Northern Peru

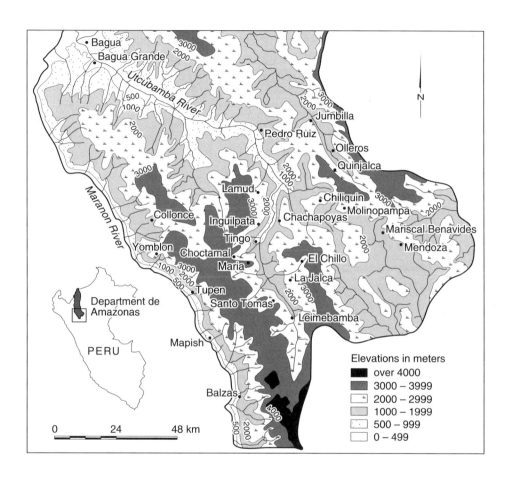

Map 2. Southern Amazonas

Modernity at the Edge of Empire

1 Introduction

Tradition, Modernity, Nation, and State

In the early afternoon of June 12, 1985, having finished lunch, I was ambling from my house on the edge of the Andean town of Chachapoyas toward the city center.[1] As I came within several blocks of the town square and market, I began to notice that something was amiss. People seemed not to be following their usual routine of slowly moving about the town, attending to their daily affairs, greeting each other as they passed. Something was drawing them in large numbers and at a rapid pace into the market area. Loud voices and angry cries could be heard emanating from the market, and it was clear that crowds were gathering around particular market stalls. Drawing nearer, I saw that the town's prominent merchants were the focus of attention, and that Chachapoyas's single television camera operator was standing to the side of one of their stalls, flanked by the town mayor and two policemen (*Guardia Civil*). The mayor was reprimanding the merchant who operated the stall in a condemning, moralizing tone while one of the policemen took notes and the cameraman trained his camera (a small, hand-held, "low-budget" device) on a small blackboard, where the day's prices for food staples were written in chalk. It seemed that the merchant had been caught charging prices higher than those allowed by the government, and the cameraman and the policemen were recording the evidence. The mayor continued on about the suffering that the townspeople were forced to endure because of the merchant's greed, singling out small children, single mothers, and all those whose incomes were insufficient for their needs (which after five years of runaway inflation included most of the people of the town), while the crowd hooted its approval and made threatening gestures at the merchant. Thereafter, one of the police-

1

men led the merchant away, while the mayor and the remaining policeman proceeded to the stalls of the town's other important merchants, repeating the drama, until a public spectacle had been made of each.

That same evening, the "surprise raids" on the merchants were shown on local television,[2] and were very favorably received by the townspeople. The conversations that came up later that night (mostly in the town's *cantinas*) in the wake of the broadcasts, and in days following, were but a continuation and elaboration of what I had been hearing about the town's merchant *forasteros* (outsiders; strangers) since my arrival during Christmas season in 1982. I reproduce several typical comments here.[3] The first contrasts what is seen as the "essential nature" of forasteros and *Chachapoyanos*:

> The *forastero* is a different kind of person than the *Chachapoyano*. He is not honorable or hospitable. He is an *egoísta* [selfish; antisocial]. The *forastero* lives in one place only—his shop! He almost never goes home. He doesn't really need a home. He spends every hour of every day in his shop, making money to make more money to make more money. [*Forasteros*] never do anything else. They never drink with us [the men], they never participate in religious processions, contribute money to town charities or sponsor fiestas [as *mayordomos*]. They even laugh at us for wasting our money on fiestas. They say we are lazy! They have spoiled our way of life. They only take from the town and its people, and never give anything back.
>
> The *Chachapoyano* is a *conformista* [which, in addition to conformity also implies agreement, harmony, and compliance]. He is honorable, generous, and hospitable. Unlike the *forastero*, he likes to spend his time with his family and friends. . . . And unlike the *forastero*, he lacks the spirit to risk, to risk his capital in business. He is content with things as they are.

Other comments bear on the disintegration of community life and values stemming from the intrusion of a modern, external world perceived as dangerous, polluting, and atomistically individualizing—a world thought to have been brought to Chachapoyas by the forasteros:

> Groups of *forasteros* come in with the trucks, get drunk in the *cantinas*, and then beat people up. You used to be able to go anywhere at any time and never be afraid. . . . The *forasteros* have also brought in *drugs* and have infected the local girls and boys. Girls used to be chaste here. Not anymore!

Before the roads arrived [from the coast, in 1960–61] the society here was cut off from the outside. The people were innocent and naive. Not now! Things have changed a lot here. Most of the good families have left. . . . The *forasteros* have brought with them the ideas of the outside world. Young people, especially, have changed. Many do drugs that the *forasteros* have shown them how to use. Today people have "woken up." They are *mas vivo* [aware, clever, but also crafty and unscrupulous].

The *forasteros* have come here with machines that make things much faster than we can by hand. They are not really carpenters, though. They are businessmen. They have no interest in the quality of what they make, but only in the quantity of what they sell. They deceive people, lying about when they can finish orders, knowing that they have months of work to do before they can start anything new. But by lying, they also insure that they never waste a moment of the working day. They are always at work. . . . As a result, they have seriously damaged the trust that our customers used to have in us, and have hurt the reputations of all carpenters. They have ruined our trade.

Since the coming of the roads the *campesinos* [peasants] have changed. They are no longer *sano* [wholesome]. Even their crops are diseased. . . . It used to be that you could trust everyone in town. There was never any need to guard your things or lock your doors. Now, the *campesinos* and *forasteros* steal. They break into people's homes at night when they are not there and they rob the houses.

As these statements suggest, a process of cultural differentiation is taking place in this region of Peru. People who think of themselves as "local" and "of the place" of Chachapoyas are attempting to fix a moral boundary between themselves and a modern, external world perceived as dangerous and foreign—one whose polluting individuality and self-serving greed have already done much to destroy a simpler, traditional, community-oriented way of life based on trust, honesty, respect for person and property, service to community, and a strong sense of sexual propriety.

The merchant forasteros epitomize this danger and disintegration to the local populace. So fundamentally alien do they seem to all things truly *of* Chachapoyas that local people have articulated a theory of their own to account for what are seen as the inherent differences between themselves and the "outsiders":

The merchants are too much like Jews. A friend explained to me why. He told me that one of the ten lost tribes of Israel came across the ocean in boats, sailed up the Amazon River and up the *Marañon* [River] to settle at Celendín [the town where most of Chachapoyas's important merchants come from; see Map 1]. The Celendinos act like Jews because they *are* Jews!

How have the forasteros managed to accumulate the considerable wealth that sets them off so clearly from local people? The following anecdote—repeated to me any number of times during my stay and applied without exception to every one of the merchant forasteros—can be regarded as the local consensus on this matter:

When Sanchez [one of the merchants from Celendín] came here in the 1930s he had nothing! He didn't even have a mule. He *walked* all the way from Celendín [a trip of eight days], and arrived looking like a peasant—dressed in a poncho, sombrero, and *llanques* [sandals made of rubber tire treads], *coqueando* [chewing coca leaves]![4] He brought with him only a little *añilín* [blue/indigo clothing dye] to sell. But in no time at all he had a big store and a beautiful house. How was that possible? How could anyone do that? Everyone knows he made a pact with the devil. [Anthropologist asks, "Does he still have this pact?"] No, now he and the other *forasteros* sell drugs.

The schism between Chachapoyano and forastero had reached alarming proportions by the mid-1980s. In addition to the televised raids already discussed, for the first time in anyone's living memory the police had been "forced" to use repression in order to break up a protest march. The march was led by market women and small *bodega* (grocery-store) operators, who were protesting price-fixing on the part of the handful of important merchant wholesalers who provided them with the staples that they sold to the public. Much of the local populace joined in this "anti-forastero" march as well.[5] The police used tear gas against the protesters in an act that was widely resented among the townspeople.[6] Shortly thereafter one of the merchants was murdered. At the time, an informant said to me:

You know, Hitler had reason to do what he did to the Jews [murder them]. Jews are not like other people. If you have a Jew for a neighbor and you are in trouble, the Jew will always stand by and just watch. It's because Jews are not concerned about anybody but themselves. They can't really *be* neighbors. They won't even help members of their own families. They spend all of their time working to get rich. Jews are interested in only one thing—making *money*![7]

The local populace has thus articulated a blatantly anti-Semitic, racist discourse to account for the differences between themselves and the forasteros—one that encompasses contrasting cultural experiences of time and space, and notions of proper personhood and collective behavior. One of the ways that the local, morally based community legitimizes itself as the real community is that it is said always to have been there. It is an unchanging, unchangeable essence—one that is in a sense outside of time because it is rooted to its original place. Its people attribute to themselves an essential nature. They are simple, uncomplicated, sincere folk who thrive on community and family and see their strongest obligation as being to one another.

The forasteros are also conceived of as a timeless essence, but one that is properly of another place. They are depicted as an intrusion, and a recent one at that. Within the context of Chachapoyas, they enter the realm of the impermanent and transitory. Their lack of autochthonous connection with the town of Chachapoyas—in short, their temporality—shows their lack of legitimacy. And their essential nature is said to be the opposite of that of local people—they are *self*-focused, mocking of community, ridiculing of tradition, and dismissive of family. Furthermore, they are obsessed above all else with a single overarching preoccupation—making money. Indeed, much of the contemporary folklore of the town revolves around showing that there is no social connection that forasteros attach more importance to than making money; that there is no form of personal misconduct that a forastero will not sink to—including lying and cheating, and even cavorting with the devil and selling drugs—in order to gain; and that there is no social obligation that a forastero will not forsake if it stands in the way of, or means a drain on, profit.[8]

This story appears at first glance to be a familiar one. We seem to be confronted here with yet another case in which a local, culturally distinct group of people seeks to defend itself from the alienating, individualizing, homogenizing processes by which modern nation-states are built—processes that in-evitably threaten cultural distinctiveness because they seek to integrate such culturally distinct groups into a unitary national community, economy, and consciousness.

Despite appearances to the contrary, however, we would be mistaken were we to interpret the case at hand in this manner. Chachapoyanos have not al-ways regarded the "outside world" in threatening, polluting terms—as some-thing against which they must defend themselves and their children. Rather, as will become clearer in the chapters that follow, in the not-so-distant past much of the local populace regarded commerce, accumulation, and "civilization" in precisely the opposite terms. These "things modern" were regarded with a kind of millenarian awe, as having the potential to help usher in an era of pro-ductivity and prosperity that would benefit one and all. Such a perception led to a radically different understanding of local community, and of the relation between community and "outside world":[9]

> Just as the cross is the symbol of mankind's spiritual redemption, thus is the highway the torch that brings moral and material well-being to the pueblos. . . . In those regions where the roads are good, the farmer has within his reach better markets, better schools, better stores, and better means with which to amuse himself and to effect the good society. (*Amazonas* I, no. I: I)

> Why is [the region] found in . . . such a lamentable state of backwardness? What is the cause of it being left behind other departments? Why does it not progress? . . . Because of the lack of good roads that would allow it to de-velop its industries and export its products to the coast. (Ibid.)

> Good roads expand the reach of civilization . . . and "cultivate" the spirit of progress in the pueblos. Good roads are the arteries of civilization, the best bonds of brotherhood among men. . . . Good roads reduce selling time, im-prove life, promote exports, and bring the best markets within reach. . . . Roads also improve the spiritual and moral conditions of the people by broadening their boorish and provincial lives. . . . Roads expedite work of all kinds, intensify and extend commerce, exorcise hunger and ignorance, [and] establish the basis for public tranquility. . . . Roads increase the value of land [and] promote industries. . . . They conquer rivers . . . and convert the steaming jungles and the frozen wastes into money. (Ibid.: 2)

In the 1920s and 1930s the people of Chachapoyas did not present themselves as a bounded, moral community that was averse to risk, thought little of monetary gain, submerged the individual into the group, and sought the security and protection of "natural" community bonds. Instead, they expressed their most heartfelt desire to integrate with rather than separate from the broader, national context, which was seen as a source of prosperity and progress rather than corruption and decay.

The unconditional positive regard with which Chachapoyanos held commerce, accumulation, and civilization in the 1920s and 1930s cannot be understood outside the context of a more general cultural movement of the era—one in which modernity and nationhood both played central roles. Circa 1930, important sectors of the local population revealed attitudes toward modernity and nationhood that mirrored their perceptions of commerce and accumulation. Actually, the expansion of commerce was seen as one element of a more general movement toward modern nationhood. It was this broader movement that was regarded as having enormous emancipatory potential. Excerpts from the local newspaper *Amazonas* will help illustrate local perceptions toward "things modern" and "things national":

To the Nation:
   In the Oriente of Peru there is a department that, despite the amazing fertility of its soil, the variety of its products, the spiritual richness of its children, and its infinite yearning for progress, writhes in backwardness and abandonment. . . . We refer to the department of Amazonas . . . whose political authorities [are] men without ideas and lacking in sentiment . . . who struggle ceaselessly over the right to exercise power . . . [who] allow women to be jailed, men to be flagellated, and the most intimate sanctum of human dignity to be sullied. . . . [Amazonas is] a region where not even a single stone is moved in the interest of progress, where the very air . . . is poisoned by traditional hatreds, by morbid passions, and by bastard ambitions . . . where a free man cannot live because he feels oppressed, because he will not resign himself to sacrificing his dignity . . . to [authorities] who hang like a curse on the collectivity. [Such a place] cannot, should not, ever call itself . . . a department of Peru. (*Amazonas* 4, no. 19 [1929])

We will endeavor to gain some of the privileges that . . . our happy brothers of the Occident . . . already have . . . the newspaper that illuminates, the investment capital that accumulates, the rights of citizens, and the library that is the source of perpetual light . . . and thus lessen the difficulties of our . . . isolated situation. We do not know when [we will succeed] . . . but we will go in pursuit of the ideal, confident in . . . the efficacious and unswerving assistance of the public will. (Ibid. 1, no. 1 [1926])

As will become increasingly clear in the pages that follow, in the 1920s and early 1930s most Chachapoyanos viewed not only commerce and accumulation but also state and nation as potential liberating forces in their lives. Indeed, as the quote above suggests, they identified the absence of strong state institutions and of authentic national sentiments as the source of the region's problems, and pleaded directly with the central government to establish a greater presence in the region. So strongly did Chachapoyanos feel about the emancipatory potential of modernity and nationhood that many risked their lives in an armed uprising to break the power of the landed elite and thus join the community with the institutions of the nation-state. For only under the protection of such institutions, and only guided by authentic national sentiments, they believed, would they be free to realize their potential as individuals and as a community. This successful uprising—which deposed the aristocratic elite—was a key moment in the process of state-building, as only in its aftermath were state institutions able to attain autonomy and independence from local landed power.

Chachapoyanos' longing for communion with commerce, accumulation, modernity, and the nation-state confronts most discussions of state-building and nation-making with an important anomaly. For most such discussions are based on an implicitly oppositional model of state-society relations. In such models, building the nation-state is depicted as a process in which the state—through a combination of coercion and cooptation—must impose its central institutions and cultural/moral values on the recalcitrant local populations found within its boundaries, who resist the state by clinging to a myriad of oppositional, local identities.[10] These identities have been seen as "primordial" in nature, as representing "rationally manipulated strategies," and as constituted by colonial and postcolonial forces of domination.[11] Regardless of the source of cultural differentiation, however, analysts agree that the dilemma the state faces in centralizing fully is that it is perceived as "imposed" and lacking in legitimacy by those it seeks to control. It is thus forced to rule by coercive means, which in turn results in a further lack of legitimacy. The dilemma the state faces in forming a national consciousness, therefore, is how to convince these many oppositional groups to abandon their local identities, and to join the community of the nation.[12]

Analysts' emphasis on state efforts to "nationalize" (Fox 1990a) those who live within state boundaries stems in part from the recognition that national cultures generally seem alien and contrived to the various groups that the state seeks to "assimilate" into the national community (Gellner 1983; Hobsbawm 1990)—because of which national traditions are highly contested, must be carefully constructed and maintained, but are inherently arbitrary and imposed phenomena.[13] Indeed, if the state is to succeed in constructing a viable national culture, it is argued, one of its primary tasks is to render as natural these cultural constructions which necessarily appear alien to much of the population living within the boundaries of the state.

In seeking to explain how the artificial has been made to appear natural in the making of national cultures, analysts have had recourse predominantly to Gramscian notions of cultural hegemony,[14] and Foucauldian arguments concerning institutional practices and technologies of power.[15] Corrigan and Sayer (1985: 4), for example, in their brilliant and influential analysis of English state formation, write:

> Out of the vast range of human social capacities—possible ways in which social life could be lived—state activities more or less forcibly "encourage" some while suppressing, marginalizing, eroding, undermining others. . . . We call this moral regulation: a project of normalizing, rendering natural, taken for granted, in a word "obvious," what are in fact ontological and epistemological premises of a particular . . . form of social order.

Similarly, Cohn and Dirks (1988: 225) argue that "the legitimizing of the nation-state proceeds . . . by constant reiteration of its power through what have become accepted as natural (rational and normal) state functions." Analysts may differ in which theory of "naturalizing the artificial" they draw on to explain how states nationalize their populations, but they share the assumption that some such form of "mystification" is essential to the making of national cultures.[16]

The national community is most effectively made to appear as part of the natural order of things, it is argued, by attributing to it and its inhabitants both permanence and distinctiveness. National cultures therefore depict themselves as organic communities, each of which represents a distinct kind of human essence. The essence may be presented in terms of singular cultural/linguistic characteristics, biological features, or some combination of the two.[17] Regardless, all who truly belong to the community necessarily partake of this essence, whereas those who do not are depicted as "out of place" (Bauman 1989). They more properly belong to/in a different natural, national community. A fundamental unity is therefore posited among those who make up the nation; each citizen is said to embody/metonymically represent what is essential about the nation as a whole.[18]

This emphasis on national distinctiveness and homogeneity of citizenship means that boundary maintenance is a key issue in the production of national cultures. The boundaries of the national community must be clearly and unambiguously defined, and great care must be taken to protect against "pollutants" who threaten the nation's integrity (cf. Douglas 1966). Threats may be cultural/biological in nature—as when large groups of non-nationals residing within the national community are perceived to be threatening to or diluting of the national essence (Haraway 1989: ch. 3; Bauman 1989; Denich 1994). Threats may also be of an explicitly *spatial* nature—as when the territory of the nation is perceived to be under attack from without. Indeed, one of the key features of national cultures is their claim to a clearly bounded, homogenous national space[19] within which the organic community of the nation is said to reside. As if to leave no question regarding its authenticity, this natural, territorial community attributes to itself a "deep history"—it claims always to have existed, to be an eternal, timeless entity.

In an effort to understand how it has been possible to naturalize such an obviously arbitrary and artificial cultural construction, analysts have stressed the ways that state institutions and technologies of power have remade the worlds inhabited and thought by the members of national communities (Lofgren 1989b; Mitchell 1988, 1991; Borneman 1993). Particular emphasis in this regard has been given to changes in the organization and conceptualization of space (via national parks and monuments, mapping, the media, and education[20]); the rewriting and recasting of history and prehistory (via education, media, ritual, and scholarly endeavors, as well as by reordering space[21]); the

standardization of language,[22] and the production of modern forms of subjectivity and citizenship (by means of the institutional gaze of state institutions[23]).
The combined effect of these forces, it is said, has been to structure everyday
life and thought in such a way as to render as natural the improbable, arbitrary, and contingent claims of national cultures.

Analysts emphasize that the particular cultural forms that become hegemonic as a national culture are anything but given. Rather, the production of
a national culture is the outcome of a struggle among various groups, each of
which endeavors to impose its own version of truth on the others, often by
"conquering" state institutions. In other words, national cultures must be actively *produced*.[24] Furthermore, once produced, national cultures remain anything but static. Rather, there is a constant and ongoing process of contestation, accommodation, marginalization, etc., in which different groups strive to
make their own voices heard—in which hegemony emerges out of struggle.[25]

The present book arises from a dialogue with this approach to building
states and making national cultures. For despite the groundbreaking nature of
much of the work cited here, and the undeniable importance of the processes
it discusses, I would argue that it leaves key aspects of state- and nation-building unaddressed. These neglected aspects of building states and making national cultures are particularly germane to understanding the historical development of state and nation in postcolonial Latin America, and I focus on them
in the chapters that follow. I do so by exploring the social processes that culminated in the modern Peruvian nation-state consolidating territorial control within the Chachapoyas region—a peripheral section of the national space
in the northern sierra—circa 1930. Unlike much work on building states and
making national cultures, however, this analysis does not examine state-making and nation-building from the perspective of state institutions, discourses,
and practices per se. Rather, my focus is a particular regional population in
the northern Peruvian Andes—the people of Chachapoyas—and its relationship to the project of making the nation-state.

National culture did not come to Chachapoyas in the form of alien beliefs
and practices that had to be naturalized by the institutions of the state. And if
people were mystified into accepting the arbitrariness and artificiality of national culture, this represents a case of "self-mystification"—one that occurred
beyond the gaze of state institutions. In Chachapoyas history was remade,

space was reconfigured, and subjectivity was reimagined *prior* to the state establishing any independent, institutional presence in the region. Furthermore, these imaginings took shape in the minds of marginalized subaltern sectors of the population—those usually depicted as having to be coerced, molded, or mystified into becoming national citizens. In addition, in reimagining themselves in this way, and in reaching out to embrace the nation, in no sense did these subaltern groups abandon local identities to become part of an undifferentiated, national essence. To the contrary: These subaltern groups looked toward identification with the nation precisely because of the distinctive kind of *local* community they understood themselves to be—because of the kind of *local* essence they believed themselves to represent. And they insisted that the central government establish a more direct presence in the region in order to help preserve and protect this essence—in order to help these groups realize their potential as a distinct regional community. Local and national forms of community and identity thus mutually constructed and enabled one another in this region.

Having succeeded in bringing the nation into the locale, and the locale into the nation, Chachapoyanos made no attempt to conquer state institutions or to impose their own local cultural understandings on the rest of the national community. They were quite content with "mutual coexistence" between region and nation. And finally, it was only because these subaltern groups embraced the national community—to the point of risking their lives in an armed uprising against the ruling landed elite—that the central government was able to establish any real institutional presence in the region. Only after the local population reimagined itself in modern form and actively sought out the institutions of the nation-state, then, was the state able to initiate the individualizing, homogenizing, institutional practices discussed at length in the literature on the making of national cultures.

In other words, the process by which state and nation took on a tangible presence in the Chachapoyas region inverts and reverses the scenario invoked by most analysts of state-building and nation-making. The present book is written in an effort to understand the reasons for as well as the implications of this inversion.

This work focuses on a social context in which commerce, modernity, and the nation-state were regarded as liberating rather than threatening forces—

forces to be embraced rather than resisted.[26] It will be argued that the regional community that generated such sentiments toward modernity and nationhood was a historically emergent phenomenon whose specific nature was contingent upon a complex field of interacting forces, from those within the locality, to those emanating more properly from the national arena, to those from beyond the territorial boundaries of the state. In order to understand how and why such a form of community came into existence in Chachapoyas, it is therefore necessary to reconstruct these evolving fields of relations.

This book thus attempts to identify a set of cultural-historical processes specific to late-nineteenth- and twentieth-century Peru that have made it possible for "things modern" to be seen as liberating and empowering.[27] This "promodern" moment in the region's history cannot be understood outside of the process of Peruvian state-building—conceived of in material/political and cultural terms—and the place of the Chachapoyas region within this process. Particularly important in generating such a response, however, was a qualitative change in the way that the state came to control this section of national space circa 1930. In order to understand how this transformation in state presence was effected, I first examine state-region relations, and the broader context in which the region was embedded prior to 1930. I then trace out the transformation of this pre-1930s organization.[28]

At the turn of the twentieth century, the emerging Peruvian nation-state was rent by contradictions of several different kinds. Although founded as an independent state in the 1820s on liberal principles of democracy, citizenship, private property, and individual rights and protections, the central government was not remotely able to make good on these arrangements even 100 years later. Although such principles were uniformly invoked in all political ritual and discourse, many parts of the country were organized according to principles diametrically opposed to these precepts of "popular" sovereignty. Chachapoyas was one such region. Dominating the social and political landscape of Chachapoyas was a group of white, aristocratic families of Spanish descent who saw it as their birthright to rule over the region's sizable mestizo and Indian peasant population. These elite families rejected all assertions of equality between themselves and the subaltern groups over which they ruled. Rather, the elite regarded and referred to themselves as a separate aristocratic caste—the *casta española*—that was naturally entitled to power and privilege due to its racial purity and cultural superiority.

Peculiarities of the Peruvian state during this period meant that the central regime in Lima, which lacked the ability to control the national territory directly during this period, was forced to ally with such aristocratic families if it was to maintain even a semblance of control in the outlying sections of its territory. Indeed, as a legacy of the *caudillo* politics of the post-Independence decades (as of the 1820s; see Bonilla et al. 1972; Gootenburg 1989; Wolf and Hansen 1967), and the devastation caused by the War of the Pacific (1879–83), at the turn of the century Peru was an internally fragmented polity.[29] The state apparatus was controlled by the Civilista party, which, during its period of dominance (1895–1919), represented the interests of select regional elites: north coast plantation owners who were involved in sugar production for the international market, mine owners (and those who provided services to the mines) in the central sierra who were also involved in export production, and Lima industrialists and merchants.[30] Not only was the mass of the population excluded from participation in the political process, but so, too, were the other regional elites scattered about the national space: mine and hacienda owners from the northern sierra, large estate owners in the central sierra, and wool merchants and hacendados from the southern highlands.[31]

The state maintained connections with these marginalized elites, and nominal control over the outlying regions in which they lived, through clientelistic ties with particular elite groups in each region (see Miller 1982; Jacobsen 1988). The strength and character of these ties, and thus the degree of autonomy from state control, varied considerably from region to region. In virtually all cases, however, much of the regional elite was denied access to political power; at any given point in time, the state favored only a few, at the expense of the remaining elite families. In many regions, this resulted in endemic conflict, as elites struggled among themselves to control the local apparatus of the state.[32]

In other words, although the state had been founded on precepts that had emerged out of the Enlightenment, the actual operation of the state apparatus depended crucially on maintaining social structures of the *ancien régime*. As a result, by the turn of the twentieth century, two opposed notions of legitimate political and social order—two different forms of sovereignty (Foucault

1980)—had been forced into uncomfortable juxtaposition in the Chachapoyas region, namely, aristocratic and popular sovereignty.[33] Each of these forms of sovereignty had its own totalizing vision of the social order, based on radically different ways of classifying social persons, of distributing material and nonmaterial rights and obligations among the social persons thus defined, and of mediating their social interactions. Each, that is, had a distinct way of controlling space, and of organizing the activities of people in time and through space. The cultural categories and the social relationships of aristocratic sovereignty acted as the foundation of everyday life. Aristocratic sovereignty was based on the assertion of fundamental, inherent, and qualitative differences among people who occupied the various categories of society. Distinctions based predominantly on race (Indian, mestizo, white), gender (female and male), ancestry (Spanish or not), and land ownership segregated the population into what were (in theory) fixed and inherited social categories that did much to prescribe the life possibilities of the people who occupied them. Roles of leadership and control in virtually all domains—economic, social, political, military, legal, and religious—were reserved for the white, male elite of Spanish descent (who likewise reaped most of the benefits of dominating the social order). These elite men were to watch over and safeguard those who occupied various "legal minor" categories—Indian and mestizo men, and women of all social classes—as these "minors" were not considered fully capable of looking after themselves. Those who occupied the status of legal minor were burdened with a range of category-specific obligations and limitations—material, social, and political. The ongoing public expression of one's relative status in the regional social order was encoded in forms of dress, in patterns of socializing and "cultural" affectations ("European" versus "Indian"), in deferential patterns of behavior and speech, in forms of livelihood, and in the ability to occupy important positions in public life. The sum total of these constantly reiterated distinctions helped lend an air of naturalness and inevitability to aristocratic sovereignty.[34]

The "modern" or popular notion of sovereignty, on the other hand, was advanced by the central government as providing the sole and exclusive set of terms by which national life would be organized. It was predicated on precepts diametrically opposed to the aristocratic order—on Enlightenment principles of equality, citizenship, individual rights and protections, and the sanctity of private property and individual labor, principles written into Peruvian constitutions since independence from Spain in 1824. The modern notion of order rejected (in theory) any form of inherent privilege as the basis of society. It posited a community of like individuals, each peacefully pursuing his (!) own self-interest to the greater good of all members of society. Popular sovereignty articulated notions of "progress," the "public good," and the community of citizens, equal in the eyes of the law, who made up "the nation."

Under popular sovereignty, in addition to being equal in the eyes of the law, all individuals were considered equally endowed with the right to use power—or, more accurately, all were considered equally powerless. It was the prerogative of no one to use power arbitrarily for his own purposes. Conflictual relations between "individuals" were never to be settled by the individuals themselves; rather, they were to be handled by the mediating institutions of the state. Under aristocratic sovereignty, on the other hand, it was not held that a separate state apparatus had the sole legitimate right to mediate conflict, to use force or violence. Rather, members of the most privileged stratum of society—the "aristocratic" white male elite of Spanish descent—saw it as their unquestionable, inherited right to occupy positions of power and influence, and to rule over their social inferiors. Furthermore, in order to be able to exercise these rights, members of the elite believed it was their prerogative to use force whenever necessary—against those who sought either to remove them from positions of power and influence, or to prevent them from occupying such positions.

Those who attempted to interfere with the exercise of elite privilege, including the central government, therefore did so at their peril—as is attested by members of elite families down to the present. In this regard, consider the following anecdote, related to me by an elderly member of the Echaiz family, one of the region's elite, aristocratic families:

> In August of 1930, [President] Leguía finally fell from power [in a military coup]. We received word from an ally in Lima by telegram, who told us to take the prefecture immediately. My grandfather [José María Echaiz], father [Eleodoro Echaiz], and uncles quickly assembled a very large group of followers and attacked the prefecture. The prefect at that time was Sr. Távara, an ally of the Rubio [the Rubio-Linch family], who along with his secretary and the military assistant of the prefecture quickly fled once the fighting be-

gan, so we had no difficulty in taking control. . . . My family had suffered for many years at the hands of the Rubio [the eleven-year period of the rule of President Leguía and his local clients, the Rubio-Linch], and my grandfather and father were very anxious to avenge themselves for all the outrages they had been forced to tolerate. After they took the prefecture, they attacked the house of Miguel Rubio [Linch], hoping to catch him and make an example of him . . . but he and [his brother] Arturo escaped to [their hacienda] *Boca Negra* [located just outside Chachapoyas]. Later, fearing my family, the Rubios left Amazonas. . . . With my father in control of the prefecture, we sent a telegram to Lima [to the Ministry of Government] informing them of what had happened. The reply came quickly—a new prefect had been appointed, and would soon be traveling to Chachapoyas. When my father received this telegram he became *very* angry, and immediately sent back his own reply: "*I rule in Amazonas!*" The new prefect never arrived. (Taped interview with Sr. Carlos Echaiz, Aug. 13, 1990)

There was a sense in which elite men regarded themselves as having no true peers, and certainly no masters. Rather, each believed he had the right to use power in defense of prerogatives that were legitimately his because of the elite station in life that he enjoyed by right of birth. No one—not even the state—had the right to interfere with these privileges.

The juxtaposition of these two opposed notions of legitimate order created several interrelated problems for the regional elite. To justify its claims to legitimately occupy the top of the aristocratic social order, it was of course necessary that such an order exist. The effort to reproduce aristocratic sovereignty absorbed virtually all aspects of elite life—from the uses to which wealth was put to the contexts in which armed force was applied to decisions regarding who was an eligible marriage partner. But although the elite was necessarily committed to reproducing aristocratic sovereignty as the "habitus" (Bourdieu 1977) of everyday life, for reasons explored in greater depth in the chapters that follow, the particular elite faction that controlled the apparatus of state was equally compelled to articulate state-endorsed notions of popular sovereignty in all public political ritual, and in all written political discourse, public and private alike. That is, the elite faction in power at any point in time was forced to offer public and private accounts of its deeds by invoking notions of equality, individual rights and protections, and the "common good" that not only directly contradicted its own actions, but also provided a critical commentary on the cultural and material logic of aristocratic sovereignty itself. Aristocratic sovereignty could not be celebrated, or even acknowledged, in formal political spheres. Popular sovereignty had to be celebrated, on an on-going basis, despite the fact that it had virtually no relation to any existing so-cial reality. Indeed, there was a conspicuous silence about the very existence of the aristocratic order in all political ritual and discourse.[35]

The ruling faction of the elite was thus in the odd position of having to reproduce aristocratic sovereignty in everyday life, but of having to invoke popular sovereignty as a way of explaining its "aristocratic" actions to society at large. The contradictions thus generated are captured in the following protest sent by a leading member of the Oyarce family—one of the oldest and most established in the Chachapoyas region—to the prefect of the depart-ment of Amazonas in 1924 (Oyarce belonged to a faction of the elite that had been driven from power five years earlier):

> For more than five years I have suffered the mortal hatred of my neighbor Sra. Laura Castañeda . . . who assisted by her sons Hector and Eloy . . . [makes] continuous attempts . . . on my life and that of my family. . . . On May 17, 1921, I was treacherously attacked by Hector . . . and others, all of whom were armed, and was seriously wounded. . . . On June 17 of the past year, in [a] public thoroughfare . . . and in the presence of Sra. Laura Cas-tañeda . . . Eloy attempted to shoot my nephew . . . who, miraculously, was able to escape this attack. . . . [Eloy] and ten other men have [also] had the cowardice to make an armed attempt on the life of my young son Estanró-filo, who is only a boy. . . . Not only our lives but also my family's economic affairs are subject to the furor of [this family] . . . and their followers who, armed with Winchester carbines and Mauser rifles, continually lay waste to my properties, killing and carrying off my livestock. . . . [Due to] the danger to my life and to the lives of those dear to me, I write to demand the indi-vidual rights (*garantías*) that the Constitution grants to all its citizens. . . . I can scarcely believe that at a time when our national culture has reached such an advanced state, scenes occur that belong more properly to the medieval epoch, for nothing else can explain the attitude of my . . . enemies, who have set themselves up as the arbiters of a life I do not owe them, as the ar-biters of my economic affairs and of my individual labor. ([APA15], no. 142)

When placed in context, this document expresses one of the central contradictions of state-society relations in the period before 1930. From Sr. Oyarce's protest, one would suppose that regional society in Chachapoyas was organized along the familiar lines of liberal democracies—in which citizens enjoy individual rights and protections, the rule of law obtains equally for all, and private property is sacrosanct. Indeed, according to Oyarce, only because his neighbors adopt highly aberrant behaviors that belong to a long past "medieval" era is it necessary for him to demand what all citizens ordinarily enjoy —the individual rights and protections guaranteed them by the Constitution.

Ironically, however, Sr. Oyarce's document emerged from a society characterized overwhelmingly by the very "medieval" privilege Oyarce deplored, one that bore no relation to the egalitarian principles Oyarce invoked. As mentioned above, regional society in Chachapoyas was divided into fixed and inherited socioeconomic strata, based on race, ancestry, property ownership, and gender, that were far from equal in any terms—economic, social, political, cultural, or even juridical.

Sr. Oyarce himself, for example, was the head of a family that was one of a small handful that made up the region's true elite. All of these elite families claimed descent from Spanish colonial forebears, prided themselves on the racial purity of their families, and carried family names of truly noble bearing.[36] All saw it as their exclusive, inherited right to rule the region free from the interference of the "common" people—to enjoy the many material and cultural benefits to which people of noble standing were naturally entitled. All went to great lengths to insure that neither their bloodlines nor their family names were tainted by admixture with "commoners"—either the despised *runa* (a derogatory term referring to "Indian" cultivators; from the Quechua for "people") or the *cholos* (urban mestizos), whose labor and product provided the elite with much of its wealth. Even social interaction with such people was kept to a minimum, and was structured in such a way as to require public subservience from the subaltern. Such deference was but one of a host of highly visible public markers whose combined effect was to proclaim the legitimacy of an entire system of privilege and hierarchy.

To invoke Enlightenment principles of equality and justice in a social context where hierarchy was naturalized and legitimated daily, and in which the very constitutional guarantees in question were an obvious fiction for all, would seem either disingenuous or absurd. And yet Sr. Oyarce's plea to be accorded his individual rights was far from unique. During periods when the political faction to which they belonged was not in power, similar appeals for justice came from "citizens" of each of the region's ascribed social categories—Indians, mestizos, and white elite, male and female alike.[37] In no sense, then, did those employing the *language* of equality and individuality even remotely resemble a true community of individual citizens, equal in the eyes of the law. Nor did they make any attempt to become such a community. Rather, those out of power used these Enlightenment notions strictly in private discourse with state officials, in an attempt to protect themselves, their belongings, and their families.[38]

In the early 1930s, the aristocratic order of Chachapoyas came undone. Key in bringing about its demise was the emergence of a subaltern social movement that mobilized around principles of citizenship, equality, progress, and individual rights and protections—principles that had long been invoked in political ritual and discourse, but that stood in glaring contradiction with the organization of everyday life. In the context of massive dislocations in culture and economy occurring across the country, the movement seized on this radical disjuncture between ritual language and social action in order to elaborate a telling critique of the existing state of affairs. It did so by affirming the legitimacy and reality of the egalitarian principles invoked by the aristocratic families, and by pointing to the elite's consistent betrayal of these principles. That is, the movement asserted that the region *did* have a general interest, that it *could* progress, that its people *did* have common enemies, and that they *could* build an effective future for themselves. They could do so by rising up against the aristocratic families, whose incessant struggles for power and domination had constantly undermined the common good of region and nation alike.

This movement attracted much of the local populace, who were drawn to the appeal made by the movement for regional unity, moral behavior, social justice, and national integration. In 1930, at a moment of crisis in the national political order, those involved in the movement succeeded in overthrowing the region's ruling elite faction in an armed uprising. Thereafter, the newly ascendant middle sectors used their recently won strength to create a new kind of public culture in Chachapoyas—one based on the egalitarian principles of popular sovereignty. As a result, by the late 1930s, the "medieval" order had been done away with, and what is referred to locally as the "*democratización*" of social life had largely succeeded.

It is the process by which the aristocratic order of Chachapoyas was replaced by what local people call a "democratized" form of society—and thus by which the modern nation-state of Peru assumed a tangible existence in Chachapoyas—that forms the substance of this book. More specifically, the present work focuses on three interrelated themes. First, it examines the juxtaposition within the Chachapoyas region of the two contrasting modes of political legitimation to which Sr. Oyarce referred in his plea to the prefect— "feudal" (aristocratic sovereignty) and modern (popular sovereignty). That is, it analyzes the ways in which notions of equality and of individual rights and protections were integrated into a regional social order in which neither individuality nor equality (in the contemporary, Western sense) existed—in which hierarchy and the arbitrary use of power were the realities of everyday life. Second, it traces the ways in which these same notions of individual rights, in the context of radical social and political transformation, became the basis for articulating an entirely new political and cultural order—one that subverted the existing terms of legitimacy and presented a serious challenge to the existing state of affairs. Third, the book analyzes the ways in which the newly ascendant middle sectors, once in control of regional affairs, used their recently established position of dominance to eliminate the host of material, behavioral, and symbolic markers of distinction upon which the aristocratic order had been based. The book thus concludes with an examination of the processes by which the formerly marginalized social sectors of the region mobilized among themselves to create a new cultural order based on the precepts of modernity and nationhood.

After placing Chachapoyas in its geopolitical context within Peru at the turn of the twentieth century, Chapters 2 and 3 present an overview of the contradictory and countervailing forces that characterized the "aristocratic" social and political order alluded to above. Chapter 4 then offers a more detailed analysis of the operation of the aristocratic order during the period prior to the first movements toward democratización. Chapter 5 presents an analysis of the way in which the regional elite managed the state-endorsed discourse of popular sovereignty, which actually strengthened and reinforced aristocratic control of the region—but which ultimately contributed to the elite's undoing. Chapter 6 begins with an analysis of the massive changes in economy and polity experienced throughout Peru in the early decades of the twentieth century—changes that contributed much to the disintegration of the aristocratic order within Chachapoyas. It finishes with a discussion of one of the two movements of democratización that emerged in Chachapoyas, and of the way that the participants in these movements seized upon the notions of popular sovereignty long present in political ritual and discourse in order to challenge the aristocratic order. Particular attention is paid to how movement participants attempted to create an alternative cultural order to challenge the hegemonic assertions of the aristocratic elite, and thus to unite the region's marginalized social elements. Chapter 7 discusses the second of the two movements of democratización that emerged in Chachapoyas in the late 1920s, and the cultural order imagined within the movement that presented its own alternative to the aristocratic order. Chapter 8 begins with a discussion of the national and regional forces that led to the breakdown of the aristocratic order in Chachapoyas; it concludes with a consideration of the ways in which the formerly marginalized middle sectors seized control of the region by force of arms, and thereafter helped construct a new cultural order based on the egalitarian principles of popular sovereignty. Chapter 9, the conclusion, draws out the broader implications of the analysis. It begins with a brief summary of the arguments of the book as a whole, highlighting the ways in which the nature of state-building and nation-making in Chachapoyas inverts and reverses the scenario of these processes invoked by most analysts. The chapter finishes with an explanation of why these processes took on an inverted form in Chachapoyas. This explanation is grounded in the historical development of state and class structures in postcolonial Latin America, and in the ways that the forces of modernity articulated with these evolving structures.

2 State, Region, and Casta

The Chachapoyas region lies on the eastern slope of the northern Peruvian Andes, within the Cordillera Oriental, midway between the high mountain sierra to the west and south and the Amazon rain forest to the east and north (see Map 1). During the period under consideration (1885–1935), the region may be said to have straddled a geopolitical fault line of sorts, simultaneously occupying the margins of two major political-ecological zones whose integration was of capital importance for the viability of the Peruvian territorial state. That is, in addition to having had considerable regional integrity of its own (see below), Chachapoyas had important lines of connection with, but also bases for separation from, each of these two zones. The first of the zones was the core of the state itself, lying to the west and south of Chachapoyas, centered on the national capital of Lima and encompassing Peru's dry coastal desert and rugged, mountainous spine. Chachapoyas's ties to this zone were of considerable historical depth, the town having been founded in 1538 as part of the initial process of Spanish conquest (Zubiate Zabarburú 1979) and having been a regional center of some import throughout the colonial period (Aguilar Briceño 1963). Chachapoyas was also intimately involved with the making of the independent Peruvian state. The battle of Higos Urco, fought (on July 6, 1821) by local inhabitants against Spanish loyalist forces during the Wars of Independence, was decisive in driving the loyalist army out of the entire eastern part of Peru and in consolidating control of the northern sierra for the opposition (Aguilar Briceño 1963; Basadre 1968–69, 2: 261–62). Chachapoyas's commitment to the preservation of Republican Peru is reflected in its response to the War of the Pacific with Chile (1879–83), which directly threatened national integrity. Despite the fact that the region was not occupied by Chilean troops, and was never directly threatened by the conflict, Chachapoyas both fielded a volunteer "regiment" during the war and contributed a considerable sum of money to help support the war effort.

The strength of Chachapoyas's ties to the Republican state, however, was mitigated by its geographic and administrative remoteness from the state center. Separating the region from national political-economic forces to the west was (and is) the canyon/valley of the Upper Marañon River. At its greatest extremes, this canyon is over 10,000 feet deep, and represents a mammoth natural obstacle to integrating efforts. The first road suitable for motor traffic was not completed across the canyon until 1961. Prior to that time, it could be crossed only by mule, by means of a circuitous and difficult trail. In 1930—the decisive year in which the central government began to make its presence more immediately felt in the Chachapoyas region—travel time by mule between Chachapoyas and the nearest city to the west (Cajamarca) was eight days in good weather (see Map 1). Trips to the national capital in Lima commonly took as long as one month, and involved a combination of travel by mule, train, and ocean steamer (see Nugent 1988: 73–109). This isolation meant that the goods and labor of the Chachapoyas region were effectively prevented from intermingling with those of regions farther west, and thus that the regional economy was very inward-looking.[1]

Chachapoyas's ties to the other main political-ecological zone—centered on the jungle city of Iquitos—were more recent.[2] During the latter decades of the nineteenth century and the first decade of the twentieth, the rubber boom helped define new political and economic relations throughout the Amazon basin (Weinstein 1983; Brown and Fernandez 1991). In Peru, the center of the new extractive economy was the city of Iquitos, which began to act as a magnet not only for rubber and its profits, but also for labor, investment capital, and a wide range of foodstuffs and other products from throughout the jungle regions of Peru.[3] Chachapoyas was located geographically on the margins of this new extractive economy. Unable to produce rubber itself, and separated from Iquitos by hundreds of miles of jungle and as much as a month of difficult, dangerous travel, it was able to participate only minimally in the expanding economy of rubber.

Other connections to Iquitos, however, were of considerable importance.

Attracted by the economic boom in rubber, several of the wealthiest families of Chachapoyas had moved to Iquitos by the turn of the century (maintaining residences in both towns),[4] a number of Chachapoyas's sons had journeyed there to seek their fortunes, and trade networks connecting the manufacturing centers of Europe with the jungle capital reached as far as Chachapoyas. Indeed, by the turn of the century, Chachapoyas was subject to growing cultural influence from Iquitos,[5] and the landed class relied on the trade networks that passed through the rubber capital for many of the luxury goods whose conspicuous consumption and display was such an integral part of elite culture. A few brave souls from Chachapoyas tried to ship cattle on the hoof over the precipitous trails of the eastern slope of the Andes to lowland river ports with steamer connections to Iquitos, but they met with limited success (Nugent 1988: 73–109). Thus, as was the case with regions to the west of Chachapoyas, despite the existence of important lines of connection, for the most part the goods and labor of the region were not able to participate in the growing markets of the rubber economy. This fact further reinforced the inward-looking nature of the regional economy.

Chachapoyas had long been the key administrative center from which central state efforts to maintain an administrative presence in its northern jungle regions had emanated. Indeed, state monies to support its thin bureaucracy in the northern jungle area were funneled directly through Chachapoyas via the heavily used mule trail that ran from Cajamarca north and east through Chachapoyas, and then continued still further east as far as Yurimaguas (and beyond via river transport), connecting jungle in the east to sierra and ultimately coast in the west. Thus, although Chachapoyas occupied a key position with regard to the integrity of the state in northern Peru, it was characterized by powerful centripetal tendencies, and at the turn of the century was as strongly pulled in the direction of Iquitos to the east as it was integrated into the national state to the west.[6]

Chachapoyas's marginal position with respect to both of the political-ecological zones it straddled combined with features of the local ecology and a distinctive pattern of land distribution to make for a singular form of political control in the region. The region lies within the northern reaches of the Cordillera Oriental, in an area where the Cordillera has splintered off into sub-chains that extend fingerlike, but in an irregular and broken fashion, toward the rain forest in the northeast. These circumstances make for an exceptionally rugged and precipitous terrain throughout much of the Chachapoyas region (Aguilar Briceño 1963: 10–24).

Punctuating the landscape further are two turbulent rivers that drain toward the Amazon rain forest, each carving in its path a steep canyon/valley (see Map 2). The larger of the two is the Upper Marañon—one of the major tributaries of the Amazon River. The canyon/valley of the Upper Marañon defines the western perimeter of the Chachapoyas region. The semitropical floor of the river canyon lies at an elevation of less than 1,000 meters. The highest parts of the canyon reach elevations of over 4,000 meters, well above the tree line, where the high *punas*, well known from other parts of Peru (called *jalcas* in the Chachapoyas region), are encountered. Because of the steepness of the canyon/valley walls, between these two extremes is found a great range of microecological zones quite close to one another. Peasant villages and elite estates in the Upper Marañon canyon/valley tend to encompass as wide a variety of these zones as possible. The tendency toward "multizonality" is a familiar pattern in the Andes (Brush 1977; Mayer 1985; Murra 1972; Orlove 1974).

Continuing east and north from the high crest of the Marañon River canyon/valley (from its eastern side), the terrain begins to slope toward the Amazon rain forest. The topography in this section of the region is made unusually rugged by the canyon/valley of a second river system, the Utcubamba. The headwaters of the Utcubamba are found to the south of the peasant village of Leimebamba. The river itself runs in a northerly direction for approximately 72 kilometers before it turns toward the northwest at the town of Pedro Ruiz, to join the Marañon River at the town of Bagua. As one follows this watercourse northward from Leimebamba, it drops steadily in elevation, and at the settlement of Churuja, what had been a narrow canyon/valley opens up to become somewhat less constricted than it is in its upper reaches. From this point onward the environment becomes increasingly tropical. By the time one reaches Bagua, the canyon has opened up into a broad and fertile valley.

The section of the canyon/valley between Leimebamba and Pedro Ruiz—the heart of the regional economy of Chachapoyas—varies greatly in its physical features, in some places appearing as a steep, stone-walled canyon, in other places as an earthen valley with slopes of somewhat more moderate grade. In general, however, the more hospitable sections of the canyon/valley are found where small tributaries enter the Utcubamba, carving out narrow valleys of their own, and depositing small amounts of rich agricultural soil on the floor of the Utcubamba canyon (Aguilar Briceño 1963: 18). Throughout most of this Leimebamba-Pedro Ruiz section, the canyon/valley slopes upward on both sides of the river to elevations in excess of 3,000 meters.

In terms of the distribution of different forms of land tenure, one of the more important features of the Utcubamba canyon/valley is the elevation of its floor. Beginning just north of Leimebamba, the floor of the Utcubamba lies at slightly less than 2,000 meters. At the town of Tingo, 33 kilometers to the north, the valley floor has fallen to below 1,000 meters, and continues to drop steadily in elevation until it reaches 500 meters at the village of Pururco, roughly midway between Pedro Ruiz and Bagua. In other words, the entire section of the canyon/valley floor between Tingo and Pedro Ruiz supports a semitropical environment.

A number of the region's most important haciendas were located on the floor of this section of the Utcubamba canyon/valley, particularly in those small and scattered areas where tributaries had deposited alluvial soils richer than those of the nearby slopes and high jalcas. Access to these fertile sections of the valley floor was particularly important to the elite, as the region's most important commercial product—cane liquor—could be fabricated from the sugarcane that grows easily there. The haciendas were involved in the production of sugarcane as a cash crop on a minor scale, but like haciendas throughout the region, they devoted most of their efforts to raising basic food crops for subsistence purposes. Indeed, the defining characteristics of estates in this region—whether on the floor of the Utcubamba canyon/valley or in surrounding highland areas—included the small areas of land they cultivated, the restricted size of their peon populations, and their subsistence rather than market orientation (see Nugent 1988: 110–85).[7] Very few haciendas marketed basic food products in anything but minor quantities. Rather, the *maiz*, *frejol*, *papa*, vegetables, and *camotes* grown on virtually all of the estates were intended predominantly for the use of the hacendado and his family ([APA18]; [AMC3]).

Haciendas claimed many but by no means all of the small fertile areas scat-

tered along the riverbed of the Utcubamba. Along the river itself, and distributed on both sides of its canyon/valley, was a series of peasant villages.
These villages tended to be quite large in size—in terms of both land area and
population—and controlled far more in the way of land and labor than did
the relatively few haciendas scattered about the countryside. Although precise figures on land holdings for the turn of the century are not available, some
indication of the size of village domains may be gleaned from the areas of land
they claimed later in the century, when some were able to obtain the legal
status of *comunidad*.[8] The peasant villages of the Utcubamba ranged in size
from approximately 1,000 to over 30,000 hectares (Nugent 1988: 161–62).

Not all of this land was suitable for agrarian production. Virtually all communities included within their holdings lands with multiple uses that spanned
a variety of ecological zones—from lands along the valley floor, to prime agricultural lands lying at middle altitudes, to high pasture lands (Aguilar Briceño
1963). In addition, most communities also controlled areas of forest and scrub.
The size of their land holdings, and the fact that these communities possessed
a diversity of productive resources, meant that most produced the vast majority of foodstuffs they required for their subsistence. In addition to consuming
products grown on village lands, most community members marketed small
quantities of foodstuffs in the town of Chachapoyas. Indeed, as the region's
most important source of commercial demand for purchased food, Chachapoyas drew agrarian production of all kinds from the entire Utcubamba
canyon/valley.[9]

Unlike many other parts of Peru, then, in Chachapoyas the peasantry retained control over most of the region's arable land, and landed estates remained relatively modest in size (Nugent 1988: 110–85).[10] Furthermore, only
a small proportion of the peasant population lived within the confines of estates, or could be considered "captured" by estates (ibid.). The historical origins of this pattern remain obscure, but undoubtedly it was key that the regional economy was so introverted, and that little in the way of regional production or labor participated in external, commercial markets. In terms of the
ability to commercialize foodstuffs, peasant and hacendado alike were limited
to regional exchange networks and regional sources of demand. By far the
largest (and almost the sole) source of demand for purchased food was the
town of Chachapoyas. In 1876 Chachapoyas had a population of only 3,380

(Peru 1878: 577; by 1940 the population had grown to 5,145 people: see Ministerio de Hacienda y Comercia 1942). Limiting the demand for marketed foodstuffs among even these people was the fact that a number of the "urban" inhabitants of Chachapoyas owned small pieces of land themselves, on which they grew food for their own families.[11]

These conditions made for an extremely limited market for would-be commercial food producers. The lack of opportunity for profit via the sale of agrarian products, either locally or extralocally, meant that there was little reason for the privileged class to attempt either to wrest control of land from the peasantry or to harness much peasant labor.[12] Thus an important feature distinguished this landed class from many others: it was removed from the realm of production. In the Chachapoyas region, the elite extracted wealth from primary producers by means of a variety of secondary, tribute-taking mechanisms (see Wolf 1982: 73–100; in Chachapoyas, head taxes, taxes on occupations, and indirect consumption taxes, as well as various forms of extralegal extortion) rather than via primary, productive relationships. Control of these tribute-taking mechanisms depended on the ability to occupy political office.[13]

Because agrarian pursuits were not an important source of wealth, struggles within the region rarely focused on control of agrarian production processes, as they did in many other parts of the Andes.[14] Nor did conflict ordinarily revolve around attempts to exploit peasant labor.[15] Instead, the available documentary evidence for the period—in the form of court cases, official communiqués, denunciations, accusations, and petitions—reveals a regional social order in which violence was endemic. And though highly patterned in time and through space, this violence was not directed at productive processes or labor. Rather, in that the key to affluence and power was to be found in occupying political office, struggles were focused overwhelmingly on control of public positions, public spaces, and public activities. Because of the poverty of rural pursuits, it was as if influential families were being thrust out of the agrarian world and into the public, political world, where all threatened to collide in their efforts to become the single, privileged client of the central state.[16]

Pressure to control public spaces was further intensified because of the nature of elite self-image. As explained earlier, members of the elite regarded and referred to themselves as a separate, aristocratic caste—one whose origins, history, beliefs, practices, and even biology were said to be wholly distinct from the mestizo and Indian commoners who made up the bulk of the social order. Members of the elite saw it as their exclusive, unquestioned right not only to enjoy the many material and cultural benefits to which people of noble standing were naturally entitled, but also to occupy positions of power and to play influential and highly visible roles in public life. At stake in the intra-elite competition over control of public positions, public spaces, and public activities was therefore the ability of any member of the elite to live according to the privileged station in life that all members of the casta española considered their birthright. To be forced out of such positions and spaces—to be made not only economically marginal, but also socially and politically invisible—was deeply shameful for people whose self-conception was that of a hereditary elite for whom privilege and rule were legitimate aspirations and expectations.

During this period, however, there were few institutionalized mechanisms that could be drawn on to routinize the understandably fierce competition for these crucial public spaces. As a result, not only were the prerogatives of each elite family openly challenged by others on an ongoing basis, but each family employed any means necessary to claim as its own the privileges of the others. Struggles among the various elite families were thus continuous, and often violent.

In the absence of institutionalized, legitimate mechanisms for mediating relations among elite families, personal displays of power, generally by men, became the most common method. As a result, in addition to being continuous, ongoing, and violent, struggles were both highly gender-specific and intensely "personalistic." That is, a key means for men to establish and maintain position was to demonstrate the ability to meet and crush any challenges. The more a man was perceived publicly as potent and dangerous, the less likely it was that he and his family would be challenged, and thus the more secure was their position. The following—a complaint made by a leading member of the elite Hurtado family to the president of Peru in the context of difficulties the Hurtados were having controlling their elite enemy and counterpart Pablo M. Pizarro—can be taken as a fair description of elite behavior when dealing with adversaries.

The uncontrollable, bad-tempered, and rebellious character of this person [Pablo M. Pizarro] is well known to the Head of State. You will remember that in 1896, [when] he was deputy, he was captured in the port city of Pacasmayo in possession of contraband weapons, a grave crime for which he was imprisoned. . . . I have begun criminal proceedings against Sr. Pizarro . . . for various crimes, especially for publicly repudiating and showing contempt for me as a legally constituted political official. ([APA45], Sept. 6, 1907)

Male members of the elite thus sought to dominate and humiliate one another on an ongoing basis, to establish for themselves such a reputation of potency that all competitors would think very carefully before confronting them.[17] A reputation of this kind was most effectively established either by dominating and shaming opponents publicly, in highly visible, face-to-face confrontations, or by staging violent encounters that were widely discussed in public (successful or unsuccessful assassinations, ambushes, attacks, rapes, etc.; see Chapter 3). Each such act had a "demonstration effect" concerning the power of the man that committed it, and made ongoing, public statements to other men, and to society at large, about each man's capacity to rule.[18]

Again the behavior of Pablo M. Pizarro provides an apt example of this general tendency. The petition quoted below was written in the direct aftermath of a failed uprising organized by Pizarro's enemies, the Burga, to drive Pizarro and his allies from power (see Chapter 4 below). Even though Pizarro and his allies had vanquished their foes decisively and secured their positions, Pizarro was not satisfied. He felt compelled to make a personal statement about the risks involved in challenging him, and about his capacity to dominate all who opposed him. Furthermore, he did so in public—by humiliating a member of the opposition that Pizarro and his allies had so soundly defeated:

At this very moment, 11:00 A.M., having gone to the prefecture, Sr. Pablo Pizarro entered as well and with club in hand uttered the following words [to me]: "Coward, assassin, one day soon I will make you sweep up the Plaza." Hurling these injurious words at me he attempted to remove a revolver from his pocket in order to kill me, but he was prevented from doing so by the [military] assistant of the prefecture; I answered him saying that . . . I had never killed anyone, and wishing to avoid a scandal I chose not to speak with him any further and left. ([APA5], Apr. 27, 1913)

This is not to say that regional politics consisted of a Hobbesian war of all against all. Strategies employed by elite families to prevail in the context of this highly charged, competitive atmosphere resulted in the emergence of broad, multiclass political coalitions. Each of these coalitions consisted of a core of elite families and a large number of artisan and peasant clients scattered about the regional space. It was these coalitions which competed with one another to control the region. The contexts in which coalition members sought to dominate and shame one another, and the forms in which they did so, were functions of the changing fortunes of the coalitions to which they belonged (see Chapter 3).

The changing fortunes of elite-led factions depended in large part on their relationship to those who controlled the central state apparatus. For if the ruling regime in Lima was to maintain even a semblance of central control in Chachapoyas, it was forced to ally with one of these elite-led coalitions. In so doing, however, the central government of necessity excluded all other coalitions from positions of wealth and power. Marginalized coalitions responded by mobilizing against the central regime's client coalition, resulting in a pattern of violent attack and counterattack. In general, however, the means of violence the central government made available to the local coalition of its choice made it possible for that coalition to prevail over its enemies.

The relationship between the central government and its client coalition was not just one of political expediency—one in which each helped the other defend itself against common adversaries. This relationship also had important ideological dimensions—dimensions that reflected the historical process of anticolonial struggle that gave birth to Peru as an independent state. Peru was a particular kind of political entity: an independent nation-state that, like other nation-states established in the nineteenth century, was founded on Enlightenment principles of popular sovereignty. As the official representative of the independent Republic of Peru within the department of Amazonas, it was essential that the ruling coalition of Chachapoyas conform to and help reproduce the state's self-image as a modern, democratic republic—one that abided by the same principles as other modern nation-states. This meant that whenever the ruling coalition represented itself and its actions to society at large—particularly in political ritual and discourse—the exclusive language of legitimacy it could employ was that of popular sovereignty. That is, the ruling coalition was obliged to present as sacred principles that everywhere figured as the only legitimate bases of modern nation-states—citizenship, private property, individual rights and protections, and equality under the law.

As we have seen, however, everyday life in Chachapoyas was organized according to principles diametrically opposed to those of popular sovereignty. Indeed, rather than a mass of equivalent and identical citizens going about their private affairs, mutually respecting one another's rights and liberties in an environment of peace and cooperation, armed factions led by privileged elites did battle with one another to control the region by force of arms. Furthermore, the central government provided one of these factions with the means of violence that was the key factor in deciding the outcome of these struggles.

In other words, political rule was contingent upon the reproduction of hierarchical social forms that directly contradicted the egalitarian principles that legitimated political rule. Thus, if it wished to remain in power, the ruling coalition was compelled to demonstrate its ability to dominate, persecute, and humiliate its enemies in the most public of manners. At the same time, however, the ruling coalition was equally compelled to contribute to the reproduction of the state's image as a modern nation-state. As a result, when representing itself to society at large (in political ritual and discourse), the ruling coalition was forced to depict its violent and self-serving actions as stemming from a concern for individual rights and protections, equality under the law, the sanctity of private property, and the common good.

The environment of violence and competition fostered by inter-casta struggles to control the region thus formed the background against which state-endorsed notions of popular sovereignty assumed concrete meaning. Although the rhetoric of popular sovereignty put forth the exclusive set of terms in which political behavior could be represented, then, the significance of the rhetoric was not in its content per se, but rather in the identity of the persons who employed it and the contexts in which it was employed. Indeed, because the ability to rule depended on constant, public assertions of the capacity to dominate and shame the opposition—to violate the principles of popular sovereignty—those principles openly contradicted the exigencies of everyday life. Those who invoked notions of equality, individual rights, and the common good therefore did so only in specific and limited circumstances—and for reasons that belied the content of these very precepts.

The remainder of this chapter and the following two chapters discuss the ways in which alliances were formed, and in which competition and violence were structured, within the aristocratic order. These chapters also analyze the contexts in which the rhetoric of popular sovereignty was invoked, and the identities of those who invoked it. The intention is to convey to the reader not only the organization of power in everyday life, but also something of the contradiction between aristocratic and popular sovereignty that characterized the period as a whole. After a brief overview of the town of Chachapoyas in 1900, and of the political coalitions that emerged out of the above-mentioned process of elite competition, I will describe the central role played by patriarchal, elite marriage strategies, and by social identities that were highly gendered and racially marked, in constructing these coalitions.

NOBLE CASTAS AND POPULAR SOVEREIGNTY

The town of Chachapoyas is located along the eastern side of the Utcubamba River at an elevation of 2,334 meters, on a thumb-shaped piece of land formed out of the confluence of the Utcubamba and its major tributary, the Sonche. The town lies in a relatively dry basin, surrounded by forested hills to the south (called "Puma Urco"), dry buttes to the east, and dry, rolling scrub land to the north and west. In most places this dry basin is not well suited to agriculture. Indeed, prior to the arrival of the Spanish, there was no aboriginal settlement where Chachapoyas lies. What is true of most of the region holds for Chachapoyas and the surrounding countryside. Rather than large expanses of fertile agricultural land, one encounters relatively small pockets of good land interspersed with much more extensive areas of scrub and forest (Aguilar Briceño 1963: 10–24).[19]

Despite the fact that Chachapoyas is not well-suited to agriculture or livestock-raising, at the turn of the century by far the greatest concentration of haciendas was found in its environs. Like haciendas in the region as a whole, most of those near Chachapoyas controlled very little in the way of either cultivated land or peasant labor (see Nugent 1988: 110–85). With the exception of two (*El Molino* and *Quipachacha*), all produced food crops only on a minor scale for the use of the hacendado's family, and marketed little or nothing in Chachapoyas. The presence of such a large number of estates near the departmental capital reflected political exigency rather than economic rationality. For reasons hinted at above, and to be explored in more depth below, it was essential for elite families to maintain an important presence in the town of Chachapoyas itself. Otherwise, they were at a distinct disadvantage in the intra-elite competition to control the public sphere. At the same time, it was unnecessary for them to remain in the countryside for anything but relatively brief periods of time.[20]

In 1876, at the beginning of the period under consideration, Chachapoyas was a town of 3,380 people (according to the national population census of that year; see Peru 1878: 577). In a pattern not unfamiliar from cities and towns in other parts of Peru (Parker 1992; Sarfatti Larson and Bergman 1969; Stein 1986), the town's residents were divided into two distinct social strata. At the top of the social structure was the casta española, a group of white families of putative Spanish origin who claimed to be the descendants and heirs of the colonial aristocracy.[21] In addition to racial purity, high levels of education, and proper last names that bespoke their colonial heritage, one factor was key in differentiating the members of the casta española from the remainder of society: if they worked at all, those who belonged to this most privileged stratum of society performed exclusively mental rather than manual labor. The casta española was made up of hacendados, lawyers, doctors, clergy, officers in the military, and high-ranking political officials. They were people who led, ordered, controlled, and dictated (the casta española was also referred to as the *casta política*).[22] Indeed, members of this elite stratum controlled virtually all positions of public prominence—political, economic, religious, military, social, and educational.

In Chachapoyas, the casta española was not extensive. There were perhaps 40 estate-owning families that could reasonably claim elite status.[23] The leading fifteen or twenty of these families lived in large, fortified, two-story homes, the biggest with fifteen to twenty rooms, several interior courtyards, and two or three kitchens. In order to maintain such a household, it was necessary to retain a number of domestic servants, for the ladies of these families did not themselves do housework of any kind. Household servants were invariably peasant ("Indian") women, drawn from a family estate if possible, who usually lived in the house on a full-time basis.[24]

Beneath the casta española in the town's social order was a much larger group, referred to by the elite as *cholos* or *runa*—terms that were at times used interchangeably with *Indio*, an appellation that normally applied to peasant cultivators of the countryside. According to the census of 1876 (Peru 1878: 578), this group numbered about 2,200. These were people of "impure" racial backgrounds and little or no education, who could make no claims to elite status or background. Unlike the casta española, the cholos did manual rather than mental labor. They were the town's artisans, muleteers, small shopkeepers, cantina owners, market vendors, breadmakers, and lower-level public employees—the people without whom the mundane affairs of life would never have been performed. Unlike the elite, members of this amorphous middle sector were systematically excluded from positions of power, prestige, and influence. They followed rather than led, and obeyed rather than ordered.

Cholo and elite were raised to think of themselves as wholly different kinds of people, with distinct (and unequal) rights, duties, obligations, and privileges. Indeed, the social worlds of the two groups were almost entirely separate. In addition to the fact that one group performed mental and the other menial labor, and that one group controlled virtually all positions of power and influence while the other occupied none, the two groups also baptized their children in different churches, attended different churches themselves, and were ministered to by different priests. They even revered different patron saints.[25] Members of these two strata never socialized. Indeed, whenever possible the elite avoided interacting with cholos entirely. Cholos rarely had occasion even to go to the homes of the elite—unless it was to attend to some chore solicited by an elite patron, to work for an elite family, or to seek the assistance of a patron on a legal or financial matter. When a cholo did go to the house of one of the elite, he or she always entered through the side rather than the front door, never ventured inside the rooms reserved for receiving "proper" guests, and was rarely allowed anywhere but in the work areas of the house.[26]

Members of these two distinct social strata also had wholly different life courses. Elite children in general attended elementary school in Chachapoyas, then boys of the casta española attended high school either in the town's Catholic seminary or at an exclusive, private secondary school in Lima.[27] A boy would normally go on to train in one of the professions in the national capital, become an officer in the military, or (less commonly) join the clergy. During his sojourn in Lima a young man of the elite had ample opportunity to mingle with others of his class from around the country, giving him political connections of crucial importance once he returned to Chachapoyas. Upon his return, he would marry a young woman of one of the other great families (after a long, formal courtship and engagement; see below), and would take up his place as one of the leading members of local society.

Children of the middle sectors, on the other hand, had an extremely limited set of life possibilities. Most boys (and some girls) attended elementary school, alongside the children of the elite, but the two groups kept largely to themselves (it was not uncommon for elite children to ridicule their less fortunate classmates because they lacked school supplies, shoes, or new clothes). Relatively few children of the middle sectors ever began high school, and even fewer finished their secondary education. Those that did attend high school did so exclusively at the local *Colegio Nacional San Juan de la Libertad* in Chachapoyas.[28] A boy generally apprenticed himself in the trade of his father (or that of a maternal uncle) from an early age, and pursued this craft as his vocation rather than continue with his studies. Most middle-sector men eventually set up a household and had children by a woman of the middle class, but very few married.[29] As a result, it was not uncommon for a man to have children by a number of different women, few or none of whom he supported after he had stopped living with their mother. Similarly, women often had children by several different men during their lifetimes, from whom they received some support as long as they lived together.[30]

Members of the casta española would insist that those beneath them in the social structure demonstrate proper forms of deference and respect at all times. Upon encountering cholos, runa, and Indios in the streets of Chachapoyas, for example, members of the elite always expected that their social inferiors would step off the sidewalk to let their betters pass. If spoken to, members of the subaltern were to use proper terms of deference (*taitito* was the term most commonly used).[31] They were never to look members of the elite in the eye when addressing them, but rather were expected to look toward the ground with their heads bowed respectfully. Men were expected always to bare their heads whenever they encountered members of the elite.

Although barriers of race, culture, education, wealth, and breeding separated these social strata, political exigency dictated that the elite establish extensive clienteles among the cholos, runa, and Indios. For only in this way could they form political coalitions extensive enough to control the region.

The structure of political economy that emerged in this isolated region, at a time when the national polity was rent by major internal divisions, had a number of peculiar characteristics. First, elite families, each highly localized within the regional space, established fragile alliances with one another via marriage in an attempt to form broad coalitions that could effectively control the region. Second, these allied families and their peasant, artisan, and merchant clients formed unstable, multiclass political coalitions that competed with one another by violent means for control of the regional political apparatus. Third, such political hegemony gave the ruling coalition temporary control over the "legitimate" use of force within the region (the police and the judiciary), which enabled it to drive members of opposing coalitions out of all political positions, and to harass and persecute the opposition in a variety of ways (see below). Such ongoing persecution fragmented other coalitions, and thus helped enable, protect, and reproduce ruling casta efforts to dominate public life. Fourth, concurrent with its persecution of the opposition, the ruling casta adopted the central state regime's discourse of popular sovereignty, progress, equal protection under the law, and the "common good." This discourse and public image, however, blatantly contradicted the violent, personalistic, and competitive actions that characterized casta behavior in general—behavior that stemmed from the particular way that efforts to reproduce aristocratic sovereignty played themselves out in the region. Fifth, control of public space, and the ability of people and products to move safely through it, was shifting and insecure for people of all social classes, and depended on having numerous and strong political allies—none of which could ultimately guarantee the security of person and property. Sixth, state-endorsed notions of citizenship, individual rights and protections, the sanctity of private property and individual labor, and the equality of all citizens assumed concrete meaning only in relation to this shifting, violent, and competitive environment. Seventh, although much of the population was involved in moving goods and people between the jungle to the east of Chachapoyas and the sierra to the west—and a number of local people described themselves as merchants—commerce had little independent existence of its own.[32] Rather, it was subsumed within and was forced to obey the dynamics of a political-economic structure (discussed below) that operated according to a noncommercial logic.

Perhaps the most serious problem facing landed elite families, the majority of whom were intent on occupying a prominent place in the overall structure of aristocratic sovereignty, was how to "capture" the regional space, extract wealth from its primary producers (the peasantry), safely move themselves and their goods through the regional space, and enjoy the station in life to which all felt entitled, considering that elite properties were scattered piecemeal throughout the region in small, isolated fragments, that elite families controlled relatively little in the way of cultivated land and peasant labor, and that the "spheres of influence" of any elite family were very restricted in spatial terms.[33] The key to resolving the dilemma was to gain control over the local machinery of state, for in this way elite families could appoint clients to bureaucratic positions involving taxation, policing, and judicial functions throughout the regional space. Such control ensured a steady flow of revenue for the ruling coalition, gave it access to the armed force it needed to contain threats from other elite families intent on taking its place, made its members' efforts to move themselves and their goods through the regional space considerably more secure than they otherwise would have been, and assured the coalition's families of a highly visible and influential role in public life. In short, this control made it possible for elite families to live according to their own self-image and to achieve what they saw as their legitimate life aspirations.

As one might guess, elite families fought fiercely among themselves to control the state apparatus, and as a single family was too "localized" within the regional space, and lacked the broad connections and resources to accomplish this alone, families of the elite sought out alliances with their peers in order to form as broad and strong a coalition as possible. Such a coalition was known as a "casta," and was referred to by the name of its dominant families. The most important of these families were the Pizarro, Rubio, Burga, Hurtado, and Echaiz.[34]

The core of a coalition was formed by means of patriarchal strategies of marriage alliance. Senior members of the region's fifteen or twenty most powerful landed families[35] used the marriages of their sons and daughters to effect alliances of several different kinds in order to absorb otherwise "free-floating" resources and spaces into the family to whatever degree possible.[36] A primary strategy for these elite families involved allying via marriage with one or more of the region's other powerful families—with distinct spheres of influence in other sections of the regional space. In that the region was relatively undifferentiated in terms of its ability to produce commercial wealth,[37] potential marital allies were not evaluated with regard to their control of commercial wealth-producing zones. Rather, for this purpose, space was conceived in political-administrative terms. Most families had strength in no more than one of the department's three provinces (Chachapoyas, Luya, and Bongará), and only in sections of that province at that. In order to construct a coalition that could successfully control the department as a whole, a family needed strength in the other two provinces, where its presence was minimal (the most important provinces being Chachapoyas and Luya), as well as in those sections of its "home" province where it had little influence. Thus, this form of marriage alliance attempted to overcome the highly localized nature of even powerful families' spheres of influence by tying them to an equally powerful ally.

This alliance—out of which the core of the coalition was formed—was in many ways the most important but also the most dangerous, for it represented the union of otherwise separate, and potentially antagonistic, power blocks. Most commonly, a single marriage between two such families was insufficient to ensure the continuity of the alliance. According to informants (and borne out by the evidence), the preferred arrangement was for two powerful families with spheres of influence in distinct sections of the regional space to exchange daughters with one another, for in this way a kind of balance could be maintained between the families. As this arrangement was not always possible, however, at times two brothers from one family married two sisters of another (which implied client status for the family of the daughters). Less stable alliances were based on a single marital union.[38]

A second form of marriage strategy was used to build ties with families that made up a somewhat less central part of the coalition, and involved either marrying daughters into less powerful landed families scattered about the regional space (who thereby acknowledged their client status to the families whose daughters they married), or marrying daughters (or sometimes sons) into the families of influential individuals who were not necessarily members of the landed class—politicians and military men stationed in Chachapoyas by the central government, and wealthy merchants (and their "muleteer magnate" clients) who moved in and out of the region on a regular basis.[39] Alliances with these additional but less influential landed families increased the geographic scope of core families' spheres of influence. Marriage with state appointees gave the casta core some control over a potentially independent and dangerous source of power. And alliances with merchants (and muleteers) gave the coalition access to key resources that could only be procured far outside the region (weapons, most importantly), as well as the means necessary to transport them to Chachapoyas.

Alliances with individuals in all of these categories gave an elite family connections with and access to resources, contacts, and "spaces" that it could not develop on its own. At the same time, however, it was essential that each landed family preserve the integrity of its own landed core—which was under threat of becoming fragmented every generation due to laws of partible inheritance. Therefore, a third strategy pursued by older family members in building a strong coalition involved marrying their children to close relatives (generally second cousins, first-cousin marriage being prohibited by the Catholic Church) with properties near or adjacent to those of the family in question—thus reconsolidating its landed estate (if only partially) every two generations.[40]

One source of instability and fragility in elite coalitions was the conflict that the pursuit of any one of these three strategies often created with the other two. That is, there were built-in contradictions between the need to maintain strength locally, and the need to ally with and absorb into the family estate those outside the local sphere.[41] The fact that marriage was the mechanism by which these "externalities" were made internal, however, indicates the importance of patriarchy and gender-specific social identity in the politics of regional control, in the control of space, and in the ability to control the movement of people and products through space.

The existence of a social order that was highly stratified according to gender, race, ancestry, and land ownership was crucial to the ability to form coalitions that could control regional space—and to the ability to reproduce aristocratic sovereignty itself. Coalitions emerged as elite men—each of whom had strength in specific but limited sections of the regional space—combined forces to form extensive, noncorporate groups that could better advance the interests of all members. The control over select sections of the regional space exercised by an elite man was a function of the many retainers of "legal minor" status (Indian and mestizo men and women) who were drawn to such a man because the elite represented virtually the only means of access to the wealth, power, and protection so necessary to the well-being, and even survival, of the subaltern.

But the alliances made among elite men to form these broad coalitions were established almost exclusively on the basis of patriarchal marriage strategies—because a small group of privileged men had the ability to manipulate the lives of their daughters and sons to better realize their own political ambitions (as well as to protect the interests and to maintain the "good name" of the family and all its members). Elite marriage thus formed the entire basis of coalition organization in particular and political alliance in general. Only by establishing strong and lasting ties via marriage with other carefully selected elite families could noble elite families create even the possibility of living according to their own self-conceptions. Elite marriage thus represented an extremely important social relationship in terms of the regional power structure, whereas the gendered social identities upon which these strategies were constructed represented one of the key bases of the entire aristocratic order.

Due to its centrality in regional political life, elite marriage was surrounded with great pomp and ceremony, was subject to strict social conventions and controls, and had great bearing on the honor and reputation of the families involved. Some sense of the importance attached to elite marriage can be gleaned from a firsthand account of the activities of order and ritual surrounding a marriage that played an important role in uniting Chachapoyas's ruling casta—the Pizarro-Rubio—with another family of the region's true elite early in the present century.

A WEDDING

On July 17, 1915, Luis Felipe Pizarro Rojas (age 23; Person A, Figure 1) and Robertina Torrejón Monteza (age 21; Person B) were joined in holy matrimony in the main cathedral of Chachapoyas by the bishop of the diocese, Emilio Lisson.[42] The ceremony commenced at 8:00 in the evening, the customary hour for weddings of the elite, and took place in the presence of godfather Salomon Rodríguez (age 72; Person C: Luis's uncle, by marriage to his father's sister), godmother Rosa Rojas Mesía (age 58; Luis's mother's sister), close members of the family, and a large retinue of specially invited friends. The bride entered the cathedral wearing a white wedding gown that had been made in France, had been specially ordered by the Torrejón family, and had been brought to Chachapoyas at great expense with the help of relatives who lived in the rubber boom city of Iquitos in Peru's jungle region. In addition to its flounced sleeves, the gown had a train four meters long, which had to be carried aloft by four young ladies, or *damitas*. Three of the damitas were grandchildren of the godparents; the fourth was the daughter of close family friend and wedding ceremony witness Alberto Hernandez. The damitas were also attired beautifully, wearing dresses modeled on the bride's, but sewn locally by the Eguren Hernandez sisters, cousins of Alberto Hernandez, who were famous for their masterful confections.[43]

After the solemnities were over, the couple and their retinue left the cathedral and began a long, rather slow, roundabout procession through the lantern-lit streets of Chachapoyas, eventually ending up at the huge, eighteen-room, colonial-style home of the Torrejón family.[44] Along the way they were accompanied by over 200 elegantly dressed elite ladies, gentlemen, and their families (who would shortly enjoy the hospitality of the Torrejóns at an all-night reception). Bringing up the rear of the long trail of people was a large group of "common people," for whom such weddings were a social happening and diversion of considerable interest. Commoners who were unable to join in the procession (due to illness or advanced age), as well as elite families who were political adversaries of the Pizarros and Torrejóns (and thus had not been invited), watched the procession pass from their windows.

When the couple finally arrived at the heavy, large, wooden front door of the fortress-like Torrejón home and stepped across the threshold, they were

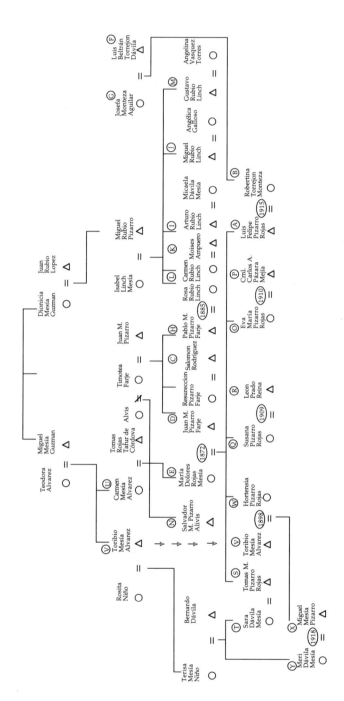

Figure 1. Marriage Strategies of the Pizarro-Rubio Casta

greeted by a group of finely dressed ladies who threw bunches of wild orchids in their direction—the flowers having been carefully gathered in sections of the high "cloud forest" outside of the town by peasant families that lived on estates owned by the Torrejón and their friends. Walking through this "hail of flowers," the couple entered one of the home's two large outdoor patios. In typical "colonial" style, the square patio was surrounded on the first floor by a series of rooms for receiving guests; a stairway led up to a second-floor balcony that continued around the entire perimeter of the patio (bedrooms and/or storage rooms were located off the balcony).[45]

When the couple entered the patio area, a band of the finest local musicians played a brief fanfare, called a "Diana,"[46] to announce the arrival of the newlyweds. As the couple posed for a photographer, the 200 or so invited guests that had made up the wedding procession crowded along the outside of the patio, up the stairs, and in every corner of the upstairs balcony to witness the events that were to follow. All wore their best attire, the women in fine dresses, the men in dress coats with tails, stovepipe hats, bow ties, white vests, and pocket watches with gold chains (Longines, wherever possible). All left generous gifts for Luis Felipe and Robertina with domestic servants as they entered the Torrejón home.

Godfather Salomon Rodríguez took his place in the middle of the beautifully decorated patio, just to one side of the fountain that was its centerpiece, and gave a memorable speech. French champagne (Cordón de Oro), which had been brought into Chachapoyas in huge quantity (and at great cost) by mule train from the coast, had been distributed to all the guests; led by Rodríguez, everyone toasted the newlyweds amidst shouts of congratulations.

The toasting temporarily over, the couple then took center stage in the patio and danced alone to a Strauss waltz played by the assembled musicians while family and friends looked on. Next the parents took turns dancing with the bride and groom, after which pairs of close relatives joined in the waltzing as well. More toasting with champagne followed, after which Robertina retired briefly to change into a dress appropriate for the night of dancing that was to follow.

Upon her return, the general party commenced, and guests crowded into the patio area in order to take part in the dancing. At this point the band began to play a wide variety of music popular with the national and local elite of this era—the French quadrille, the "one-step," the *famosa jota española de la corrida de toros*, the *waltz Peruano*, and the *marinera*.[47] And at midnight, to mark the success of the party and the joy of the event, the patio was cleared of guests and the bride and groom performed a ceremonial *Chumaychada* (a local, more elaborate form of the marinera) for all assembled.

The party continued well into the next morning, as did the dancing, drinking, and feasting. The Torrejón home's three kitchens and numerous domestic servants were hard-pressed to provide the assembled guests with the huge quantities of food and drink the reception required, but in the end succeeded admirably. The first round of food was served at 11:00 P.M., and consisted of coffee and baked finger food. At 1:00 A.M. a hearty soup and innumerable loaves of locally baked bread (in four varieties) were provided to the guests. At 5:00 A.M. another round of coffee was served, and at 7:00 A.M. the guests enjoyed a full breakfast buffet. Rumor had it that Robertina's older brother Eusebio had chosen five steers from the family's *Tincas* estate to be slaughtered for the occasion. Throughout the night and morning the guests were served prodigious quantities of locally produced alcoholic drinks (most of them made from sugarcane).

Although the party wore on into the early morning hours, and was accompanied by much drinking and dancing, at all times "proper" formalities and patterns of respect were strictly adhered to. If, for example, a young man wished to dance with a young lady, he first asked the permission of one of her parents, and he might easily be refused. It was not uncommon for families with daughters under twenty years of age to refuse to let them dance at all, or to allow them only a few dances with very select partners. Young men and women were not allowed to stray from the watchful eyes of their parents or relatives.

The marriage of the Pizarro Rojas and Torrejón Monteza families—which united two of Chachapoyas most established families, both of which were recognized as belonging to the casta española—was the culmination of almost two years of discussion, negotiation, socializing, and visiting. The father of the groom, Juan M. Pizarro Farje (Person D, Figure 1), first conceived of the marriage and, after discussing the matter with his wife, María Dolores Rojas Mesía (Person E), decided to approach Robertina's parents, Luis Beltrán Torrejón Dávila (Person F) and Josefa Monteza Aguilar (Person G), in October 1913. Once agreed on the feasibility of the marriage, the parents advised their respective children of the plan, and at this point were begun a series of parties, trips to country estates, moonlight guitar serenades, and other social activities—always under the careful supervision of both families—so that the young people could get to know one another. Six months later, when no extreme form of antipathy developed between them (even had it done so, it is unclear whether the marriage plans would have been called off), the future plans of the couple were formalized, and the families made the engagement known publicly. There were two separate ceremonies involved in formalizing the engagement—a family ceremony, in which the couple exchanged rings (with the godparents actually placing the rings on the fingers of the future husband and wife), and a public ceremony, which took place in the main cathedral.

With the engagement made official and public, for the first time Luis Felipe was granted what were called "free visitation rights." That is, for the first time he was allowed to enter the house of his future in-laws, and was allowed to visit his future bride, unannounced. The social space of the Torrejón home was thus opened to him as if he were less of an outsider. But even at this stage of the engagement the activities of the *novios* (the engaged couple) were carefully monitored. As was the custom, "visiting hours" commenced at 3:00 P.M. and never extended beyond 9:00 P.M. Even so, the young couple was virtually never left alone, an older (generally female) relative usually being on hand as chaperone, even within the confines of the Torrejón home. After six months of "preliminaries" and a formal engagement of fifteen months, the couple and their respective families were at last joined together.

This particular marriage connected the Torrejón family to an extensive coalition of allied families referred to by the local populace as the Pizarro-Rubio casta, which ruled the region from 1909 to 1930. Key in establishing and maintaining regional control was the ability of the casta to monopolize elected and appointed political positions for the department, for by this means the casta was able to establish an important presence in all sections of the regional space. Concerning elected positions, by the time of the wedding, Pablo M. Pizarro Farje (Luis Felipe's father's brother; Person H, Figure 1) was one of two senators for the department of Amazonas—a position he had enjoyed since 1909;[48] Pablo's casta ally and brother-in-law, Arturo Rubio Linch (Person

I), was deputy of Chachapoyas province; Arturo's brother, Miguel Rubio Linch (Person J), was deputy for Bongará province,[49] and Luis F. Martinez Pizarro (nephew of Senator Pizarro) was the substitute deputy of Luya province.[50] Thus, for all intents and purposes, by 1915 the Pizarro-Rubio casta had succeeded in monopolizing all elected political positions for the department of Amazonas.

The elected representatives of the Pizarro-Rubio casta were involved in a constant struggle with the central regime in Lima to control the distribution of the key appointed political positions of the region: departmental prefect, comptroller (*tesorero fiscal*), district attorney (*agente fiscal*), and the departmental heads of the region's two police forces (the *mayor de la Guardia Civil* and the *comandante de la Gendarmería*), as well as provincial subprefects, judges of the first instance (*jueces de la primera instancia*),[51] and provincial heads of the Guardia Civil and Gendarmery. The casta sought to consolidate and expand its power as much as possible by granting these posts to relatives and friends, while the state attempted to check the casta's pretensions toward expansion by filling the positions with career politicians from Lima.[52]

By 1915, however, the state had (temporarily) relinquished virtually all the key positions to the casta. By this date Moises Ampuero (Person K, Figure 1; husband of Carmen Rubio Linch [Person L], sister of the above-mentioned deputies of Chachapoyas and Bongará provinces, and sister-in-law of Senator Pizarro) was departmental comptroller (*tesorero fiscal*),[53] Gustavo A. Rubio Linch (Person M; brother of the above-mentioned deputies and brother-in-law of Senator Pablo Pizarro [Person H]) was subprefect of Chachapoyas province, while Juan M. Pizarro Farje (Person D; brother of Senator Pizarro, and father of Luis Felipe Pizarro Rojas, whose wedding ceremony was described earlier) was subprefect of Luya province.[54] Senator Pizarro and Deputies Arturo and Miguel Rubio Linch had also used their influence in Lima with the minister of justice to have *jueces de la primera instancia* (provincial judges) sympathetic to their cause appointed for the provinces of Chachapoyas and Luya-Bongará.[55] The judge of Luya-Bongará was Salvador M. Pizarro Alvis (Person N, half-brother of Juan and Pablo M. Pizarro Farje), who had long been a key member of the Pizarro-Rubio casta. Equally attuned to casta needs was the judge of Chachapoyas, Daniel Araña—relative of Iquitos rubber baron Julio César Araña—the latter being a close business associate of Miguel A. Rojas

Mesía (whose sister, María Dolores [Person E], was the wife of Luya subprefect Juan M. Pizarro Farje [Person D], and mother of recently married Luis Felipe Pizarro Rojas [Person A]).

Only the appointed positions of district attorney, departmental heads of the Guardia Civil and the Gendarmery, and the departmental prefect consistently remained in the hands of career politicians sent to the region from Lima during this period. The Pizarro-Rubio casta was able to absorb (generally via marriage; see below) or coopt a number of the most important of these appointees. Those that remained immune to the casta's overtures of alliance generally found their efforts to administer the region—and to check the unrestrained use of power by the Pizarro-Rubio casta—thwarted informally by the casta's extensive clientele and the ample resources it was able to command. Most of these career politicians spent a relatively brief period in their posts before demanding to be transferred. Indeed, as an active part of its socially recounted memory, the Pizarro family maintains the following tradition:

In 1913[56] the president [of Peru] . . . was [Coronel Oscar] Benavides, an old friend of my great uncle Pablo M. Pizarro, who was senator of Amazonas. The two had gone to military school together. . . . Benavides appointed a new prefect for Amazonas, who traveled from Lima to Chachapoyas, where he expected to begin his duties. My great uncle [who as senator was living in Lima], however, was opposed to the appointment . . . and when the new prefect attempted to take up his post he was informed that Senator Pizarro would not allow it; he [the new prefect] was denied entrance to the prefecture. After waiting for several weeks at *El Molino* [a hacienda of an opposing casta, located just outside Chachapoyas], he returned to Lima. Shortly thereafter the president called my great uncle into his office for an explanation. Challengingly, he asked my great uncle, "Who rules in Amazonas, you or me?" My uncle replied, "It looks like I do, doesn't it!" The president then told my uncle, "I am going to send an army battalion [to Chachapoyas]," to which my uncle replied, "The battalion will never enter the department, because I will have my men dismantle the bridge [across the turbulent Marañon River] at Balzas" [the only bridge joining Chachapoyas with the core of the state to the west]. . . . At this point Benavides . . . [and] my great uncle laughed, Benavides came around the table, and the two men embraced each other, and Benavides said, "Forget your vanity and do me a favor. I will put the prefect I chose in office for 24 hours, in observance with the law [the

man had already been appointed prefect, and thus had to be allowed to occupy the prefecture], and after the 24 hours [are over] you can choose whoever you want." (Interview with Sr. Mariano Rubio Pizarro, June 27, 1991)

By virtue of the fact that its members occupied these high-level appointed
positions, the Pizarro-Rubio casta also controlled appointments to a wide
range of lower-level administrative posts, which gave it an important presence
in virtually all sections of the regional space. Particularly important in this regard was casta control over the positions of subprefect and judge of the first instance.

A subprefect had extensive powers of appointment. In consultation with
the prefect, the subprefect chose the governors and lieutenant governors who
were the official representatives of the central state in the districts and subdistricts of the subprefect's jurisdiction. Along with the district-level justices of
the peace, these appointees administered people, helped collect taxes, mediated
disputes, organized public works, maintained "law and order," located fugitives
from authority, provided mule drivers for the transport of official travelers and
communications (when so ordered by the prefect or subprefect), and reported
on and contained any challenges to the existing regime on a daily basis. Because the Pizarro-Rubio casta succeeded in placing its leading members in all
three subprefectures, it was able to fill all governorships and lieutenant governorships with its clients as well.

In consultation with the deputies of the province, a subprefect also controlled appointments to all positions in education via his power to appoint a
provincial inspector of education. Each provincial inspector of education appointed all teachers and school administrators for every school in every district
in his province. In that teaching and administrative positions came with a
modest salary (and gave especially teachers the opportunity to call on their
students to provide them with labor services and "gifts" in kind), they were
much sought after, were filled with faithful clients, and helped expand the
webs of influence of the ruling casta.

In conjunction with the prefect and the chief of police of the provinces, a
subprefect also helped choose individuals to staff the region's two police forces.
Members of the Guardia Civil and the Gendarmery were usually concentrated in the capital of the province, along with the subprefect, and played a

key role in supporting not only his activities and decisions but also those of the governors and lieutenant governors outside the provincial capital (when the subprefect so instructed the police at his command).

A subprefect was also involved in appointments to the lucrative post of provincial tax-collector. The collection of most kinds of tax was farmed out to the *Compañía Nacional de Recaudación* (a state-endorsed, publicly owned entity that collected taxes for the central state on a commission basis) during this period.[57] The Compañía generally appointed its own departmental head (relying on nonlocal personnel), but relied on provincial-level appointees (who were usually local) to go through the countryside to collect the taxes due in each district (working in conjunction with the district governor). These individuals, who usually found it necessary to go about their work escorted by a group of armed policemen (who were partially beholden to the subprefect for their appointments), were in theory chosen by the Compañía's departmental head. In that provincial appointees had to rely on the armed force provided by the subprefect (as well as on the assistance of district governors, who had been appointed by the subprefect) in order to actually collect the taxes, however, the departmental head of the Compañía was forced to "consult" with the subprefect in making the appointments. Should the departmental head of the Compañía appoint someone who was not to the subprefect's liking, the latter would simply refuse to provide the protection necessary for taxes to be collected, or would instruct his governors not to cooperate with the tax-collection process (see Chapter 4). As a result, provincial-level tax-collection appointments generally went to prominent casta members.

Subprefects, then, were involved, directly or indirectly, in making the most important decisions regarding both who would do the day-to-day work of managing political life within their jurisdictions and who would be responsible for extracting wealth from their jurisdictions' primary producers.

A judge of the first instance did not have as broad a range of influence as a subprefect. He did, however, have the formal power of appointing justices of the peace for each of the districts in his jurisdiction (as mentioned above, a justice of the peace worked closely with the governor and lieutenant governors in managing day-to-day political life at the local level, and was the official representative of the Ministry of Justice within the district over which he presided). A judge of the first instance was also the highest criminal and civil magistrate in his province. He had great latitude to decide upon legal matters of all kinds with virtually no interference. He could unilaterally order that particular individuals be apprehended in any section of the regional space, and then jailed. Or he could unilaterally order that individuals already in jail be freed. He could choose to ignore cases brought to his attention, or to pursue cases with great zeal. In short, the ability to enjoy legal recourse depended in large part on one's relationship to the judge of the first instance. Appeal was possible only with the Court of Appeals of Cajamarca—located eight days' ride away (in good weather)—which rarely intervened in legal matters internal to Amazonas.[58]

Because the Pizarro-Rubio casta held all elected departmental positions, by 1915 it had managed to assert its control over all appointed positions as well. To the extent that its district-level appointees (governors, lieutenant governors, and justices of the peace) worked in concert, then, the casta could monitor the movements and contain the activities of members of the opposition with considerable efficiency. It could also prosecute, persecute, ignore crimes committed against person and property, manufacture evidence, and even seize and/or destroy the property of those who belonged to other castas—regardless of their social class. And to the extent that the ruling casta's provincial-level appointees (subprefects, judges of the first instance, and chiefs of police) and departmental appointees (the prefect, and the two departmental police chiefs) worked in concert, and cooperated with district-level appointees, the ruling casta effectively denied members of opposing coalitions any alternative to the structures of power they encountered within district arenas. The ruling coalition was thus well able to advance its own interests, and to contain threats from opposing castas.

This position of casta dominance had been built up in large part by means of a series of strategic marriage alliances—of which the marriage of Luis Felipe and Robertina described earlier in this chapter was but one example. That is, this particular marriage was one element of a much broader set of strategies pursued by the Pizarro-Rubio casta—and by castas in general—which had a "dual" character. As discussed earlier, it was essential that all members of the elite preserve the racial purity of their own families and mix only with other families of truly noble bearing. For the right claimed by the elite to rule over their social inferiors was in part culturally validated. It could be legitimated only by conforming to culturally defined rules concerning who was aristocratic (who, that is, was white, wealthy, and could legitimately claim Spanish ancestry) and how aristocratic purity had to be maintained.

At the same time, castas pursued marriage strategies that would allow them to advance their own interests, to safeguard the members of their families, to enjoy security of person and possessions, and to live according to the elite station in life to which all members of the elite believed themselves entitled. Juan M. Pizarro Farje and María Dolores Rojas Mesía arranged the marriages of all of their children with the goal of absorbing into the Pizarro Rojas family—which was itself part of the Pizarro-Rubio casta—resources, spaces, people, and connections that would not otherwise have been available to the family or the casta. For example, the family into which the Pizarro Rojas had just married in 1915—the Torrejón Monteza—owned small estates in several sections of the regional space where the Pizarro Rojas family had a weak presence (in various districts of Luya and Bongará provinces), and thus the marriage brought the Pizarro-Rubio casta access to additional spheres of influence in its attempt to maintain regional control.[59] As discussed earlier, marriage alliances with such elite but nonetheless "second-tier" families, who could help a casta overcome the spatially limited nature of its own spheres of influence, were key to building up a strong coalition.

There was an additional consideration in joining with the Torrejón Monteza family, however, that was of much greater importance to the Pizarro Rojas family and the Pizarro-Rubio casta as a whole. Luis Beltrán Torrejón Dávila, Robertina's father and the Pizarro Rojas family's new in-law, was an important local military figure. He was a colonel in the army (specifically, in the cavalry), had served with distinction in the War of the Pacific (1879–83), and thereafter had on several different occasions been the departmental head (*comandante*) of the Gendarmery. As an ally, he could provide important military backing for the Pizarro-Rubio casta.[60] As a foe, however, he could place his *contingente* (the contingent of people loyal to him) at the disposal of the opposing Burga-Hurtado casta, which, although out of power, was constantly hatching plots to challenge the hegemony of the Pizarro-Rubio.

The marriages of Luis Felipe's siblings attempted to realize similarly strategic goals of absorbing into family and casta important, and otherwise free-floating, resources and spaces. Several took place at key moments in the consolidation of the casta's position vis-à-vis the state and other castas. On New Year's Day 1910, five years prior to Luis Felipe's marriage to Robertina and less than a year after the Pizarro-Rubio casta had begun its ascent to a position of regional dominance, Juan M. Pizarro Farje and María Dolores Rojas Mesía married their 20-year-old daughter, Eva María Pizarro Rojas (Person O, Figure 1), to 40-year-old Colonel Carlos A. Pázara Mejía (Person P). Like Luis Beltrán Torrejón Dávila, Pázara was a military man. Unlike Torrejón, however, he was not from the Chachapoyas region. Rather, he had been appointed departmental prefect by the central government, and had come to Chachapoyas in February 1909 to replace the outgoing prefect, opposing casta leader Manuel Hurtado.[61] His marriage to a daughter of the Pizarro-Rubio casta signified an important victory for the casta, for the prefect—in his role as the highest-ranking representative of the central government in the entire region—exercised control over a myriad of departmental affairs. He was the ultimate arbiter of most forms of regional conflict, decided in whose favor and in which sections of the regional space the armed force of the state would be applied, and decided whose appeals for protection or redress would be acted on and whose would not. The timing of his marriage to Eva María was important for the casta as well. The fact that Pázara was able to put the machinery of state at the service of the Pizarro-Rubio casta so early in 1909 was a key factor in the casta's rise to power: it significantly reduced the threat from opposing castas, and made it that much easier for the Pizarro-Rubio to persecute and ultimately cripple their main enemies, the Burga-Hurtado and the Ocampo-Eguren (see Chapter 4).

Pázara's recruitment to the cause of the Pizarro-Rubio had an extra advantage. The prefect's brother—Alberto Pázara—had been sent to Chachapoyas at the same time as Carlos, and shortly thereafter become *mayor de la Guardia Civil*, or departmental head of the Guardia Civil. Because the new *mayor de la Guardia Civil* and his brother, the new prefect, were so closely tied, by means of the marriage of Prefect Carlos to Eva María Pizarro Rojas, the Pizarro-Rubio casta was able to transform two individuals whose positions represented potentially dangerous and resistant forms of outside power into important legitimizing links with the central regime in Lima. The marriage thus allowed the Pizarro-Rubio casta to absorb into itself the power of the central state, rather than have the state define and limit the activities of the ruling casta.[62]

Just months prior to the marriage of Eva María Pizarro Rojas and Colonel Pázara, the marriage of Eva María's sister, Susana Pizarro Rojas, provided the family with a different kind of resource, and a different set of connections, which were equally important in forming a strong coalition. On September 20, 1909, 19-year-old Susana (Person Q, Figure 1) was married to 35-year-old Leon Prado Reina (Person R). Like Prefect Pázara, Prado Reina was not native to the Chachapoyas region, but unlike Pázara, he did not have a military background. His family had moved to Chachapoyas from the southern city of Arequipa, and had acquired considerable wealth from involvement in long-distance merchant activities. The marriage link to Prado Reina provided the Pizarro Rojas family, and the Pizarro-Rubio casta, with an expanded set of market ties to the national economy located to the west of the Chachapoyas region.[63] Such ties were particularly important not only in giving the casta access to the luxury goods whose conspicuous consumption was such an integral part of elite culture, but also in procuring such essential goods as firearms, necessary to help maintain their position as ruling casta.

While each landed family used the marriages of its sons and daughters to overcome the geographic limitations of its own spheres of influence within the region, and to absorb into the family important military men and state political officials, it was also essential that each landed family preserve the integrity of its own landed core, which was under threat of becoming fragmented every generation due to laws of partible inheritance.[64] The marriages of the other Pizarro Rojas children were arranged with the goal of preventing this fragmentation. Tomas Pizarro Rojas's (Person S) marriage to Sara Dávila Mesía (Person T: his maternal second cousin) exemplified this. Tomas's maternal grandmother was Carmen Mesía Alvarez (Person U). His wife Sara's maternal grandfather was Carmen's brother, Toribio Mesía Alvarez (Person V). Tomas was thus married to his maternal second cousin. Siblings Carmen and Toribio Mesía Alvarez had inherited adjacent properties in Levanto district, sections of which had been passed down to their grandchildren, Tomas and Sara. The marriage of the second cousins thus allowed the reconsolidation of property divided between siblings two generations earlier.

Making the situation more complex, however, was the marriage of another of the Pizarro Rojas daughters. In October 1898, during an earlier period of Pizarro–Rubio ascendance, 18-year-old Hortencia Pizarro Rojas (Person W, Figure 1) was married to her own great-uncle, 69-year-old Toribio Mesía Alvarez (Person V: brother of her mother's mother, Carmen Mesía Alvarez [Person U])—the same man who was Sara Dávila Mesía's (Person T) maternal grandfather. Hortencia had inherited land formerly in the Mesía Alvarez family through her mother (María Dolores Rojas Mesía [Person E]), who had been left the property by her mother, Carmen Mesía Alvarez (Person U). As already mentioned, Carmen's brother Toribio, Hortencia's aged husband, had been left land adjacent to that of his sister Carmen. At the death of Toribio, Hortencia and her children would also be able to reconsolidate the lands formerly divided between Hortencia's grandmother, Carmen, and great-uncle (and husband), Toribio. In this way, lands divided between Carmen and Toribio Mesía Alvarez were reconcentrated in the hands of two siblings of the Pizarro Rojas.[65]

Preservation of the landed core of the family estate was further reinforced, however, by means of the marriage of Miguel Mesía Pizarro (Person X), the only son born to Hortencia and her aged husband/great-uncle Toribio. In 1918 Miguel was married to Meri Dávila Mesía (Person Y), sister of Sara Dávila Mesía and maternal granddaughter of Toribio. Meri thus stood in an unusual relationship to her husband, Miguel: her grandfather (Toribio Mesía Alvarez [Person V]) was Miguel's father![66] She had inherited land through her grandfather Toribio, as Miguel had from his father (also Toribio). Upon receiving their inheritances, the children of Miguel and Meri would thus be able to recombine pieces of family property divided through several generations.

In sum, the senior members of the Pizarro Rojas family—like the other families that made up the core of the Pizarro-Rubio casta (the Pizarro Rubio and the Rubio Linch)[67]—used the marriages of their sons and daughters to control space, to absorb into the family potentially threatening forms of independent (state-endorsed) power, to effect ties that would enable them to control the movement of goods and people through space (via marriage ties to merchants, who were in turn connected to muleteer magnates), and to preserve the landed core of the family estate to whatever degree possible. Each of the core families also arranged the marriages of its children so as to preserve the racial purity of the family and the nobility of the family name. For only families of truly noble bearing and noble lineage could legitimately claim the right to rule their social inferiors—the mestizo families of the towns (who were tolerated by the elite, but from considerable social distance) and the Indio families of the countryside (who were looked down upon as children and therefore were pitied, but who were also despised as irrational and somewhat less than human). The wedding of Luis Felipe Pizarro Rojas and Robertina Torrejón Monteza, described earlier in the chapter, is but one example of the dual nature of all such marital alliances.

Elite marriage—and the hierarchical gender roles upon which it was based—was thus the sole means of effecting a series of key relationships upon which depended both the reproduction of aristocratic sovereignty and the formation of casta coalitions. For marriage was virtually the only secure means by which alliances could be made between otherwise separate family groups. Thus, while marriage represented a potentially dangerous set of ties—which could at best effect relations that would remain fraught with tension—it was the only means by which coalitions broad enough in scope to control the entire department could be formed.

3 The Contradictions of Casta Rule

At any given point in time there were generally two main, and opposed, coalitions in existence, whose "cores" had been formed using the kinds of patriarchal marital alliance discussed in Chapter 2.[1] Each of the castas counted among its members landed families of varying degrees of prominence, past or present representatives of the central state, merchants who specialized in long-distance exchange, and "muleteer magnates" (with their peasant mule-driver clients). Along with the numerous clients among the peasantry and artisans that elite families of necessity maintained (their spheres of influence were established largely on the basis of such clienteles), these castas made up extensive, multiclass coalitions (of a noncorporate character; see Schneider, Schneider, and Hansen 1974) whose cumulative spheres of influence were scattered irregularly about the region. In terms of inter-casta struggles to control the regional space, vertical linkages between families of different social classes were therefore more important than horizontal, class-based divisions.

In the period under consideration, the two castas that struggled with one another to control the region were the Burga-Hurtado and the Pizarro-Rubio.[2] Both of these castas had emerged out of the dissolution of the Hurtado-Rodriguéz casta in the first half of the 1880s, when the contradictions inherent in casta rule (see below) asserted themselves in the context of the chaotic conditions that prevailed during this period of foreign invasion (the War of the Pacific, 1879–83) and civil war (1884–85).[3] Thereafter, the Burga-Hurtado and Pizarro-Rubio castas controlled regional affairs in alternating periods. From 1886 to 1890, the Pizarro-Rubio were dominant within the region, although the Burga-Hurtado were not completely marginalized. The period from 1890 to 1895 saw growing Burga-Hurtado influence, even though the Pizarro-Rubio held certain key elected positions. The Burga-Hurtado expanded its sphere of control by means of Machiavellian political intrigue. During the period from 1895 to 1902, the Pizarro-Rubio enjoyed virtually complete hegemony within the region, having swept the Burga-Hurtado forces from power as an outgrowth of civil war, in which the Pizarro-Rubio chose the winning side. The next seven years, 1902 to 1909, featured an uneasy alliance between the Burga-Hurtado and the Ocampo-Eguren, who joined forces against their common enemy, the Pizarro-Rubio. From 1909 to 1915, the Pizarro-Rubio seized power from the Burga-Hurtado, consolidated its position thereafter, was almost overthrown by Burga-Hurtado forces, temporarily faced an equally hostile central state regime, but in the end prevailed. The years 1915–24 were a period of virtually uninterrupted Pizarro-Rubio control. During the final period, 1924–30, the Rubio Linch family led the ruling casta, the Pizarros having been forced into invisibility as a result of Pablo M. Pizarro having been a key participant in a failed, nationally organized attempt to oust his compadre Augusto Leguía from the presidency.

Casta rule was characterized by a series of contradictory and countervailing forces. A ruling casta began its tenure strong and united, but as time passed found its position increasingly undermined by its adversaries. This chapter presents an overview of these contradictory forces, and offers an explanation for why they existed. I use examples from each of the periods in order to illustrate particular dimensions of the model and show the general applicability of the model to all seven periods outlined above.[4] What emerges is a composite picture of the political dynamics underlying all seven periods as a whole. The next chapter presents data from 1908 to 1913 in order to show how these contradictory forces worked themselves out during a particular period.

I have chosen to focus on what the various periods have in common not because there were no differences among them, but because of the larger problematic that I wish to engage—the contradiction between aristocratic and popular sovereignty, and the way in which subsequent state-building processes grew out of and can only be understood in relation to this contradiction. For these purposes, the seven periods outlined above can indeed be dealt with in terms of their commonalities, for the contradiction between aristocratic and popular sovereignty in which they were grounded was not overcome until the 1930s. It is precisely the process by which this contradiction was eventually overcome that is one of the major foci of the book.

THE RISE OF A RULING CASTA

As explained in Chapter 2, because of the poverty of agrarian pursuits in the Chachapoyas region, control of political office was the key to affluence and power. Indeed, the ability of any of the "aristocracy" to live according to the privileged station in life to which all members of the elite aspired was critically dependent on occupying political office. The competition between the Pizarro-Rubio and Burga-Hurtado castas thus focused predominantly on occupying the region's most important elected and appointed political positions—congressmen (*diputados*), senators (*senadores*), prefect, and subprefects. Control of these positions enabled a casta to demand (at least temporarily) that the central regime in Lima allow the casta to staff the remainder of the local state bureaucracy with its own clients (see below). Only by succeeding in appointing clients to lower-level administrative positions throughout the department could a ruling casta construct a political machine able to extract revenue, persecute and marginalize members of opposing castas, and reproduce ruling casta power.

There were three means by which a casta could establish monopoly control over the machinery of state. The first was to seize it by armed force, in open combat, often (but not always) in the context of national political upheaval. In this case, a formerly out-of-power casta rose to prominence by acting as the local client of new leaders in the national capital, thus becoming part of a new national political alliance. The rise of the Pizarro-Rubio casta in 1895, when civil war brought Nicolas de Piérola to power in the nation's capital (Basadre 1968–69, 10: ch. 123), exemplifies this process. With the backing of the Piérola regime, the Pizarro-Rubio deposed the Burga-Hurtado, which had dominated regional affairs during the preceding five years.[5] The Pizarro-Rubio remained in undisputed control of the region until 1902 (when a change in the presidency partially undermined its hegemonic position within Chachapoyas). Similarly, in the aftermath of the coup of August 1930, which removed dictator Augusto Leguía from power, Leguía's local clients, the Rubio-Linch, were deposed by the Burga-Hurtado.[6]

A second way of establishing monopoly control over the departmental political apparatus was to help an existing regime defeat opposition forces intent on seizing control by force of arms, often (but not always) in the context of political conflagration in the nation as a whole. In this case a local casta helped preserve an existing national political alliance. The successful defenses of Chachapoyas organized by the Hurtado-Rodriguéz casta (out of which emerged both the Burga-Hurtado and the Pizarro-Rubio castas) against the armed assaults mounted by its foes, the Santillán-Becerril, in the late 1860s and early 1870s illustrate this second option.[7] The Hurtado-Rodriguéz went on to dominate the region throughout the entire decade of the 1870s, in large part on the basis of its contribution to preserving the position of its national political patron, Manuel Pardo, and his Partido Civil (Basadre 1968–69, 6–7).[8] Similarly, in September 1886, Pizarro-Rubio forces played a key role in helping central government forces retake control of the department after a reconstituted Santillán-Becerril casta, led by Justo Villacorta, had seized control of the prefecture and the department by force of arms several months prior.[9] On the strength of its role in determining the outcome of the conflict, the Pizarro-Rubio casta was awarded all three deputyships for the department—a vantage point from which they were able to control the region until 1890 (when their position was undermined by political maneuvers of the Burga-Hurtado).[10]

A final way of achieving regional hegemony occurred more in the context of "politics as usual": winning elections. The victories of the Burga-Hurtado in the elections of 1894, 1902, 1908, and 1931, as well as those of the Pizarro-Rubio in the elections of 1909, 1912, 1913 (see Chapter 4), 1915, 1919, and 1924, illustrate this method.[11] The electoral approach posed unique problems, however. The elected positions that were essential to controlling appointments to the remaining posts in the state bureaucracy were the two senatorships for the department of Amazonas and the three deputyships—one for each of the department's three provinces. The most effective way to influence elections for these positions was to gain control over the membership of the various bodies responsible for implementing the electoral process: the *asambleas de mayores contribuyentes*;[12] the *juntas de registro electoral*, or voter registration boards, which formulated lists of those eligible to vote; the *juntas es-*

crutadoras, or electoral review boards, which were responsible for reviewing the results of and vouching for the veracity of elections; and the *mesas receptoras de sufragio,* or voting tables, where individuals cast their votes.[13]

All of these bodies had significant influence over the outcome of elections, but perhaps the key role was played by the mesas receptoras de sufragio. The outcome of elections was in large part decided by which coalition controlled the mesas, because their members "tallied" the voting results. As a result, as elections approached, castas began to scheme, plot, maneuver, and machinate in an attempt to control the mesas.[14] Most commonly, either the night before or early on the morning of election day, each coalition assembled a group of armed retainers in the three provincial capitals of the department, where most individuals cast their votes.[15] As voting commenced, the various armed groups did battle with one another for control of the mesas until one prevailed. Deaths were common occurrences (in addition to the examples in this and the following chapter, see Basadre 1980; Taylor 1986).[16]

An equally common and often complementary electoral strategy consisted of attempting to prevent members of the opposition from ever participating in elections. There were three means of doing so: manipulation of the courts so as to disqualify opposing casta leaders by having them jailed or prosecuted for real or supposed crimes;[17] persecution of members of the opposition via armed attacks and/or threats, which had the effect of driving them out of the region during the elections;[18] and assassination of leading members of the opposition.[19]

The following incidents, which took place during the month leading up to the presidential and congressional elections of June 1924, typify the violence and intrigue that surrounded the electoral process. At this time, the Pizarro-Rubio casta, which had ruled the region since 1909, was intent upon reproducing its dominant position in the face of challenges from the Burga-Hurtado, which was attempting to field José María Echaiz as a candidate for a deputyship. Despite its domination of regional affairs during the preceding decade and a half, the Pizarro-Rubio was in a vulnerable position. This was because Pablo M. Pizarro, recently deposed senator of Amazonas and leader of his casta, had been involved in a failed plot to overthrow President Augusto Leguía. Thereafter, Pizarro had led a failed secessionist movement to establish Amazonas as an independent state.

In retaliation for his traitorous activities, President Leguía had sacked Pizarro as senator, placed him under house arrest in Chachapoyas, and undermined the ability of Pizarro's casta to control regional affairs by naming individuals who were not members of the Pizarro-Rubio casta to important political posts. Among these individuals was Pedro Bautista, who was named subprefect of Luya province. Bautista was responsible for insuring that Pizarro and his followers did not mount another revolt against the central government in Luya, and did not steal the upcoming election by force of arms.

The Burga-Hurtado casta sought to take advantage of Pizarro's weak position—and the presence of political appointees who would not act on behalf of his casta—to bring to an end its own marginal position. It hoped to do so by claiming at least one deputyship for its casta—by electing José María Echaiz as deputy of Luya province. (Eloy Burga, leader of the Burga-Hurtado casta, also ran for office as deputy of Chachapoyas province at this time.)

In response to this state of affairs, the members of the Pizarro-Rubio hatched an elaborate plot in which they took advantage of their remaining control over select political positions (the justice of the peace of the town of Lámud, capital of Luya province) in order to hold secret nighttime meetings among relatives and friends. At these meetings they planned a complex and carefully orchestrated ambush of José María Echaiz, several of his relatives, and Subprefect Bautista—all of whom were seen as standing in the way of definitive electoral success for the Pizarro-Rubio. In this way they hoped to eliminate Echaiz as a candidate, to demonstrate the ability of their own casta to dominate the opposition, and to make a public statement about the dangers of interfering with their designs on elected office. Such a demonstration of force was the most effective means of restricting the field of candidates to members of their own casta.

Petition for Individual Rights and Protections. Sr. Subprefect of the Province [of Luya]. José María Echaiz, native and resident of this city [Lámud], respectfully informs you that: several days past a meeting took place in the home of Noé Lopez [justice of the peace of Lámud], over which Lopez presided, which was attended by Juan Ignacio Collantes [son of Hortencia Pizarro Rojas, niece of Pablo M. Pizarro]; Manuel H. Malaver; Lizardo, Hernan, and Josué Pizarro [nephews of Pablo M. Pizarro]; Elías and Florentino Chavez Arroyo; Benjamin Villegas [an aspiring merchant]; Buenaventura Santillán;

Eloi Zegarra; Virgilio Mori; and others, at which it was decided to assassinate me, my brother Fabriciano [Echaiz], Marcial Ponce de Leon [Echaiz's brother-in-law], Francisco Merino, and you, these having been the orders the men received from their *jefe político* Pablo Pizarro.

This fact has been made known to the aforementioned Sr. Ponce de Leon by Doña Aurora Mori de Pizarro [who was a relative of Sr. Ponce de Leon].

As these declarations comprise a threat to my life I appeal to you to accord/provide me with the individual rights and protections granted me by the Constitution . . . 25 of May, 1924. ([APA16], decreto no. 142)

Several weeks later it became clear that Sr. Echaiz's information was extremely accurate, and his fears well-founded. In mid-June the very men he named in his "Petition"—all either relatives or close confidants of Pablo M. Pizarro—did indeed attempt to murder him.

Subprefecture of Lámud/Luya to Sr. Prefect of the Department. 13 of June, 1924. On June 8, at 9:30 P.M. a homicide was perpetrated on the person of don Antonio Guevarra in this city [Lámud].

On the date indicated, exercising my functions as *autoridad* [political official], I left my home at 8:00 in the evening with the intent of making my normal rounds through the city, whose tranquility has been threatened for some days by a group of armed men [followers of Pablo M. Pizarro] who place the lives of some citizens of this town in danger, as is demonstrated by the accompanying Petition for Individual Rights and Protections [of Sr. Echaiz; see above]. After having passed along several streets I arrived at the home of Srta. Delfina Arévalo, where I found Francisco Merino, José María Echaiz, and David and Antonio Guevara, with whom I entered into conversation. As we spoke Antonio Guevara, who was my young friend, asked me if I could provide him with alfalfa for the pack animals he and Sr. Echaiz had brought with them from [the town of] Luya. I responded that I did not have any alfalfa close at hand, but that if he and Sr. Echaiz wished to accompany me to a place called "Gache" on the outskirts of the town, there was a place where they could pasture their animals. Sr. Guevara accepted my offer, and he and I proceeded to lead the animals to the place indicated [Echaiz decided to stay behind]. Having accommodated his animals at "Gache" we returned to town; when at the corner of the house of Apolinar Ramos, we encountered two individuals, one of them wearing a poncho, [acting] as if he was attempting to conceal something [underneath it], and [coming nearer] I discovered that it was Eloy Zegarra and Florentino Chavez Arroyo, adepts of [Pablo Pizarro], who has of late sought to disrupt public order, and informing these men that they were to be detained so that an investigation could be made [of Pizarro's plans], when I tried to take them to jail they attempted to escape, Zegarra running down the alley that runs behind the house of don Manuel Malaver to the ravine of Gachi [sic] and Chavez running along the main road in the direction of the house of doña Cruz Malaver. With the object of capturing them again I sent my young friend Guevara after Zegarra, and I followed Chavez Arroyo.

While in pursuit of [Chavez Arroyo], I encountered a group of men at the corner of the house of Sra. Malaver, who I mistakenly thought were *gente de orden* [law-abiding citizens], and to whom I called out to help capture the man who was fleeing. . . . Having made this appeal I changed direction in order to help [my young friend] Guevara who, being from Chachapoyas and thus not knowing the town, I doubted could catch [the other fleeing man, Eloy] Zegarra . . . when I heard a gunshot from the direction in which Guevara had run and . . . hurrying to the spot where the gun had been fired I found my friend Guevara, lying on the ground, who in an agonized voice cried out, "Don Pedro, they have killed me, Virgilio Mori has shot me in the chest!" Filled with anger at realizing that this was indeed true, I immediately went in search of the assassin . . . going in the direction of the group of men whose assistance I had asked in capturing Chavez . . . [approaching them] again I was surprised to discover that Chavez himself was among them, along with [justice of the peace] Noe Lopez, Benjamin Villegas, Buenaventura Santillán and others . . . who approached me menacingly. . . . Before they could do anything to me I returned to the house of Srta. Arévalo, where I had left Sr. Guevara [brother of the murdered man], Sr. Echaiz, and Sr. Merino, so as to enlist their help . . . along with that of Manuel Ponce de Leon, Francisco Rojas, and others whom we found close by. . . .

This is the way in which the murder took place. . . . The authors of the death of the young Guevara are: don Pablo M. Pizarro, instigator of the crime . . . Virgilio Mori, who provided the criminals with weapons . . . Florentino Chavez, Eloy Zegarra, Lizardo Pizarro, Wilfredo Altamirano . . . Noe Lopez, Benjamin Villegas, and Benjamin Santillán . . . Juan Ignacio Collantes, Manuel H. Malaver y Hernan Pizarro . . . and Josué Pizarro . . . [who] are in jail. . . . In my capacity as a [government] functionary I denounce this cowardly crime, directed against my person. ([APA16], decreto no. 140)

A final petition from the mother of the murdered young man makes explicit the connection to José María Echaiz, whom the Burga-Hurtado wished to field as a candidate for deputy.

> *Denunciation of the homicide perpetrated on the person of her son.* Sr. Prefect of the Department. Rosa D——— [?] de Guevara, native and resident of this town [Lámud] . . . respectfully informs you: that on June 8, at 9:30 P.M., taking advantage of the shadows of night, a numerous and premeditated plot [resulted in] the assassination . . . of my son Antonio Guevara. The facts . . . of the crime . . . are the following. At the invitation of the Srs. Echaiz, for some time my son Antonio had been working at the [Echaiz's] hacienda *Shañi*, doing various jobs of carpentry, which was his profession. On the aforementioned date my unfortunate son and his "uncle" don José María Echaiz went to [the town of] Luya in order to obtain wood . . . returning as far as Lámud by late in the afternoon, they decided to spend the night in Lámud in order to avoid the ambushes that, according to public rumor, political allies of Pablo M. Pizarro have been preparing for Sr. Echaiz, so as to kill him. At about 9:00 at night the interim subprefect, don Pedro Bautista, friend of my son, arrived at the house of Srta. Arévalo, where [my son and Sr. Echaiz] had arranged to spend the night, whereupon my son asked if [Bautista] could provide pasture for their pack animals . . . to which Sr. Bautista responded yes, offering "Gache," to which the subprefect and my son took the two animals. Returning from . . . "Gache," [and approaching the] property of don Manuel Malaver, they came upon two individuals . . . Eloy Zegarra and Florentino Chavez Arroyo . . . [to whom the subprefect] explained that they were to be detained, being known followers of those who had recently committed numerous scandals, but when he tried to take them to jail they escaped . . . my son was . . . shot with a Mauser rifle near the larnyx, which caused his death.
>
> The authors of this odious crime, committed by mistake, since the person they wished to assassinate was Sr. José María Echaiz, are Virgilio Mori, Florentino Chavez Arroyo, Lizardo Pizarro Mori, Eloy Zegarra . . . Noe Lopez, Benjamin Villegas, Buenaventura Santillán . . . [and] Josué Pizarro. . . . The premeditation and additional aggravating circumstances are proven; the form in which the murder was carried out makes it clear that Pablo M. Pizarro had the principal role, since, as has been stated publicly in Lámud, it is he who gave the orders to carry out the crime and also provided the arms for its

execution. . . . I therefore denounce, in legal and due form, the assassination of my son, Antonio Guevara, committed by Pablo M. Pizarro. ([APA16], decreto no. 143)

In other words, the Pizarro-Rubio forces had met in secret at the home of Justice of the Peace Noe Lopez, and had decided to assassinate several individuals who stood in the way of definitive electoral success—most notably, two high-ranking members of the Burga-Hurtado casta (brothers José María and Fabriciano Echaiz) and the subprefect (who was not cooperating with the Pizarro-Rubio's election plans). Having reached this decision, members of the Pizarro-Rubio began to lay in wait for a time when they could catch these individuals unaware and do away with them. Ambush by night presented the best opportunity for success, and thus groups of armed Pizarro-Rubio clients began to roam the streets, committing "outrages" of various kinds, and waiting to find the individuals they sought unprotected. Despite the precautions taken by the Echaiz and the subprefect, the night of June 8 presented such an opportunity, and nearly ended in success for the Pizarro-Rubio. Only extreme caution on the part of José María Echaiz caused him to remain at the home of Srta. Arévalo, where he was to spend the night, rather than accompany the subprefect and Antonio Guevara to the edge of town in order to pasture their animals. Thereafter, as the subprefect and Guevara pursued the Pizarro-Rubio clients who sought to escape capture by the authorities, only a quirk of fate took the subprefect down a street different from the one where the ambush was planned. Even so, only a hasty retreat on the part of the subprefect once he encountered his enemies in the street saved the subprefect from a fate similar to that of young Guevara—who had been shot by mistake.

Just days after this failed attempt to murder José María Echaiz and the subprefect of Luya province, the members of the mesas receptoras de sufragio (the voting tables) in each of the districts of the province of Luya were chosen ([APA16], resolution no. 111 [June 27]). Alert to the possibility that Pablo M. Pizarro and his followers would try to impose their own outcome on the elections, members of the ruling casta took special care to safeguard the selection process for members of the mesas. Shortly thereafter, the elections themselves were held, and José María Echaiz stood as a candidate. The attempt made by

Pablo M. Pizarro to eliminate leading members of the opposing coalition by means of assassination—and thus to "simplify" the outcome of the elections—had failed.[20]

The results of elections were therefore satisfactory to only one coalition—that which successfully controlled the mesas receptoras de sufragio (and/or the other electoral bodies). Those who lost out in elections often organized competing and parallel elections after the fact—referred to as *dualidades*—where they elected their own candidates.[21] As a result, several individuals would journey to the national capital in Lima and present themselves to Congress as the "real" deputies and senators from Chachapoyas. It was then up to Congress to declare which of these candidates were the actual winners.[22]

Regardless of who was eventually recognized as legitimate, the "victorious" candidate represented an important coalition of forces within the Chachapoyas region. If the central regime in Lima was to have any real presence in Chachapoyas, and if it was to maintain itself against competing national coalitions (whose clients included out-of-power castas in Chachapoyas), the central regime could not ignore the desires of the casta it had chosen to support. As a result, the executive branch of government, which in theory made appointments to the positions that controlled the machinery of state within the region—departmental prefect, provincial subprefects, judges, and chiefs of police—in practice heeded the desires of "elected" representatives concerning who would fill such posts.[23]

In effect, the elected congressman represented a coalition of forces that promised to control a particular section of the regional space for the central regime in the face of threats from mutual enemies. In order to do so effectively, the congressman needed to be granted powers of appointment that in theory rested with the executive. It was for this reason that deputies (who represented particular provinces) were given the right to name the subprefects and judges for the provinces from which they came. Senators (who represented the entire department) were affiliated with a potentially different, department-wide coalition. They were given the right to name the departmental prefects and chiefs of police. Elections are thus best understood as a reciprocal pact between the central government and local castas that represented particular sections of the regional space.

During such times of political transition—when out-of-power coalitions often mounted armed assaults on the ruling casta—the central government was forced to depend on "strong" clients who acted in concert to maintain regional control. A ruling coalition that controlled the offices of prefect, subprefect, judge, and chief of police was in an extremely strong position vis-à-vis other coalitions.[24] By monopolizing these offices, the coalition in question was able to control coveted appointments to all lower-level administrative, extractive, and judicial posts for the entire department. These powers enabled the ruling casta to elevate individuals of its own choice to positions of governance in every province, district, and subdistrict—and thus to recruit a contingent of loyal followers who were distributed throughout the entire department, and who could be counted on to control the opposition. In addition to acting as the official representatives of the central government (and thus the ruling casta) within their zones of jurisdiction, appointees were responsible (directly or indirectly) for collecting the taxes (and for extorting the wealth) that were among the ruling casta's main sources of revenue.[25] This revenue provided the ruling casta with another key resource in recruiting and maintaining its network of clients.

In addition to recruiting clients by awarding them political posts, the ruling casta generated followers among the peasantry and artisans by simply relieving them of the duty to pay taxes.[26] In return, such individuals were expected to perform various tasks for their patrons—from helping defend their patrons in times of political unrest, to occasionally providing their patrons with labor services. Needless to say, tax relief was a "favor" that could be withdrawn at any time, and thus was an effective way of disciplining peasants and artisans— of compelling them to obey the dictates of their patron.

By virtue of these powers of appointment and extraction, the ruling casta attempted to construct a single, department-wide political machine whose members were united behind the common causes of extracting tributary revenue, persecuting members of opposing castas, and reproducing casta power. To the extent that it controlled appointments to administrative positions throughout the department, the ruling casta was assured of an official presence in all sections of the regional space, even where estate ownership made opposing coalitions strong, and thus could more effectively carry out its duties of maintaining "law and order" for the regime in Lima.

Upon rising to power, the ruling casta also used its position of dominance to assume control over commercial activity within the region. Long-distance merchants with marriage ties to the ruling casta found their commercial activities favored and protected,[27] while merchants allied with the deposed casta found themselves harassed and persecuted. Elite men at or near the core of the ruling casta were able to expand their involvement in mercantile activities after having been forced to abandon their commercial involvements in the period prior to the rise of their casta.[28] Some members of the elite seized upon the opportunity presented by the ascent of their coalition to form new commercial partnerships. Indeed, all seven of the alternating periods of casta rule that took place from 1885 to 1930 were marked by the establishment of new mercantile companies.[29] And finally, governors, lieutenant governors, and justices of the peace in the rural districts commonly used their positions to assume control over the commercial activities that took place within their zones of jurisdiction. For example, these appointees decided who (among the peasantry) would be allowed to transport and sell products for which there was an ongoing commercial market—*chancaca* (brown sugar), *trago* (cane liquor), *guarapo* (cane beer), salt, and tobacco. Needless to say, appointees invariably charged those who wished to exercise this privilege.[30] It was also quite common for governors and lieutenant governors to charge tolls for the use of roads that passed through their districts. These functionaries also made decisions regarding which peasant *arrieros* (part-time mule-drivers) would be employed for official and unofficial business.

Governors and lieutenant governors also assumed control over the commercial activities that passed through their districts, and in the process often initiated their own mercantile activities. Many of these appointees purchased manufactured goods from merchants in neighboring departments (Cajamarca and San Martín), which they then distributed and sold either within their own districts or in the town of Chachapoyas.[31] In order to reduce costs and maximize profit, governors and lieutenant governors commonly forced peasants within their zones of jurisdiction to travel considerable distances with pack animals (usually to the departmental border) to retrieve the merchandise in question. The peasants might or might not be offered what was at best a minimal monetary compensation for providing this service.[32]

The deepening involvement of district-level political appointees in long-distance commerce often became a major distraction from their duties as government functionaries. Indeed, it was very common for these appointees to request formal and extended leaves of absence from their political posts so that they would be free to pursue commercial dealings considerably more lucrative than their activities as political appointees.[33]

The ability of the ruling casta to maintain control over this tributary-commercial structure was in large part a function of a key power it exercised as the central government's privileged client—its control over the region's two police forces, the Gendarmery and the Guardia Civil. During periods of political transition—when the survival of the central regime depended on the strength of its regional allies—the ruling casta was able to control virtually all appointments to both police forces. At times, the departmental heads of the Guardia Civil and the Gendarmery were prominent members of the kin-related, landed families that led the ruling casta. At other times the individuals who filled these positions were appointed from the national capital (often according to the dictates of the elected representatives of the department of Amazonas). In consultation with the prefect and subprefects, the heads of each of the two police forces chose the men who made up its rank-and-file, invariably local men with limited economic opportunities, little education, and no training, who would feel deeply indebted to casta leaders for the opportunity afforded them.

Even so, the loyalty of the police could not be taken for granted. Because of the key role they played in maintaining the status quo, in order to ensure their allegiance, the ruling casta added funds of its own to the rather meager salaries provided by the Ministry of Government in Lima (drawing on the local tax revenues over which it exercised monopoly control).[34] In addition, the police were allowed considerable latitude to engage in what might be called "private extraction" from the local populace, as long as this did not interfere too much with more general casta objectives and operations. The following incident, which involved robbery, housebreaking, and the rape and attempted murder of an underage girl, typifies the kinds of police abuse to which members of opposing castas were continually subjected.

Sr. Judge of the First Instance. November 21. In compliance with my duty, I
write to inform you that at 9:00 P.M. yesterday don Esteban Santillán [a client
of the Pizarro-Rubio casta] appeared before me on behalf of his underaged
niece, Roza [sic] Gamarra, both residents of this town [Chachapoyas], accus-
ing don Genaro Reyes Alvares [a foot-soldier in the Guardia Civil] and don
Ramon Hurtado [a high-ranking officer in the Guardia Civil] . . . of having
broken into the house of the aforementioned minor, of having robbed her,
of having raped her, and of having attempted to kill her, acts . . . committed
at 4:00 P.M. in the home of Gamarra. Political authorities being charged with
the preservation of order and of public morality, immediately upon receiving
the denunciation I had the aforementioned Reyes Alvares apprehended, and
this morning had Hurtado [apprehended], both of whom are now in detention in the barracks of the Guardia Civil. . . . From the investigation . . . that
I have conducted, I have discovered that don Santos Vigil knows something
of what occurred, as he assisted Srta. Gamarra when, fleeing from her attackers, she managed to escape by the roof of her house. ([APA63], *Subprefecto del
Cercado al Juez de 1ra Instancia,* Nov. 21, 1893)

Symptomatic of the importance of the Guardia Civil's loyalty to the ruling
casta—and thus the latitude its members had to be allowed in their dealings
with the local population—was the fact that foot-soldier Reyes Alvares received a slight reprimand for his possible involvement in the crimes, whereas
Officer Hurtado received no punishment whatsoever.[35] Focusing the abuses
of the police on members of opposing castas was an effective means of granting them extra privileges without alienating the ruling casta's clientele.

The police were concentrated in the town of Chachapoyas, but were also
distributed in smaller numbers in select provincial and district capitals throughout the department. Working in concert with the casta's local political appointees, they maintained "order" according to the dictates of their patrons,
patrolling their jurisdictions with rifles, constantly on guard against challenges
from other castas.[36]

Because the people that filled these administrative, extractive, judicial, and
"surveillance" positions were united in their opposition to other coalitions,
the ruling casta was generally able to contain threats from and ultimately
weaken and even cripple the opposition, and thus was able to maintain order

for the central regime (while simultaneously strengthening its own position). For in these moments when the survival of the central regime was so dependent on the strength of its regional allies, the ruling coalition used its nearly hegemonic position to persecute members of competing castas throughout the entire department, secure in the knowledge that the central regime would ignore even the most blatant abuses of authority. Members of opposing coalitions were removed from as many influential positions as possible, and their leading members were often subject to criminal prosecution for past "crimes," committed when they controlled the machinery of state.[37] Such persecution did much to fragment opposing castas, making united action against the ruling casta difficult or impossible. This in turn helped reproduce the dominant position of the ruling casta.

The ruling casta, however, did not simply eliminate or neutralize members of other coalitions. In the process of driving opposing casta members out of public spaces, public positions, and public activities, members of the ruling casta actually flaunted their ability to belittle and humiliate their enemies, to "misuse" the machinery of state for blatantly self-serving and partisan ends—to accuse falsely, harass unnecessarily, and punish unjustly. In short, members of the ruling casta flaunted their ability to violate the individual rights and protections granted to all citizens (including casta enemies) by the central state.

One way the ruling casta might belittle its opponents was with face-to-face encounters involving personal domination and humiliation—elements of which can be found in virtually all of the violent encounters of the era. The example below, however, is typical of the encounters of shame and countershame in which leading members of the region's castas were involved during periods of political transition. This particular case comes from just prior to the fall of the Rubio-Linch casta in August 1930. At this time members of the opposition were emboldened by the knowledge that the ruling casta had lost its national political patron—President Augusto Leguía—who had been deposed in a coup led by army officer Luis M. Sanchez Cerro. This case illustrates the danger to the ruling casta when it was *not* able definitively to show its ability to dominate and humiliate the opposition.

> We received the news that an airplane was going to fly in to Chachapoyas! This was the first time an airplane had ever come to the town . . . the next

day two small planes arrived . . . the planes arrived in August of 1930, at the time of the fall of Leguía . . . when the prefect of Chachapoyas was Sr. Tavara [a close confidant of the Rubio-Linch]. . . . Before the planes landed a friend of the Echaiz approached the prefect and vilely insulted him to his face, in the presence of the whole town, because the entire populace had gone to see the airplane. . . . The prefect was outraged and called upon several Guardia to seize the man, but they were unable to do so, as the man jumped on a horse and rode away. The prefect was even further enraged and humiliated by this failure to impose his will over the man who had shamed him, and vowed to take revenge. He returned to town and immediately ordered that the police apprehend the man . . . and Officer Sevillano together with six or seven armed men began to ask where the man—Sr. Ramos—was hiding, and if anyone had seen him, and Ramos was in the house of Sr. Pedro Castilla, who had many children. The second of his sons, Germán, was sixteen years old and was a very strong and impulsive boy . . . and when the soldiers arrived at his house . . . he told them that they could not enter and they told him yes they could . . . and Germán punched the sergeant, who took out his revolver and shot, "Ya, ya" [the gunshots], and from inside the house firing started against the police, and Germán fell dead to the ground. . . . It was a terrible thing because Germán was my mother's nephew, son of her sister . . . the prefect was blamed for the death . . . it was a tragedy. . . . [Just] a few days later the Echaiz rose up against the prefect . . . and the [town's] population was up in arms about the death of the boy and they blamed the prefect, so the prefect was in a very difficult situation and could not defend himself in any way, as everyone was against him and [thus] came his downfall. (Taped interview with Mariano Rubio Pizarro, Aug. 10, 1990)

A second means of shaming opponents was via the court system. Court cases were often brought against members of the opposition, for real or supposed crimes, and dragged out for very long periods of time, while the accused languished in jail. Witness after witness was called, often brought in from distant sections of the regional space, requiring further delays. Testimony gradually piled up, while the ruling casta showed its ability to dominate, broadcasting publicly, far and wide, its power to persecute those who were foolish enough to have offered opposition. Constantly throughout, the fact that the accused was subject to the denigration of the ruling casta was kept in the public eye.[38]

A third way to belittle opponents was by physically abusing the leading members of other castas who were unfortunate enough to be captured. This abuse could range in form. At times it included outright torture, usually in a room inside the prefecture—control of which the victim's casta had just lost. Oral testimony from Mariano Rubio Pizarro, members of whose family were tortured by the Echaiz when the latter seized power from the Rubio-Linch casta in 1930, provides a description of the kind of torture employed by one casta against another.

> The Echaiz took advantage of the triumph of Sanchez Cerro [an army offi-
> cer who led a coup against Augusto Leguía, patron of the Rubio-Linch, in
> 1930] to rise up against [us] . . . [once] they knew that Leguía had fallen they
> organized a group of armed men who attacked the prefecture and took con-
> trol of it . . . they wanted to capture my parents and relatives . . . [especially]
> Miguel Rubio [Linch] . . . head of the family . . . but he escaped . . . so the
> Echaiz committed a series of outrages against all of my family's friends [who]
> they put in jail and tortured. . . . Inside the prefecture of Chachapoyas there
> were a set of stocks [*el Cepo*], and a *barra*. The Echaiz hung [these men] by
> their arms, with their legs behind them, tied together on a piece of wood . . .
> and tortured them . . . and afterward they put these men on the ground on
> their backs, and placed their legs in a *barra*—a piece of wood divided length-
> wise in two—and closed the [pieces of wood] and locked the men in with
> their feet elevated . . . and the sharp edges of the wood cut into them, and
> [the Echaiz] threw water on the floor . . . and left them there on their backs
> with their legs locked in the *barra* for the entire night. . . . Sr. Beltran Vilca,
> who was a shoemaker and who lived opposite my house and was a good
> friend of my father, was tortured [in this way] along with Sr. Flores, who was
> tortured to death . . . the people could do nothing about this, they were
> afraid, everyone was afraid . . . there were more than 30 friends of my father
> [being held] in the prefecture, and they heard the screams and the blows. . . .
> I hope that [the torture] never returns, [it was of] the kind of the Spanish In-
> quisition. (Taped interview with Mariano Rubio Pizarro, Aug. 10, 1990)

The physical abuse of opposing casta members also included extended prison terms in the Chachapoyas jail, during which captives were often badly neglected, denied food, and beaten.[39] Frequently the physical condition of a captive deteriorated so severely that he had to be sent to the hospital (under close guard). Such was the case with Felix Ocampo in 1894, and with Luis Bonifaz in 1895.[40]

Such ongoing demonstrations of the ability to dominate and humiliate were necessary because other castas refused to accept the dominant position of the ruling coalition as legitimate. Out-of-power castas regarded their own claims on regional power as inherently more valid than those of the ruling casta, and thus constantly sought to actualize what they saw as their own legitimate aspirations by undermining ruling casta control. Often, they attempted to do so by means of the kinds of personalistic attack mentioned above. Consider, for example, the following incident, which took place in 1893, in which out-of-power casta leader Pablo M. Pizarro publicly assaulted and attempted to kill ruling casta leader Eloy Burga and his close associate Felix Obando. The Burga-Hurtado casta had just completed its marginalization of the Pizarro-Rubio by ousting Pizarro and his allies from the municipal council of Luya province—the Pizarro-Rubio's single remaining sphere of influence.

> *Sr. Judge of the First Instance.* Along with the present *oficio* [official letter] I remit to you the report sent to this office by Sergeant Major Don José Miguel Cabrera, chief of the Guardia Civil . . . informing me of a scandalous affair committed by Lieutenant Colonel Pablo M. Pizarro. On the 24th of last month this subprefecture posted an edict in conformity with articles 18, 19, and 22 of the "Law of Public Morality" prohibiting the use of firearms. In spite of this prohibition, Sr. Pizarro has committed the acts described in the enclosed report. Armed with a revolver [he] fired two shots, the second of which was directed at the provincial mayor [Eloy Burga], which fortunately did not strike him because the chief [of the Guardia Civil] alluded to, being present at the time, obstructed [Pizarro's attempt].
>
> *Sr. Colonel Prefect of the Department.* July 22. I inform you that at 6:00 P.M. today . . . a grave scandal has taken place, originated by Don Pablo M. Pizarro in the [commercial] establishment of Felix Obando,[41] [where he] fired two revolver shots, the second directed at the mayor of the province, Don Eloy Burga. . . . Chief of the Guardia Civil, Sergeant Major José Miguel Cabrera, . . . has placed the revolver and a long knife . . . that Pizarro was carrying at the disposal of the judge of the first instance, along with Pizarro, who is presently being held incommunicado in jail.
>
> —*[signed] Luis Arce [subprefect of Chachapoyas Province]*[42]

Ongoing demonstrations of force by the ruling casta were thus necessary in order to answer challenges to ruling casta control of the kind offered by Sr. Pizarro above—to act as "object lessons" to opposing coalitions and to the general populace concerning the ruling casta's power and potency. The more dangerous the ruling casta was perceived to be publicly, the less likely it was to be challenged, and thus the more secure was its position.

Symptomatic of the role of public demonstrations of domination and submission in the reproduction of the casta order was an incident involving Justo and Melquiadez Inga, two brothers, both peasant cultivators, whose casta (the Rubio-Linch) had been driven from power on August 22, 1930, in an armed uprising (see Chapter 8). In the months following the fall of the Rubio-Linch casta, the position of the region's new power holders was anything but secure. Although the leaders of the Rubio-Linch casta had been forced out of the prefecture, they had taken refuge in their estate, *Boca Negra*, located on the outskirts of Chachapoyas. From there the deposed casta leaders were attempting to mobilize a force of followers large enough to retake control of the department.

The Rubio-Linch's first attempt—which came just days after it had itself suffered defeat—consisted of an armed assault on public buildings in Chachapoyas and in several peasant villages. Despite much fighting and many deaths, this attempt failed.[43] Instructed by their leaders at *Boca Negra*, clients of the ousted casta took a new approach. They began to engage in an ongoing struggle with the appointees of the new ruling casta for control of the regional space. Although the new ruling casta had the means of force provided by the central government at its disposal, Rubio-Linch clients countered this with personalistic attacks on ruling casta functionaries—attacks in which they sought publicly to humiliate and discredit the representatives of the new order. In this way members of the ousted casta hoped to weaken their adversaries, and to recruit a sufficient number of followers to the Rubio-Linch cause to make possible a successful assault on the prefecture.

The Inga brothers were central to this campaign within their home district of Lónguita. From the fall of their casta in August 1930 until the end of that year, they had continually insulted, defied, and publicly humiliated the new governor and justice of the peace of their district. These functionaries had protested to the prefect in a series of oficios, in which they asked that

gendarmes equipped with rifles be sent to Lónguita to capture the men. The
prefect had responded by issuing an order for the arrest of the Inga brothers,
and by sending gendarmes to Lónguita on two separate occasions. Both efforts to apprehend the brothers had failed, however, and the Ingas continued
to harass and humiliate the ruling casta appointees of Lónguita without suffering any ill consequences.[44]

By January 1931, however, conditions had changed considerably. The region's new power holders had secured their position of dominance by driving
the leaders of the ousted Rubio-Linch casta out of the region entirely. Indeed, the latter had been forced (temporarily) to give up any hope of recruiting enough followers to mount an assault on the prefecture. Instead, they
looked to a more long-term strategy of undermining the ruling casta by seeking powerful political allies outside of the regional space.[45]

When its most prominent members quit the region entirely to seek out
new allies, the Rubio-Linch casta lacked any centralized leadership or coordinated plan of attack, and thus low-level, rural clients like the Inga brothers
quickly found themselves isolated and unprotected. In these changed circumstances, after months of insulting, humiliating, and threatening ruling casta
appointees, and after defying all efforts made to capture them, the Inga brothers opted for a radically new course of action: they decided to turn themselves in voluntarily to the very appointees they had formerly attacked and
offended. The Inga brothers offered a public apology to these officials, and in
this way acknowledged their obeisance to the region's new power holders.

The public nature of this act of contrition was perhaps its most important
dimension. The act was carried out not only before the town of Lónguita's
"notable citizens" (local representatives of the ruling casta) but before the entire population, in the town's main square, during a public tribunal convened
for this very purpose by the governor of the district.

> In the pueblo of Lónguita on the twenty-second day of the month of Febru-
> ary of 1931 in a public tribunal held in the Plaza de Armas of this locality
> under the presidency of the governor and in the presence of the [town's] no-
> table citizens and other residents, the individuals Justo and Melquiadez
> Inga . . . appeared [before the tribunal] . . . the first [Justo Inga] having
> agreed to confess before the tribunal his crimes committed against the gover-
> nor, having slandered and repudiated him in his position as [political] author-

ity, in the same fashion the second [Melquiadez Inga] having shown contempt to the justice of the peace, threatening to strike him, as has already
been reported to the prefecture; both [Ingas], in full exercise of their liberties
and of their own free will acknowledged the crimes they had committed . . .
humbly offered their submission, and pleaded to be pardoned. In light of
this, the injured authorities as well as the remaining citizens decided to accept the apology . . . but only on the condition that [the Ingas] refrain from
ever offending their authorities or fellow citizens in the future. ([APA46],
Feb. 23, 1931)

For the ruling casta, then, one of the conditions of successful rule was that
it publicly demonstrate its ability to dominate and shame members of the opposition, and to crush any challenges offered to its hegemonic position. Doing
so helped contribute to the reproduction of the particular form of aristocratic
sovereignty encountered in the region, in which the ability to prove oneself
potent and powerful was essential to being perceived as a ruler.

Faced with such conditions, upon falling from power or failing in a bid to
seize it, leading members of opposing castas often chose to retreat into their
haciendas, where their peasant clients would gather in considerable numbers to
protect them from armed assaults by the ruling coalition.[46] As already mentioned, deposed casta leaders who failed to reach the sanctuary of their estates
and the protection of their clients often found themselves tortured in the prefecture by members of the new ruling casta. A second option was to leave the
region entirely. When leaving the department, a failed leader often looked
elsewhere for disgruntled allies who might shore up his position. A broad alliance of such disaffected caudillos might help effect a change in who controlled the central state apparatus, allowing the self-exiled casta leader to return
to his home region triumphantly, and to impose his will on his enemies. A
successful attempt of this kind was that of Prefect Gaspar LaTorre, who in
1886 returned to Chachapoyas at the head of a battalion of 900 men—complete with cavalry and cannon—to wrest control of the department from Justo
Villacorta, who had earlier driven LaTorre out of Amazonas entirely.[47] A failed
attempt was that of Toribio Rodriguéz, in 1857. Rodriguéz was forced to flee
the region due to the persecution he suffered at the hands of the ruling casta,
later linked up with opposition forces to the west in the department of Cajamarca, and then led a failed revolt against his enemies in Chachapoyas.[48] Pablo

Pizarro and Felix Ocampo, at the end of the civil war of 1895, were more successful.[49] Having been forced to quit the region by the forces of the Burga-Hurtado casta, Pizarro and Ocampo returned to Chachapoyas as the local clients of the new president, Nicolas de Piérola (the victor in the civil war), and swept the Burga-Hurtado from power.[50]

An additional dimension to the establishment of hegemony over the regional space by one casta, and flight from such control by other castas, was that once out of the regional space, castas that had fallen from power (or had failed in a bid to seize it) were able to publish public accounts of the persecution to which they were subject—usually in the form of handbills that were distributed either in the national capital or in highland capitals near Chachapoyas.[51] Within the regional space itself, however, the ruling casta enjoyed complete control over the print media—which allowed it to define how the "truth" of events would be cast for the reading public at large. In this regard, it is revealing that publicly spoken challenges to the ruling casta were considered serious matters, were frequently heard, and were generally prosecuted as criminal offenses.[52] Equally revealing is the fact that the small handful of printing presses in Chachapoyas were often attacked and vandalized by out-of-power castas, who sought to challenge those who controlled the department.[53]

Members of a casta that had been deposed, or that had failed in an attempt to seize power, suffered continual violations of their individual rights and protections, regardless of their social class. During periods when the ruling casta was at the height of its powers, its persecution fragmented opposing castas, making it difficult for their members to act in concert. Forced to act in isolation, as individuals, their only recourse was to protest against the violence done to them in private discourse with state officials (the subprefect and/or prefect). In these protests they invoked the central regime's discourse of popular sovereignty, individual rights and protections, and the sanctity of private property.[54] Though such pleas were rarely acted on immediately, they left a written record of abuses, available for review and possible action when a new casta seized power.[55] Consider, for example, a petition sent to the subprefect of Chachapoyas by Pablo M. Pizarro, leader of the Pizarro-Rubio casta, in December 1924. During the previous year Pizarro had been involved in one failed coup attempt to seize control of the national government by force, as well as a regional movement of secession that followed on the heels of the failed coup attempt when the central government sent troops to Chachapoyas to capture him. The protest thus came when Pizarro had been isolated politically (he was under house arrest at this time), and cut off from his once strong and numerous following.

Sr. [Subprefect and] Intendant of Police. Pablo M. Pizarro, of this locality [Chachapoyas], with the utmost respect declares that: I have learned that some of my enemies, taking advantage of the fact that my relations with the prefecture are not good, have told the prefect that I am preparing an attempt to disrupt the public order of this city [Chachapoyas]; [I have also learned that] the prefect, due to the ill will he has toward me, [plans to] exercise his authority against me.

These claims upset me greatly, since my political affiliations are well known, and because to the contrary I have always been prepared to place my *contingente* on the side of order; . . . I [write] to make a formal protest to you [the subprefect] concerning any and all calumnious assertions [concerning the claims of my enemies] and to make known the following facts: First, that the conspirators and revolutionary agents [in reality] are Eleodoro Echaiz and Fernando Luque Seoane, a dangerous criminal, who at present is in this city in his house on Belén Street, where he enjoys complete liberty. Second, that the aforementioned Luque and Echaiz have received documents and appointments from the revolutionaries in Chota, by means of an express [letter] sent by [Sr.] Carrera, communication agent of the revolutionaries. Third, that . . . Luque and other accused individuals . . . meet in groups and roam the streets with intentions that the public assumes to be subversive. . . . Fourth, that taking advantage of the lack of harmony between the prefect and myself they have sent [men] disguised as gendarmes to my home with the object of provoking an armed conflict. . . . This occurred last night when a group of individuals . . . surrounded my house with the intention of attacking or at least of provoking me.

The object of this petition is: first, to clarify my behavior in these events; second, to indicate the names of the people whom the public identifies as revolutionary agents; . . . third, to put on record the fact that there have been continuous attempts to attack my house; [and fourth,] to demand that you provide me with the individual rights and protections to which I am entitled, and that you shield me . . . from the attacks directed against me, as it is not right that members of my family live in constant alarm because of . . . indi-

viduals who have it as their goal to molest me without cease. ([APA15], decreto no. 255 [Dec. 8, 1924])

Pablo M. Pizarro's claim that he was always prepared to place his forces on
the side of order, and that the prefect had nothing to fear from a law-abiding
citizen such as he, was preposterous—especially in light of the two large-scale
armed uprisings Pizarro had led *against* the forces of order during the previous
year. It was precisely because of "strong" opposition leaders like Pizarro that
the central state had to appoint powerful individuals to the positions of prefect,
etc. For only such "strong" clients could contain people like Pizarro. In the
example above, he has been reduced to pleading for his individual rights and
protections. But this is only because he had been defeated and isolated in the
previous year.

Just as the central regime in Lima was forced to rely on "strong" prefects,
subprefects, etc., in order to meet challenges from the leaders of opposing castas, so, too, did the prefect have to appoint "strong" clients to administer outlying sections of the regional space—where lower-ranking members of opposing castas mounted their own challenges to ruling casta control. To a certain extent, the ruling casta could rely on its marriage alliances with less
influential landed families in appointing these "strong" clients (to positions of
governor, lieutenant governor, and justices of the peace). Ultimately, however, there were many more positions to fill in these outlying sections of the
regional space than there were affines to fill them.[56] Moreover, affines were
not always the safest choices for such positions; it was not uncommon for
them to cut the ties they had established via marriage with the ruling casta
and seek out other alliances in the context of the constant changes that occurred in regional politics (see below). A final, recognizably distinct section of
a coalition was therefore formed out of influential individuals with whom the
ruling coalition lacked even a marriage tie, who were appointed to govern in
the districts where their spheres of influence were strongest. These individuals made up what might be called the "coalition periphery." Control of the
state apparatus thus allowed the ruling casta to extend its control over the regional space, and over the movement of people and products through this
space, considerably beyond what would have been possible via marriage alliance alone.

Prefects were forced to rely on "strong" clients to govern the rural sections of the region because no one else would, or could, contain the members of opposing coalitions who threatened the ruling casta's control there (either electorally or through outright armed attack). These "strong" clients, who occupied the positions of governor, justice of the peace, and lieutenant governor (the governors playing the key role), administered people, collected taxes, mediated disputes, organized public works, maintained "law and order," located fugitives from authority, provided mule-drivers for the transport of official travelers and for communications (when so ordered by the prefect or subprefect), and reported on and contained any challenges to the existing regime on a daily basis in the region's many districts, subdistricts, and villages.[57]

In order for the prefect to be sure that these "strong" clients could maintain control over their sections of the regional space, he had to be confident that all local representatives would work together in the defense of the ruling regime. That is, it was essential that these local administrators be strongly allied to one another. To this end, the prefect and subprefect, who in theory appointed governors, justices of the peace, and lieutenant governors,[58] in practice heeded the advice of the local governor regarding appointments to the other two positions.[59]

As did the prefect and his immediate circle, a district governor and his allies used their positions to persecute the members of opposing coalitions operating within their more local jurisdictions, subjecting them to criminal proceedings for supposed crimes, interfering with their activities in whatever way possible, jailing them, ignoring crimes committed against their property and person, etc. This persecution of the opposition within more local, rural jurisdictions contributed to the breakdown of opposing castas, thus strengthening the position of the ruling casta throughout the regional space.[60] A typical case was that of Noe Oyarce, longtime client of the Burga-Hurtado, in mid-1924—by which point the combined forces of the central government and the Rubio-Linch casta had retaken control of the department after the Burga-Hurtado had held it for approximately a month (see Chapter 8).

For more than five years I have suffered the mortal hatred of my neighbor Sra. Laura Castañeda . . . , who, assisted by her sons Hector and Eloy . . . makes continuous attempts . . . on my life and that of my family. . . . On

May 17, 1921, I was treacherously attacked by Hector . . . and others, all of whom were armed, and was seriously wounded. . . . On June 17 of the past year, in [a] public thoroughfare . . . and in the presence of Sra. Laura Castañeda . . . Eloy attempted to shoot my nephew . . . who, miraculously, was able to escape this attack. . . . [Eloy] and ten other men have [also] had the cowardice to make an armed attempt on the life of my young son Estanró-filo, who is only a boy. . . . Not only our lives but also my family's economic affairs (*intereses*) are subject to the furor of th[is family] and [its] followers who, armed with Winchester carbines and Mauser rifles, continually lay waste to my properties, killing and carrying off my livestock. . . . [Due to] the danger to my life and to the lives of those dear to me, I write to demand to be provided with the individual rights (*garantías*) that the Constitution grants to all its citizens. . . . I can scarcely believe that at a time when our national culture has reached such an advanced state, scenes occur that belong more properly to the medieval epoch, for nothing else can explain the attitude of my . . . enemies, who have set themselves up as the arbiters of a life I do not owe them, as the arbiters of my economic affairs and of my individual labor. ([APA15], decreto no. 142 [Aug. 1, 1924])

In the process of persecuting and harassing the opposition, these district-level members of the ruling casta demonstrated their power and potency by showing their ability to dominate and humiliate their enemies in the most public and visible of manners. As was the case with the demonstrations of force against the leaders of opposing castas, these more localized applications of force had an important "demonstration effect" concerning the power and scope of the ruling coalition, and discouraged opposing castas from attempting to challenge the status quo.

The effect of such localized displays of force was to help reproduce the particular form of aristocratic sovereignty that characterized the region, in which hierarchy, privilege, and the arbitrary use of power by some was matched by servility and powerlessness for others. As a result, upon falling from power or losing a bid to seize it, opposing coalition members who lived in rural districts often chose either to leave the region entirely or to retreat into the confines of their estates until the political environment changed. Either response might include sending written pleas to the subprefect or prefect of the kind quoted above, in which the language of popular sovereignty was invoked in protesting against the violence to which these members of deposed or unsuccessful castas were subject.[61]

THE BREAKDOWN OF RULING CASTA CONTROL

There were two interrelated sets of contradictions that continually worked toward the breakdown and reconstitution of ruling coalitions. The first relates to the centrality of marriage in forming coalition alliances. The second concerns the difficulties of maintaining centralized political rule in tributary contexts.

The powerful landed families that came together in forming the casta core were immediately faced with a dilemma. It was their alliance that made regional hegemony possible, and thus each family reasonably expected that its members would be appointed to key positions of power, influence, and extraction. Specifically, at the center of each of these formerly independent family power blocks was the senior male who presided over the family's landed estate and his sons; somewhat further afield was the set of relatives united around the preservation of the family's landed core via (generally) second-cousin marriage. There were no rules for how the most important positions in the state apparatus would be distributed among these individuals, either within or between the families of the casta core. And there were many more aspirants than there were important positions to fill.[62] Working out who would be given which positions was therefore a very delicate undertaking. Each family had to safeguard its own interests while ensuring that the other family was satisfied with the arrangement as well.

It was inevitable that some members of both families got less than they felt they deserved, and that others got nothing. With little to tie them to the coalition, these individuals often looked elsewhere for opportunities to improve their situations, which often meant allying themselves with a different casta.[63] Thus, in the very act of being born, the ruling casta generated powerful opposition from within its center.

Alliances formed by marrying daughters to somewhat less influential landed families with properties scattered about the region—the "second tier" of the coalition—were also fraught with weakness. Like the casta core families, these "second-tier" families were highly localized within the regional space, and had their own local spheres of influence (where they had their own clients), from which they extracted a limited amount of wealth. Furthermore, like the casta core families, these "second-tier" families were particularly concerned with preserving the landed core of the family estate—via marriage to relatives with adjacent properties. They had only two reasons to put their localized spheres of influence at the disposal of a broader coalition: the expectation of deriving benefits that came from the ruling casta's control of the machinery of state;[64] and the need to ally with a powerful coalition in order to safeguard themselves, their property, and their families from competing local landed families.

Should either of these two needs fail to be met, there was little to prevent affinal allies from cutting their ties to the casta core and seeking out a new alliance with a different patron. This was equally true for the "peripheral" members of the coalition—those with whom the casta core lacked even a bond of marriage. As we shall see presently, it was inevitable that many "second-tier" and peripheral members of the ruling coalition ultimately became disillusioned with the coalition core—for they were almost sure to be eased out of the ruling coalition as a function of the contradictions in casta organization mentioned above.

The "second-tier" and peripheral members of the ruling coalition—who were appointed to positions of governor, lieutenant governor, and justice of the peace in the region's many districts and subdistricts—received no salary from the state.[65] As a result, they had to be allowed considerable latitude in organizing extractive processes (collecting taxes and organizing public-works projects) and in overseeing commercial activities within their zones of jurisdiction. Leaving such responsibilities in the hands of unpaid rural functionaries presented the casta core with something of a dilemma. On the one hand, the prefect was compelled to rely on "strong" clients in the districts who would act in unison to contain threats from opposing coalition members and thus maintain "order" for the ruling casta. On the other hand, however, because these appointees controlled wealth extraction, labor use, and commodity movements directly, they had a tendency to use these powers to strengthen and enrich themselves at the expense of the casta core. For ultimately, the prefect and the core of the ruling coalition assisted them only minimally in the daily work of managing political life. In such circumstances, these "second-tier" and peripheral members of the coalition had a tendency to disengage from the coalition core. As they used their administrative control to extort wealth from local populations, they also generated increasing hostility toward the ruling casta, and encouraged those they governed to seek alliances with out-of-power castas in the hope of easing their burdens (see Chapter 4).

In order to guard against such developments, when periods of instability passed, the prefect began to replace these "strong" clients with "weak" or true clients—people who had relatively little power and few clients of their own, who would be truly beholden to the prefect for their positions.[66] These individuals could not use the relatively meager resources made available to them by virtue of their positions to build up much of a clientele because they had no existing sphere of influence, or *contingente*, upon which to draw in the districts where they were appointed. They were unable to be as coercive as the strong clients had been, but then strong coercive abilities were not as necessary in these more stable conditions.

Weak clients posed much less of a threat to the integrity of the casta.[67] They also were less prone to disengage from the coalition core than their stronger counterparts. Indeed, because they had little autonomous power of their own, and were in a certain sense "surrounded" by people more powerful than they were, they were forced to appeal to the higher authorities for armed assistance whenever they had difficulty getting those who were stronger than they were to obey their commands (see Chapter 4).[68]

At the beginning of a ruling casta's period of tenure, strong clients played an essential role in fragmenting the opposition, and thus in establishing the calmer and more stable conditions in which administration by weak clients became feasible. It was nonetheless the case that weak clients were far less able than their strong counterparts to persecute the opposition, and thus to maintain the fragmented state of other castas. They were also less able to demonstrate the capacity to wield power arbitrarily, and thus could not communicate as effectively the ongoing public lessons about the ruling casta's ability to dominate that were so important to the reproduction of ruling casta control. These differences between strong and weak clients meant that under the latter, opposing castas could begin to regroup, and could more easily engage in united action against the ruling casta (see Chapter 4).

The same contradictory relationship obtained between the central regime in Lima and the regional coalition headed by the prefect. Because of the powers it had bequeathed to the prefect and the coalition he represented—out of necessity and in periods of instability and/or crisis—the central regime had in effect provided the coalition core with powers and resources it could use to strengthen itself at the expense of the central state. Ruling casta members monopolized administrative and extractive positions, thereby denying the central government an important source of revenue. Further, to the extent that the ruling casta continued to persecute and harass its enemies, it generated increasing hostility among much of the population. Such hostility was not conducive to the long-term stability of the central regime. As a result, when moments of political instability passed, the executive branch would gradually try to undermine the hegemonic position of the ruling group, often by appointing a new prefect, subprefects, or chief of the Guardia Civil or Gendarmery, who were not members of the ruling coalition, and often were not even from the region.[69] The central regime also used the formal independence of the various branches of the central government (judiciary, finance, government, etc.) to make appointments to regional-level positions in the judiciary and the police force without consulting the deputy and senator, who were the elected representatives of the ruling casta. These newly appointed individuals did not so much oppose as attempt to contain the consolidation of ruling casta power.[70]

As often as not, the individuals assigned to occupy high positions in the Chachapoyas region were unsuccessful, or only partially successful, in their efforts to control the ruling casta. The ruling casta used a variety of means, formal and informal, to thwart such independent appointees—at times going so far as to organize armed resistance or attempts on the lives of Lima appointees. Consider the following example, from 1898, when the Pizarro-Rubio was the dominant force in the region, and the central state was attempting to contain its consolidation of control by assigning prefects to Amazonas who were not from Amazonas. On November 14, Prefect Anselmo Huayapa wrote to the Ministry of Government in Lima about the latest of a series of protests in which he outlined an elaborate plot carried out by the Pizarro-Rubio forces to rid themselves of Huayapa's presence, and to place Pablo M. Pizarro in the prefecture.

Sr. Minister of Justice, Religion and Education . . . Sr. Minister. In compliance with your decree, [and] in obedience with the dictates of the truth and of justice, I remit the report that you have requested. . . . I have read the note of the Sr. President of the Departmental Council [a Pizarro-Rubio client] that motivates this report with the greatest of care, and I have found that it abounds in so many incoherent and inexact claims that I find in it not a single charge that could justifiably be used against the position that I exercise due to the generosity of the Supreme Government. Said document can only be seen as inflammatory libel, in which a public functionary, a *jefe* of a respectable institution [the Departmental Council], far from employing the noble and moderate language that is appropriate in official matters, [and far from] rendering homage to the truth, reviles the highest political authority of the department, the delegate of the Supreme Government in [this] section of the territory of the Fatherland, with false imputations, with fraudulent [and] disloyal words, and [with] coarse epithets, . . . which not only denigrate and discredit my person, but which also cast the principle of authority [itself] into the dirt. ([APA45], Nov. 14, 1898)

Having made plain his position regarding the accusations made against him by the president of the departmental council, Prefect Huayapa goes on to detail the elaborate scheme hatched by the Pizarro-Rubio to oust him from the position of prefect:

In order to refute this series of . . . false accusations, I believe it necessary to counter all the points [made by the president of the Departmental Council] with the truth . . . and to this effect I ask for your conscientious attention.

Having been appointed prefect of this department on August 20 of this year, after having been subprefect of [Chachapoyas] for more than a year and interim prefect for nine months, during which time no one formulated any charges against me whatsoever, the mail of Sunday, Sept. 4 brought me the news of my appointment as prefect, with which the president of the Republic has had the goodness to distinguish me; but the mail did not bring the authorization to the Sr. Judge of the First Instance to give me the oath of office. No other mail deliveries followed, depriving this locale of communication with the coast for the space of a month, as a result of the blockages of the roads carried out by the groups of armed bandits (*montoneras*) that maraud about in [the departments of] Cajamarca and La Libertad; because of which I remained the prefect, but in exercise of my duties in a provisional capacity. In these circumstances news arrived of the appointment of . . . Samuel Eguren as the new subprefect of [Chachapoyas], as a result of the influence of Deputy . . . Juan M. Pizarro, as well as the authorization [to the judge of the first instance] to give Eguren the oath of office; documents that were brought from Lima to Cajamarca by special messenger, who avoided the bandits in transit, and that were remitted [the documents] via special delivery from Cajamarca to this capital [Chachapoyas].

Desiring to merit the confidence the Supreme Government has shown in me, and being apprised of specific data and official information that a large group of bandits was in Jaen . . . and was advancing on this department, in order to contain the possible further advance that the bandits appeared to intend, I deployed the entire detachment of gendarmes at my disposal. Not wishing to leave control of the department in the hands of someone [Eguren] I believed, with reason, not to be completely loyal, I suggested to Sr. Eguren that we wait for the next mail, in which I was sure the authorization to swear me in would arrive, and that he and I could take the oath of office together at that time, which Sr. Eguren accepted . . . [and this was] the point that was to act as the basis of a local uprising . . . which I was able to prevent. . . .

[When the authorization to give me the oath of office did not arrive,] believing in the rule of law, I resigned myself to delivering the prefecture to Subprefect Eguren, who assumed control of the prefecture in a provisional capacity; but that same afternoon, as I walked about the town, I encountered a group of people in the street, among them the new prefect, his brother Julio [Eguren], and an uncle of both named Francisco Hernandez, and this last individual approached me and said to me in an irritating, ironic, and deprecatory tone, "Sr. Huayapa, now you are nothing; now Samuel is prefect and so he should be," . . . to which his nephew added some additional remark. . . . I guarded my silence and withdrew without giving the slightest recognition to their disrespect, using the moderation . . . proper to my character and to the circumstances. . . .

Twenty-four hours had not passed, Sr. Director, before a local revolutionary movement broke out. Sergeant Major Don Alfredo Concha, head of the Guardia Civil . . . the only police force in the town at the time [the gendarmes having been sent to combat the "bandits," who were actually Pizarro-Rubio clients] advancing from Jaen, came to see me . . . to inform me that the interim prefect, Sr. Eguren, had gone to his barracks just hours earlier to inform the head of the Guardia Civil that he [Eguren] was going to change the entire personnel of the Guardia Civil from the chief to the last soldier, and that to this effect he had available dependable people brought [to Chachapoyas] from the pueblo of Santo Tomas. In a word, the entire corp of loyal servants was to be disbanded. . . .

It was also communicated to me that same day, very early in the morning (because Sergeant Major Concha and I spoke all night long, into the dawn, and did not sleep), that the same night two political meetings of a subversive character had taken place . . . one . . . in the home of D. Manuel Vasquez [brother-in-law of Pablo M. Pizarro] . . . and the other in the home of Priest Julian Caro . . . who has on diverse occasions declared that I should be deposed and held. These meetings were attended by the principal actors in the revolt, Prefect Sr. Eguren, D. Pablo M. Pizarro . . . and other more-or-less important individuals. Their purpose was to hatch a plot proclaiming D. Pablo M. Pizarro as prefect, to order the immediate imprisonment of the particular group of people [who oppose them], to seize me, and to spread the revolution in all directions, [which would be] accompanied, of course, by the full range of crimes and outrages that these movements of disorder invariably provoke.

Having discovered this wicked and odious plan, I prevailed upon the judge of the first instance to give me the oath of office (because the note authorizing me to be sworn in had been held up in Lima, Juan M. Pizarro being the person charged with delaying it), and he swore me in [as prefect]. . . .

The judge having accepted my demand [to be sworn in], the plans of the conspirators were completely frustrated, as was the advance of the bandits [organized by the Pizarro-Rubio casta] from Jaen. (Ibid.)

The Pizarro-Rubio had gone to great lengths in order to rid itself of an "uncooperative" appointee from Lima, attempting to undermine Huayapa's position as prefect in both military and legal terms. Concerning the former, the Pizarro-Rubio had organized a large group of "bandits" (in actuality its own followers) to march on Amazonas from a frontier section (Jaen) of the neighboring department of Cajamarca, requiring Huayapa to send a sizable armed contingent (the entire Gendarmery) to meet their advance. The Pizarro-Rubio had also arranged for a second group of men, a large number of clients from the peasant village of Santo Tomas, to come to Chachapoyas to replace the other military unit at the disposal of the prefect—the Guardia Civil. In this way it hoped to render Huayapa defenseless in military terms.

The Pizarro-Rubio made similarly elaborate plans to dispose of the legality of Huayapa's position as prefect. From his position of influence in Lima, Deputy Juan M. Pizarro had tampered with the mail, thus preventing the delivery of the order to the judge of the first instance of Chachapoyas to swear Huayapa in as prefect. Furthermore, the Pizarro-Rubio leaders fabricated orders to have their own client, Samuel Eguren, sworn in as prefect, and arranged for these orders to be rushed to Chachapoyas via special delivery. Ultimately, only the fact that Huayapa was able to count on the support of the head of the Guardia Civil—himself a Lima appointee—kept the Pizarro-Rubio casta from realizing its aims.

Prefect Huayapa ended his appeal with a condemnation of Pablo M. Pizarro in particular, and of the Pizarro-Rubio in general—a condemnation that clearly expressed the contradiction between the power of the central regime in Lima and that of the ruling casta in Chachapoyas:

> Sr. Minister, at the heart of this entire, contemptible scheme is D. Pablo M. Pizarro, today mayor of the province of Chachapoyas, against whom I have begun criminal proceedings, together with the other members of the municipal council over which he presides, for various crimes, and especially for repudiating and showing contempt for my acts as a legally constituted authority, as I have had the honor of relating to you in various *oficios* [official letters] in the past.
>
> . . . How sad it is and how deserving of blame and punishment are these men [the Pizarros] who put themselves in opposition to all the prefects who come to this beautiful region and who are not willing to become the blind instruments of their wickedness and their willfulness . . . they . . . have raised unjust charges and false accusations against Prefect Dr. Mariano Velit, and afterwards against Sr. Colonel Alejandro Herrera, and later still against D. Marcial Ruiz Murga, and presently . . . against me [these being the prefects sent to Chachapoyas from Lima during the period 1895–98 who attempted to contain the consolidation of power of the Pizarro-Rubio]. (Ibid.)

Faced with such determined and hostile adversaries, appointees from Lima could curtail the power of the ruling casta by naming governors, lieutenant governors, and justices of the peace to govern in the districts, and by appointing police rank-and-file, who would not be so beholden to the ruling casta for their positions. Indeed, as the petition above demonstrates, in light of the elaborate lengths gone to by ruling castas to dispose of "uncooperative" prefects and subprefects, it was foolhardy for such people *not* to appoint lower-level functionaries who were independent of the ruling casta. For if prefects and subprefects assigned to the region from Lima were to rely on clients of the ruling coalition to fill these posts, they would be contributing to their own demise.

These more "independent" lower-level functionaries were much less likely than ruling casta clients to act in a united manner as the local cogs in a de-partment-wide political machine. Therefore, their appointments made it that much more difficult for the ruling coalition to persecute its enemies, to main-tain the fragmented state of opposing coalitions, and even to keep up ade-quate surveillance of the activities of its enemies. In such circumstances, out-of-power castas did indeed begin to mobilize to change the existing state of af-fairs. At times, opposing coalitions were able to recruit some of these new "independent" appointees to their cause (see Chapter 4).

As individuals with no ties to the ruling casta were appointed to adminis-trative positions throughout the government bureaucracy, the ability of the coalition in power to dominate all commercial activities likewise began to de-teriorate. In such circumstances, individuals who had been forced out of com-merce during the period of ruling casta strength were able to take up these activities once again, in town and country alike—leading to complaints from district-level appointees of the ruling casta that "contraband" was on the rise, or that the people of their districts refused to obey their commands, defied their authority, etc.[71] In fact, such charges generally indicated that those mem-bers of the ruling casta who continued to occupy high-level positions were unable, for example, to specify who would be allowed to transport and sell products for which there was an ongoing commercial demand, to charge their customary fee for extending this privilege to select individuals of their own choice, to charge tolls for the use of roads, or to force peasants to haul mer-chandise for them for little or nothing.

Similarly, as appointees from Lima undermined the ability of the ruling casta to harass its enemies, commercial rights granted to leading members of the ruling casta were also called into question. The following case is typical of such developments. It occurred in mid-1902—toward the end of a period of rule by the Pizarro-Rubio casta (1895–1902). By this time the presence of numerous appointees from Lima who were independent of the ruling casta was interfering with the ability of the Pizarro-Rubio to control its adversaries, the Burga-Hurtado, because of which the latter had succeeded in mobilizing against the ruling casta along multiple fronts. The ability of the Burga-Hurtado to move against the Pizarro-Rubio in turn threatened the latter's control over the region's commercial activities.

> August 26, 1902. Oficio no. 83. Sr. Minister of Government.
> . . . It is without question, Sr. Minister . . . that Amadeo Burga, lacking any authorization, based only on his own will, and taking advantage of the protection afforded by the impenetrable jungles of this locale, along with a group of armed men . . . has prevented the peaceful exploitation of the rubber trees to which the priest David Muñoz has been granted a concession and thus has the legitimate right to exploit. . . . It is also without question . . . that this man [Burga] is arbitrarily charging a toll for the use of roads, although he has been granted no such right by the Government. ([APA45], Aug. 26, 1902)

In light of this complaint, what action was taken to protect the concession granted to the priest Muñoz (a member of the Pizarro-Rubio casta), and to preserve free transit in the section of the regional space recently claimed by Amadeo Burga and his men? The weakened Pizarro-Rubio forces were unable to do anything to punish Burga, even though Burga's transgression was both a serious affront to the honor of the Pizarro-Rubio and a public sign of the deterioration of their control over commercial privileges. Indeed, later that year Amadeo Burga's brother Eloy Burga was elected deputy of Luya province, marking the (temporary) ascent of the Burga-Hurtado casta and the demise of the Pizarro-Rubio (until 1909). Within months of having been branded a criminal for interfering with the rights of priest David Muñoz, Amadeo Burga was granted the legal concession to the same area of rubber trees formerly granted to Muñoz ([APA45], Jan. 18, 1904). The ability to exercise economic privileges was indeed a function of the changing fortunes of one's casta.[72]

There was thus a series of internal contradictions in this form of organization, contradictions that produced weakness out of strength, and strength out of weakness. Coalitions rose to positions of regional hegemony in conditions sufficiently unstable for the state to grant them extensive powers to monitor regional affairs in a relatively autonomous manner. Similarly, coalition cores were forced to grant their more peripheral members virtual carte blanche in policing their jurisdictions. In both regional and local arenas, these extensive powers allowed ruling coalition members to do much to neutralize leading members of the opposition, and to weaken opposing coalitions. In the process, however, ruling coalition members (temporarily) transformed the very conditions of instability that made them indispensable to those higher in the coalition structure. They also increasingly threatened those in these higher positions, because strong clients tended to strengthen themselves at the expense of those higher in the coalition structure. And finally, their tendency to extort wealth and labor services from the primary producers within their jurisdictions encouraged the latter to seek alliances with out-of-power castas.

As steps were taken to replace strong with weak clients throughout the coalition, the ruling casta generated its own opposition and undermined its own organization.[73] For those who were eased out of positions of governance often resented this fact considerably. It was not uncommon for governors, lieutenant governors, and justices of the peace to refuse to step down, or to refuse to hand over the seal of office and/or the files to their would-be successors, forcing the subprefect to send in the police in order to effect the change in office.[74] Equally common was for a former appointee to harass his successor once the latter was in office, at times with the help of former and/or new political allies.[75]

Nor was it unusual for these former district-level appointees to seek an alliance with any of the ruling casta's growing number of enemies: those who were at one time closely associated with the casta core, but who had disassociated themselves because they had received less than they thought they deserved when key appointments were made; those (generally landed families) who had been important members of opposing castas, and had found themselves persecuted in the period of the ruling coalition's greatest strength; and those in the towns and village districts (generally artisans and peasants) who had not played much of a role in coalition politics but who found themselves and their products and labor increasingly subject to the arbitrary exactions of ruling coalition members.

As new alliances formed among such displaced individuals, the ruling casta's task of administering the regional space became ever more difficult. For in the absence of any institutionalized, legitimate means of controlling public life, these displaced individuals seized upon the same pattern of personalistic confrontation pursued by the ruling casta—but in order to reveal the weaknesses in ruling casta control. They generally began such challenges in a somewhat peripheral, if still public, space—often a district where the ruling casta had no viable sphere of influence. A common strategy was to organize a group of local people to accost the district mayor or governor—both appointees of the ruling casta—as he attempted to collect taxes or to force people to labor at public-works projects. The appointee would be insulted and ridiculed in a highly visible public place, and would be prevented from carrying out his duties. During the encounter the "rebels" often denigrated the ruling casta by name, and boasted of the power and protection of the casta to which they belonged.

Santo Tomas. August 15, 1887. Sr. Prefect of the Department of Amazonas.

From the 9th of the present month, when the *apoderado fiscal* [the official who collected the Indian head tax] arrived in this pueblo, the collection of the head tax has proceeded without the least novelty, even if a little slowly; but unfortunately . . . yesterday morning José Eulogio Maycelo appeared in the [main] plaza insulting and threatening me and the *apoderado fiscal*, saying that the Sr. *Fiscal* was a thief who had come to steal from Maycelo's labors, at which point I approached Maycelo and struck him several times, giving the order that he be arrested, because the Sr. *Fiscal* gave me the order to send him to the prefecture, but no one in the pueblo made any attempt to take him [prisoner] using the pretext that they were not inspectors [assistants of the governor] . . . a number of Maycelo's group continued to scream [at us].

This is not the first time that Maycelo has committed such acts, [rather] he is one of the constant perturbors [of order] in this pueblo along with others who accompany him and since the [time of the revolutionary] movement of Villacorta [an out-of-power casta leader] they never leave this pueblo in peace, [spreading] false news of Villacorta and of Yoplac [a lieutenant of Villacorta], but I have not wanted to bother you about this until now, thinking that [his behavior] would improve, but this act [represents] contempt of my authority and that of the *apoderado fiscal*, and sets a bad example for the remaining people of the pueblo. . . . I ask you, Sr. Prefect, to assist me by sending the police necessary to make these scoundrels understand their duty and to make them respect authority and not to act as they did yesterday, by the end of which they were very drunk and were screaming messages to Yoplac.

The Sr. *Apoderado Fiscal* will inform you of my behavior yesterday in the public plaza when only he and I attempted to take the troublemakers prisoner but were not able to because the rest of the people there watched with their arms folded across their chests, condemning me to fail. . . .

The Sr. *Apoderado* has taken the precaution of leaving early in the morning today, carrying with him the money that he has collected and leaving me with 64 receipts to collect. . . . I hope that you can assist me. . . .

　　　　　—*[signed] José Mori, governor of Santo Tomas, August 16, 1887*
　　　　　　　　　　　　　　　　　　(*[APA54], Aug. 16, 1887*)

Appointees of the ruling casta responded to these challenges in large part by sending communiqués to their superiors protesting a state of affairs in which the appointees were confronted with what they called "contempt of their authority," and by demanding that criminal charges be brought against the people responsible for the crime—a request that was usually heeded.[76] However, as the "hegemony" of the ruling casta was increasingly undermined by the contradictions of casta rule, the appointees of the ruling casta were confronted with an escalating number of such acts of public disrespect and defiance, which put growing strain on the ability of the courts and police to respond to them.[77]

Such acts forced the ruling casta to expend much time and effort if it was to answer the affront to its authority. Should it fail to do so decisively, the challenger's success had a "demonstration effect" of its own—generating additional allies, and leading to new challenges in other spaces of perceived weakness. As the contradictions inherent in casta rule produced a growing number of disgruntled individuals, challengers seized upon the potential thus created to recruit new allies. Additional allies with spheres of influence in new sections of the regional space made it possible for out-of-power castas to widen the scope of their transgressions, coming ever closer to the centers of power. Consider the attack on two clients of the Burga-Hurtado casta, carried out in broad daylight in the streets of Chachapoyas in April 1895. The attackers were a group of Pizarro-Rubio adepts, emboldened by the knowledge that the successful conclusion of the civil war was soon to bring their casta to power, ending the reign of the Burga-Hurtado.

Sr. Judge of the First Instance. Today at 11:00 A.M. a criminal act has taken place
that I will now relate to you: José Chapa Solsol was returning from [the es-
tate] *Murcia* [whose owner was Chapa's patron, casta leader Manuel Hur-
tado], where according to information obtained by this subprefecture he
plants a few *chacras* [small fields] of maize, and having passed by several streets
of Yance barrio [one of Chachapoyas's four barrios, or neighborhoods] José
Santos Valdez, José Picón, Justo Lopez, and Ciriaca Villacorta, Valdez's
woman, advanced upon Chapa with the clear intent of killing him. Between
them they managed to throw Chapa to the ground, and once having done so
they proceeded to completely destroy Chapa's head, with clubs and stones,
inflicting on him more than a dozen wounds, all of them grave. . . . I must
add that several days ago José Picón attempted to kill priest José Lopez Zu-
maeta [also a Burga client], but was prevented from doing so when the priest
seized the weapon that Picón was carrying. ([APA63], *Subprefecto del Cercado
al Juez de 1ra Instancia del Cercado*, Apr. 5, 1895)

The report on a second attack further conveys the personalistic nature of
such confrontations—the way that they were designed to humiliate the casta
whose member was the subject of the violence. In this particular case, followers of Pablo M. Pizarro—under house arrest in Chachapoyas for his involvement in the failed national coup attempt of 1924—attempted to resurrect
their patron by persecuting his enemies in the countryside:[78]

Sr. Prefect of the Department. Isaías Barrera, resident of the town of Santo
Tomas . . . with the greatest respect informs you that: For some time don
Pablo Pizarro, in his murderous endeavors, pursues me tenaciously here [in
Santo Tomas], where I have my house, family, and economic affairs, by
means of his appointees and armed killers that he has at his disposal, because
of which I . . . appeal to you to provide me with the individual rights and
protections that all citizens are granted by the Constitution. Pizarro's son-in-
law, Nemesio Ramos, is the person entrusted [by Pizarro] to carry out this
criminal labor, because of which Ramos, . . . the governor Dolores Yoplac,
the justice of the peace Maximiliano Zabaleta, and the tax collector Tomas
Cáseres, assemble daily in this pueblo, armed with revolvers. Not having
found me here they have fired their weapons at my wife, who escaped
miraculously. . . . I have had to hide myself and my family in [the pueblo of]
Cocabamba, because of these savages, who are armed with a great many

Mauser rifles, who shamelessly announce that they have been ordered to deliver my head to the aforementioned Ramos, in exchange for rewards or
money. . . . I was not there [in Santo Tomas] when don Pablo Pizarro arrived, and Ramos together with the aforementioned authorities went to the
house of my sister-in-law, Josefina LaTorre, robbed her of everything she had
in her house, beat her, Ramos grabbing her by the hair and in a cowardly
way dragging her to . . . Colonel Pizarro. . . . The poor woman would have
suffered [an ill fate] had Captain Moran not defended her . . . refusing to
consent to more outrages. . . . Immediately [thereafter] they went in search
of her husband Isaac LaTorre. They captured him, incarcerated him, and tortured him miserably and made him sign statements swearing that no robbery
or other outrages had been committed against his family. . . . The present
governor, at the order of Ramos, whom [the governor] obeys blindly, jails
people [without cause], and under the pretext of [levying] fines, extorts 10,
15, or 20 soles from peaceful citizens, dividing the money among the aforementioned group [of authorities]. He [the governor] commits outrages that
were unknown even in the time of the Roman Inquisition. In Santo Tomas
there are honorable people who suffer such a fate simply because they do not
obey Ramos . . . for no other reason than they are not servile to him. . . . I
firmly believe, Sr. Prefect, that your impartial authority will find a remedy
for the situation of many honorable citizens, and will apply the [legal] sanction that such unspeakable and monstrous crimes deserve. . . . In light of
what I have explained, I ask that you provide me with the constitutional
guarantees to which I refer in this petition.

—Cocabamba, June 17, 1924, [signed] Isaías Barrera ([APA15], decreto no. 138 [June
21, 1924])

During moments of political transition (elections, coups, civil wars)—such
as those which obtained during the "outrages" described above—the ascend-
ing casta would attempt to publicly humiliate even the highest-ranking officials
of the outgoing casta—who did their utmost to avoid such a fate by disap-
pearing.[79] A typical example can be seen in the failed plot of Pizarro-Rubio
followers to demonstrate their ability to dominate and punish the opposition
in May 1895, when the same civil war mentioned above was about to depose
the Burga-Hurtado and to bring the Pizarro-Rubio to power. This particular
attack was focused on José María Echaiz, a high-ranking member of the
Burga-Hurtado.

Sr. Judge of the First Instance. With the present oficio I have the honor of send-
ing to your office the enclosed letter signed by Ildefonso Chavez and Leon
Melendez. . . . In the letter . . . sent to Timoteo Cachay, principal agent in
Luya and Lámud of Toribio Lopez [one of Pablo Pizarro's oldest and most
trusted clients] and his followers, [Chavez and Melendez] incite Lopez and
his armed gang to rob José María Echaiz of everything he has at . . . *Shañi*
[Echaiz's hacienda] . . . to burn *Shañi* to the ground . . . and to kill
Echaiz. . . . In addition, the aforementioned letter also includes [plans to
make an] attempt on the life of the new prefect recently appointed to this
department. ([APA63], *Subprefecto del Cercado al Juez de 1ra Instancia del Cercado*, May 10, 1895)

Having risen to power, the new ruling casta would begin to flaunt *its* ability to violate the rights of its competitors, and thus the whole cycle would
begin anew. For out-of-power coalitions, then, one of the conditions of rising
to preeminence was that they demonstrate their ability to dominate, humiliate,
shame, and abuse members of the ruling casta—to violate the constitutional
garantías granted to all citizens by the central government.

The ruling casta's control over the police force and over tributary extraction
and bureaucratic appointments, and its ability to impose sanctions and taxes selectively, generally allowed it to retain a strong following through all the vi-
cissitudes of local politics. In the context of the opposition that grew out of
contradictions of casta-based control, however, it was forced to rule in an increasingly arbitrary and autocratic manner through time—and to do so via
"weak" clients who were obliged to rely on higher authorities (often the police) in order to impose their will within their localities. The longer the regime
of any particular casta endured, then, the more coercive it was perceived to
be by a growing number of the regional population. Ultimately, the pretensions of opposing coalitions were kept in check only by the knowledge that
the ruling casta could count on the armed support of the central state.

Consequently, opposing coalitions chose moments when the central state
had a difficult time backing its local clients with armed force to mount attacks on the ruling casta—either during times of political transition (congressional and presidential elections) or during the frequent coup attempts and
outbreaks of insurrection and civil war that characterized the period. For at
these moments coalitions fought one another on more equal terms.[80]

The political organization described above formed the context within which all "individual" actions and all commercial transactions were necessarily embedded. Virtually no one was able to go about his daily affairs as an autonomous individual, enjoying security of person and property, without the protection of numerous and powerful political allies. And virtually no one was able to move himself and his goods through the regional space in a sufficiently safe and secure manner for a sufficiently long period of time to make "commerce" a viable form of livelihood—although many people attempted to participate in and gain from the general movement of goods and people within the region itself, and between it and the adjacent jungle and sierra regions to the west and east.[81] One's ability to do either in any stable and consistent manner was perpetually at risk because of the continually shifting nature of political alliances, which varied according to whether the ruling coalition was in a "strong" or a "weak" phase.

During "strong" phases—when the ruling coalition monopolized the key positions of prefect, subprefects, judges, and chiefs of police, and had the support of strong clients in the districts—members of the ruling casta could count on enjoying virtually complete security of person and property, as guaranteed them by the Constitution. At the same time, they were able to deny these rights to members of opposing castas—to violate the latter's individual rights and protections without suffering any ill consequences. Indeed, members of the ruling casta were *obligated* to do so in order to establish the kind of reputation for potency and power that successful rule required.

As an outgrowth of its position of (temporary) strength, the ruling coalition was also able to specify who would and would not be involved in commercial activities, from merchant/hacendado to peasant mule-driver. Furthermore, the casta in power could effectively enforce its will because of its ability to monitor the movements of people and goods through space.[82] As a result, during such periods, there were relatively few individuals involved in major commercial undertakings. Those who were so involved had been granted this right by the ruling casta. And those associated with other castas were either forced entirely out of the commercial realm (thus weakening the opposing casta by cutting off its commercial links), or were allowed minimal involvement in ways that did not threaten the ruling casta.

During a "weak" phase, on the other hand—when the ruling casta did not monopolize key political positions, and could not count on the assistance of strong clients in the districts—its ability to control the regional space in an effective manner deteriorated concomitantly. As a result, members of the ruling coalition could not count on complete security of person and property— did not unproblematically enjoy the "individual rights and protections granted to all citizens" by the central state. Other castas were able to expand their involvement in the general movement of goods and people both within the region and between it and adjacent regions (although often by means of "alternative" transport routes and outside the gaze of regional authorities). Further, a wider range of people from all social classes was able to become involved in commercial activities.

During this period as a whole, then, neither individual actions nor commercial transactions had any independent existence. Rather, both were subsumed by the dynamics of the unstable, unpredictable, constantly shifting political organization described above.

These political struggles underscored the importance of "aristocratic privilege" as the true basis of political order, and showed the degree to which regional political dynamics subsumed the state's notion of "popular" political legitimacy. The "individual rights and protections granted to all citizens" by the central government did nothing more than provide a consistent frame of reference in relation to which each individual's standing in the "aristocratic" power structure could be publicly evaluated: the ability to enjoy one's rights and to violate those of others qualified one as powerful; the inability to defend one's rights marked one as servile. Far from expressing equalitarian social realities, "rights" acted as a perverse measure of one's changing place in an unstable structure of hierarchy.

In addition, ordering regional affairs according to casta affiliation produced a series of what might be called "dysfunctional bureaucratic institutions"— from the police to the courts to tax collection to education. Because virtually all bureaucratic appointments were made in order to create/reward allies and clients, it was rare indeed for the individuals appointed to particular posts to have any training in, aptitude for, or interest in the positions entrusted to them. Rather, bureaucratic posts were generally regarded as means of personal enrichment for those who (temporarily) filled them. As a result, the police did not truly police, the courts/judges did not adjudicate, and teachers rarely taught. The purpose for which the institution in question had been created was at best incidental, and most commonly in opposition, to the interests and desires of those who worked within them.

As a result, it was impossible for the institutions of the state to attain any independence from the particular interests of the casta currently in power. It was obvious to all that *el Supremo Gobierno* served no general interest, and played no disinterested role within regional affairs.

4 Casta Contradictions Historicized

The developments of 1908–13—when the Burga-Hurtado was deposed as the ruling casta of the Chachapoyas region by the Pizarro-Rubio, which then went through strong and weak phases of control and was subsequently challenged by the Burga-Hurtado forces—will help illustrate the contradictions inherent in casta rule outlined in Chapter 4. It will also underscore several other points: the importance of patriarchal strategies of marital alliance in constructing coalitions that could control the regional space; the subsumption of individuality by broad social categories of race and gender, which acted as "building blocks" for the entire order of domination and control; the position of aristocratic sovereignty (although not voiced in public, political ritual or in public or private political discourse) as the reigning social reality of the era; and the fact that the state-endorsed rhetoric of popular sovereignty (involving notions of individual rights and protections, the sanctity of private property and individual labor, and the formal equality of all citizens in the eyes of the law) acquired concrete meaning in relationship to a political and economic order based on inherited hierarchy and inequality.

During 1909 a major shift in power relations occurred in the department of Amazonas. For the previous six years, departmental affairs had been dominated by an uneasy alliance between two family groups—the Burga-Hurtado and the Ocampo-Eguren—who, with considerable effort, had managed to forestall the efforts of the Pizarro-Rubio casta to seize control of the department. Leading the Burga-Hurtado casta as deputy of Luya province was Eloy Burga Valdez; at the head of the Ocampo-Eguren coalition was Felix Ocampo

Bustamante, deputy of Chachapoyas province. Burga and Ocampo were the regional clients of two different national political parties—the *Partido Civil* (Burga) and the *Partido Constitucional* (Ocampo). These two parties had formed a temporary and ad hoc alliance prior to the presidential elections of 1903 in order to defeat their common adversary, Nicolas de Piérola, and his *Partido Demócrata*, of whom the Pizarro-Rubio casta was a regional client. The national alliance between the two parties was short-lived, however, and relations between the Burga and Ocampo forces in Chachapoyas were always strained.

Finding coordinated action difficult, the Burga-Hurtado and Ocampo-Eguren forces had been somewhat less successful than the Pizarro-Rubio casta would subsequently be in restricting elected and appointed positions to their own allies, and in winning the constant struggle with the executive branch of government to control high-level appointed positions (which meant that the Burga-Hurtado and Ocampo castas were less able to fill lower-level appointed positions with their own clients). As a result, even prior to the rise of the Pizarro-Rubio casta in 1909, several of the latter's high-ranking members had attained positions of importance.[1] The Burga-Hurtado/Ocampo alliance thus exercised something less than complete hegemony within the regional space.

Nonetheless, the Burga-Hurtado and Ocampo families did succeed in controlling the majority of the most important elected and appointed positions from 1902 until 1908. And during the period immediately prior to the rise of the Pizarro-Rubio casta in 1909, they controlled the prefecture, the deputyships of Chachapoyas and Luya provinces, the subprefectures of both provinces, the position of departmental comptroller, and the judgeships of Chachapoyas and Luya-Bongará.

By mid-1909, however, Eloy Burga and Felix Ocampo had lost their deputyships of Luya and Chachapoyas provinces, despite the fact that during May of the previous year, when presidential elections had taken place, their two families had controlled most of the important elected and political positions in the department, had used the armed force of the state (which they monopolized) to manipulate elections in their favor, had placed their own clients in charge of the provincial voters' registration boards (which decided who was and was not eligible to vote; see [APA13], decreto no. 75 [Mar. 30, 1908), and had the advantage of being able to use state funds to support "election costs" (100 soles in each province; [APA13], decretos no. 106 [May 26,

1908], 107 [May 27, 1908], 119 [June 10, 1908]). In addition, they had expended a huge sum of money (5,724 soles: [APA13], decreto no. 170 [Sept. 9, 1908]) in putting down simultaneous rebellions staged in early May by the Pizarro-Rubio casta (assisted by José María Echaiz) in Luya and Bongará provinces. The Pizarro-Rubio had staged the uprisings with the goal of seizing control of both provinces by force so as to impose their own results in the elections that were to follow later in the month.

The violence surrounding attempts to control the presidential elections of May 1908 will convey something of the centrality of electoral politics, and of elected political position, in giving a casta control over regional affairs. The presidential elections were particularly important because a president sympathetic to the cause of a marginalized casta could do much to help that casta rise to power. In the uprisings staged against the Burga-Hurtado/Ocampo alliance in Luya and Bongará provinces, the Pizarro-Rubio were attempting to bring their marginalization of the previous six years to an end by helping to "elect" a new president who would act as its political patron in the nation's capital.[2]

In the late afternoon of May 3, 1908—three weeks prior to the presidential elections—Pablo M. Pizarro, his nephew Javier M. Pizarro (son of Pablo's half-brother Rosendo), Pablo's brother-in-law Gustavo Rubio Linch, another in-law of the Pizarros (José del Carmen Tuesta), Javier Pizarro's father's cousin José María Echaiz, and Echaiz's son Francisco led a group of armed men into the town of Lámud, capital of the province of Luya. They quickly assembled at the door of the *Casa Subprefectural*, or subprefectural building, located on the town square, where they expected to find the subprefect, Felipe Rodriguez, who was also a high-ranking officer in the Guardia Civil. The interlopers broke down the door of the Casa Subprefectural and poured in with the intention of killing the subprefect and assuming control of the province. Finding him not at his desk, however, they immediately made their way to his residence, where he was in conversation with the governor of Luya district, Manuel Chavez. Once they had surrounded the house, the attacking forces began their assault, firing their weapons into the Rodriguez home. Rodriguez and Chavez were both unarmed, and attempted to escape by the rear balcony of the house. Once outside, however, they found a number of armed men waiting for them, who summarily executed them.

The seven members of the Guardia Civil quartered in the town heard the shooting, left their barracks to investigate, and immediately ran into the fire of the attacking Pizarros and Echaiz. Thus ensued a gun battle of several hours in the streets of the town, which ended only at nightfall when the attackers withdrew. Three members of the Guardia Civil were wounded in the fracas ([APA13], decretos no. 108 [May 29, 1908], 109 [May 30, 1908], 110 [May 30, 1908]).[3] In the weeks that followed, the *montonera* (the band of armed men) continued to harass the towns of Lámud and Luya, forcing Prefect Manuel Hurtado to authorize the expenditure of a considerable sum of money in order to put more men in arms. By the end of May, the montonera had been driven from the region.

Despite this serious challenge from the Pizarro-Rubio casta, the ruling Burga-Hurtado/Ocampo alliance managed to capture the presidential election within the department of Amazonas for the ruling political party in Lima, the Partido Civil. This was the surest means for it to reproduce its own position within the department when elections were held for the deputyships of Chachapoyas province and Luya province the following year. Indeed, so thoroughly did the ruling alliance overcome its enemies that, after the failed Pizarro-Rubio bid to seize power, the most important members of the unsuccessful casta first went into hiding and then fled the department entirely. For they could be sure that the Burga-Hurtado/Ocampo would seek retribution for their transgressions via one or more of the mechanisms used by ruling castas to humiliate leading members of the opposition—torture, lengthy public trials, and physical abuse/neglect during extended prison terms (see Chapter 3). Indeed, by late June, the substitute senator for Amazonas—José A. Urteaga, a close ally of Eloy Burga—and the prefect of Amazonas, Manuel Hurtado, were pressuring the prefect of the neighboring department of Cajamarca to capture the Pizarros, Echaiz, and other "*revoltosos*," and to return them to Chachapoyas so that "justice" could be done ([APA13], decreto no. 136 [June 27, 1908]).

Developments outside the region of Amazonas, however, ultimately confounded the local successes of the Burga-Hurtado/Ocampo alliance.[4] Prior to the election of 1908, the national political party that controlled the central government—the Partido Civil—split into traditional and progressive wings (Basadre 1968–69, 11: ch. 140; 12: ch. 148; Taylor 1986: 38, 40). The Burga-

Hurtado/Ocampo alliance had the misfortune of backing the traditional wing of the party. It was the progressive wing, however, under the leadership of Augusto Leguía, that triumphed at the polls. Adding to the difficulties of the Burga-Hurtado/Ocampo alliance, Colonel Pablo M. Pizarro, military head of the Pizarro-Rubio casta and leader of the failed election uprising of 1908, was the spiritual compadre of the new president[5]—in fact, Pizarro was the godfather of Leguía's children. Further, President Leguía chose as his first minister of government the senator for the department of Loreto, Miguel A. Rojas Mesía—brother-in-law of Juan M. Pizarro Farje, and close business associate of Iquitos rubber baron Julio Cesar Arana. Thus, two prominent members of the Pizarro-Rubio casta were confidants of the president.[6]

Nonetheless, at the end of 1908 the Burga-Hurtado/Ocampo alliance was in a strong position. Allies and/or appointees of Chachapoyas deputy Felix Ocampo and Luya deputy Eloy Burga filled most important positions in the police, in the military,[7] and in public administration (including subprefects of both provinces, the district attorney, the comptroller general, and both judges of the first instance. The all-important post of prefect was occupied by Eloy Burga's close casta ally and father-in-law, Manuel Hurtado. The strength of the Burga-Hurtado/Ocampo alliance was particularly important because Deputies Burga and Ocampo were up for re-election in the spring of 1909. The outcome of these elections would determine which casta, if any, emerged to rule the region.

In 1909, President Leguía began to take actions that favored the casta of his compadre Pablo M. Pizarro—actions that ultimately proved decisive in allowing the Pizarro-Rubio casta to triumph over the Burga-Hurtado/Ocampo. Despite the protests of Amazonas Substitute Senator José A. Urteaga (a close ally of Eloy Burga and judge of the first instance of Chachapoyas province), in January 1909 President Leguía appointed a new prefect (career politician Carlos Pázara), a new departmental head of the Guardia Civil (Captain Juan Mancilla), and a new commander of the Gendarmery (Luis Pantoja) for the department of Amazonas.[8] Appointed at this time as well was a new subprefect for the province of Chachapoyas, career politician Alejandro R. Santander. Accompanying Pázara, the new prefect, was his brother Alberto, a high-ranking officer in the Guardia Civil, who was given the post of military assistant to the prefecture over which his brother Carlos was to preside.

In making these appointments President Leguía did not choose members of the Pizarro-Rubio casta itself—which would have been dangerously and unnecessarily provocative considering the strength of the Burga-Hurtado/Ocampo alliance at the time. But because these new appointees would be the ultimate arbiters of most forms of regional conflict—they would decide in whose favor and in which sections of the regional space the armed force of the state would be applied, and whose appeals for protection or redress would be acted on and whose would not—wresting these positions away from the Burga-Hurtado/Ocampo alliance was a means of restoring some semblance of balance in the relations between the ruling alliance and the Pizarro-Rubio casta. This was a particularly important consideration in light of the upcoming elections, for if the Pizarro-Rubio casta was to have even a remote chance of success at the polls, it was essential that the machinery of state not remain entirely in the hands of the Burga-Hurtado/Ocampo forces. This was true even though President Leguía's faction of the Partido Civil controlled the National Election Board, which would ultimately rule on the outcome of the elections. Local casta leaders had learned through painful experience that decisions made in Lima about the outcomes of elections in the provinces reflected political exigencies in the national capital as much as or more than they did the interests of provincial allies, especially when no one casta was able to definitively control the electoral process and to marginalize the opposition.[9] It was best to settle election matters within the region if at all possible, by leaving no trace of doubt as to their outcome.

President Leguía's decision to appoint a new prefect and new heads of the Guardia Civil and the Gendarmery for Amazonas brought important changes in the balance of power between the two castas, and gained for the Pizarro-Rubio casta a definitive victory at the polls. It allowed the casta to follow a time-honored election strategy in the Chachapoyas region—eliminating members of the opposition as even *potential* competitors by preventing them from ever participating in the elections.

As explained in Chapter 3, castas had traditionally attempted to exclude members of the opposition from participation in elections by one or more of three possible means: by physically eliminating members of the opposition via assassination (an option that would have been dangerous for the Pizarro-Rubio casta in early 1909 because it would have forced the central state to intervene, since Ocampo and Burga were both congressmen); by manipulating the justice system and the courts to disqualify members of the opposition temporarily by having them jailed or sought for some crime, real or imagined (an option that was not available to the Pizarro-Rubio casta at the beginning of 1909 because its members did not control the local courts or system of justice); and by driving members of the opposition out of the region entirely with threats and attacks (an option not available at the beginning of 1909 because the Burga-Hurtado/Ocampo alliance controlled much more in the way of armed force than the Pizarro-Rubio).

The second and third of these options became real possibilities for the Pizarro-Rubio casta as a direct outgrowth of changes in regional political relations that took place during the first half of 1909. Once it became widely known that President Leguía had removed Manuel Hurtado as prefect, and had chosen new heads of the Guardia Civil and the Gendarmery,[10] an extensive "changing of the guard" began in the most important political positions in the department, seriously undermining the position of the Burga-Hurtado/Ocampo forces.[11] A number of key positions in the police departments and elsewhere changed hands as clients and allies of the Burga-Hurtado/Ocampo alliance, sensing that the rise of Leguía and the arrival of his powerful appointees made conditions too dangerous for them to remain, resigned and/or left the region.[12] They were replaced either by individuals who came from the national capital,[13] or by interim appointees from within the region who were beholden to the new prefect for their positions. Simultaneously, members of the Pizarro-Rubio casta, interpreting the president's decision to change the prefect and the heads of both police forces as an unspoken endorsement of their casta, initiated a wave of violence and intimidation that was intended to purge the region not only of clients of the opposing casta who had not left of their own accord, but also of new appointees who did not fully cooperate with the Pizarro-Rubio's bid to seize control of the region. A number of Burga-Hurtado/Ocampo clients and several important, recently arrived appointees deserted their posts due to the threats they received from members of the Pizarro-Rubio casta (see below). And at least one position in one of the police forces was vacated due to assassination by members of the Pizarro-Rubio casta.[14] The result was that the Burga-Hur-

tado and Ocampo families lost virtually all their important allies among the officers of both branches of the police, and also in high- and low-level positions in public administration.

Perhaps the key roles in effecting these changes were played by the new
prefect, Carlos Pázara, and the prefect's brother Alberto, who was military assistant of the prefecture. Soon after the arrival of Prefect Pázara, it became
clear to all that he was willing to put the armed force of the state at the disposal only of members of the Pizarro-Rubio casta, would respond only to
their appeals for protection and justice, and would ignore the complaints of the
casta's enemies. The fact that Pázara was so quickly swayed in the direction
of the Pizarro-Rubio casta was undoubtedly related to his growing attach-
ment to Eva María Pizarro Rojas, whom he subsequently married.[15]

Prefect Pázara's ability to favor the casta of his future in-laws was hampered
initially, however, by the new mayor de Guardias, Captain Mancilla, who was
unwilling to side exclusively with the Pizarro-Rubio casta in its struggles with
the Burga-Hurtado/Ocampo alliance. Equally uncooperative was Sr. Santander, the new subprefect of Chachapoyas province. Santander refused to replace the governors of each of the districts of the province with Pizarro-Rubio clients. This was a pressing matter because most of the existing governors
were Burga-Hurtado clients, appointed at the end of 1908 by Prefect Manuel
Hurtado (and Subprefect Jorge A. Guadiamus, a career politician from Lima,
who took up his post in June 1908). If the Burga-Hurtado clients remained in
their posts, it would be very difficult for the Pizarro-Rubio casta to control the
upcoming elections in April. If members of the Pizarro-Rubio casta were to
succeed in placing their own appointees in these positions, they could be
much more certain of capturing the electoral process for themselves.

Within just one month, the Pizarro-Rubio casta had succeeded in removing these formidable obstacles to its rise to power. On March 10, Mayor de
Guardias Mancilla resigned his post, citing "ill health," and made a hasty retreat
to Lima ([APA13], decreto no. 78 [May 1, 1909]). Three days later, Subprefect
Santander resigned and was transferred out of the region (ibid., decreto no.
40 [Mar. 13, 1909]). Popular memory in Chachapoyas has it that both decided
to quit their posts in the face of threats they received from members of the
Pizarro-Rubio casta—an interpretation that is strongly reinforced by the im-

mediate appointment of Alberto Pázara, brother of the new prefect Carlos Pázara, to replace Mancilla as mayor de Guardias (ibid., decreto no. 62 [Apr. 1, 1909]; *Guardia Civil de Amazonas al Subprefecto del Cercado*, May 12, 1909).

A new subprefect for Chachapoyas (Sr. Colina) did not arrive from Lima until April 12 (ibid., decreto no. 75 [Apr. 15, 1909]), by which time the all-important elections for the two provincial deputyships had already taken place. In the interim, Nestor Alvaro Santillán, governor of Chachapoyas district, became temporary subprefect (as stipulated by law), and Santillán did nothing to obstruct the efforts of the Pizarro-Rubio casta to control the elections. As a result, Prefect Pázara took it upon himself to appoint new governors for most districts of Chachapoyas province.[16] As district governors always did, these new officials "oversaw" the electoral process—making sure that the *asambleas de mayores contribuyentes* (see Chapter 3) were made up strictly of individuals chosen by the National Election Board (controlled by president's faction of the Partido Civil), and that they were able to meet and carry out their functions without being disrupted by violence from opposing castas. Governors also helped ensure that those individuals listed in the official voting registers did not meet with "accidents" while making their way to the district and provincial capitals where they were to cast their votes. An edict published and distributed by the prefecture just prior to the elections of 1913 succinctly expresses this problem:

> All those who provoke disorders that interfere with the freedom of suffrage or who create turmoil by means of the use of firearms, clubs, or any other means of aggression in the places where the electoral councils or their respective commissions meet will be subject to trial and punishment . . . consisting of a fine of from 50 to 500 soles or of a prison sentence of from fifteen days to six months, with the additional penalty of losing their right to vote for a period of two years. ([AMC6], 3, no. 15 [Jan. 25, 1913]: 2)

The particular individuals chosen by Pázara to act as governors to safeguard the electoral process, the sections of the regional space they were assigned to control, and the Burga-Hurtado/Ocampo clients they replaced reveal much about the way that castas used "strong" governors and appointees in outlying sections of the regional space to control space effectively during periods of political transition. Chachapoyas district was both the seat of regional power and the residence of the majority of individuals who were eligible to vote—and therefore was key in controlling the outcome of elections. High-ranking casta member Gustavo A. Rubio Linch, brother-in-law of Pablo M. Pizarro Farje (soon to be substitute senator for Amazonas) and brother of Miguel and Arturo Rubio Linch (who would subsequently become deputies of Chachapoyas and Bongará provinces), was appointed governor of Chachapoyas.[17] Working with the mayor de Guardias, Alberto Pázara, he was able to prevent any disruptions in the electoral process "by means of the use of firearms, clubs, or any other means of aggression," and thus to capture the elections for the Pizarro-Rubio casta within this key section of the regional space.

"Strong" Pizarro-Rubio clients were also placed in the governorships of four strategic districts in outlying sections of the region. Leimebamba sat astride the main road linking Chachapoyas to Cajamarca and the national capital beyond; in this district, Governor Neptalí Ocampo (brother of Deputy Felix Ocampo) was replaced by José M. Escobedo, a landowner with close ties to the Pizarro-Rubio casta. In Molinopampa, which protected the main road to Moyobamba and the jungle beyond, Luis E. Rimache was appointed governor (and in nearby Taulia, Luis's brother Benito Rimache was named to this post; the Rimaches belonged to a landowning family with long-standing ties to the Pizarro-Rubio). The Burga family owned land and had many clients in Chuquibamba, located in the extreme southwest corner of the region, where it borders on the neighboring department of Cajamarca; here, the Pizarro-Rubio casta replaced Governor Isidro Burga (first cousin of casta leader Eloy Burga) with its own strong client, Eusebio Reyes. In Chiliquin, located along the road to Jumbilla (capital of Bongará province), where the Hurtado family owned estates and had established an important sphere of influence, Manuel A. Pizarro was appointed governor. Each of these districts was located along a major transport route linking Chachapoyas to other regions, or to important population centers within the region. These routes, along which arms and men had often been moved in great amounts rapidly into and out of the region during large-scale conflagrations, had in the past decided the outcome of inter-casta political conflicts.[18] In order to preclude the possibility that the Burga-Hurtado and/or Ocampo would use them in this way to "steal" the elections (as they attempted to do in 1913; see below), it was essential for the Pizarro-Rubio casta to place in these districts "strong" clients who could monitor and contain the movements of casta enemies.

The appointments of strong governors in two other districts reflected somewhat different strategic considerations. The district of Levanto is located just above and outside of the town of Chachapoyas, and is therefore potentially a site from which the town can be easily attacked. The Hurtado-Eguren family owned several large haciendas (most notably *Quipachacha*) along the common border of Chachapoyas and Levanto, and had a long-standing and important sphere of influence in the latter district.[19] In order to guard against the possibility that the Burga-Hurtado would mount an attack on Chachapoyas from Levanto during election time, or that it would attempt to "steal" the election within the district itself, the Pizarro-Rubio casta appointed Manuel Rubio as governor. The Rubio family was the perfect choice for containing any potential threats from the Burga-Hurtado, for the Rubio also owned an important estate (*Condechaca*), in Levanto itself, and thus had its own long-standing sphere of influence in the district.

In this way the Pizarro-Rubio casta filled the governorships of the most important districts of the province with its own high-ranking members. In each case, the individuals in question had pre-existing spheres of influence and *contingentes* (contingents of people loyal to them) in the districts where they were appointed (or had relatives with such spheres and contingentes), which they could draw on in imposing control during the electoral process. Their mere presence in these districts signaled to members of the opposition that the Pizarro-Rubio casta would be carefully monitoring the activities there.[20]

The general insecurity both of those who did not comply fully with the wishes of the Pizarro-Rubio casta and of those who had been clients of or were associated with the Burga-Hurtado or Ocampo families increased markedly from the time that Alberto Pázara assumed command of the Guardia Civil. From this point onward, it became increasingly clear that Prefect Pázara and Mayor de Guardias Pázara could not be counted on to intervene on behalf of *anyone* whom members of the Pizarro-Rubio wished to persecute[21]—neither private citizens nor appointees of the central state. Thus ensued not only great insecurity of person and property for people of all social classes, but also a power vacuum that members of the Pizarro-Rubio casta were quick to fill. For when political appointees found that the prefect and the Guardia Civil were deaf to their pleas for protection in the face of violence and threats, they either resigned their posts or ceased taking any decisive action against the Pizarro-Rubio. And when former Burga-Hurtado and Ocampo clients realized that the Pázaras would do nothing to protect them from the Pizarro-Rubio casta, they either attempted to retrench and defend themselves without the help of the authorities or left the region entirely.

In addition to Mayor de Guardias Mancilla and Subprefect Santander, one of the early targets of the Pizarro-Rubio casta was the judge of the first instance of Luya-Bongará, Dr. Leonardo del Mazo. Del Mazo had been judge in 1909, at the time of the Pizarro-Rubio's failed attempt to seize control of Luya province by force of arms so as to impose their own electoral results in the presidential elections.[22] On May 13, 1909, Judge del Mazo made the mistake of issuing an order of detention for Javier M. Pizarro (one of the leaders of the 1908 electoral insurrection) and several other men who had attacked and publicly beaten a former low-level appointee of Deputy Eloy Burga.[23] On that same day, Judge del Mazo sent a communiqué to Prefect Pázara protesting that his life had been threatened by Pizarro. Furthermore, del Mazo pleaded with the prefect to provide him with the constitutional rights and protections to which all citizens were entitled according to the Constitution ([APA13], decreto no. 95 [May 13, 1909]).

Judge del Mazo's response to Pizarro was strange indeed. Ordinarily, a judge who was threatened in this way would immediately begin criminal proceedings against the person who threatened him, and would instruct the subprefect of the province first to have the person thrown in jail, and at some later date to have the person appear before the judge for sentencing. The subprefect in turn would instruct the provincial head of the Guardia Civil (or of the Gendarmery) to have one of his men imprison the man and to be sure that the person did indeed appear before the judge on the appointed date.

Dr. del Mazo knew, however, that he could count on neither the subprefect of Luya (Sr. Maza) nor the provincial head of the Guardia Civil (Major Vargas) to comply with such an order. Subprefect Maza had already bowed to pressure from the Pizarro-Rubio casta by appointing its clients to governorships in many of the districts of Luya province, and thus was unlikely to assist del Mazo in his attempt to jail one of the casta's more prominent members. Nor was Major Vargas, head of the Guardia Civil in Luya province, likely to assist in the jailing of Pizarro. The close ties between the Pizarro-Rubio casta and Vargas's superior officer, Alberto Pázara, mayor de Guardias for the entire department of Amazonas, were a matter of public record. For Vargas to help del Mazo imprison Pizarro would thus be to go directly against the wishes of his immediate superior.[24]

Without allies and fearing for his life, Judge del Mazo appealed to Prefect Pázara—not for Pizarro to be brought to justice, but only for protection from him. The prefect, however, already closely allied with the Pizarro-Rubio casta (he was soon to wed one of the casta's daughters), did nothing more than send the subprefect of Luya the following instruction: "Be sure that the [constitutional] guarantees to which all citizens are entitled are observed" ([APA13], decreto no. 95 [May 17, 1909]).

Predictably, Subprefect Maza did nothing. Judge del Mazo went into hiding immediately, and was replaced as interim judge of the first instance by Salvador M. Pizarro Alvis, uncle of Javier M. Pizarro, the man who had originally threatened del Mazo's life.[25]

By means of this wave of violence and intimidation, combined with the assistance of the prefect and the mayor de Guardias, the Pizarro-Rubio casta succeeded in shifting the balance of power within the region in its own favor, so that when the National Election Board named high-ranking casta member Ezequiel Bardales (brother-in-law of Arturo Rubio Linch, who was soon to become deputy of Chachapoyas province) as departmental president of the *Asamblea de Electores Contribuyentes* (see [APA13], decreto no. 55 [Mar. 30, 1909]), the political environment was such that he and his activities could be carefully protected. These changes helped ensure victory at the polls for the Pizarro-Rubio.[26]

The casta went even further, however, to ensure that neither Eloy Burga nor Felix Ocampo had any opportunity either to participate in or to disrupt the electoral process. As mentioned above, Salvador M. Pizarro replaced Dr. Leonardo del Mazo as (interim) judge of Luya-Bongará in mid-May. One of Judge Pizarro's first acts was to declare enemy casta leader Eloy Burga guilty of

murder, and to begin first a regional and then a national manhunt to bring
Burga to justice. On June 1 Judge Pizarro (half-brother of Juan and Pablo
Pizarro Farje) declared Eloy Burga guilty of the murder of an officer of the
Guardia Civil (no evidence that Burga was guilty of the crime was ever produced), and ordered that Burga be sought out and detained. Judge Pizarro
sent a communiqué to Prefect Pázara to this effect ([APA13], decreto no. 116
[June 1, 1909]), and Pázara then ordered the subprefects of all three provinces
to comply with the order. The subprefects informed the governors of their
respective districts that Burga was to be apprehended and detained—at which
point Burga first went into hiding and then fled the department (apparently in
the direction of Cajamarca). On June 4, 1909, Judge Pizarro followed his first
communiqué to the prefect with a second. Here he asked the prefect to inform the central government in Lima of Burga's crime, and solicited the help
of the central authorities in conducting a nationwide search so that Burga
could be brought to justice.[27]

Just four days later, on June 8, the Electoral Review Board of Luya (the
Junta Escrutadora de Sufragio) met to decide who had been elected deputy of
the province. With Eloy Burga in hiding, accused of a capital crime, and the
subject of a departmental and national manhunt—and with his casta in disar-
ray and its members in flight—neither he nor his compatriates could have any
influence over the outcome of the electoral contest. The Pizarro-Rubio casta
had succeeded in eliminating Burga as even a potential competitor.[28]

A similar fate befell Felix Ocampo, deputy of Chachapoyas province. In
the context of the violence and lawlessness precipitated by the Pizarro-Rubio casta in the early months of 1909, Ocampo retreated into the confines of
his hacienda *Cocochó* (located in Lonya Chico district, Luya province). He was
forced to do so because none of the political officials who ordinarily would
have protected him were willing to defend the sworn enemy of the Pizarro-
Rubio casta.

Within the confines of his hacienda, Ocampo was for a time relatively safe.
But when Salvador M. Pizarro became (interim) judge of Luya-Bongará in
mid-May, the attacks on Ocampo began to extend even to his hacienda. Un-
able to leave the relative safety of his property, and under attack even there,
Ocampo was not able to run for a second term as deputy of Chachapoyas.
On June 8 the Electoral Review Board reviewed the election results and de-

clared Arturo Rubio Linch—who had run unopposed—deputy of Chachapoyas.

Once the Pizarro-Rubio casta had seized control of the department's
elected political positions,[29] it began to pursue its enemy Felix Ocampo with
even greater zeal. Shortly after the elections, Gustavo A. Rubio Linch
(brother-in-law of Pablo M. Pizarro) was appointed subprefect of Luya, and
Gustavo initiated a vicious series of attacks against Felix Ocampo, who was
still attempting to protect himself inside his hacienda. By March 1910, however, Ocampo was forced to abandon even his hacienda and had to quit the region altogether. On April 2, 1910, relocated in the city of Cajamarca, Ocampo
sent a protest to the prefect of Amazonas concerning his treatment at the hands
of his enemies, and included with it a handbill that he had had printed in Cajamarca under the title "Assault and Robbery at the Hacienda *Cocochó.*" In his
protest, Sr. Ocampo demanded that his constitutional rights be protected, and
protested that he had been driven out of his home by the relentless attacks of
the subprefect of Luya province, Sr. Gustavo Rubio. The prefect, in accor-
dance with the accepted procedure for investigating such protests, sent it on to
the judge of the first instance of Luya-Bongará, Salvador M. Pizarro Alvis (the
accused Sr. Rubio's close casta ally) to investigate the charges.[30] Judge Pizarro
in turn queried Subprefect Rubio, the very man who stood accused by
Ocampo, as to the veracity of Ocampo's claims—again following standard
procedure for the investigation of protests. Concerning the question of his
own guilt in violating the constitutional guarantees of Ocampo, Subprefect
Rubio responded:

> Sr. Ocampo enjoys and always will enjoy the constitutional guarantees to
> which all citizens are entitled according to the Constitution and laws of the
> land . . . the other accusations are pure invention on his part.[31]

The wave of violence and intimidation initiated by the Pizarro-Rubio casta
in March 1909 extended far beyond the persecution of leading members of
opposing castas. As soon as it was clear that the Pázaras would do nothing to
obstruct even the worst abuses of members of the Pizarro-Rubio casta, the
latter began to extort, beat, rob, rape, and steal from those who had been even
low-level Burga-Hurtado and Ocampo clients during the preceding six years—

abuses that accelerated by early June, after the Burga-Hurtado/Ocampo alliance had been definitively deposed. The result was a stream of protests, from people of all social classes, that their constitutional rights were being violated—and the demand that the representatives of the central state (most notably, the prefect) intervene to protect them. The letter sent to the prefect by rural cultivator Juan Mendoza, former lieutenant governor of Lonya Chico district (Luya province) under Eloy Burga, captures the insecurity of person and property faced by many people during this difficult time of political transition, as well as the outrage they felt about the treatment to which they were subject. On May 31, 1909, Mendoza wrote a protest and plea to Prefect Pázara. He titled his remarks, "Denunciation of Criminal Acts Committed in Lonya Chico and Request That Those Who Have Been Kidnapped Be Freed":

Juan Mendoza, citizen of Lonya Chico, province of Luya, department of Amazonas . . . swears that during the night of the 30th of the present month scandals so atrocious that they are without precedent were committed against the peaceful and defenseless inhabitants of the town of Lonya Chico. The famous governor of Lonya Chico [José del Carmen Tuesta], author of the assassinations that took place in Luya and Lámud in May of last year [the election uprising led by the Pizarro-Rubio], who stole weapons and ammunition of the state, appeared in our house in order to take us prisoner. During the night of the 30th the governor put the following citizens in prison: Francisco Chavez, Vicente Chavez, Juan Pio Chavez, Rufino Tuesta, and José Dolores Mendoza. All were taken to prison cells while being beaten with clubs, and all at present have serious wounds. Afterward, José Dolores Mendoza was freed because he was able to produce the sum of 4 soles. The rest, being unable to pay, were taken to Lámud and I suppose that they remain there even still. *Sr. Prefecto, how is it possible that such criminal acts have been committed when we are enjoying a period of peace, and when we should be under the protection of authorities who have sworn to comply with the law?* [Emphasis in original.] How is it possible that various honorable individuals have been taken prisoner, and that those who are able to pay are freed while those who are not able to pay are mistreated and taken to other towns as prisoners only because they could not satisfy the desires of abusive authorities? I believe that in light of these facts you will order an immediate investigation and will free the honorable citizens [in question] . . . the mothers, wives, and other relatives of the victims have escaped to Cajamarca . . . where we will remain until justice is done. ([APA13], decreto no. 108 [June 2, 1909])

How did Prefect Pázara respond to these rather astonishing accusations? He denied the request for an investigation because he said the way that the protest was worded cast aspersions on the honor and dignity of the authorities. Rather than investigate the charges and be sure that people were not being held against their will for ransom, and were not being physically abused by his own appointees, Pázara instructed the judge of the first instance of Luya-Bongará (Salvador M. Pizarro Alvis) to begin criminal proceedings against the man who wrote the protest—Juan Mendoza—for lack of respect for the legally constituted authorities.[32]

THE CONSOLIDATION OF THE PIZARRO-RUBIO CASTA

Once the Burga-Hurtado/Ocampo alliance had been deposed (by early June, 1909), the Pizarro-Rubio casta went about the important work of consolidating its position. There were three separate elements to its efforts. First, it endeavored to fill as many positions in the state bureaucracy as possible with its clients, and to expand its clientele and influence by distributing government largesse of other kinds (for example, handing out work contracts and making available commercial opportunities), in order to swell the ranks of its members and extend its influence into all sections of the regional space. Concomitantly, casta leaders began to use their nearly complete control over public administration, the courts, and the justice system to persecute all those associated with the Burga-Hurtado and/or Ocampo forces. Their ability to do so with impunity both reduces the influence of members of the opposing casta in much of the regional space and served as an object lesson to society at large concerning the power and potency of the ruling casta. Finally, the Pizarro-Rubio placed or kept "strong" clients in key sections of the regional space—generally where opposing casta leaders had important spheres of influence—to guard against the possibility that its enemies would organize revolts.

In general, it was a fairly straightforward procedure for the Pizarro-Rubio casta to rid itself of the appointees of the previous coalition; in most cases, the new Pizarro-Rubio appointees had the legal authority to make their own lower-level appointments (to the posts of governor, lieutenant governor, justice of the peace, etc.). There were some positions, however, that were protected from such purging activities by the formal independence of the various ministries and bureaucratic arms of the central government. In order to gain control over these positions, more circuitous and/or informal means of cleansing were employed.

Appointments to the important positions of provincial tax collectors for the *Compañía Nacional de Recaudación*—the entity to which the government farmed out tax collection—were in theory protected from the purging efforts of the dominant casta. Formally, it was up to the departmental head of the Compañía (who was usually a Lima appointee; at this time, it was Limeño Pedro Torres) to choose provincial representatives. As discussed in Chapter 3, however, because provincial appointees could only collect taxes if they were assisted by district governors and accompanied by an armed contingent of the Guardia Civil (both of which were provided by subprefects), the departmental head of the Compañía usually consulted with the subprefects of each in making his own provincial-level appointments.

In June 1909, however, the provincial representative for Bongará province was José E. Zabarburú—a man chosen by and closely tied to the previous casta—whereas the Pizarro-Rubio casta controlled the subprefecture of Bongará. On June 1, Prefect Pázara, responding to a protest he had received from a group of "notable citizens" (clients of the Pizarro-Rubio casta) of San Carlos district (in Bongará province), sent a communiqué to the head of the Compañía, Sr. Torres, demanding that Zabarburú be fired. At issue was the need to put a stop to the supposed "abuses" to which Zabarburú had subjected the people of San Carlos (demanding more money than they were obligated to pay; embezzlement). Jefe Torres did his own investigation into the matter, and responded that there was absolutely no proof that Zabarburú had done anything illegal. Zabarburú likewise protested his innocence, and claimed that he was the simple victim of slander. But in order to avoid what Zabarburú referred to quite literally as the "fatal consequences" of remaining in his position, he offered his resignation.

Without the support of the ruling casta to protect him, Zabarburú realized that tax collection put his life in mortal danger. Indeed, many tax collectors re-ferred to the danger of attempting to collect taxes without the support of an armed guard (see [APA4], Jan. 10, Mar. 11 and 14, Aug. 5, 10, and 31)—a fact that made tax collection an issue around which out-of-power castas could rally supporters with relative ease (ibid., Jan. 10, Aug. 31). Within months, a new provincial representative of the Compañía had been chosen—José María Echaiz Alvis, one of the main participants in the failed Pizarro-Rubio election uprising of May 1908, and cousin of Luya-Bongará judge Salvador M. Pizarro Alvis ([APA13], decreto no. 129 [May 20, 1910]).

By means of such legal and extra-legal mechanisms, within just months of its electoral triumph the Pizarro-Rubio casta had removed all the remaining clients of the previous Burga-Hurtado/Ocampo alliance from important po-sitions in the state bureaucracy. The new ruling casta had also placed its own clients in virtually all administrative positions in most sections of the regional space, and had expanded its clientele and its influence by distributing largesse provided by the central regime in Lima to select individuals. The ruling casta's district-level appointees were closely allied to one another at this time, strong governors having been given leave to choose their lieutenant governors and justices of the peace in the interest of containing potential threats from op-posing castas. Because the ruling casta enjoyed monopoly control over the machinery of state within these localities, members of the casta were free to prosecute, persecute, ignore crimes, manufacture evidence, and even seize and/or destroy the property of those who belonged to other castas—of all so-cial classes (including the peasantry; see below). And because the casta's provin-cial and departmental appointees were closely allied with its district-level ap-pointees, the ruling casta as a whole effectively denied members of opposing coalitions any recourse or alternative to the structures of power they encoun-tered within district arenas.

At this point the ruling casta, at the height of its powers, began to exploit its control over the machinery of state within the region in order to settle old scores with clients of the Burga-Hurtado and Ocampo—secure in the knowl-edge that, for the time being, the central regime in Lima would ignore even the worst abuses at the local level. The result was considerable insecurity for people of all social classes—as well as continual protests concerning a state of affairs that was perceived by all as fundamentally unjust.

On June 21, 1910, Sr. Angel F. Reyna, owner of the hacienda *Shelica-huaico*, located in Colcamar district, wrote to the new prefect of Amazonas, Sr. Arellano (Carlos A. Pázara having ended his tenure on January 15; [APA13], decreto no. 17 [Jan. 17, 1910]), imploring the prefect to protect him and his family from the depredations of his neighbor, Sra. Josefa Pizarro Farje de Astequier (sister of Juan M. and Pablo M. Pizarro Farje), and her sons, who, Reyna claimed, had been attacking him and destroying his crops. Upon receiving the protest, the new prefect instructed the subprefect of Luya province, Gustavo A. Rubio Linch (close casta ally and brother-in-law of Sra. Pizarro Farje de Astequier), to look into the matter. Subprefect Rubio then asked the governor of Colcamar district (Miguel A. Torrejón, a "strong" client of the Pizarro-Rubio casta) to investigate. Torrejón reported back that one of Sra. Pizarro de Astequier's sons had indeed uprooted a few maize plants—that he had found growing on his own property. Sr. Reyna's accusations were declared false (ibid., decreto no. 25 [Jan. 22, 1910]).

Two days later, Sr. Reyna sent the prefect another plea, this time asking that his constitutional rights and those of his peons be protected, as the Pizarro de Astequier family continued laying waste to his crops. They also persisted in scaring away his peons with rifle fire, because of which no work could be performed. One of Sra. Pizarro de Astequier's sons (Juan Gustavo), Reyna explained, was a former officer in the Guardia Civil. Juan Gustavo had (illegally) kept his rifle when he left the service, and was using it not only to drive away Sr. Reyna's peons but also to threaten Sr. Reyna's life (ibid., decreto no. 29 [Jan. 24, 1910]).

Again the prefect instructed Subprefect Rubio to investigate, and Rubio again turned to Colcamar governor Torrejón for clarification. Torrejón responded in the same manner as he had two days prior, adding only that he had assured Sr. Reyna that his constitutional rights would be protected. Shortly thereafter, Sr. Reyna was forced to desert his hacienda, to abandon his agrarian labors, and to seek safety in his home in the town of Chachapoyas (ibid., decreto no. 60 [Feb. 16, 1910]).

Other cases parallel that of Sr. Reyna. The following month, Sr. José Aguilar, a mestizo cultivator who owned a small farm in Jumbilla district, Bongará province, and who had been a lieutenant governor in 1904, appealed to Prefect Arellano to do whatever was necessary to ensure that his and his family's constitutional rights were safeguarded in light of the persecution the family faced by the subprefect of Bongará. The prefect responded by instructing the subprefect of Bongará—the very man accused by Aguilar of violating Aguilar's rights—to be sure that Aguilar and his family enjoyed the constitutional rights to which they were entitled (ibid., decreto no. 62 [Feb. 24, 1910]).

By May 1910, however, the Pizarro-Rubio casta went further still. On May 7, Manuela Tejada de Burga—wife of deposed casta leader Eloy Burga, who had been forced into hiding by the persecution of the Pizarro-Rubio—wrote to the prefect, pleading that the individual protections to which all citizens are entitled according to the Constitution be extended to her and her family. They had all been threatened by Alejandro Anduaga, a nephew (by marriage) of Pablo M. Pizarro and a powerful landowning member of the elite.[33] Sra. Tejada de Burga had good reason to consider Anduaga's threat as more than idle. Anduaga was widely feared and respected due to his willingness to inflict injury on others. During the six years of rule by the Burga-Hurtado/Ocampo alliance prior to the rise of the Pizarro-Rubio casta, Anduaga had intermittently raped and castrated peasant clients of Eloy Burga, who lived in the same district as Anduaga (Lonya Chico), and had then retreated into his hacienda, where it was difficult to pursue him.[34]

The Pizarro-Rubio went still further in persecuting the Burga-Hurtado. On May 12, David Burga (cousin of Eloy Burga) appealed to the prefect for assistance in freeing his young son Manuel from jail. The boy had been "unjustly conscripted" into the Gendarmery by the subprefect of Bongará. (Each subprefect was also the head of the draft board for his province, giving him almost complete discretion over who would be drafted into the armed services.)[35] The prefect, however, did nothing more than inform the subprefect—the very man who stood accused of abuse of authority—of Burga's complaint, and left the matter to be settled by the subprefect (ibid., decreto no. 125 [May 12, 1910]).[36]

By means of legal and extra-legal mechanisms of the kinds outlined above, the Pizarro-Rubio casta extended its influence into virtually all sections of the regional space, and drove both leading members and clients of the deposed casta as deeply underground as possible. These cleansing and purging activities did more than just reduce the influence of members of the opposing casta in much of the regional space. They also served as an object lesson to society at large concerning the power and potency of the ruling casta—and therefore of the risks of challenging its position.

The ruling casta further consolidated and maintained control over the regional space by placing "strong" clients of its own in those sections of the regional space where opposing casta members were particularly influential. Some of these "strong" clients were the governors, lieutenant governors, and justices of the peace that had been appointed to oversee the electoral process in the various districts of Chachapoyas and Luya provinces prior to the elections of 1909, who remained in their positions after the electoral contest was over. Others were appointed after the election. Regardless, these strong clients played an essential role in supporting the consolidating efforts of their casta even after the Burga-Hurtado/Ocampo alliance had been definitively deposed. Their presence in key sections of the regional space helped preclude the otherwise strong possibility that Burga-Hurtado and/or Ocampo forces would regroup where they were strongest and attempt to lead revolts against the ruling casta.

The strategy of appointing strong clients to control the regional space was accompanied by important risks. To the extent that such clients remained in their posts for a long period of time, they used their control over labor, product, and the movement of goods and people within the zones they administered to enrich themselves at the expense of the casta that had appointed them. Because these appointees received no salary, they used their positions to extort wealth from primary producers—peasant and nonpeasant alike.

Indeed, the prefect of Amazonas received a large number of protests from peasant communities concerning "abuses" committed by district governors, lieutenant governors, and/or justices of the peace. Consider the following protest, written in 1913:

PETITION. Made by the *comuneros* of the pueblo of Colcamar protesting the outrages and abuses of authority committed continually by the governor of the district Nestor P. Tenorio [brother-in-law of deputies Arturo and Miguel Rubio Linch] in conjunction with his lieutenant governors.

In the pueblo of Colcamar, capital of the district of the same name in the province of Luya in the department of Amazonas on the 15th day of November of 1913 the citizens who have signed [this petition] gathered in the public plaza with the object of discussing the mode and form that should be employed in raising their dissatisfactions to the subprefect of the province concerning the abusive and unjust procedures of the present governor Nestor P. Tenorio, and taking into consideration:

1st: That the governor accompanied by his lieutenant governors and forgetting his sacred duties goes from house to house in this pueblo, taking sheep, chickens, eggs, and ——— [?], claiming that his superior has asked for them and without paying a single centavo [and] only by the imposition of his authority.

2nd: That he has made himself into the agent of a number of merchants and [therefore] forces the owners of pack animals to carry freight and merchandise from the ports of Tupen and Mendán [several days' difficult journey from Colcamar, on the eastern bank of the Marañon River], paying the owners almost nothing, making up for what he lacks in wisdom and prudence with force.

3rd: That these procedures constitute the shameless theft of other people's property, that is totally inconsistent with the dignity that a political authority should have.

4th: That the property, the honor, and the life of the citizens of society in general are protected by the Constitution but despite this fact it appears that the inhabitants of this district do not enjoy these rights, because the governor, who [should be] the first to comply with the law and to make others do the same, tramples upon it, mistreating the defenseless citizens, seizing their goods without paying them a centavo and levying fines without providing the respective receipt.

5th: That the governor referred to has named eighteen citizens to the position of inspector and all of them are forced to work in his [the governor's] haciendas *Alfalfar* and *Utcubamba* without being paid a single centavo, all the while subjected to blows from clubs, kicks, and punches, the governor saying that he receives no salary and has orders from his superior allowing him to do this.

6th: That in December of last year the governor was denounced for identical abuses to Sr. García Rosell, prefect at the time, and this authority in compliance with his duties and with the law sacked Tenorio and liberated this pueblo from the abuses of said governor for a period of days, but that he [Tenorio] was reappointed by the interim prefect that followed Don Juan Olivera.

7th: That such a disastrous situation cannot and should not persist, because if it does this pueblo will be delivered into a [state of] brutal despotism by a governor who lacks the most basic notions of sagacity and insight necessary to manage the affairs of this pueblo.

Taking into consideration [the above] the citizens agreed:

1st: To invoke the Constitution of the country as the only means of guaranteeing individual rights and of re-establishing administrative equilibrium in this district [so] vilely managed by Nestor P. Tenorio.

2nd: To raise in the name of said Constitution this letter to the subprefect of the province; so that in light of our clamorous protest he might have the goodness to end the abuses of the wretched authority referred to and liberate this pueblo from his outrages, from the direct attack on other people's property, and from all types of suffering and threats of which we the honorable citizens of this locality are the victims. ([APA59], Nov. 15, 1913)

By acts of extortion such as these, strong governors like Sr. Tenorio produced growing resistance on the part of those they sought to rule—which made such populations unusually receptive to allying with out-of-power casta leaders like Eloy Burga and Felix Ocampo.[37] The casta core sought to guard against such developments by replacing "strong" with "weak" clients once periods of political transition or instability had passed. Following such a procedure was dangerous in the long run, however, because it was that much more difficult for the casta core to maintain adequate surveillance over the activities of its foes. And when the ruling casta did attempt to replace strong with weak clients, it was likely to provoke the former to seek alliance with an out-of-power casta. For in this way strong clients could preserve the extraction privileges exercised by virtually all "strong" clients (particularly governors)—some sense of which can be gleaned from the petition just quoted.

Despite these dilemmas—which were contradictions inherent in casta-based domination—the Pizarro-Rubio coalition exercised nearly complete hegemony in the Chachapoyas region from 1909 to 1912. The central state attempted to curb the excesses of the casta by assigning a series of career politicians to important political posts within the region (most consistently to the positions of prefect and mayor de Guardias), but none ever posed a serious threat to the prerogatives enjoyed by the ruling casta.

With the Burga-Hurtado and Ocampo forces driven from power and made publicly invisible, members of the Pizarro-Rubio casta were free to assume the leadership and domination of public life to which all members of the elite felt entitled by right of birth. For the next several years, elite members of the casta directed virtually all aspects of public life—economic, social, political, educational, legal, bureaucratic, and religious. Indeed, from mid-1909 until November 1912, it was difficult to participate in any dimension of public life or public ritual without finding Pizarro-Rubio clients at center stage.

THE CHALLENGE OF THE BURGA-HURTADO

Political developments in the nation's capital surrounding the presidential elections of 1912 upset the monopoly control over public life exercised by the Pizarro-Rubio casta and threatened its domination of regional politics. They did so by subtly shifting the balance of power between Chachapoya's opposing castas, creating the possibility of the return of Eloy Burga. Burga's "rebirth" in turn set the stage for further armed conflict between his (radically reconstituted) casta and the Pizarro-Rubio as the two forces struggled to control the region.

The presidential elections of May 1912 had a surprising outcome, and reflected what might be called a form of "extra-electoral democracy." The faction of the Partido Civil controlled by outgoing president Augusto Leguía had a majority in both houses of Congress, and controlled the National Election Board, which ruled on the outcomes of elections. The pro-Leguía forces had chosen candidate Antero Aspíllaga as Leguía's successor, and used their control over the electoral process to engineer a victory for Aspíllaga. But the Partido Civil was faced with what one prominent historian has referred to as a "popular uprising" against Aspíllaga and the machinations of the pro-Leguía forces. "The masses" in Lima backed a candidate that had emerged at the last minute to challenge Aspíllaga—Guillermo Billinghurst. Faced with a popular insurrection, despite the fact that the Partido Civil had already manufactured a victory for Aspíllaga, the party felt compelled to give the election to Billinghurst. Billinghurst took office on September 24, 1912.[38]

Although Billinghurst had gained the presidency, both houses of Congress remained pro-Leguía and anti-Billinghurst. This conflict within the national government bureaucracy led to a somewhat anomalous situation in the provinces, as appointees of the executive branch of government (prefects and subprefects) and the elected representatives of the departments administered by these clients of the executive were involved in an escalating conflict (Basadre 1968–69, 12: 230–31).

In terms of regional politics in Chachapoyas, the election of Billinghurst and the conflict between the executive branch and Congress were important in that they created an environment in which Eloy Burga could once again come "above ground" (there was never any evidence produced concerning his supposed murder of an officer of the Guardia Civil), and could return to Chachapoyas without being openly persecuted. An article that appeared in the local newspaper *La Ortiga* (The Nettle) on January 25, 1913, announcing Burga's arrival, suggests the scale of his following even after several years' absence—and also the scope of potential opposition to rule by the Pizarro-Rubio.

> At 4:00 P.M. today Sr. Eloy Burga, prestigious political caudillo of the department, arrived in the city, accompanied by more than 200 of the most distinguished members of our society, who went to his hacienda *El Molino* with the object of bringing him here.

The timing of Burga's return was particularly apropos, as elections for both senatorships of the department of Amazonas were to be held later that year, in April. Burga's return to Chachapoyas as an honored and respected citizen just prior to the elections put the Pizarro-Rubio casta on notice that they would not enjoy the luxury of an easy victory at the polls—and thus that their position of dominance within the region was threatened.

The Pizarro-Rubio casta did its utmost to control the outcome of the elections for the two senatorships.[39] Its ability to do so, however, was severely constrained by the fact that the new president was intent on gaining as many seats as possible for his followers in these same elections, and was determined to undermine the pro-Leguía majority in Congress as a whole. As a result, he appointed to key positions in Chachapoyas individuals who could help engineer the election results in his favor. To do so effectively, it was essential that appointees of the president control the most powerful political positions of the department—prefect, subprefects, and mayor de Guardias. It was equally important, however, that clients of the pro-Leguía Pizarro-Rubio casta, who occupied most governorships and lieutenant governorships, be replaced with clients of the president who could steer the election in his favor in rural sections of the regional space.

By November 1912—about a month after Billinghurst had taken office—the new president and his followers in the executive branch of the government began to implement this plan within the Chachapoyas region. They started by making a series of political appointments that undermined the position of the Pizarro-Rubio casta. Coronel José Manuel Vivanco, who had been prefect of Amazonas since April 1911 (and who had very close ties with the Pizarro family), was replaced by Ricardo García Rosell—a career politician from Lima. Subprefect of Chachapoyas Gustavo A. Rubio Linch (brother-in-law of Senator Pablo M. Pizarro Farje and brother of deputies Miguel and Arturo Rubio Linch) was replaced by Juan Olivero, whereas the subprefect of Luya, Rosendo Pizarro (half-brother of Pablo M. and Juan M. Pizarro Farje), was replaced by Sergio Bendejir—the new subprefects both being career politicians with no links to the Pizarro-Rubio casta. At the same time, a new mayor de Guardias, Wenceslao Roca, was assigned to the region in place of Teobaldo Vivanco, brother of outgoing prefect José Manuel Vivanco, who had been appointed to his post in April 1911, when his brother assumed the prefecture.

Supported by Subprefects Olivero and Bendejir, and Mayor de Guardias Roca, Prefect Rosell began to assign new governors to many of the department's districts, in the process replacing Pizarro-Rubio clients with individuals who would support the electoral efforts of President Billinghurst. By year's end, the powerful appointees from Lima had chosen new governors for most districts, and were well on their way to orchestrating electoral results favorable to the new president.

This attempt on the part of the executive branch of government to act in isolation, without the assistance of provincial political allies who represented real power blocks within their home regions, violated the most fundamental bases of electoral politics. As argued in Chapter 3, candidates who were successful in local elections were only able to overcome their adversaries because they represented an extensive coalition of allied families who, acting in concert, were able to control important sections of the regional space by force. The candidate who represented such a coalition in effect entered into a pact with the executive branch of government to control the regional space for the executive—in return for which the executive granted the representative's coalition extensive privileges of "administration."

President Billinghurst, however, attempted to circumvent this process and to disregard regional power relations entirely. His faction's efforts to engineer the electoral process in his favor had a curious side effect. The district governors who were appointed by the new prefect and subprefects at the end of 1912 as a group represented neither the Pizarro-Rubio nor the Burga-Hurtado—the region's two main castas. Rather, they were an odd mix of a few clients of both along with a larger number of people with strong ties to neither. As a group, they and the new prefect and subprefect did not represent an existing power block that could effectively control the regional space. And unlike ruling casta behavior prior to elections under "normal" conditions, this group, which had been "imposed from above," was not in a position to engage in an effective and coordinated effort to prevent existing power blocks from mobilizing their forces. To a significant extent, this was because the governors chosen to oversee the electoral process throughout the regional space were not "strong" clients who could draw upon existing spheres of influence and "contingentes" to monitor and contain the movements and activities of those within their zones of jurisdiction.

The ultimate folly of this policy became apparent in the early morning hours of April 25, 1913—the first of two days of voting to decide who would occupy the two senatorships for the department of Amazonas.

Express Telegram. President of the Republic.
No. 342. April 25, 1913.
[Sent by Prefect Gaspar de la Puente.]

[At] daybreak today, the police detachment commanded by [the] mayor [de] Guardias that was guarding [the] house [of] Eloy Burga, [due to a] petition [from] him [asking that] he be provided with his constitutional guarantees, despite having had them always, was attacked by two groups of armed men.

Said individuals [consisted of a group who] came from this capital [Chachapoyas] led by Santiago Rodriguéz [nephew of Pablo M. and Juan M. Pizarro Farje] [and another group] from various districts commanded [by] Julian Castro, resident [of] Leimebamba.

Mayor [de Guardias] Roca repelled [the] attack of these [men] and put out fires they had started on [the] balconies [of the] Burga house. Guardia Vargas and Gendarme Chuechas [were] wounded in the battle as well as countrymen [local individuals] Santiago Rodriguéz, and Lizardo Hurtado from the group of Castro, who swore [that they] had been pressured by Eloy Burga to surprise [the] detachment [of Mayor Roca] and [then] take control of this plaza [of the city], various other captured [members] of [the] rebels swear [the] same.

Five carbines [of] diverse types and [assorted] ammunition [was] seized.

[A] search carried out [of the] houses [of] Santiago Rodriguéz and Eloy Burga turned up [in the] house [of the] first one box [of] ammunition [of distinct] types and two packs of Manlincher ammunition and 32 sticks of dynamite with percussion caps and in the house of the second [of Burga] twelve cases [of] Manlincher ammunition.

Immediately upon hearing [a series of] dynamite explosions I hurried [to the] place where they were coming from [and] taking [the] necessary steps [I] managed to re-establish order that up to the present moment remains unaltered; [the] military judge [of Amazonas] [is] preparing [an] indictment [of] all [the] events. Santiago Rodriguéz, wounded [in the fighting] [is being] cared for [in the] home [of] his father Sr. Salomon Rodriguéz, [who] guarantees [his son's] whereabouts.

The *Mesa Receptora* [de] *Sufragios* [voting table] [is] operating without incident [in the] plaza.

Voters [are] casting their votes peacefully; [the] subversive movement [was] without question [arranged through an] agreement with [elements of] the police [and] also [with] José María Echaiz and his sons in [the] province of Luya [who] were contained due to [the] appropriate measures [having been] adopted.

I have given an account of everything that occurred to the director [of] government.

Being unable to pursue [the subversives] much of a distance due to a shortage of men and in order to guard against a repeat attack tonight [I am] dictating [the measures] necessary to avoid a surprise [attack] and if possible a new conflict.

I will inform [you of] any [additional] occurrences.
—*[signed] G. de la Puente [prefect of Amazonas] ([APA17], Apr. 25, 1913)*

The fighting was intense. When the conflict finally came to an end, government forces had been forced to expend over one thousand rounds of ammunition in order to put down the revolt.[40]

Sporadic fighting between the rebel forces and Mayor de Guardias Roca and his men continued for several days in the countryside surrounding Chachapoyas, while within the town Pablo M. Pizarro Farje, outraged by events that had taken the lives of several associates and had almost succeeded in deposing his casta, reasserted the dominant position of his casta by insulting and attempting to kill a close ally of Eloy Burga in a highly visible public place (Burga having gone into hiding immediately after the failed uprising; see [APA5], Apr. 27, 1913).

By April 29, the forces of the subversives had withdrawn, and the subprefects, following instructions from the prefect, ordered that the following edict be posted throughout the town in the "customary public places," and that it be distributed as well to all district governors, who likewise were to post it in public places and generally to inform the people of their districts of its contents:

> *Considering*: that the prefecture of the department, in oficio no. 100, dated yesterday, has authorized this office to make it known to the inhabitants of its jurisdiction that public order has been definitively re-established, dictating the measures necessary so that all citizens may enjoy their constitutional rights and protections;
>
> *It Is Decreed*: That all the inhabitants of this province can dedicate themselves to their daily labors safely, enjoying as always their constitutional rights and protections.
>
> [Dated] April 29, 1913[41] ([APA59], Apr. 29, 1913)

Revealingly, the same day that the prefect commanded that it be publicly decreed that order had been re-established, that all could be sure of enjoying their constitutional rights and protections, and that all might go about their daily affairs untroubled by violence and threats, Eloy Burga's wife was forced to plead with the prefect that he provide her with precisely this kind of protection ([APA59], Apr. 29, 1913). The señora wrote rather than her husband because once again Eloy had been forced "underground."

In the weeks that followed, the main outline of the rebellion emerged.[42] The preparations had been extensive. The plan had been for simultaneous uprisings to be staged in Chachapoyas, the departmental capital; in the town of Lámud, capital of Luya province; and in Jumbilla, capital of Bongará province. The rebels hoped to seize control of the voting tables in each town and to impose electoral results favorable to the reconstituted Burga casta.

The specific strategy employed by the Burga-Hurtado reflected its awareness that the Pizarro-Rubio casta was not in a position to control space and to monitor the activities of its enemies, as it had done prior to the 1909 elections. Indeed, the Burga-Hurtado forces prepared and launched their assault in precisely those sections of the regional space that the Pizarro-Rubio had been most careful to control in 1909—Chachapoyas itself, Leimebamba, Molinopampa, and Chiliquin.

The success of the entire rebellion depended on "taking" Chachapoyas, the departmental capital, and it was toward this end that the rebels devoted the bulk of their men and resources. Several forces were to converge on the town at once from different directions. One column of men was to come from the direction of Molinopampa, where pro-Billinghurst forces had appointed Leocadio Montoya as governor in late 1912 to support the president's electoral efforts. Montoya had struck an alliance with Eloy Burga shortly after the latter's return to Chachapoyas in January 1913. Prodded by Burga, Montoya had successfully recruited followers to the Burga cause in Molinopampa and neighboring districts. He was able to do so because of the deep resentment harbored for the ruling casta by much of the rural peasantry, who had been subject to the abuses of Pizarro-Rubio clients for the previous four years.

Assisted by Amadeo Torrejón,[43] a landowning member of the elite whose petition inciting the local population to rise up against the abuses of the Pizarro-Rubio casta was distributed in a number of rural districts, Montoya also helped organize uprisings in the pueblos of Chiliquin and Quinjalca. Both towns were located along important transport routes linking Chachapoyas with Jumbilla, capital of Bongará province. One of the purposes of staging uprisings in these pueblos was to cut the constabularies of Chachapoyas and

Jumbilla off from one another during the uprising. To this end, Montoya had distributed a number of Winchester rifles smuggled to him by Eloy Burga.

Another column of armed men was to converge on Chachapoyas from the direction of Leimebamba, where Neptalí Ocampo, brother of former deputy Felix Ocampo, had been appointed governor at the end of 1912 to support the electoral goals of President Billinghurst and his clients. This second force was led by elite landowner Julian Castro, and consisted of peasant followers from a number of different communities located between Chachapoyas and Leimebamba who had been drawn to the Burga-Hurtado cause with the hope of ending the abuses they had suffered at the hands of Pizarro-Rubio officials.

Within Chachapoyas, Eloy Burga was to divert the attention of the Guardia Civil toward his house by asking that his life and property be protected in light of threats he had received from the Pizarros ([APA62], Apr. 19 and 22, 1913). A force from within Chachapoyas, led by Santiago Rodriguéz, and the force coming from Leimebamba were to feign an attack on Eloy Burga's home. During the attack, which was intended to look like an assault by Burga's enemies, Rodriguéz and Castro were to overwhelm the police. In the meantime, the force that advanced on Chachapoyas from Molinopampa was to overcome the remainder of the Guardia Civil, and with the support of Rodriguéz and Castro was to take control of the city.

The simultaneous uprisings in Lámud (led by José María Echaiz, and assisted by Felix Castro, the ranking officer of the Guardia Civil stationed in Lámud and brother of Julian Castro) and Jumbilla (led by Aniceto Rojas) were intended to give the pro-Burga forces control over the subprefectures of both provinces—a vantage point from which they could dictate their own election results.

The identities of the leaders of the uprising reveal much about weaknesses inherent in casta organization. There were, of course, several people whose involvement was not surprising. For example, given the powerful ties that united the Burga and Hurtado families at the core of a single casta, the participation of Lizardo Hurtado, son of Manuel Hurtado and brother-in-law of Eloy Burga, was to be expected. Andres A. Arce, brother-in-law of Eloy Burga and a long-standing member of Burga's casta, was another whose involvement is easily understood. Arce owned an estate (*El Chillo*) located along the Leimebamba-Chachapoyas road about half a day's march to the south of Chachapoyas. Footpaths that bypass Chachapoyas run from *El Chillo* to Molinopampa, where one of the two forces that converged on Chachapoyas originated, and the main mule trail that connects Chachapoyas to the coast runs between *El Chillo* and Leimebamba, where the other force originated. Arce's estate was ideally located for passing messages between Leimebamba and Molinopampa without either the authorities loyal to President Billinghurst or the Pizarro-Rubio being any the wiser. Arce thus helped coordinate the preparations and activities of the Leimebamba and Molinopampa columns prior to the outbreak of hostilities so that they could converge on Chachapoyas at the same time.

The participation of several other individuals, however, is noteworthy. José María Echaiz and his sons were entrusted by the Burga-Hurtado forces to lead the uprising in Lámud, capital of Luya province. Just five years prior, Echaiz had been one of the organizers and main participants in another armed re-volt in Lámud—one that took the lives of several state representatives—and was likewise intent on seizing control of elections by force. In 1908, however, Echaiz had been allied with his relatives, the Pizarro family, and with the Rubio as well, in an effort to oust the Burga-Hurtado casta from its position of re-gional domination. In 1913, on the other hand, he allied himself with the Burga-Hurtado in an attempt to overthrow his relatives, the Pizarro family.

Echaiz's "defection" to the cause of the Burga-Hurtado was symptomatic of the forces toward dissolution generated whenever casta cores were formed out of the union of previously unallied family groups. As argued in Chapter 3, when powerful families united via marriage to form a casta core, there were no rules for how the relatively few important political positions available would be divided among the family members. It was inevitable that some members re-ceived less than they felt they deserved. José María Echaiz was such a person. Although he was given the post of provincial tax collector of Bongará in 1909, in light of the fact that he had put his life in danger for the Pizarro-Rubio casta during its failed election uprising of 1908, he was far from satisfied. Echaiz subsequently defected to the Burga-Hurtado in an effort to achieve a more prominent role in public life. Several years later, he deepened his com-mitment to the Burga-Hurtado by marrying his son Francisco to Rosa Vic-toria Hurtado Cubas.

Similar concerns were behind the decisions of several other prominent members of the elite who had been part of the Pizarro-Rubio casta to involve themselves on the side of the Burga-Hurtado forces. Santiago Rodriguéz (Pizarro) led the armed uprising in Chachapoyas against the casta of his own mother and father, Resurección Pizarro Farje (sister of casta leaders Pablo M. and Juan M. Pizarro Farje) and Salomon Rodriguéz Tuesta. Despite the fact that Santiago was a grown man at the time of the uprising, he had been consistently passed over when important posts were distributed among the various members of the Pizarro-Rubio casta. By "defecting" to the Burga-Hurtado, he, like José María Echaiz, hoped to escape the limitations imposed on his ambitions by the casta of his parents.

Elite landowner Julian Castro, who led the Leimebamba column's assault on Chachapoyas, and his brother Felix, the officer in the Guardia Civil who assisted José María Echaiz in organizing the revolt in Lámud, were resentful of the Pizarro-Rubio as well. The Castro family belonged to the true elite of regional society—the racially pure casta española that claimed descent from Spanish forebears. The Castros owned several large estates (*Tambillo, Lluy, Potreros,* and *Chilingote*) in Leimebamba district, and had an important sphere of influence within the district. In previous decades the Castro family had intermarried extensively with members of the Pizarro-Rubio casta. As a trusted member of the casta, Julian Castro had been appointed governor of Leimebamba in 1911, but had been replaced at the end of the year by a "weaker" client, Grimaldo Escobedo. Thereafter, despite their social prominence and their close ties to the Pizarro-Rubio, the Castros had been virtually ignored by the ruling coalition. Julian and Felix Castro defected to the Burga-Hurtado forces and rose up against their own casta in the hope of ending the shameful and unjust treatment they had received at the hands of the Pizarro-Rubio.

The same motivations were behind the decision of Amadeo Torrejón, a landowning member of the elite (whose petition inciting rebellion was distributed among the peasants of Molinopampa, Chiliquin, and Quinjalca), to side with Eloy Burga. Except for several small "favors" he had been granted early in the period of Pizarro-Rubio rule (a work contract, an honorary title), Torrejón had been left out of the distribution of the spoils since 1909. By joining forces with Eloy Burga, he hoped to right this situation.

The decisions of Molinopampa governor Leocadio Montoya to actively participate in the rebellion, and of Leimebamba governor Neptalí Ocampo not to obstruct it, reflected the different kinds of conflict inherent in casta rule. The central government had appointed Montoya and Ocampo as governors to support its efforts to steer the election in favor of pro-Billinghurst candidates because of the known animosity between these two men and the forces of the Pizarro-Rubio. Montoya was considered an appropriate choice to safeguard the electoral process in Molinopampa because of his ties to the Burga-Hurtado and Ocampo families. Montoya had been governor of the district in 1904, when Felix Ocampo was deputy of Chachapoyas province and Andres A. Arce, brother-in-law of Eloy Burga, was subprefect. Though not a large estate owner or member of the regional elite, Montoya did have medium-sized landholdings in Molinopampa, maintained a house on the town square, and was a prominent local citizen. During the period of Pizarro-Rubio rule, however, Montoya had been persecuted and marginalized by appointees of the ruling casta, and thus could be counted on to oppose the electoral efforts of the Pizarro-Rubio ([APA13], decreto no. 223 [Nov. 8, 1909]).

Neptalí Ocampo was the brother of former deputy Felix Ocampo, and on this basis alone could be counted on to oppose any attempts by the Pizarro-Rubio forces to seize control of the elections. Adding to Neptalí's resentment of the ruling casta was the fact that he had served as governor of Molinopampa in the first months of 1909, at the end of the period of Burga-Hurtado/Ocampo rule, but had been removed from his post by the Pizarro-Rubio forces. Since that time he had played no role in public life. The Ocampo family owned several large estates in Leimebamba (*Teaben, Monteseco, Chilingote*), had a long-standing sphere of influence in the district, and thus was in a good position to safeguard the elections.

The appointment of these "independent" clients thus represented a special case of a more general tendency on the part of the central regime to name appointees independent of the ruling casta so as to the contain the latter's consolidation of power (although in this case, in a period of political transition during which the executive hoped to strengthen itself at the expense of the Pizarro-Rubio casta). In general, such independent appointments were dangerous for the ruling casta because they made the ruling casta less able to monitor the activities of its enemies—which was precisely the effect the appointments had on the Pizarro-Rubio casta in 1913.

Because of the special circumstances surrounding the election of 1913, however, the appointment of "independent" clients like Montoya and Ocampo ended up being as dangerous for the pro-Billinghurst forces as it was for the Pizarro-Rubio. With little to tie these clients to the Billinghurst regime in Lima, and with the ruling Pizarro-Rubio casta unable to take the usual pre-election precautions, there was little to prevent Eloy Burga from activating old ties (for example, those between himself, Andres A. Arce, and Leocadio Montoya) and from cultivating new ones to strengthen his position.

The contradictions of casta rule thus produced a growing number of disgruntled individuals from all walks of life between 1909 and 1913—peasant cultivators, district-level administrators, and elite landowners. The Burga-Hurtado forces seized upon these dissatisfactions to recruit numerous new clients to their cause from all social classes. At a moment of weakness in ruling casta control, the reconstituted Burga-Hurtado casta mounted a major assault that almost succeeded in wresting control of regional affairs from the Pizarro-Rubio.

Ultimately, however, the national-level forces of President Billinghurst and the local-level forces of the Burga-Hurtado were unsuccessful in deposing the Pizarro-Rubio casta. Billinghurst's efforts to undermine the pro-Leguía majority in Congress foundered when Congress refused to recognize the candidates elected during the 1913 campaign. Thus, the candidates who won the senatorial posts in Amazonas never took office. Instead, Pablo M. Pizarro was assigned the position of (substitute) senator by the pro-Leguía Congress.[44]

By early 1914, the tensions between Congress and the president had reached crisis proportions, resulting in a military coup by Coronel Oscar Benavides on February 4. By July 1914, Benavides had reached an accommodation with the pro-Leguía forces in Congress (Basadre 1968–69, 12: 290, 303, 323). This accommodation ended any hope on the part of the Burga-Hurtado forces in Chachapoyas of being able to return to power, for the Pizarro-Rubio casta had once again arranged to become the privileged local client of the central regime in Lima.

With the defeat of the reconstituted Burga-Hurtado casta in 1913, a new era in regional political and economic affairs had begun. Prior to this, no single casta had the ability to "hold" the region for any appreciable length of time. Between the internal contradictions of casta rule and the constant changes in who held power in the national capital, castas replaced one another locally on a regular basis. The defeat of the Burga forces in 1913, however, marked the first of a series of similar defeats that continued throughout the teens and the 1920s.

Symptomatic of this shift in favor of the Pizarro-Rubio casta was the marriage of Luis Felipe Pizarro Rojas and Robertina Torrejón Monteza, whose wedding ceremony was described in Chapter 3. For the decision of Robertina's father to ally with the Pizarro-Rubio was a kind of defection of its own. As mentioned earlier, Robertina's father (Luis Beltrán Torrejón Dávila) had long been an important local military figure, and had been the head of the Gendarmery on several occasions. A few decades prior to the marriage of his daughter to a son of Juan M. Pizarro Farje, in his capacity as head of the Gendarmery, Torrejón had played a key role in frustrating the attempts of the Pizarro-Rubio casta to overcome its primary political adversary within the region—the Burga-Hurtado casta—and thus to establish unquestioned hegemony within the region. As a direct result of Torrejón siding with the Burga-Hurtado and against the Pizarro-Rubio, the former casta was able to marginalize and ultimately drive the latter out of positions of prominence. The Pizarro-Rubio was only able to re-emerge several years later in the context of civil war, which allowed it to sweep the Burga-Hurtado forces from power. Included among the Burga-Hurtado casta members who were deposed was Torrejón.[45]

The fact that a marriage with the Pizarro, the family of his old enemies, was ever contemplated thus represented the severing of old ties, a commitment of new alliance, and an attempt to heal old wounds.[46] It was also symptomatic of more general processes that helped make the Pizarro-Rubio period of control so long and uninterrupted.

It was this prolonged period of Pizarro-Rubio control that formed the context within which much of the local population became involved in a movement to democratize regional social relations in the late 1920s. In Chapter 6 I turn to a consideration of the national-level processes of state-building that made possible the extended rule of the Pizarro-Rubio casta—and that precipitated the movements of democratización. First, however, in Chap-

ter 5 I discuss the more cultural dimensions of casta rule, that is, how the ruling casta leaders—presiding over a structure of aristocratic sovereignty—managed the central state's rhetoric of popular sovereignty in such a way as to
strengthen the aristocratic order, even though the principles of popular sovereignty stood in direct contradiction to the everyday public behavior of those
who ruled.

5 The Cultural Politics of Casta Rule

> Well-intentioned governments, like that which currently
> controls the destiny of the Republic, seek to gather the
> family that is Peru into a single body that works in concert
> for the progress of the country; but . . . I believe that . . .
> those individuals whose foreheads are marked with the
> stigma of general condemnation as a result of their
> previous history . . . could never merit a pardon for their
> evil ways . . . especially the nearby caudillo of abominable
> nature [Pablo M. Pizarro] . . . and although I believe he
> would not dare to rebel against the legally constituted
> authorities at present . . . it is my duty to make plain the
> difficulties caused by [his presence].
>
> *Coronel Don José Alayza, presenta al*
> *Sr. Director del Gobierno, 1893*

As has been shown in previous chapters, in the period of strength and solidarity that characterized its initial phase of control, the ruling casta used its
monopoly on political positions and its control over armed force to persecute
and harass members of the opposition in a systematic and comprehensive manner. In the process, the ruling casta indiscriminately violated its adversaries'
constitutional rights and protections, and thus made a public mockery of the
state's legitimating rhetoric of popular sovereignty.

Continuous persecution of the opposition was necessary because opposing castas refused to accept the position of the ruling group as legitimate.
Rather, opposing castas saw their own claims to power as inherently more
valid than the pretensions of those who controlled the prefecture, and thus
constantly sought to take the place of those who ruled. Only by engaging in
consistent and coordinated persecution of opposing castas could the ruling

casta fragment this hostile opposition sufficiently to make united action on the part of its enemies difficult or impossible. In this way, the ruling casta was able to reproduce its position of regional dominance.

In the period of growing weakness that followed, however, ruling casta members suffered many of the same violations of person and property as did members of the opposition. As contradictions inherent in casta rule made themselves manifest, political appointees from Lima who were not beholden to ruling casta leaders took on roles of growing importance in local affairs. Their presence, which broke the ruling casta's monopoly on political positions and weakened its control over armed force, made systematic and coordinated persecution of casta enemies increasingly difficult. At the same time, members of the ruling casta began to struggle among themselves for access to key political positions and for control of tributary revenue. In these transformed conditions, members of the opposition were able to unite against the ruling casta, and eventually to drive it from power. Just as the ruling casta was forced to demonstrate its ability to violate the "rights" of others in public in order to reproduce its position of dominance, the only way opposing castas could rise to power was by publicly violating the "rights" of members of the ruling casta. These conflictual dynamics of shame and countershame, violence and counterviolence, characterized the particular form of aristocratic sovereignty encountered in the Chachapoyas region.

Although committed to making constant attacks upon the life and property of the opposition, the ruling casta was equally compelled to present itself in all political ritual, and in all political discourse, as the sole and true defender of the principles of popular sovereignty. In these rhetorical and ritual spaces, the ruling casta elaborated a mythical social order that was the antithesis of casta organization and aristocratic sovereignty. In place of the violence, insecurity, and privilege that characterized everyday life, in the realms of ritual and discourse the ruling casta asserted the existence of a "peaceable kingdom." In this alternative world, the ability to rule was not contingent upon public demonstrations of force that humiliated the opposition. Indeed, there was a conspicuous silence about the very existence of power in all political declarations and performances of ruling castas. Instead, governance was depicted as consensual and orderly, and individuals were portrayed as responsible, peaceful, and respectful of one another—as universally enjoying the protections of life, liberty, and property granted them by the Constitution. In the realm of political drama, the ruling casta never appeared in its true guise—as an entity that wielded power arbitrarily to advance its own interests, to punish and persecute its enemies, and to allow a small handful of upper-class individuals to live according to the privileged station in life to which all members of the elite aspired. Rather, in the symbolic space elaborated in ritual and discourse, castas were made to disappear entirely. And ruling casta leaders were transformed from dangerous and powerful men into servants of the "general good," who had sworn to uphold and defend the rights of all "citizens" as a patriotic duty. In ritual and discourse, unity and harmony prevailed, and distinctions of race, gender, and caste—upon which the entire aristocratic order was based—ceased to exist. In place of such distinctions, the ruling casta asserted the existence of a mass of identical citizens, all of whom were united behind the cause of promoting "progress" and "advancement."

Ironically, in ritual performances and in rhetorical addresses, adversarial castas were disparaged in terms that were largely accurate (if highly partial), but that applied equally to *all* castas, ruling and ruled alike. Opposing casta leaders were reviled as dangerous "caudillos" who, along with their numerous followers, constituted a major threat to the region's progress and to the forward march of civilization. It was said that these caudillos sought, solely for their own private gain, to disrupt the reigning peace and tranquility established with great difficulty by the ruling casta. Ruling casta leaders thus used the rhetoric of popular sovereignty to oppose the "self-interested" behavior of enemy caudillos with their own selfless and patriotic commitment to the common good, to progress, to the nation—even though their actions were equally self-serving, and were known publicly to be so.

In depicting their actions to society at large in this way, ruling casta leaders were not attempting to deceive anyone about the true nature of their actions. Considering the importance of publicly deployed violence and intimidation in reproducing political rule, it would have been impossible for casta leaders to so deceive people even if they had wanted to. Rather, casta leaders were responding to a particular historical conjuncture in which the terms available for the representation of political life had no relationship to the organization of political life. That is, because the language and concepts of popular sovereignty offered the exclusive terms in which moral and immoral attitudes and behaviors could be represented, the actual nature of the region's social groups, and the reasons for their struggles, were consistently masked and distorted. This was especially true of the behavior of the ruling casta. For within the rhetoric of popular rule, the hierarchy, privilege, and purposive use of violence that characterized ruling casta behavior defied representation in anything but illegitimate form. And since the ruling casta was the official representative of the independent republic of Peru within Amazonas—a modern nation-state founded on Enlightenment principles of equality, citizenship, progress, and private property—the ruling casta could not represent its actions to society as they truly were. Neither, however, could it conceal the violent and dominating nature of these actions from the public eye and still remain in power. As a result, the ruling casta employed the language of popular sovereignty to create a wholly imaginary social order in ritual and discourse—one based on consensus, cooperation, and concern for the common good—and embraced this imaginary social order wholeheartedly. Simultaneously, however, the ruling casta continued to pursue actions that violated virtually every principle of popular rule, and thus demonstrated its power and potency to all.

This "schizophrenic" presentation of self can be seen in virtually all contexts in which the ruling casta offered public accounts of its political behavior to society at large. Consider, for example, the following lead article, written by high-ranking members of the ruling Hurtado-Rodriguéz casta and published in *El Registro de Amazonas*, the official government newspaper (which was distributed weekly, without charge, to all district governors in the department). This particular issue of the *Register* appeared on the heels of an attempt to assassinate President Manuel Pardo in the nation's capital, and was intended as a commentary on the assassination attempt.[1]

> PROGRESS, that inexorable law of Humanity, cannot be realized with perfection, but there does exist a social order that is based on compliance with the laws that govern the advance of the pueblos and that requires respect for the authorities duly constituted by these laws. This principle, which serves as the fundamental basis of stability for those Nations organized as Monarchies, is even more important . . . in Republics [like Peru], which are the cradle of Democracy. In a Democracy, the progress of the pueblos depends on strict observance of the law, while the pueblos regress when the law is not obeyed.

From this we may deduce that those individuals who violate legal mandates can rightly be considered outcasts from society, and that it is fully within the rights of society to impose severe punishment on those who make attempts against its existence. Possessed of this truth, the Peruvian People have hurled a terrible anathema in the face of those who attempted to subvert the public order . . . in the most treacherous manner, by [means of] the crime of homicide on the person of the president of the Republic.

The department of Amazonas has joined its unanimous vote to that of the nation, and has demonstrated in a splendid manner its respect for the established institutions and the government, as is demonstrated in acts realized today in this capital [Chachapoyas]. The municipal council, the highest representatives of the clergy, of the Beneficent Society, the National High School, the judiciary, the public employees, and, in a single word, all the people, have made their solemn protest against the assassination attempt . . . and have offered the chief of state their material and moral support in order to thwart any and all attempts to disrupt the public peace.[2]

This public declaration of the ruling Hurtado-Rodriguéz casta was a prime example of the way in which the violence, insecurity, and arbitrary use of power that characterized everyday life was made invisible in ritual and discourse, and was replaced by the chimera of a consensual social order based on peaceful coexistence and concern for the common good. The article asserted the existence of a series of mythical entities—"the Peruvian People," "the department of Amazonas," "society," and "all the people." Each of these entities was depicted as being internally undifferentiated, as having a single set of unitary interests and concerns that *had* to be respected if "progress" was to be achieved. Explicit as well was the notion that the Hurtado-Rodriguéz sought to guide the mythical entities in question toward a brighter and more promising future according to the inexorable laws of Progress. The legitimacy of the ruling casta, and the justice of its position, stemmed from its respect for the laws of order and progress, from its attempts to do everything in its power to make advancement possible for "all the people." The criminal nature of the opposition resulted from the fact that they threatened to disrupt this natural process of such great potential benefit to all. The great mass of the people recognized the legitimacy of the Hurtado-Rodriguéz, and felt deeply grateful to the ruling casta for its efforts to promote the common good. This was at-

tested to by the huge numbers of people who participated in mass demonstrations against the treacherous attempt made by a small criminal element to
subvert these general interests, to derail this forward path of advancement.

This public declaration made by the ruling Hurtado-Rodriguéz casta bore
virtually no relation to the events the declaration depicted, and presented such
a distorted view of the region's social groups and their interactions that they
became unrecognizable. What the newspaper article failed to mention was
well known to all in Chachapoyas at the time. The attempt on the president's
life had been part of a more general plot to seize control of the national government by force of arms. Sizable political factions in several departments in
northern Peru, including Amazonas, San Martín, and Cajamarca, had participated in the plot.[3] Participants in the plot had attempted to take government
representatives by surprise by staging simultaneous uprisings in all three departmental capitals, thus seizing control of local government for the opposition, and ousting President Pardo's Partido Civil from power regionally and
nationally.

In Chachapoyas, the revolt had been led by Pablo E. Santillán—leader of
the Santillán-Becerril casta, which had been driven from power locally in
1872 with the ascendance of the Partido Civil and its local client, the Hurtado-
Rodriguéz casta.[4] Santillán and a large coterie of his followers had organized
and carried out a carefully planned armed assault on the prefecture, which
was only put down with much blood spilled on both sides.

The Santillán-Becerril had been driven to act by the severe persecution they
had suffered at the hands of the ruling Hurtado-Rodriguéz casta. Had the Santillán-Becerril been victorious, it would have been able to liberate itself from its
oppressors, to promote its own interests and affairs, and to punish and persecute
the Hurtado-Rodriguéz. Instead, Pablo E. Santillán spent the next five years
under careful guard in the Chachapoyas jail, his allies were mercilessly harassed
and persecuted, and his casta ceased to exist for all practical purposes.[5]

It was thus hardly surprising that the political, educational, and religious
elite of Chachapoyas turned out in number for the demonstrations alluded to
in the article, protesting the attempt to assassinate President Pardo. For these
members of the elite owed their prominent positions to the regime of President Pardo, and had just come very close to losing these positions. Contrary to
what the article asserted, however, it was not "the people of Amazonas" who

appeared en masse to express their outrage at the attempt on the life of the president, for "the people" did not exist. Rather, those who participated in the protests were members of the Hurtado-Rodriguéz casta. This casta consisted of a highly select group of people who enjoyed special powers and privileges not available to the rest of the population by virtue of having seized these powers by force of arms. But the members of the ruling casta were not only especially privileged; they also actively differentiated themselves from the rest of the social order by publicly displaying the powers and privileges that they alone enjoyed.

In other words, the leaders of the demonstrations alluded to in the article were not public servants who selflessly guided the interests of the department toward a brighter future of hope and progress for all. Actually, they were dangerous men who publicly flaunted their ability to advance their own interests, and to dominate, shame, and dispossess all who opposed them. Furthermore, it was common knowledge that this was the case. There was no pretense that the Hurtado-Rodriguéz actually represented or defended some abstract "general interest." Quite to the contrary; only by continually demonstrating the *lack* of such a general interest—by means of ongoing violations of the persons and property of its adversary, the Santillán-Becerril casta—had the Hurtado-Rodriguéz managed to remain in power during the previous two years.

Nonetheless, the Hurtado-Rodriguéz casta was the official representative of the independent Republic of Peru within the department of Amazonas—a republic founded on Enlightenment principles of popular sovereignty, and born of struggle against aristocratic, colonial privilege. As the local representative of such a central regime, it was essential that the Hurtado-Rodriguéz conform to and help reproduce the state's self-image as a modern, democratic republic—one that abided by the same principles as other modern nation-states. Since the exclusive language in which it could do so was that of popular sovereignty, the ruling coalition was obliged to present as sacrosanct principles that were known everywhere to provide the only legitimate basis for life in modern nation-states—principles of citizenship, private property, individual rights and protections, and equality under the law.

In responding to events such as the attempt to assassinate President Pardo, the universalistic principles of popular sovereignty thus provided the sole terms in which political leaders could represent moral and immoral forms of behav-

ior, legitimate and illegitimate forms of society. The discursive account of local reaction to the assassination attempt crafted by the ruling casta reflected
this fact. Casta leaders seized upon the crisis provoked by inter-casta struggle
and the nearly fatal attack on the president to project a wholly imaginary social order based on harmony and consensus, a social order of which they
claimed to be the true representatives. This consensual social order was depicted as having been temporarily threatened by a few deviant individuals
who could not possibly have had any legitimate grounds for insurrection—
who could only be regarded as "outcasts from society." Thus, by recasting the
crisis in the language of popular sovereignty, the ruling casta erased not only
casta conflict but the very existence of castas themselves. In place of warring
groups led by privileged elites, casta leaders asserted the existence of a mass of
patriotic citizens and a handful of deviants. The former were united behind
the cause of progress and advancement. The latter were determined to disrupt these processes, which would otherwise lead to the betterment of all.

The contradictory nature of the position of the ruling casta, forced as it
was to reconcile conflicting forms of sovereignty, is revealed in two ways. First,
those in power released this account of "the people and their common interests" in the direct aftermath of a violent encounter between highly differentiated groups with blatantly opposed interests—an encounter that demonstrated
precisely the opposite of what was asserted in the ruling casta's public declaration. Second, they offered this fabrication not to strangers, who might be expected to accept it uncritically, but to the very people whose *lack* of common
interest led to endemic violence and constant insecurity of person and property for people of both castas.

Clearly, the ruling casta did not offer accounts that contradicted its behavior and undermined its authority by choice. That it was compelled to do so
speaks to the historical process that gave birth to the postcolonial Peruvian
state—and to the contradiction between the two forms of sovereignty that
had been forced into uncomfortable juxtaposition in the region as a result:
aristocratic sovereignty, whose cultural categories and social relationships acted
as the organizational basis of everyday life; and popular sovereignty, whose
concepts and language provided the sole terms in which political life could
be represented.

There was, however, a subtext to the ruling casta's public demonstrations and protestations concerning the assassination attempt on the president—one that contradicted the very principles of popular rule expounded upon with such force by casta leaders. The Hurtado-Rodriguéz casta's ability to seize notions of the common good, the general interest, and the people, and to assert that its particular interests *were* these general interests, that it *was* the people, that its progress *was* progress, sent very powerful messages to society at large. For everyone knew the opposite to be the case. It was therefore apparent that the ruling casta was potent enough to make public assertions in ritual contexts that directly contradicted both everyday life and the principles endorsed by the central state—and to do so with impunity. By the very act of proclaiming as public truths what everyone knew to be false, the ruling casta was able simultaneously to ridicule its enemies (by violating their rights while claiming to defend these rights), popular sovereignty, and the central government.

Those who governed thus made continual reference to "the common good" and "the general interest." They asserted that it was the patriotic, moral duty of each individual, without distinction, to rise above his particular interests, and to contribute to the great and noble effort of advancing the interests of "the nation," of "the people"—entities that transcended the individual. And they employed the moral contrast between the common and the private good, between the general and the particular interest, between selfless and self-interested behavior, each time they sought to persecute their enemies or to advance their own affairs.

Consider, for example, the struggle between the Burga-Hurtado and the Pizarro-Rubio castas in 1893 over the all-important question of where to build the first bridge across the turbulent Marañon River, which separated the department of Amazonas from the core of the state located to the west and south (see Map 1). The construction of a bridge across the Marañon was a matter of considerable import. The bridge would act as a conduit by means of which new political and economic forces would enter the department—forces that threatened to disrupt existing power relations between castas. Specifically, the bridge would make it possible for large numbers of armed men and large quantities of merchandise to enter the department on a scale, and with a degree of ease, never before possible.

Prior to 1893 it had been necessary to transport all human and commercial traffic across the Marañon on small rafts, which had to be poled from one side of the river to the other. Not only was the crossing a time-consuming and dangerous endeavor, in which loss of cargo and life was frequent, but it was carried out at many points along the river. A bridge promised to eliminate these difficulties, and thus to allow much greater quantities of goods and people to enter the region. It would also, however, eliminate what had been the spatially dispersed manner in which people and goods had entered the region, and would concentrate their entry at a single strategic point. As a result, each casta sought desperately to define where that point would be.

In 1893 the Ministry of Public Works sent an engineer to Amazonas to determine which of two possible locations—the river port towns of Balzas or Tupen—would be the better location for the bridge. The Pizarro-Rubio favored Balzas, as its members owned properties adjacent to the town. By locating the bridge within its sphere of influence, the casta hoped to reap the benefits the new bridge offered, and to deny these benefits to its adversaries.

Fortuitously, the Central Highway, which had been the main transport route linking Amazonas to Cajamarca since the colonial era, crossed the Marañon River at Balzas, and in reality Balzas was the only reasonable site for the bridge. The Burga-Hurtado forces, however, owned estates at the river port of Tupen, downriver from Balzas, where a different, and considerably more marginal, mule route connected Amazonas to the department of Cajamarca. The Burga-Hurtado was determined to have the bridge built at Tupen, as its members believed that a bridge at Tupen would benefit them greatly and would hurt the Pizarro-Rubio forces. It mattered little that Tupen was an inappropriate and out-of-the-way site for the bridge, and that building the bridge there would require a major reorganization in the entire system of mule transport between Amazonas and Cajamarca.

Geopolitical considerations also made the location of the bridge a pressing matter for both castas. Each sought to locate the bridge within its own sphere of influence to better control the new political and military forces that the bridge's construction would introduce to the region—forces that could be decisive in helping a casta prevail over its enemies. The casta that succeeded in locating the bridge within its own sphere of influence could easily welcome friendly government or rebel troops into the department, and could protect these troops from attacks by opposing castas. Similarly, the casta that controlled the bridge could more easily prevent hostile government or rebel troops from entering the department at all.[6]

In 1893, when the government engineer arrived, the Burga-Hurtado had the advantage of being the ruling casta. It was thus able to exert tremendous influence on the engineer concerning what eventually stood as the "truth" regarding the best location for the bridge. In light of their marginal position in regional affairs at this time, the Pizarro-Rubio forces were compelled to form an organization they called the "Union of Amazonas" in order to protect their interests. They used this organization to lobby the Congress and the Ministry of Public Works in favor of placing the bridge at Balzas. After the engineer had completed his work, Prefect Alayza wrote to the Ministry of Public Works to justify the engineer's improbable decision that the bridge should be built at Tupen rather than at Balzas.

> Don Nazario Castro, in his capacity as president of a society known as the Union of Amazonas, has asked that the Supreme Government choose the port of Balzas as the most appropriate site for the construction of the [Marañon] bridge . . . putting forward reasons, however, that are not acceptable. . . . Not being a native son of this department, nor having had occasion to travel the routes of Balzas and "Tupen," I believed it best to listen to the opinions of the respectable citizens of this locality . . . who have practical knowledge of the routes; to this end, on the 2nd of the present month I met in the prefecture with those persons who, in my judgment, would be able to provide me with the truth regarding this matter. The claims put forward by Sr. Castro having been discussed in detail, the conclusion was reached that the only appropriate site for the construction of the bridge is that identified by Engineer Hohagen, "Tupen." . . . This [conclusion] has been stated by Sr. Hohagen in his report, and it has also been recognized by the [respectable citizens] referred to earlier, who include among them some who would benefit directly if the bridge were to be built at Balzas. These same people are [also] convinced . . . that it would be impossible to maintain a bridge built [at Balzas].
>
> The residents of Balzas [most of whom were members of the Union of Amazonas] are accustomed to exploiting passersby, imposing their unappealable will on [these travelers], and are accustomed as well to idleness, for the time that remains available after [they have provided] the service of transporting people and cargo from one side of the Marañon to the other, they em-

ploy neither in agriculture nor in any other useful occupation; and divided as they are into various groups that seek only their own personal ascendancy rather than the triumph of any political ideal, which they lack, they perpetrate atrocious crimes. . . . Of course they do not view with favor [the possibility that] they would lose the only source of livelihood currently available to them. . . . Balzas is not an appropriate site for the project: the roads that lead to said point from this department as well as those that continue from it to Cajamarca are the biggest obstacle with which to deal; and even if it were possible to improve these roads it would still be necessary to invest more money than is available in the construction of the bridge. . . .

In light of these difficulties, there remains no option other than to follow the opinion of Engineer Hohagen, and to adopt "Tupen," a route that offers conveniences and facilities that the other lacks . . . and that will put the productive haciendas of this entire route [namely, those of the Burga-Hurtado] in constant and easy communication with Cajamarca. . . .

As I have said, this report is the summary of the opinions expressed in the general meeting [of respectable citizens] held on the 2nd of this month, and in taking it upon myself to echo their ideas, I believe that I am complying with a sacred duty.

The claim made by the president of the "Union of Amazonas," that the designation of "Tupen" as the site for the construction of the bridge is an attempt to promote private interests, which can never be allowed to come before the general interest, is totally without foundation. . . .

Roads must never be built to favor particular interests, but rather for the general good, since they are the most powerful elements of progress and civilization, and if I had known that an attempt was being made [by the Union of Amazonas] to promote the interests of the few at the expense of the many, I would have been opposed to it from the very first moment. ([APA36], Feb. 4, 1893)

The idea of placing the new bridge at Tupen rather than at Balzas was preposterous, and was known by everyone to be so. This, however, did not prevent the ruling Burga-Hurtado forces from attempting to impose Tupen as the construction site to advance their own interests. The manner in which they did so reveals much about the prevailing contradiction between aristocratic and popular sovereignty.

In order to resolve the question about where to locate the bridge, the prefect pretended to initiate a public discussion in which "respectable citizens" who were intimately familiar with the two routes met in the prefecture to weigh the competing claims of the Union of Amazonas and the engineer sent by the Ministry of Public Works. This measure was necessary, the prefect confessed, because he personally lacked sufficient knowledge of the routes to make a sound judgment himself. In this way, the prefect emphasized his impartiality in and his distance from the entire matter. The prefect also took special pains to emphasize the disinterested nature of the group who met—it was an impartial group that represented no single interest, consisting as it did of "respectable citizens" and including as it did individuals whose interests would have been better served were the bridge to be built at Balzas. These knowledgeable, respectable, impartial citizens met, debated, and evaluated the various competing claims. They concluded that the government engineer had made the correct choice; that the Union of Amazonas was motivated by self-serving greed; and that its members cared little for the general interest or progress of the department.

There were a few things that the prefect failed to mention. As was known to all, the prefect was firmly allied with the forces of the Burga-Hurtado, and had been since his arrival in the region in March 1892. He had spearheaded a movement to oust Pizarro-Rubio clients from all important political posts, had succeeded in removing them from the subprefectures of all three provinces, and had allowed Burga-Hurtado clients to replace them. He had also been responsible for members of the Pizarro-Rubio casta being sacked from high posts in the Guardia Civil. Thereafter, he had helped the Burga-Hurtado seize control of the Pizarro-Rubio's last stronghold in the region— the municipal council of Luya province—going so far as to appoint Burga-Hurtado clients as auditors to "inspect" the account books of the council. Predictably, the auditors "discovered" graft on a massive scale, because of which the prefect was legally obligated to dissolve the council, initiate criminal proceedings against its members, and organize new elections (in which the Burga-Hurtado candidates were victorious).[7] In the course of these investigations, the prefect also discovered that the man who collected the Indian head tax in Luya province (the *apoderado fiscal*), a high-ranking member of the Pizarro-Rubio casta, had misappropriated tax revenue. The law required that the prefect, as the highest representative of the central government in the region, instruct the judge of the first instance to prosecute the man for his crime. Thus began a drawn-out judicial investigation in which many other members of the Pizarro-Rubio casta were ultimately implicated.[8]

By the time the prefect called the meeting of "citizens" to debate the location of the bridge, members of the Pizarro-Rubio casta had suffered persecution at the hands of the Burga-Hurtado for several years.[9] Many had gone underground in order to avoid further abuse. In light of the prefect's hostility toward the Pizarro-Rubio, and his role in driving them from all positions of prominence, it is not surprising that the "citizens" he called to his meeting were exclusively members of the Burga-Hurtado casta.[10] The conclusions reached as a result of their "democratic debate" spoke of their casta affiliation.

Here as elsewhere, in the realms of ritual and discourse, the rhetoric of popular rule was used to create the illusion of consensus, democracy, and selfless concern for the common good—even while inter-casta political struggles were played out publicly in fundamentally different terms. That is, because the ruling casta was forced to adopt the central state's standards of representation in certain specific and limited domains, events that were carefully orchestrated to show everyone the ruling casta's ability to dominate and shame its enemies were transformed into something virtually unrecognizable when recast in ritual and discourse. They became egalitarian, consensual, and democratic events in which power played no role. Thus, in depicting the controversy about the bridge to the central government, the ruling casta, the violent behavior of its members, and their efforts to impose their will on their adversaries were made to disappear entirely. All underwent a metamorphosis into their polar opposite. The ruling casta became indistinguishable from society itself, while the interests and desires of casta members became society's interests, the nation's interests, general interests that were synonymous with progress and civilization.

Similarly, the history of persecution of the Pizarro-Rubio effected by the prefect—which drove the Pizarro-Rubio from public life and ultimately allowed the Burga-Hurtado to impose its own version of the truth regarding the best location for the bridge—was also rendered invisible. It was replaced by a public political ritual—the meeting of knowledgeable citizens held in the prefecture that rationally and democratically settled the question at hand so as to best promote the common good, progress, and civilization—and by a legitimating report about the meeting sent to the central government.

All this occurred, however, without the existence of the ruling casta ever having been acknowledged. Ruling castas were simply not available or present as elements of discourse to be regarded, evaluated, embraced, or dismissed.[11] For to acknowledge that such entities as ruling castas existed would be tantamount to asserting that an exclusive, hierarchical, self-serving group could promote interests and ideals to which it was diametrically opposed—the inclusive, egalitarian, selfless principles of popular sovereignty. By its very nature, then, such a thing as a "legitimate ruling casta" was unimaginable within the moral logic of popular rule.

Although the ruling casta was never named as such in political discourse, its existence was anything but a secret. The Burga-Hurtado made no attempt whatsoever either to conceal itself from society at large or to deceive anyone about the true nature of its actions. To the contrary: The manipulations of the Burga-Hurtado casta were common knowledge in Chachapoyas, and could not have been otherwise. There was no pretense that democracy was actually at work in the struggle over the location of the bridge, or that the Burga-Hurtado were truly attempting to promote the common good. After all, one of the ways that the ruling casta demonstrated its power and potency was by showing its ability to impose its will on its enemies, and by doing so in blatantly self-serving ways even though the consequences were intensely negative for others.

The success of the Burga-Hurtado in removing members of the Pizarro-Rubio from positions of power during the previous several years, for example, sent powerful messages to society at large concerning the might of the ruling casta. This was equally true of the casta's ability to dictate its choice of Tupen as the construction site for the bridge—the culmination of this process of persecution and marginalization. The bridge would demonstrate the power of the Burga-Hurtado in the most glaring manner by its very inappropriateness for that locale. It would become a permanent part of the built, physical environment that would act as a monument to the potency of the ruling casta, as well as a daily reminder to all of the victory of the Burga-Hurtado over the Pizarro-Rubio.[12] The ruling casta's ability to represent the events that led to Tupen being chosen as the bridge site as a process of democratic debate and rational argument—when everyone knew the opposite to be the case—likewise demonstrated to society at large that the ruling casta was able to make public assertions in ritual contexts that were known to be blatantly untrue—and to do so with impunity. In so ridiculing the central government and the opposing casta, the Burga-Hurtado demonstrated publicly that it had neither masters nor peers.

The dilemma for the ruling casta, however, was that it was not able to celebrate or legitimate this dominating behavior in ritual contexts. Rather, in representing itself to society at large, it was forced to invoke principles of equality, consensus, and the common good that were the very antithesis of its everyday presentation of self. The content of these popular notions was such that they had the potential to subvert the authority of the ruling casta, as they provided a critical commentary not only on ruling casta behavior, but also on the cultural and material logic of aristocratic sovereignty itself.

Within the moral universe of popular sovereignty, there was no way to represent the hierarchy, privilege, and purposive use of violence that characterized actual casta behavior in legitimate terms. Nor was there any way to depict the dynamics of shame and countershame, attack and counterattack, that characterized competition between castas in legitimate terms. Rather, the assertion common to all political discourse was that the only legitimate form of society was one of consensus and harmony, in which an honorable group of citizens peacefully cooperated with one another to advance the common interests of community and nation. If a casta wished to legitimate itself, it therefore did so by representing itself not as a casta, but as a group of citizens who sought to advance these very causes. Similarly, if a casta wished to discredit its foes, it did so by depicting them as the enemies of progress and the common good. In such attempts to discredit, reference might be made to various "outrages" perpetrated by members of the opposition. But this abusive behavior was relevant only to the extent that it demonstrated that the adversarial casta had violated the ethical principles upon which legitimate society was based.

Opposing castas therefore sought to present themselves as advancing the causes of democracy, equality, progress, and the common good, and sought to vilify their foes as representing a threat to these noble ideals and principles. But these two alternatives (or gradations of them) largely exhausted the realm of what was possible or imaginable within the rhetoric of popular sovereignty. In this way, discourse about political conflict uniformly misrepresented the actual nature of the region's social groups and the reasons for their struggles.

In the inter-casta competition for legitimation, the ruling casta was at a distinct advantage. For the moral logic of popular rule was such that it precluded the possibility that an exclusive, hierarchical, self-serving group like a casta could be the legitimate representative of the modern nation-state of Peru. Rather, this moral logic *required* that the local representative of the central government be the guardian of progress and advancement. And so the ruling casta was obligated to represent itself as such. In being compelled to so depict its behavior, however, the ruling casta was obliged to alter nothing about its actual behavior. Rather, it was free to dominate, shame, and persecute members of the opposition, and thus to reproduce its own position of dominance. In representing these self-serving actions to society at large, however, the ruling casta was indeed compelled to use the language of popular sovereignty, and thus an important metamorphosis took place. The particular interests and desires of ruling casta members were converted into the general interests of the people and of the nation. And the ruling casta became transformed into society itself.

Because the language and concepts of popular sovereignty offered the exclusive terms in which moral and immoral attitudes and behaviors, and legitimate and illegitimate forms of society, could be represented, those who sat in the prefecture were able to use political discourse to convert challenges to ruling casta privilege into threats to progress, civilization, and the general good. Prefect Eloy Burga, leader of the ruling Burga-Hurtado casta, provides a particularly vivid illustration of this process. The prefect reported to the central government about what was actually an attempt by the Pizarro-Rubio to challenge the hegemonic position of Burga's casta. The Pizarro-Rubio had elected its own municipal council in the province of Luya, and was attempting to assert this council instead of the Burga-Hurtado's as the province's legal municipal council. The prefect's report clearly illustrated the way that popular political discourse masked ongoing social processes, for nowhere was any mention made of either of the region's warring casta groups. The Pizarro-Rubio casta was made to disappear, converted into a group of "evil residents" who sought to seize control of public office by illegal means for its own private gain—

and who threatened to undermine "the common good" and "the public will" as a result. The ruling Burga-Hurtado casta was likewise made invisible in the account. Prefect Eloy Burga depicted his actions as being in defense not of his casta, but of an imaginary social order based on consensus and the common good.

> Municipal elections were held without incident on March 1st, 2nd, and 3rd, in the three provinces that make up this department . . . although . . . in Lámud, capital of the province of Luya, a group of evil residents, seeing the lucrative dealings that they had formerly conducted under the protection of an irresponsible municipal council slipping through their fingers, made an attempt to elect an alternative municipal council; however, opportune measures having been taken by this office . . . the legal election triumphed. . . . The alternative municipal council of Lámud has been undermined by the illegality of the means employed [to organize it]; . . . the inexorable sanction of the law will now fall upon those who were involved, as before they felt the weight of moral sanction. ([APA43], "Ramo de Gobierno")

In this way, the entire casta order was subsumed by a discourse that represented political life exclusively in terms of popular sovereignty. Burga's report was based on the clear and unmistakable claim that the political dynamics of the region consisted of a struggle between two groups: a broad circle of honorable, just, and selfless citizens who made up legitimate society—those who were interested only in progress and the common good; and a small criminal element that was forever seeking its own private gain at the expense of legitimate society. Because the "evil residents" to whom Burga referred in his report had betrayed the public interest in the past, and clearly wished to do so again, they had proved themselves to belong to the latter group—to be outcasts from legitimate society. It was precisely the honorable and just citizenry, on the other hand, that Burga had sworn to protect.

The true nature of the unscrupulous individuals who made up the illegal municipal council, implied Burga, was clearly perceived by those honorable and just citizens who made up legitimate society. For even prior to the collapse of the illegal municipal council, the evil residents had felt "the weight of moral sanction" from society at large. And because of opportune measures having been taken by Prefect Burga, this criminal element would also feel "the inexorable sanction of the law." In other words, legitimate society and its political representatives concurred on the threat posed by such illegal activities and such unscrupulous individuals. In taking action against these "evil residents," the prefect was therefore not acting on his own behalf. Rather, his actions reflected and complemented the collective will of society. As a result, the prefect was able to use the position entrusted to him by the central government to punish the wicked and to protect the worthy—all of which culminated in the triumph of those "legally" elected to the new municipal council (who were all members of the Burga-Hurtado; the election had been controlled in its entirety by the ruling casta).

This is a clear example of the way that the ruling casta used its control over political discourse to make existing social divisions and struggles disappear, to replace them with an entirely imaginary social order based on consensus, and to transform challenges from casta enemies into threats to this imaginary social order. For what Prefect Burga failed to mention was that it was not "legitimate society" that was under attack, but rather the casta of which Burga was the leader. Nor did he explain that the people he characterized as "evil residents" were in fact members of the Pizarro-Rubio casta, which Burga and his allies had forcibly removed from the municipal council of Luya the year before with the most blatant and arbitrary abuse of power. Nor did Burga mention that the municipal council that his casta had installed in Luya province at the fall of the Pizarro-Rubio council was guilty of precisely the same "abuses" that Burga here cited to discredit his foes—as the Pizarro-Rubio demonstrated the following year, when they swept the Burga-Hurtado from power in the aftermath of civil war.[13]

In short, because he was compelled to use the rhetoric of popular rule to represent a conflict that defied characterization in such terms, Prefect Burga systematically masked and distorted the true nature of social groups, and transformed them into something they were not. Specifically, he concealed the fact that it was in the very nature of political offices like the municipal council to be used as a source of "lucrative dealings" (see Chapter 3)—but more, that it was in the nature of casta rule itself to continually betray the common interest and the general good. And yet Burga could not have done otherwise. In (mis-)representing casta behavior in the terms of popular sovereignty, Burga was making no attempt to deceive anyone regarding the true nature of his own actions or those of his casta. Rather, he was simply responding to a historical conjuncture in which the terms available for the representation of political life had no relationship to the organization of political life.

The ruling casta was compelled to offer public accounts of political behavior not only in dramatic moments of crisis, but also in the course of managing the more mundane affairs of life—what might be called "politics as usual." The ongoing public administration of these daily matters resulted in the production of an endless stream of official documents, communiqués, orders, petitions, and requests. These ranged in form from official documents sent periodically to the central government by the departmental prefect, reporting on the state of affairs in the department as a whole (*memorias*); to the daily messages sent back and forth between prefects, subprefects, judges of the first instance, governors, lieutenant governors, and justices of the peace in the course of administering their zones of jurisdiction; to communiqués sent to private citizens by all of these political officials, again in the context of day-to-day public administration. Ruling casta members thus communicated their intentions and represented their actions to one another and to society at large on an ongoing basis.

Revealingly, the principles of popular sovereignty provided the sole terms in which moral and immoral attitudes and behaviors were represented in virtually all of this correspondence. That is, political communiqués as a whole were framed as if the social order were one of peace, harmony, and cooperation, peopled by patriotic citizens who were united behind the causes of progress and advancement, and who were more than prepared to give of themselves to help realize these goals. This social order, these citizens, and the causes for which they strove were depicted as occasionally being put at risk by the irresponsible or self-interested behavior of particular individuals or groups. Public administration could thus logically be represented as consisting of the noble task of protecting this citizenry, of assisting their efforts to achieve progress, of punishing those who intentionally posed a threat to this citizenry and their cause, and of reprimanding those who inadvertently interfered with either.[14]

As noted above, however, this social order of harmony, consensus, and progress imagined discursively in political communiqués had little or no relation to the aristocratic order of power, privilege, and violence that existed on the ground. Actually, "public administration" involved casta leaders in a range of conflicts and struggles that had nothing to do with protecting honorable citizens or with contributing to the cause of progress. Rather, these recurrent conflicts were a function of the difficulty of maintaining control of the region amid the general contradictions of casta rule. Casta leaders were constantly dealing with conflicts arising from disagreements among members of the same casta over how the spoils of casta rule were to be divided, from the difficulties of imposing tax and corvée labor obligations on a large minority population (the region's "Indians"), from the need to harass and persecute members of enemy castas in order to effectively fragment the opposition, and from the pressure to constantly reassert the potency of the ruling casta in the face of ongoing challenges from the opposition. However, because ruling casta members consistently employed the rhetoric of popular rule to represent conflict and their response to it, social reality was consistently distorted and masked.

As argued at length in earlier chapters, casta control was characterized by a complex set of contradictions between casta leaders and their subaltern appointees. Most of these contradictions turned on attempts by casta leaders to assert sufficient control over the region and its populace to be able to live according to the elite station in life to which all members of the casta española felt themselves entitled—to enjoy special privileges and powers, rights and resources not available to their social inferiors. As we have seen, individual elite families lacked the resources and connections necessary to do this, and thus established alliances with families of all social classes in an attempt to realize their own elite aspirations. Many of the contradictions that emerged out of the process of reproducing ruling casta control grew out of conflicts between the lower- and higher-ranking members of this coalition of allied families. For it was the former—the region's rural governors, lieutenant governors, and justices of the peace—who did much of the actual work of managing political life (collecting tribute, organizing corvée labor, controlling commerce, containing threats from and persecuting the opposition). It was the latter, however—the elite families in Chachapoyas—who expected to reap most of the benefits of political control (see Chapter 3).

The exercise of ruling casta control thus inevitably led to a situation in which the higher-ranking members of the coalition called upon lower-rank-ing members to do more than the latter were able or willing. This in turn led to almost countless instances in which the performance of rural appointees was found wanting by casta leaders. Whenever low-ranking appointees did not comply with the wishes of higher-ranking officials, the failure of those responsible was never depicted in terms that reflected the actual conflicts be-tween local and central control that were a built-in feature of casta rule; for these conflicts stemmed from disagreements over who would enjoy the rights, and who would be burdened with the obligations, of engaging in activities that were unethical, immoral, even unthinkable according to the moral logic of popular rule. That is, the conflicts concerned who would extort, coerce, dispossess, dominate, and shame members of the opposition—things that no one, in theory, was allowed to do.

Indeed, the legitimacy of those who occupied political office was predi-cated on their opposition to these very kinds of activities. As a result, in po-litical discourse, the inability or unwillingness of subaltern appointees to carry out the wishes of their superiors was consistently recast or metamorphosed into a more legitimate form of deviance—one that bore no relation to the actual conflicts. Lower-level functionaries were depicted not as resisting their superiors' commands to extort, coerce, dispossess, etc., but as being guilty of a different kind of failing—a moral failing. They were uniformly represented as having compromised one or more of the mythical entities that figured so prominently in popular political discourse—the nation, the people, progress, and the common good.

An oficio sent by the subprefect of Chachapoyas to the governor of Chuquibamba concerning the latter's negligence in apprehending several men wanted for murder provides an example of this transformation. The subprefect had already sent orders to the governor to capture the men twice before. In at-tempting to compel and reprimand the governor in this third order, the sub-prefect subtly evoked the same scenario encountered in virtually all political discourse of the era—a legitimate social order of peace, harmony, and con-sensus that those in power were sworn to protect, and a handful of deviants whose behavior threatened that social order. With this as background, the governor's resistance to carrying out the order of his superior could only appear as a moral failure on the part of the governor to protect the region's legitimate citizenry and its interests.

> *To the Governor of Chuquibamba.* This office has learned that the criminals [responsible for] the death of don Feliciano Rojas are to be found . . . in the place called Opaban, located in your district.
>
> This being the case, I prevail upon you to capture the delinquents immediately and send them to this subprefecture, accompanied by an armed guard.
>
> This office finds the lack of vigilance on your part strange, [considering that] acts of this nature compromise the life and economic affairs (*intereses*) of all the citizens of this province. ([APA61], *Subprefecto del Cercado al Gobernador de La Jalca*, June 7, 1898)

In representing social life, social conflict, and the moral obligations of political officials in these terms, the subprefect masked and distorted ongoing social processes to such a degree that they became unrecognizable. The governor's resistance to apprehending the murderers sought by the subprefect had nothing to do with the governor having failed in his moral obligations to protect the lives and economic affairs of the region's citizenry. For there was no legitimate social order, no general citizenry, and no stable or disinterested set of economic affairs for the governor either to protect or to compromise.

Casta conflict provided the background necessary to understand the true nature of the murders themselves, the desire of the subprefect to apprehend the murderers, and the resistance of the governor to carrying out the command of his superior. The men being sought were actually members of the Burga-Hurtado casta. They had killed Feliciano Rojas—governor of Balzas district—in the course of an armed uprising organized by their casta in February 1898 in an attempt to seize power from the ruling Pizarro-Rubio.[15] The uprising failed, and these particular fugitives were attempting to take refuge in a remote part of the neighboring district of Chuquibamba, where their political patrons owned estates. The Pizarro-Rubio forces did not want this affront to their authority to go unanswered, and appealed to the governor of Chuquibamba to apprehend the men. That is, casta leaders attempted to compel the governor to assume the mortal risk of attempting to capture heavily armed and dangerous men who were hiding within a section of Chuquibamba district where the governor's authority was tenuous at best, all because the aggressive acts of these men reflected badly on the honor of the ruling casta. Not having been totally lacking in good sense, apparently, the governor refused to obey the command.[16]

The homicide for which these men were sought had done anything but compromise the lives and economic affairs of "all citizens." To the contrary; it had been carried out as part of a more general plan, whose goal had been to protect the lives and advance the economic affairs of a determinate group of citizens—members of the Burga-Hurtado casta, who had been subject to persecution by the Pizarro-Rubio for the previous three years.

All this was common knowledge at the time, and could not have been otherwise. Nonetheless, in reprimanding the governor of Chuquibamba (who had good reason to resist apprehending known killers who were more heavily armed than he), the subprefect chose to employ the rhetoric of popular rule. He chose to render the region's warring castas invisible, and their violent and aggressive members nonexistent. In their place, he asserted the existence of a mythical social order of consensus and harmony, made up of honorable and peaceful citizens, all of whom were equally threatened by "violence." The subprefect did so even though both he and the governor with whom he corresponded knew otherwise. No mention was made of competing castas, or of the dynamics of violence and counterviolence, persecution and counterpersecution, in which they were constantly involved. All were subsumed within a wholly imaginary social order fabricated from the principles and ideals of popular sovereignty.

Recasting the unending and inevitable conflicts between subalterns and their superiors as stemming from individual, moral failings rather than from the structural contradictions of casta rule was not the only use to which such popular notions were put. The discourse of popular sovereignty reached what was perhaps its most mythic dimensions when it was affixed to official demands for labor services from subaltern groups. Whenever the ruling casta imposed its unending and onerous demands on the labor power and/or the wealth of the subaltern, it would make no reference to the group's actual status as disadvantaged minorities (Indians) subject to status-specific obligations that were encoded in law (most notably, corvée labor obligations). Rather, in all political discourse, the material, behavioral, and symbolic markers that distinguished elite from commoner from Indian—distinctions whose ongoing public expression was the basis of the entire order of aristocratic sovereignty—were made to disappear. In their place, a mythical, egalitarian social order was created in which everyone became a "citizen," equivalent to and indistinguishable from everyone else.

It was on this basis that the ruling casta appealed to its Indians for labor services and production—by characterizing them as "citizens" who helped make up "the nation," which could only progress by means of such necessary and patriotic "sacrifices" made by "one and all." It was obvious to everyone, however, that those who were forced to make these "sacrifices" were most often members of a particular social stratum, that they were invariably enemies of the ruling casta, and that they were forced to labor in the interest of the particular rather than the general good.

In a communiqué that was typical of such demands for labor service, the subprefect of Chachapoyas wrote to the governor of the district of La Jalca, requesting that the "citizens" of his district contribute their labor in the interest of what the subprefect called "the common good."

> *To the Governor of La Jalca.* The prefecture has instructed me to direct the present oficio to you . . . ordering that at the end of the present month the citizens of La Jalca are to deliver 1,500 loads of stone to Chachapoyas . . . each stone should be of the length and width specified in my previous oficio . . . an additional quantity of stones is needed in order to finish paving the street that leads to the cemetery . . . and also to repair the *cañaría* that carries potable water [to Chachapoyas]. . . . [Therefore] . . . between the 15th and the 20th of next month, taking advantage of the good weather, you are to deliver to this city . . . [an additional] 2,000 loads of stone, [dividing the work] between the citizens of the pueblos of Zuta, Magdalena, and [La Jalca], always being sure that the stones conform to the size and width indicated in my previous oficio, that is, three-quarters [of a meter] in length by one-half [in width] and with a thickness of four and a half inches . . . one pack animal can carry four stones . . . [or] two loads. ([APA61], *Subprefecto del Cercado al Gobernador de La Jalca,* Apr. 27, 1898)

It was a two-day mule trip from La Jalca to Chachapoyas. The ruling casta was demanding that the "citizens" of La Jalca (including the villages of Zuta and Magdalena) provide the drivers and animals necessary for 1,750 trips by pack animal, each of which required a four-day commitment (without rest), in the course of half a month. These were extremely onerous obligations for a district whose total adult population (men and women) was 886 (in 1876; see Peru 1878: 603–8).[17] After converting the predominantly Indian population of La Jalca into an imaginary citizenry, the subprefect justified these astonishing demands for labor service by invoking additional and equally fictitious notions derived from the discourse of popular sovereignty—patriotism, and the common good:

> I am sure, Sr. Gobernador, considering your known patriotism and [concern for] the common good, that you will comply with this request with exactitude . . . [and will be] decisive and clear in taking the measures necessary for its faithful compliance.

By depicting discriminatory labor obligations imposed exclusively on Indians as a universal obligation of "citizenship," the ruling casta used the rhetoric of popular sovereignty to create a wholly imaginary, egalitarian social order. For the use of popular rhetoric in this realm had the effect of rendering the region's highly stratified racial hierarchy invisible, and of replacing it with an undifferentiated citizenry that enjoyed the same rights, and was subject to the same obligations.

In this particular case, however, something more was involved than just transforming Indians into "citizens" in certain specific contexts and for very limited purposes (to justify exploitation). Two months prior to the subprefect's order that the citizens of La Jalca gather in order to contribute to the common good, these same people had been implicated in assisting the out-of-power Burga-Hurtado casta in its attempt to mount an armed assault on the ruling Pizarro-Rubio (as described above). The unusually heavy labor demands (which were exceptional by local standards) imposed on these people were in part retribution for their lack of loyalty to those in power.

Similar appeals to the "common good," "patriotism," and the obligations of "all citizens" accompanied many of the subprefect's monthly orders to various district governors to provide the hundreds of mules and mule drivers needed to haul salt from the state-controlled salt mines at Yuromarca to Chachapoyas (a difficult two-day journey) and elsewhere.[18] Exhortations about the obligations of patriotic citizens also accompanied orders to governors to organize military conscription among the eligible men of their districts, as in a communiqué sent by the subprefect of Chachapoyas to the governor of the district of la Totora that subtly erased distinctions of race and caste by converting Indians (the only people forced to register for the draft) into "citizens," and the task of draft registration into a patriotic duty:

> *Sr. Governor of la Totora.* Despite the fact that copies of the Law and Supreme Decree concerning regulations for service in the Guardia Nacional were sent to you along with *The Official Register* [the official government newspaper] . . . I again send you copies of the law and decree alluded to, so that without further delay the citizens [of your district] proceed to register with the respective [registration] board. . . .
>
> The registration should be completed by the 30th of the present month, and my office is counting on your patriotism to carry out this disposition.
>
> —*[signed] Manuel Chavez [subprefect of Chachapoyas province]*[19] (*[APA61], June 14, 1898*)

The same process of social erasure was effected by subprefects in their unending series of commands to district governors and lieutenant governors to assemble the "citizens" of their districts to carry out the repair of roads and bridges washed out by the region's heavy rains—and thus to fulfill their obligations to the nation.[20] Virtually the same discourse was invoked yearly when the subprefect ordered the governors of districts adjacent to the departmental capital to provide hundreds of Indian laborers to come to Chachapoyas in late July in order to clean and generally prepare the town for the celebration of Independence Day, July 28.[21]

The rhetoric of popular rule also performed crucial work in relation to ruling casta efforts to contain threats from its enemies. Ruling castas employed a variety of means to prevent their adversaries from being able to mount serious challenges to the status quo, from persecution and harassment to the careful monitoring of enemy movements and activities. Regardless of the means chosen, the ruling casta routinely employed the rhetoric of popular rule, representing its actions as stemming from a concern for the common good. A notable example in this regard was the "Rules of Public Morality," first invoked in 1893, which remained in force for decades thereafter, relevant sections of which were posted for public scrutiny at times deemed appropriate by the ruling casta. The "Rules" were declared in force whenever the ruling casta was threatened by opposition forces, and were invoked with the goal of monitoring and containing the threat to the existing regime. The "Rules" included restrictions on carrying firearms (which gave the ruling casta an excuse to confiscate weapons and arrest members of other castas—considering the violence endemic to the region, and the general insecurity of person and property, many men went about armed); imposition of a curfew (which made nighttime assaults by opposition forces more difficult); restrictions on the right to assemble in groups (which made organized activity of all kinds more difficult and dangerous); and restrictions on freedom of speech (which made popular expressions against the ruling regime illegal).[22] All these restrictions were phrased in terms of protecting "the general citizenry" and "public order" from those characterized as "greedy and self-serving individuals who wished only to take advantage of the chaos they created for their own personal benefit"— even as the regulations were used to promote the self-serving interests of the ruling casta, and to protect it from its enemies.

In certain contexts, armed confrontations with opposing castas were unavoidable. In such circumstances, it was essential that the ruling coalition demonstrate its ability to crush its adversaries, and to assert its unquestioned control over regional affairs. In representing these actions to society at large, however, the ruling casta was compelled to employ the language of popular rule, and the moral logic of popular sovereignty, invoking principles that blatantly contradicted its own publicly enacted behaviors. In this regard, consider an edict posted after the end of fierce inter-casta fighting had brought the Pizarro-Rubio to power in 1895 and had driven the Burga-Hurtado from the prefecture.

> *Considering*: that the prefecture of the department . . . has authorized the subprefecture to make it known to all inhabitants of the province . . . that public order has been reestablished, the necessary measures having been taken so that all citizens may once again enjoy the individual rights and protections granted them by the Constitution;

It Is Decreed: that all inhabitants can return to their daily labors, secure in the knowledge that they once again enjoy their individual rights and guarantees.[23]

The triumph of the Pizarro-Rubio over the Burga-Hurtado casta did anything but allow "all citizens" to return to their daily labors safely, did anything but reestablish individual rights and protections for the general citizenry. Rather, it heralded the beginning of a period of intense persecution of members of the Burga-Hurtado casta, and extreme insecurity of their lives and goods. Furthermore, it was common knowledge that this was the case. Nonetheless, the Pizarro-Rubio employed the language of popular sovereignty in announcing its triumph because this language offered the exclusive terms in which political behavior could be represented as legitimate.

In sum, the principles of popular sovereignty were invoked in virtually all forms of political discourse. In addition to those discussed above, these included edicts and circulars issued by the prefecture and subprefectures announcing local political developments germane to the lives of the populace— such matters as curfews, new taxes or labor obligations, registration for military conscription, the return of stability after a period of inter-casta struggle, and so on.[24] These same principles were also voiced in other forms of print media announcing national political developments (the death of a president, the celebration of Independence Day, the progress of government versus opposition forces during a period of civil war, etc.).[25] Edicts, circulars, and newsprint of this kind were posted in "customary public places" in all provincial and district capitals, and subprefects and governors were responsible for making their contents known to those who lived within their jurisdictions. In each case, however, the language of popular sovereignty was used to justify and legitimate actions that were blatantly partisan—that represented the interests and concerns of particular individuals and groups (those involved with the ruling casta) rather than with anything remotely resembling a "common good" or a "general interest."

All this was public knowledge at the time, and could not have been otherwise. This radical disjuncture between ritual language and social action was a function of a particular historical conjuncture in which political life had to be discursively represented in terms that bore no relation to the way political life was actually organized.

It is significant that both rulers and ruled employed the language of popular sovereignty in political ritual and discourse, not because these precepts represented people's "actual beliefs," and not because those who employed the precepts believed that they were involved in promoting patriotic endeavors that would help realize the common good,[26] but because, regardless of the beliefs of the individuals concerned, and despite what was often the blatantly abusive nature of the actions involved, popular sovereignty offered the exclusive terms in which moral and immoral attitudes and behaviors could be depicted. That is, notions of individual rights and protections, the sanctity of private property, the equality of all citizens in the eyes of the law, the priority of the common good over the particular interest, and the liberating potential of progress formed a common language of representation, employed by people of all social classes, racial categories, and gender positions. These precepts simultaneously provided the sole moral justification for rule, defined the outer limits of just rule, and provided everyone with the means to challenge or delegitimate the actions of others—rulers and ruled alike.

As has been argued at length in previous chapters, however, all castas were compelled to adopt "self-serving" behaviors that threatened the "common good" on an ongoing basis—whether they were in or out of power—and were equally compelled to broadcast their ability to do so far and near. Because aristocratic sovereignty acted as the basis of the social order, there was thus a built-in contradiction between the kinds of behavior that had to be adopted in order to exercise positions of power and the kinds of explanation that could be uttered publicly and privately in accounting for these behaviors. Thus, each time casta leaders employed the language of popular sovereignty in offering public accounts of their behavior to society at large—whether in rhetoric or performance—they were forced to invoke principles that provided a critical commentary not merely on their actions, but also on the cultural and material logic of aristocratic sovereignty itself. That is, they were forced to declare publicly the lack of legitimacy of their own behaviors, of their own raison d'être, and to endorse as legitimate and just the very principles they violated on an ongoing basis.

Nonetheless, it was clear to all that aristocratic sovereignty was the reigning social reality of the time. Conformity with the precepts of popular sovereignty *never* went beyond the limited domains of ritual and discourse, *never* had any concrete impact on the daily lives of the people of the region. Rather, these principles remained in blatant contradiction with the aristocratic order throughout the period. Pretending to embrace the principles of popular sovereignty within the limited domains of ritual and discourse was thus in one sense a concession that the aristocratic elite made in order to maintain a relationship of mutual noninterference with the central state. Indeed, whenever the state attempted to go beyond these realms, and impinge on elite privilege directly, it encountered outrage and fierce resistance. In this regard, it is revealing that to the present day, each of the leading casta families maintains as an active part of its publicly recounted memory a story parallel to the one related by Sr. Echaiz in Chapter 1 and by Sr. Rubio in Chapter 2. In each case, the central government is depicted as having attempted to interfere with important decisions or actions of the ruling casta, and as having been prevented from doing so by the ruling casta—by threat of force. Each of the stories concludes with a statement emphasizing that the casta, rather than the state, ruled in Amazonas.

In another sense, then, invoking the principles of popular sovereignty in ritual and discourse was anything but a concession to central state. For what was important about ritual performances and discursive statements was not the egalitarian, consensual, selfless principles that figured so prominently within them, but rather which casta group was able to give voice to these principles—which group was able to make ritual pronouncements that were so opposed to the reality of the time.

The ruling casta's ability to represent its particular interest as the general interest, and to depict the abuse of power as rule by consensus, did much to transform the potentially subversive nature of the principles of popular sovereignty into a legitimating mechanism for the structure of aristocratic sovereignty. It did so not because the ruling casta hid its abuse of power from view, but because it did not. That is, the principles of aristocratic sovereignty required that rulers show their ability to dominate, shame, and impose their will upon those who would challenge their position. The ability to represent what was known publicly to be the vicious persecution of casta enemies as the principled protection of individual rights and the common good accomplished precisely this for those in power. For in this way, the ruling casta demonstrated that it was powerful enough to make public claims in ritual contexts that were known to be untrue. Furthermore, those in power showed that they could make these false claims with impunity, despite the fact that both society at large and the central government knew its ritual claims to be wholly fictitious.

Ultimately, by elaborating a mythical social order in ritual and discourse—one that stood in blatant contrast to the existing state of affairs, and that castas made a mockery of on an ongoing basis—the regional elite unwittingly contributed to its own undoing. The image of a world in which the material, behavioral, and symbolic distinctions of aristocratic sovereignty were made to disappear, in which violence and insecurity were eliminated, and in which individual rights and protections truly obtained for all, proved very powerful for people of all social classes. For it provided a vision of social justice and social order that could act as a radical alternative to the casta order. Furthermore, this vision of equality, progress, and nationhood was one that casta leaders embraced publicly as valid and just, but that they violated on an ongoing basis. By seizing upon the notion of an alternative social order that had already been declared legitimate, but had yet to be realized, those who sought to free themselves from casta control simultaneously found an ally in the central state, and a scapegoat for the "ills" of the region and its people.

6 Modernity as Emancipation I

The 'Partido Laboral Independiente Amazonense'

What local people in Chachapoyas refer to as the "democratization" of society was a complex process that had many contributing influences. The result of the process, however, was that in a surprisingly short period of time (surprising, that is, for those who witnessed, participated in, and lived through it) the entire aristocratic order was undermined and then crumbled. Personal displays of power—by men whose goal was to humiliate and dominate members of the opposition—ceased being viable as a means either of consolidating ruling casta strength or of revealing ruling casta weakness. Elite strategies of patriarchal marital alliance arranged by such men ceased being important as a means of effecting broad alliances that could control the regional space. Coalitions of such families (along with their clients in other social classes) ceased to engage in armed combat with one another for control of the region. The extreme forms of insecurity of person and property that characterized the period of casta rule came to an end, and in their place, a more general regime of "law and order" came to be imposed on growing numbers of the population. Interdependent constructions of race, caste, gender, and ancestry ceased being the basis of a highly stratified social structure in which hierarchy was actively celebrated and naturalized. And deferential and subservient forms of behavior ceased being expectations that people of high social standing could insist upon from those lower in the social hierarchy.

These changes imply sweeping transformations in the definition of a whole series of interrelated social categories and relationships: gender, race, property, law, and citizenship. Interestingly, the entire transformation occurred without changes in *productive* relationships having taken place. Rather, the

174

most important changes had to do with a series of new social and political relationships that coalesced after 1930 as the result of combined action by the central government and local social elements.

Key in effecting these changes was the actualization of notions of citizenship, private property, equality before the law, and progress that had been present in state discourse for decades. To a significant degree, the story of "democratization" in Chachapoyas is the story of the precepts of popular sovereignty taking on a tangible reality for important new sectors of the population.

Many of the transformations that took place in Chachapoyas had as their impetus changes occurring in Peru as a whole—in particular, changes emanating from the national capital of Lima. These nationwide transformations were in turn related to a particular moment in the transformation and reorganization of capitalism on a global scale, and the consequences of this expansion for Latin America in general, and for Peru in particular.

STATE-BUILDING AND THE CONTROL OF SPACE

Beginning in the late nineteenth century, the crisis in and reorganization of North Atlantic capitalism resulted in a flood of new laboring people, social doctrines, religious dogmas, political ideologies, and investment capital pouring into Peru at an unprecedented rate—changes that permanently altered Peru's class composition, the balance of its political power, and the organization of its state apparatus.[1] Within Lima itself, the early decades of the twentieth century witnessed the emergence of a working class, and a working-class movement, of growing proportions (Blanchard 1982; Collier and Collier 1991; Sulmont 1975). By 1920, the working-class movement had joined forces with a radical student movement, giving birth to a form of populist mass politics that for the first time in the country's history presented a fundamental challenge to Peru's traditional aristocratic elite (Burga and Flores Galindo 1979; Caravedo 1977; Deustua 1984). By the end of the 1920s, the populism of the masses had emerged as the most important new factor on the national political scene (Stein 1980).

Outside of Lima, conditions were increasingly chaotic. In some parts of the country, new economic configurations were emerging in relation to the rapid influx of capital. The most important of these came about as a result of the Amazonian rubber trade, focused on the jungle city of Iquitos (see Weinstein 1983; Brown and Fernandez 1991). In other regions, existing economic configurations were being transformed from within. The northern coastal plantations, which became involved in the export of cotton and sugarcane, increasingly resembled "factories-in-the-field" (Gonzales 1985). The Cajamarca highlands began to produce and transport foodstuffs and labor for the coastal export economy (Gonzales 1985; Taylor 1986; Deere 1990). The central highlands were transformed due to the increasingly capital-intensive nature of mining, the emergence of a full-time labor force at the Cerro de Pasco mine, and the growing commercial nature of the regional economy (Mallon 1983b; Manrique 1988). In the southern highlands, haciendas grew dramatically in size and number in response to the wool-export trade (Collins 1988; Spalding 1975; Jacobsen 1993). Because the central government had only a minimal presence in most parts of the countryside—and could not guarantee safety of person or property—these changes within and between regions resulted in a degree of violence and individual insecurity that was unusual even by the standards of the time. Regional elites, anxious to retain their traditional powers and privileges and to claim whatever they could in the way of new prerogatives, were left to fight among themselves, with newcomers, and with the subaltern, in deciding how the emerging set of economic possibilities would be institutionalized. And regional elites employed any means available to prevail.

The opening decades of the century witnessed not only changes in class composition, in the balance of political power among political groups, and in widespread economic dislocation and transformation, but also a reorganization of and expansion in the central state apparatus. This process had two main elements. First, in order to weaken the hold that regional elites exercised over local resources, territory, and people, the state expanded its apparatus in the countryside, absorbing many powers and privileges previously enjoyed by regional elites.[2] In the process, the state sought to undermine the position of these elites as mediators, controlling the flow of local resources from region to state and dominating subaltern classes within their spheres of influence.

Second, the central government also began a more concerted effort to form a unified political, economic, and cultural community of national proportions at this time. Until the early twentieth century, there was a very limited basis upon which to conceive of the nation as a single community. Virtually all important interdependencies—material, social, political, and religious—were regional in nature. The government was greatly hindered in any attempt to replace regional with national interdependencies by the physical difficulties of moving people, material goods, and cultural messages through the tortuous topography of coast, sierra, and jungle. Although successive central regimes in Lima attempted to overcome these difficulties from the turn of the century onward,[3] it was particularly during the administration of Augusto Leguía (his second period in office, from 1919–30) that the most concerted effort took place. Under Leguía, the central government made massive investments in road construction and transport. During the eleven years of Leguía's rule, the road network of Peru was increased by approximately 11,000 miles (Basadre 1968–69, 13: 257).[4] One result was to vastly increase the circulation of commodities within the country, which in turn helped create new material dependencies among Peru's population and helped link individuals to a growing national economy.

Under Leguía, the government also expanded and integrated central control over the means of cultural production—most importantly, newspapers and education. Furthermore, the government used its growing control over the dissemination of public knowledge to advocate new notions of citizenship and nationhood—those based on the principles of popular sovereignty. This change in part reflected the political struggles that had brought Leguía to power. The rise of Leguía to the presidency in 1919 represented a major break with the elite politics of the past and the demise of elite political institutions. Leguía's constituency consisted predominantly of state employees, elements of the middle class, the radical student movement, the labor movement, and the military, who joined forces under Leguía to oppose the continued political dominance of the traditional elite (Burga and Flores-Galindo 1979; Cotler 1978; Sulmont 1975). In order to clearly differentiate his regime from the politics of the past, Leguía referred to Peru under his administration as the *Patria Nueva*—the New Fatherland. The Patria Nueva broadcast the legitimacy of principles of citizenship, progress, individual rights and protections, the sanctity of person and property, and equality under the law in an attempt to build a new kind of nation, and a new national constituency, within Peru (Burga and Flores-Galindo 1979; Cotler 1978; Klaren 1973: 24–49; 1988).

At the same time that the central government was attempting to form a more cohesive national community based on a discourse of popular sovereignty, then, it was confronted with increasingly chaotic, transformative, and violent conditions that violated these very principles. Elite and "commoner" responded differently to these conditions. In many regional arenas, those elites who did not prevail in the struggle over the new economic opportunities of the era responded by organizing armed resistance to the central government and its local clients (those members of the elite who did prevail). In the 1920s and 1930s, both before and after the world economic crisis of 1929, large-scale movements of secession or revolt broke out all across the nation—resulting in a pattern of escalating violence and personal insecurity for nonelite groups.[5] In regions like Chachapoyas, these nonelite groups responded by embracing the principles offered by the central government as providing the basis of the national community—individual rights and protections, sanctity of person and property, and equality under the law.

It was thus in the context of massive dislocations in culture and economy that new forms of regional and national community came to mutually construct one another in Chachapoyas circa 1930. Notions of popular sovereignty, progress, modernity, and nationhood played a central role in this process of redefinition. That is, precepts that ruling factions had long given voice to within the limited domains of political ritual and discourse were seized upon by marginal "middle sectors" of the local population, and were made the basis of a political mobilization that challenged elite privilege in virtually all domains of social life. These marginal middle sectors were made up of artisans and muleteers, merchants and shopkeepers, cantina owners and public employees, people whose life possibilities had been severely restricted by the ability of the elite to reserve positions of influence and power for themselves. They were also made up of people who had been denied social recognition and respect because they occupied social categories that were devalued within the cultural logic of aristocratic sovereignty. As a result, such people harbored deep resentment toward the "undeserving" elite class for restricting their lives materially and socially, and for devaluing them culturally.

Two overlapping political movements—both intent on "democratizing" the aristocratic social order—emerged in Chachapoyas as a result of these forces. The first, which began to solidify in the mid-1920s, eventually became the *Partido Laboral Independiente Amazonense*, the Independent Labor Party of Amazonas. The second, which made its appearance in 1929 and grew in scope thereafter, was the local manifestation of a national political party—the *Alianza Popular Revolucionaria Americana*, the Popular American Revolutionary Alliance, or APRA. These movements attracted many members from the local populace, drawn to the appeal made by the movements for regional unity, moral behavior, social justice, and national integration. By 1930, those involved in the movements joined forces and, at a moment of crisis in the national political order, together succeeded in overthrowing the region's ruling elite faction in an armed uprising.

In the late 1910s, Ricardo Feijóo Reina—son of a landed family that was to suffer progressively more difficult circumstances as the period of rule by the various Pizarro-Rubio-Linch coalitions (1909–24) wore on—traveled to Lima to pursue a professional career. In so doing, he followed a time-honored strategy for those who were denied opportunities within the region because they did not belong to the ruling casta—that of (temporarily) quitting the regional space in order to seek out new opportunities and allies that would help them bolster their position within the region (see Chapter 3). Lima of the late 1910s, however, was a far different place than it had been in decades prior, and offered possibilities not formerly present. At this time the national capital was in the throes of crisis and contestation as the labor movement and the student movement joined forces to challenge the country's traditional political elite. The National University of San Marcos in particular was an important center of political activism. It was at San Marcos that Feijóo enrolled to pursue a degree in law.[6]

Feijóo soon became involved in student politics at San Marcos. In 1926 he was instrumental in establishing a "regional association" in Lima that was made up largely of other individuals who, like Feijóo, had fled their department during the extended period of rule by the Pizarro-Rubio and Rubio-Linch.[7] That same year, under Feijóo's guidance, this "Amazonas Association" began publishing a newspaper that was distributed in Chachapoyas—one that articulated many of the egalitarian, progressive ideals voiced within the student movement.[8] The paper was originally called *Amazonas*, but was changed several years later to *The Voice of the People* (*La Voz del Pueblo*).

The lead article on the front page of the newspaper's first issue reflects many of the paper's most general concerns:

> We seek to fill no void, nor to achieve success, nor to win glory.
>
> We offer ourselves voluntarily in order to keep vigil over the interests of Amazonas, and we will live only to contribute to its progress.
>
> But material progress without a foundation of culture and morality, in our judgment, has no solid base. Therefore, the road to material progress must be accompanied by ideas, and together . . . with the overturning of the earth, fertile or infertile, the pen should vibrate in the columns of a newspaper that, in whatever modest way possible, can build or guide good intentions.
>
> Our role will be modest, our value meager, and our actions ponderous, as long as the force of our number and conviction is not accompanied by discipline and cohesion. . . . But we will be elements of light and of good, whatever the magnitude of our contribution. . . .
>
> In any event our motive will always be high and our actions unselfish. To indifference and coldness we will endeavor to oppose concern and perseverance. To natural or intentional barriers we will oppose persistence and courage.
>
> We will endeavor to make heard reason and truth, and not the moribund harp of misfortune. And of course, we will embrace whatever comes in order to invigorate the progress of the department. . . .
>
> One of the suspect dimensions of new newspapers is their relationship, clear or obscured, to local politics, generally preferring to ally themselves with the dominant. We will endeavor not to enter into this kind of activity and to escape from its seductive web.
>
> But we will be ready to brand as such any acts that are in conflict with the good of the department, as well as to support those which concur with its effective progress and the building of its future.
>
> Of course our columns will always express the predominant ideas of the Amazonas Association, which today, by means of its organ *Amazonas*, sends its greetings to the national press, to the department that it wishes to serve, and to the readers of good will, who interest themselves in our *Oriente*, prodigious stronghold where the greatest hopes of Peru are guarded and from which will come the riches, brawn, and brains that will assist our happy

brothers of the *Occidente* that already have in their hands—to our great satisfaction—the steamboat, the railroad, the mechanical tractor, the rights of citizens, the newspaper that illuminates, the investment capital that accumulates, the telegraph cable that allows ideas to take flight, [and] the library that
is the source of perpetual light.

We will endeavor to gain some of the privileges that . . . [would] lessen
the difficulties of our . . . isolated situation. We do not know when [we will
succeed] . . . but we will go in pursuit of the ideal, confident in our own
courage and in the efficacious and unswerving assistance of the public will.
(*Amazonas* 1, no. 1 [Oct. 15, 1926]: 1)

From the first issue, Feijóo and his association thus presented their paper as
an instrument that would work for the good of the department and all its
people, that would promote the progress of the region. Feijóo promised to
rise above the destructive partisan political struggles of the past, but also to
expose the evil ways of those who worked against good in the region. Indeed, the epigraph written just below the title of newspaper's first issue reads,
"To be issued monthly, to defend the interests of the department of Amazonas, and to promote its progress" (ibid.). Feijóo called upon all "Amazonenses" (all the people of Amazonas) to join with him in this struggle for the
general good.

The appearance of *Amazonas* and its commitment to the common good
signified a major rupture in the regional order of things. For although those in
power were compelled constantly to invoke notions of "the common good"
and "the general interest" in political ritual and discourse, the dynamics of
casta rule were such that it was impossible for them to sustain the illusion that
anything like a common good existed. Actually, only by publicly demonstrating that the opposite was the case were those in power able to remain in control. That is, members of the ruling casta used their positions in the least "ethical" and most blatantly self-aggrandizing manner possible—to dominate and
shame members of the opposition, to seize their property, and to do harm to
their person.

In the context of this radical disjuncture between ritual language and social
action, Feijóo seized upon the very egalitarian principles long declared legitimate by the elite in order to critique the aristocratic order as a whole. For the
first time in the region's history, a public pledge had been made to make a

reality of the precepts of popular sovereignty, and a public appeal had been heard to make this a community effort. Feijóo asserted that the region *did* have a general interest, that it *could* progress, that its people *did* have common enemies, and that they *could* build an effective future for themselves. They could do so by rising up against those who had betrayed the common good, which would allow them to unite the prodigious natural wealth of Amazonas with the progressive forces of the modern world.

A large proportion of the local population rallied around Feijóo and his appeal for regional unity, moral behavior, and progress, so that he soon found it necessary to print far more copies of *Amazonas* than he had originally anticipated.[9] Feijóo actively solicited letters and even pieces of writing for the paper from the local populace, and people from all social classes complied. Indeed, on the front page of many issues of the paper, written in bold print for all to see, is this message: "*Amazonas* willingly offers its columns to the indigenous class so that the indigenous may denounce the abuses to which they are subject by their exploiters and so that they may demand their rights." The paper also made an offer and a pledge to its readers (*Amazonas* 1, no. 4): "*Amazonas* will applaud and will give its decided assistance to all good initiatives and actions, and will censure all abuses that are committed by public employees, *tinterillos* [shyster lawyers], priests, *gamonales*, and other exploiters."

In the process of opening its pages to those who formerly had little or no public voice, and in subjecting the actions of authorities to public scrutiny and censure, *Amazonas* became something of an open forum that not only articulated a self-righteous critique of the casta order, but also elaborated an alternative to aristocratic rule—a social order based on principles of democracy, equality, progress, and the common good. In the newspaper's columns, Feijóo, his small staff,[10] and the "Amazonenses" who contributed to the paper were thus able to make of the principles of popular sovereignty something more than empty phrases repeated mechanically in political ritual and discourse. As a result, a social movement of broad proportions coalesced around Feijóo and his newspaper. This movement was of sufficient scope that in 1930, at a moment of crisis in the national political order, those involved in the movement rose up en masse and seized control of the regional political apparatus in an armed confrontation with the ruling casta (see Chapter 8). Thereafter, in 1931, Feijóo's constituency—in control of regional affairs since the "revolution" of the previous year—elected Feijóo as deputy for Amazonas to the Constituent Congress that drafted Peru's new constitution. Feijóo was the first politician in the history of the department to successfully oppose the ruling castas.

The new image of regional society presented in *Amazonas* was in stark contrast to the existing state of affairs. The newspaper depicted the rule of the powerful castas as fundamentally immoral, based on inherited privilege, brutal coercion, greed, and outright theft:

To The Nation

The Department of Amazonas Has Been Converted into a True Fief.
Twenty Years of Prostration and Servilism

In the *oriente* of Peru there is a department that, despite the amazing fertility of its soil, the variety of its products, the spiritual richness of its children, and its infinite yearning for progress, writhes in backwardness and abandonment due to the negligence of its representatives.

We refer to the department of Amazonas, that since its creation in 1832 up to the present is nothing but a fief, a hacienda of useless and hateful castas, who believe that they have the inherited right to rule and to exploit [people] iniquitously and scandalously.

A wretched population ours, struck cruelly by Destiny and by Nature, we have never had the good fortune of having acceptable [political] representatives before the Parliament . . . [but rather] men without ideas and lacking in sentiment . . . [who] have struggled ceaselessly over the right to exercise power, to lord over their spoils . . . to benefit themselves alone, increasing their substantial fortunes. . . .

1909 [was] a sad hour for the department [because] one of its sons, Doctor Miguel A. Rojas, taking advantage of a high political position that he precariously occupied [he was minister of government under President Leguía], believed it to be in the interests of his family to demolish the ill-fated Burga-Hurtado casta, and in a moment of obfuscation sent to [Chachapoyas] a . . . political authority [Prefect Pázara; see Chapter 4] who permitted women to be jailed, men to be flagellated, and the most intimate sanctuary of human dignity to be sullied, all with the goal of enthroning the Pizarro-Rubio-Linch family [see Chapter 4].

Thus was born, and thus ascended this casta, that [since then] has monopolized everything in its favor, that allows no act of rebellion, nor even of independence, that divides what are virtually life-long public positions that are loaded with "extras" among those of its circle . . . that has taught servilism as if in a school and has introduced abjection and what amounts to a thinly masked form of slavery among the men, who in order to gain a livelihood, [to gain] bread for their children . . . must necessarily beg for a job after having had to submerge their dignity in humiliation.

Taking into account this moral corruption, one distinguished professional from Amazonas has said with reason that "Amazonas is not a department, but rather a poorly administered hacienda." And in effect, thus it is, for a region where all are abandoned to their own fate, where not even a single stone is moved in the interest of progress, where the very air that is breathed is poisoned by traditional hatreds, by morbid passions, and by bastard ambitions . . . where a free man cannot live because he feels oppressed, because he will not resign himself to sacrificing his dignity, offering homage to this casta that weighs like a curse on the collectivity, cannot, should not, ever call itself . . . a department of Peru.

"Amazonas belongs to us," this sad but celebrated phrase spoken before a group of Chachapoyanos by Sr. Hernán Monzante Rubio in an outburst of bragging and ambition, clearly reveals the truth of what we claim. . . . The department of Amazonas is the patrimony of no one family, but is a free section of Peru. (*Amazonas* 4, no. 19 [May 1929])

This oppressive state of affairs, the paper argued, weighed heavily on the defenseless and powerless people of the region who, in the absence of adequate protections by the state, had been left to be abused and mistreated by the casta families. Indeed, because the citizenry did not enjoy even the most basic of individual rights and protections, the department seemed not to belong to the twentieth century, but rather to a long-past feudal or colonial epoch. In this article, Amazonas is depicted as not worthy of being considered a real department—that is, as a section of national territory not truly *of* the modern nation-state of Peru. Rather, it is organized along premodern, "feudal" lines (as a fief) and is ruled by the barbaric emotions of its arbitrary rulers, who keep all in a state of abject servility. Neither freedom nor dignity nor progress would obtain in Amazonas as long as the "traditional hatreds," the "morbid passions," and the "bastard ambitions" of its ruling castas were allowed to hold sway within the region.

1. (*above*) Chachapoyas, Peru, seen from the western edge of the
town, looking east. (SOURCE: author's collection.)

2. (*below*) A typical street scene from Chachapoyas. (SOURCE: author's collection.)

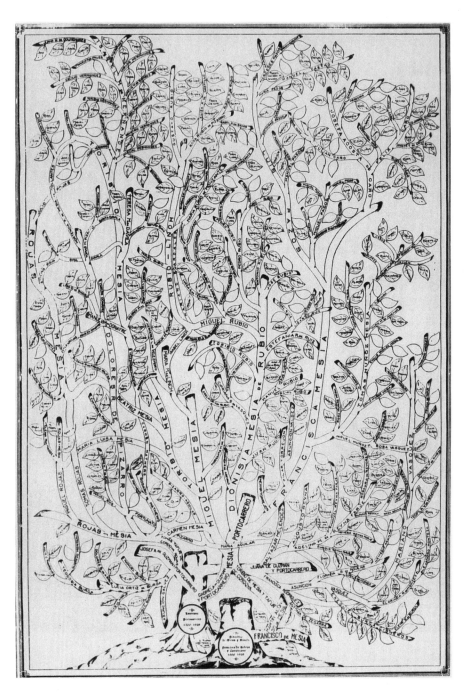

3. Genealogical tree of the Mesía Rubio family. (SOURCE: private collection, Lima.)

4. A passport issued for travel within the Chachapoyas region. (SOURCE: private collection, Lima.)

AMAZONAS

Organo de la Asociacion Amazonense

Año II   No. 15 | Lima, Marzo y Abril de 1928   6 Páginas 15 Cts.

Caminos-Arterias vivificadoras.
Colonización-Innovación de Sangre.
AGRICULTURA-FUENTE VITAL.
Instrucción-Espíritu y luz.
Miguel U. Rostegui

5. (*opposite, top*) Masthead of the newspaper *Amazonas*.
(SOURCE: private collection, Lima.)

Two views of the pre-Colombian (but non-Inca) ruins used by Apristas to impress upon the local population the unity and strength of the Inca empire.

6. (*opposite, bottom*) Ruined walls of the fortress, Kuélap. The two men at the foot of the wall indicate the scale. (SOURCE: author's collection.)

7. (*above*) Remains of the site, Yálape. (SOURCE: author's collection.)

8. Procession honoring the Virgin of Asunta, named Patron Saint
of Chachapoyas after the "revolution" of 1930.
(SOURCE: author's collection.)

Amazonas continually asserted that the abusive nature of the region's political authorities and the lack of individual rights and protections condemned the department to languish in a decadent, oppressive, premodern state.

The Martyrdom of a Town and Bossism in Action

In the department of Amazonas, the town of Colcamar does not enjoy its liberty, because its inhabitants have for many years been exploited in the most iniquitous manner by governors and local political bosses (*gamonales*). This is demonstrated by [a] letter that we [received from Colcamar], bathed in the blood of tragedy and the tears of martyrdom. . . .

According to information provided to us by people we trust . . . in this oppressed pueblo the poor Indians are not owners of their liberty, their economic affairs, their animals, and at times—according to what we have been told—not even their women. They are obliged to work one week of every month on the haciendas of the political bosses, who pay them a miserable salary. . . . They are [also] sent by force to the haciendas of the Marañon Valley and to the salt mines of Yuromarca, in order to carry cargo, and for every pack animal they are paid . . . miserable sum[s] . . . and not being satisfied with this degree of exploitation, [the political authorities] go to the extreme of offering [the Indians] minuscule prices, or nothing at all, for their chickens and ducks, upon which the political authorities in question then dine.

That is to say, in the midst of the republic there are pueblos in Peru that live out lives of oppression, whose children, in the midst of the twentieth century, are still forced to endure the regimen of the *encomiendas*, from which their ancestors suffered so terribly during the colonial period. . . .

These abuses and these injustices must end forever in Amazonas because the Indian, above all else, is a free being and as such, no one has the right to coerce him, to obligate him to work without his previous consent and without fair remuneration; no one has the right to exploit in a cowardly way his ignorance and his humility.

To the contrary, a moral imperative tells us that we must protect our aboriginal race, so as remove it from the misery in which it struggles; that we must lavish on these simple and hardworking Indians, a little more love and humanity.

We must study with care their customs, the psychology of their intimate lives, and we must educate them wisely, so that the light may shine upon their dormant aptitudes and, conscious of their rights and duties, they may become efficient elements for our nation, haughty men, capable of rebelling when anyone tries to soil their dignity. (*Amazonas* 2, no. 15 [Mar.–Apr. 1928])

Insecurity of person and property was not restricted to the indigenous population. Rather, as related in the pages of *Amazonas*, the greed of the region's political authorities created a situation in which the "forces of order" were woefully inadequate, because of which no one was truly safe:

Shameless Authorities that Discredit the Regime They Serve and the Posts They Fill

Individuals as bald as an egg [penniless] go to the provinces and return to Lima buying cars and chalets

Some day we must punish the rascals

Every day we receive telegrams from every province . . . in which it is said that banditry scours the countryside, that there are no forces of order to contain it . . . [that] it is not possible to go for a walk without feeling the threat of death hanging over one's head . . . that the number of gendarmes is insufficient. . . . Of course [the number of gendarmes] is insufficient; . . . there should have been 50 gendarmes [but] there are only 10 because [the subprefect] pockets the difference [in salaries] between 50 and 10 . . . and 40 [gendarmes] are pure fantasy. As a result many people hope that the number of police assigned to the provinces will increase . . . the Sr. Subprefect believes that increasing the personnel will make it easier to pocket more money. What is happening is simply wicked and repugnant and . . . we believe that it is necessary to reveal the truth, if we don't want the devil to carry away with him all the progress we have made. No country can prosper with so many scoundrels loose in the town and completely free of punishment; there is no country in the world where sanctions are reserved only for the poor devils that steal a loaf of bread or a sheep and leave unpunished those who loot the national treasury. . . .

There are well-known cases in which individuals have left Lima as bald as an egg [penniless], that have been sent to the provinces with a political position [that] paid 200 soles, for example, that have not received a centavo of their salary, because in the end there is such irregularity in their payments, that have returned to the capital, however, only to buy luxurious cars, . . . to choose [for themselves] a chalet and to lend money daily. . . . No one asks

how the auto and the chalet could be purchased with a salary of 200
soles. . . . They already know how; the poor, dispossessed Indians; [and] their
unfortunate neighbors, attacked and robbed. (*Amazonas* 1, no. 4 [Feb. 1,
1927]: 4)

Amazonas gave prominent place in virtually all of its issues to discussions
of the department's political authorities, exposing to public view their abuses
and their outrages. Simultaneously, the newspaper engaged in extended discussions of the characteristics of "good" political authorities—those who rose
above petty, partisan interests, who did not attach themselves to the powerful,
and who respected the democratic aspirations of "the people." One article
identified the problematic nature of local politics with unusual clarity:

Political Authorities

The day that political position is emancipated from the influence of the privileged circle of regional potentates a moment of national joy will have arrived; there are cases—and these unfortunately are not few in number—in
which political authority within a section of the territory of Peru is delivered
to a single family, as if it were a fief: subprefects, governors, lieutenant governors and gendarmes, judges of the first instance, scribes and bailiffs, inspectors of education and teachers, telegraph operators, priests, all these people
who should be servants of the state and who should add to the prestige of
the government, are nothing other than the members of a single family who
work for themselves and for their relative and leader [in Lima] who from the
parliamentary trenches . . . has given them their positions, without having
failed even a single time to auction off these posts, setting the price necessary
to obtain them.

Meanwhile, in the distant pueblos, where the pernicious influences of
these defects in our administration are endured, the poor citizens and the af-
flicted families suffer all the hardships and the difficulties that inevitably follow from this state of affairs. . . .

Today, when the entire world enters into a new age of love and justice
and when Peru shows it uncontainable determination to seek out [such] a
new life, it is necessary to carry to the most remote corners of the national
territory the renovating winds and the modern ideas of the current evolutionary era, in which the imperative of justice and humanity must triumph.
(*Amazonas* 2, no. 15 [Mar.–Apr. 1928]: 1)

According to *Amazonas*, the region's oppressive, premodern political structure was the single most important obstacle standing in the way of progress. The paper argued that if local people were liberated from their archaic casta overlords, if they were guaranteed their constitutionally granted individual rights, if they were led by responsible politicians, and if they were united with the liberating forces of the modern world, the region would at last be able to realize its true potential, and great things would result for all. For the region lacked nothing in the way of natural wealth or human bounty. Indeed, these were its very strengths:

Information About the Department of Amazonas

As can be seen . . . the department . . . is an emporium of natural resources and an inexhaustible source of spiritual riches. . . . The . . . people of Amazonas . . . [are characterized by] their intelligence, their love of work, their love of liberty, their peculiar pride, their honesty in the face of any test, [and] their unquenchable eagerness for progress. (*Amazonas* 1, no. 1 [Oct. 15, 1926]: 1)

In general, the *amazonense* is honorable, good, industrious, strong, active, intelligent, a fighter, traveler, [and] artist . . . a lover of Amazonas and of his country. With greater unity [and] discipline . . . he can have an enviable future, and thus the natural resources of the ground can be joined with the spiritual superiority of his poor class and of his workers and [can be] joined together with the scientific and economic orientation of the numerous students and professionals of our department who have stood out everywhere. (*Amazonas* 1, no. 2 [Nov. 15, 1926]: 1)

Constantly reiterated in the columns of the paper was the idea that, by working together, people liberated from casta control would be free to form a new kind of collectivity, one based on consensus and organic interconnection rather than on coercion and conflict. Such a collectivity of freed individuals would create a new future for the region, one in which the squandered opportunities and resources of the casta-controlled past would be replaced by material progress and prosperity that would benefit all.

Progress could only be achieved, however, by bringing to an end what was seen as the region's "isolation" and "backwardness." And while it was crucial to eliminate the *political* barriers (the casta structure) that prevented the department from extricating itself from its premodern state, it was equally important to do away with the *physical* barriers that contributed to the region's remoteness (in both senses of the word). That is, it was essential to conquer the mountain fastness that put Amazonas beyond the reach of the modern world—that condemned it to languish in a state of decadence and decay. Only in this way could the "renovating winds and the modern ideas of the current evolutionary era" be felt in the region. Only in this way could the region's "cornucopia of natural treasures of incalculable value" and the "immense spiritual richness of its people" be joined together with "the steamboat, the railroad, the mechanical tractor, the rights of citizens, the newspaper that illuminates, the investment capital that accumulates, the telegraph cable that allows ideas to take flight, [and] the library that is the source of perpetual light" (*Amazonas* 1, no. 1 [Oct. 15, 1926]: 1). Only by joining east with west could the region escape from its decadent premodern state, achieve its unrealized potential for growth, truly become a part of the Peruvian nation.

The liberating potential of overcoming the region's remoteness was seen as virtually limitless. As implied above, *Amazonas* became positively obsessed with annihilating the physical barriers that separated the region from the broader national context—roads, railroads, steamships, air travel, were all regarded with a kind of millenarian awe in the pages of the paper. Roads in particular were seen as having an almost magical transformative power because they could open the region to all the outside world had to offer. *Amazonas* goes on almost endlessly about roads, often quoting European philosophers and literary figures in articles and even poems that wax eloquent about the wonders of roads, about all that they make possible, about the hidden potentials that they unlock:

Thoughts

Just as the cross is the symbol of mankind's spiritual redemption, the highway is the torch that brings moral and material well-being to the pueblos. . . . In those regions where the roads are good, the farmer has within his reach better markets, better schools, better stores and better means with which to amuse himself and to effect the good society. (*Amazonas* 1, no. 1 [Oct. 15, 1926]: 1)

WITH GOOD ROADS:

The harvests are not lost;
Men do not sleep too much;
The land does not lie unused.
The pessimists are comforted or consoled;
The optimists radiate more joy and enthusiasm.
The scientists better understand nature.
The ignorant ones begin to see the supreme light.
The cultured find vast fields where they may plant their ideas.
Broad highways dilute or reduce to ashes the hate felt of the government by
     some towns.
Good roads contributed to the aggrandizement of the ancient realm of the
     Incas and to the undeniable greatness of the France of today.
By means of good roads the cross, the balance of justice and the torch of sci-
     ence walk alone . . . and together.

(Ibid.)

Road-Building. Basis of National Progress

Good roads augment the area of cultivation, improve regional cultivations,
and "cultivate" the spirit of progress in the pueblos.

Good roads are the arteries of civilization, the best bonds of brotherhood
among men, . . . the threads by which the present is linked to the future.

Good roads reduce selling time, attract transport, improve life, promote ex-
ports, bring the best markets within reach, and make men more hard-working and progressive. . . .

The road and the automobile also bring newspapers, books, ideas, ideals,
and of course noble aspirations that know [how] to plant [themselves] in
hearts and minds.

Roads . . . open new horizons to men of action, reinforce public tranquility, and help stabilize the legally constituted authorities.

Roads bring greater clarity and comprehension of patriotic duties, [make
available] the impressive . . . results of science, . . . [and] reinforce . . . as definitive the conviction that progress and advancement are possible.

Roads . . . promote the growth of industries, and multiply, improve, and
introduce new raw materials. They conquer rivers, probe the innermost recesses of the mountains, and convert the steaming jungles and the frozen
wastes into money. (Ibid.)

Thoughts

A good highway is a magic wand that converts shacks into palaces and villages into cities. . . .

Joy. (*Amazonas* 1, no. 2 [Nov. 15, 1926]: 4)

This faith in the liberating potential of roads meant that, when the central government announced its decision in 1926 to build a highway suitable for vehicle traffic from Chachapoyas to the coast (specifically, to the port town of Pimentel, near Chiclayo), the "Amazonas Association" was overjoyed. The project was considered to be of such import that the association sent a delegation to the presidential palace to meet with Peru's president in order to express their deep gratitude to the government. For they were confident of the profound transformation that the project's successful completion would work on their department. *Amazonas* included the text of a petition presented by the delegation to the president of Peru for all its readers to see:

Petition Presented to the President of the Republic

Señor President of the Republic [Leguía].

The petitioners, natives of the department of Amazonas, resident in the Capital [Lima], have met in general assembly.

—Considering:

That given the transcendental importance of the work that your government has proposed to carry out, constructing the highway that will join the city of Chachapoyas with the port of Pimentel;

That the construction of said highway will result in immense benefits to the departments of: Lambayeque, Cajamarca, Amazonas, San Martín, and Loreto;

That the department of Amazonas, due to its geographic location, its mineral riches, and its prodigious fauna and flora, is destined and called upon by its good fortune to escape from the state of backwardness in which it is disastrously found [at present] and to enter the path of progress;

That [Amazonas] will only progress when it can develop all its latent activities and export its different products, utilizing a good highway;

That therefore, now that your government has resolved to make a reality of this dream of the Amazonenses, carrying out the construction of the highway alluded to:

—It is agreed:

To humbly ask that you maintain all government assistance until the Chachapoyas-Pimentel road has been completed.

In the name of the department of Amazonas we want to offer our full cooperation; we wish to express our most sincere gratitude; and we recognize that your government will have contributed in the most efficacious manner to the progress of this privileged region of the Oriente and to the aggrandizement of Peru.

Lima, 27th of July, 1926. (*Amazonas* 1, no. 1 [Oct. 15, 1926]: 3)

The road project became one of the paper's foremost preoccupations, and commentary upon its progress, the natural and human obstacles placed in its path, and those who were its true defenders figured prominently in virtually all issues of the newspaper. A subsequent issue of *Amazonas* elaborated in greater detail the perceived importance of the "Amazonas Highway" to the people of the region:

Beloved Native Land

To remember a far-off land, with love and respect, is a worthy thing for men that have heart and conscience in their [proper] place.

Without a doubt, the practice of this noble ideal, generous and good, has been the main reason that the sons of Amazonas, whose culture and manliness are traditional in the republic, have joined together and, uniting their yearnings and their hearts in a single desire, have formed an institution that centralizes dispersed forces, and makes a good and honorable home for the family of *amazonenses* . . . [who] work together because at last they dream of the hour of resurgence of their beloved land, [as] today [begins] the redemptive work of joining the jungle and the puna of our beloved department with the expansive and progressive coast of our country.

Amazonas, which has given illustrious children to the Nation, which has known how to honor the land of its birth in all the fields of human activity; Amazonas, which guards fantastic treasures in the innermost recesses of its forests; Amazonas, which possesses precious metals of incalculable value in the sands of its rivers and in the interior of its mountains; and, Amazonas, above all, which has in each one of its cultured sons and in its lovely and hard-working women elements of virtue and beauty, valuable elements for the exaltation of the nation, lives, however, enclosed by its own halo of gold and diamonds, without its moral and material importance being known, even by the rest of the republic.

Now, when we want to bring the moral and material treasures that Amazonas guards nearer the coast, constructing a highway that brings to the Pacific the general products of that exuberant and marvelous zone, it is the duty of all the children of that department to let the bells of their happiness ring forth; and for everyone, each according to their ability and their spirit, to collaborate in that great work that promises to bring a favorite daughter closer to her beloved mother, and that promises to be the salvation of an appreciable portion of the territory, that for many years past has lived dying. . . .

The law [approving the road project] has already been passed, and the pickax that plants civilization, progress, and exaltation each time it strikes the earth has already begun to deliver its redeeming blows in the highway under construction; and very soon, with shouts that the heart pushes to the lips, the happy moment will be announced in which a machine [a motorized vehicle] proclaiming civilization and progress will emerge from the obscurity of the jungles of our beloved land and will arrive at the shores filled with light and hope, crossing distances that until today have been the shackle of steel against our advance, and announcing a new era for that territorial zone where there is more than enough of everything for it to become one of the first pueblos of the Peruvian nation.

There in the native land, where nostalgia and inaction mean that everything aches of misery and death . . . the children of Amazonas, without distinction of any kind, collaborate in the nationalist and civilizing work of the opening of the road from the montaña to the coast. . . . Already dead are the errors and selfishness of the past, and today we are thinking only of being great, strong and good. (*Amazonas* 1, no. 2 [Nov. 15, 1926]: 1)

Some sense of the importance that the highway assumed in the local imagination can be gleaned from the front-page article that appeared in the third issue of *Amazonas*, by which time unforeseen problems had delayed the road's progress:

The Amazonas Highway

Great obstacles almost always have accompanied great works. A few days after the departure of Columbus from the port of Palos, one of his caravels suffered damage and to his dismay sank. But the great genius knew to calm the storm of his spirit. In the end he discovered a world.

In like manner, the highway [from] Chachapoyas to the coast has suffered a hard blow in its beginnings. The public officials, prefect, mayor, and engineer have not had the power to conduct the work with the normalcy that was hoped for. The evil has not yet been exorcised. And the country [Amazonas] that more than any other necessity always longed for a highway, a people that have always contributed above all else with their muscles to the execution and maintenance of local roads, cannot, in the midst of their fervent devotion to road-building, afford to lose the primordial artery that, with its roots in the heart of Peru, will allow [the region] to bloom rapidly once it is united with the waves of the Pacific. (*Amazonas* 1, no. 3 [Jan. 1, 1927]: 1)

The highway that would connect east with west, the paper argued, would result in redemption and rebirth, for it would join the natural wealth of Amazonas with the renovating winds and the modern ideas of the coast. Such integration with the nation, it was believed, would release the latent potentialities of the region and its populace, and would result in a veritable explosion of creative energy—commerce would grow, industries would develop, and prosperity would come to all. Indeed, *Amazonas* included as a regular part of its offerings an agricultural column, which engaged in lengthy discussions of the potential for various "scientific" agricultural techniques to revolutionize local production. Similarly, the paper frequently expounded upon the boon to local (small) industries that would surely come with the completion of the highway to the coast—and went into considerable detail about the particular industries that would benefit the most, why, and how all could respond to the opportunity presented to their maximum advantage.[11]

This vision of redemption and future prosperity is crystallized in the masthead surrounding the title of *Amazonas* on its front page. In the center, at the top of the page in large, bold print, is the newspaper's name, *AMAZONAS*. The masthead surrounding it is presented as a kind of map of the region's troubled present and bright possible future (themes repeated endlessly in the newspaper itself). Chachapoyas (in the east, and thus to the right of the newspaper's name) is shown as isolated, but surrounded by the luxurious bounty of the *ceja de selva* (the montaña zone intermediate between jungle and sierra)— represented by banana trees and coconut palms. Arching upward and toward the west (and its coastal urban centers) is a short section of projected road that would link the town to the rest of the nation. The coast (located to the west, and thus to the left of *AMAZONAS*) is represented by sugarcane (its most important industrial cash crop) and maize. Here as well, a short section of road arches upward and toward Chachapoyas in the east, holding out the hope of national integration and all the benefits it would bring (also common themes in the newspaper). Integration with the rest of the nation is frustrated, however, by the formidable natural obstacles of high sierra and Marañon River canyon, depicted in the drawing as rising up between Chachapoyas and the coast (as they do in fact). Above the entire scene, however, conquering cordillera and jungle alike, are an automobile similar to a Model-T and a ("Curtis") biplane successfully making the journey between the two regions, with the sun shining brightly between them.[12] Accompanying the logo and newspaper title are the following epigraphs: "Roads—Life-Giving Arteries. Colonization [of the Jungle]—Infusion of New Blood. Agriculture—Vital Life Force. Education—Spirit and Light."

FORMING NEW SUBJECTIVITIES, FORGING NEW SOCIAL RELATIONS

Though it was essential to free the department of Amazonas from its oppressive, premodern political structure, and though it was equally important to incorporate the region fully into national life, Feijóo and his newspaper argued that still more was needed if the region was to truly be delivered into the modern world of progress and prosperity.[13] The people of Amazonas would have to undergo a series of profound individual purifications and social transformations if they were to free themselves from the legacy of their casta-controlled past. In addition to elaborating a critique of the aristocratic political order and presenting integration with the outside world as the salvation for the region's difficulties, *Amazonas* devoted considerable space to expounding these much needed personal and social transformations.

The paper held up idealized images of "democratized" personal behavior and egalitarian forms of association that all people were to emulate—forms of behavior and association that struck at the very heart of the aristocratic order by challenging a series of elite assertions acted out on a daily basis in the course of reproducing aristocratic sovereignty. Most fundamentally, these new forms of subjectivity and association imagined in the pages of *Amazonas* undermined the elite's claim to represent a superior stratum of people entitled by right of birth to rule over, impose their will on, and demand deferential behavior from those they disparaged as their social inferiors—to enjoy privileges, opportunities, and status not available to these "lesser beings." In place of such privileges and distinctions, *Amazonas* proposed a "democratization" of life possibilities and behaviors. It advanced a single set of moral and ethical principles that was to guide the behavior of *all* individuals regardless of race or caste. Adherence to these ethical principles of honesty, fair play, and mutual respect was to be a new means of achieving social recognition and respect open to all—one based on individual merit rather than inherited social position.

The new social world envisioned by *Amazonas*, however, was not entirely undifferentiated and egalitarian. In place of what were characterized as the "immoral" and "artificial" caste categories of the aristocratic order, *Amazonas* asserted the priority of categories given in *nature*—male, female, child, youth, the elderly.[14] The reality of these categories was apparently so obvious as to place them beyond dispute, for nowhere in the pages of *Amazonas* was any attempt made to justify or defend them. Rather, as part of a more general discourse running through the paper that subtly but continuously asserted the reality of "things natural" (see below), the paper simply presumed the existence of these categories.

It was in the course of its extensive discussions of the characteristics of men, women, youth, and so on, that *Amazonas* attempted to transform notions of proper personhood and social behavior. That is, although the new cultural categories proposed by *Amazonas* were depicted as "natural/biological," the features of each had to be carefully explained to the local populace.

THE MAN OF PRINCIPLE

Amazonas devoted considerable space to explaining the characteristics of the democratized *male*, undoubtedly because the male of the aristocratic order represented such a formidable obstacle to realizing the transformed social order that was the paper's main preoccupation. The modern man imagined publicly in the pages of *Amazonas* was the very antithesis of the aggressive, dominating, violent, unpredictable, Machiavellian, self-aggrandizing male of the aristocratic order—the male who constantly sought to establish a reputation of public potency by preying on others. In opposition to such a man, *Amazonas* elevated as representing the greatest possible good a male image distilled from the principles of popular sovereignty: a peaceful, autonomous, rational, hard-working individual, whose behavior was characterized by moderation, restraint, discipline, and respect for himself and for others—an individual who posed no threat to anyone. The actions of such a man did not need to be constantly monitored or controlled by any external body because he policed *himself* according to generally accepted principles of fair play, truth, and ethics. His motive in doing so was not to gain material rewards or riches—an excess of which was considered profligate and suspect on moral grounds. Rather, being this kind of person was depicted as its own reward—knowing that one lived up to the ethical ideals to which all should aspire in order to live just lives, in order to be responsible members of community and nation.

Amazonas presented this cultural critique of the casta order, this alternative vision of proper personhood and social behavior, throughout its pages. Consider an article from the front page of the newspaper's first issue:

The Superior Man

Is known by the following signs:

1.— To succeed in what he desires he is single-minded in purpose.
2.— He scorns nothing in the world except falsehood and baseness.
3.— For the mighty and powerful he feels neither envy nor admiration nor fear.
4.— He neither shuns nor goes in search of danger.
5.— He neither offends nor does harm to anyone voluntarily.
6.— He does not desire what belongs to others, nor show off what he has, and lives in simplicity.
7.— He is humble in the face of success and strong in the face of adversity.
8.— He is prompt and firm in his resolutions and precise in his commitments.
9.— [He] does not believe anything precipitously; he first considers the purpose behind what is being said.

10.—   He does what is right without bringing it to the attention of or re-
minding the person for whom he has done it. He does not harbor
bad feelings toward anyone. (*Amazonas* 1, no. 1 [Oct. 15, 1926]: 1)

The general dynamics of casta rule meant that members of the ruling casta
were compelled to use their positions of power not according to principles
of moderation and restraint, nor in selfless pursuit of the common good, but
just the opposite: they were obliged to dominate and shame members of the
opposition, to jail them arbitrarily, to seize their property, and to do much
harm to their persons, all in pursuit of the particular good—their own and
that of their casta. In so doing, members of the ruling casta violated every
conceivable principle of "ethical" behavior—at least as defined within the
precepts of popular sovereignty. And they demonstrated the dangerously inappropriate nature of behaviors that would be characterized as "moral,"
"right," and "honest" within the universalistic frame of reference of popular
sovereignty.

Amidst these ongoing public assertions of power and privilege, reinforced
by violence and coercion, *Amazonas* appealed to its male readers to adopt behaviors that were the antithesis of the casta order. They were to live in peace
and simplicity, desire not what belonged to others, nor do anyone harm. They
were to adhere to general principles of integrity and truth, honesty and humility. And they were to free themselves of all feelings of fear, admiration, or
envy for the powerful. In other words, they were to become disciplined, principled individuals who were neither abusive of nor obsequious to others, who
possessed the "inner strength" to be fully self-reliant, independent, and autonomous. Furthermore, they were to evaluate the worth of all, regardless of
social position, in terms of the same ethical standards of behavior.

Two other articles from the same issue of the newspaper echoed many of
these themes:

What Should Never Be Done

Never exaggerate.

Never leave a house with harsh words.

Never laugh at other people's misfortune.

Never offer to do what you cannot carry out.

Never send a gift hoping for repayment.

Never talk at length of your own accomplishments.

Never fail to be punctual at the hour indicated.

Never be a hero of your own account.

Never fail to respond courteously to a thoughtful person.

Never question a servant or a child about family matters.

Never read the letters of other people.

Never fail, if you are a gentlemen, to be polite and tactful with women.

Never put yourself in bad company, [rather] search out someone good, or no one at all.

Never when traveling in foreign lands talk much of your country.

Thoughts

It is necessary to seek the truth with a simple heart.
The truth is found only in Nature.
Happiness can be found only by practicing good works and fulfilling one's duty.
The Truth is the finest pearl and evil is a crocodile who cannot put the pearl in his ears because he has none. . . .
Poverty is a rampart that defends us from thieves.
The ills of man are multiplied immeasurably by his pleasures and material riches.
Here dwells a good conscience and a spirit that knows not how to deceive.
(*Amazonas* 1, no. 1 [Oct. 15, 1926]: 3)

Like "The Superior Man," these articles idealized universalistic principles of truth and honesty, simplicity and humility, and thus acted as an implicit critique of several interrelated aspects of aristocratic life: its ostentatiousness and tendency toward the display of wealth (as a marker of elite status), and the Machiavellian character of casta political intrigue (as a means of gaining social position). Indeed, "What Should Never Be Done" reads like a litany of what was *always* done by the men of the aristocratic order as they sought to establish for themselves a public reputation for potency, aggressiveness, and unpredictability—brag, threaten, promote, intimidate, deceive, and degrade.

In contrast to the aristocratic man, these articles extol the man who is empathetic, humble, courteous, and dependable, one who neither promotes himself nor belittles others. He is a man who can be counted on to be honest, forthright, and fair—who is what he appears to be. He finds happiness not by pursuing his own self-interest, but rather by serving causes that transcend the self—by doing "good works," by doing "one's duty." He is thus a highly principled individual. Much of the newspaper's moralizing, democratizing discourse on the man of principle is captured in the following front-page article:[15]

Dignity

He who aspires to be renounces his being. In few men are gathered creativity and virtue in a dignified whole; they form a natural aristocracy, always few in number compared to the far greater number of flawed spirits. Supreme credo of all idealism, dignity is unique, intangible, intransmutable. It is the synthesis of all the virtues that strengthen man and wipe away darkness: where it is lacking the sentiment of honor does not exist, and just as the peoples who lack dignity are herdlike, individuals without it are slaves.

With temperaments of *steadfastness and light*—the dignified stand apart from all complicity, challenge all uninformed and ignorant opinion . . . refuse everything mundane that requires any abdication, deliver up their own lives before betraying their ideals, go upright, alone, without contaminating themselves with factions, [and] convert themselves into a living protest against every villainy or servilism. . . . Without courage there is no honor. . . . With its help the wise undertake the exploration of the unknown, the moralists undermine the sordid sources of evil, the daring risk the heights and the expanses in order to fly, the just affix their signatures in adverse fortune . . . the martyrs go into the blaze to unmask hypocrisy, the saints die for an ideal. . . . He who aspires to be an eagle must look far and fly high; he who is resigned to drag himself along like a worm renounces the right to protest if he is squashed.

Feebleness and ignorance favor the domestication of mediocre characters, adapting them to a life of timidity; courage and culture exalt the personality of the excellent, flowering it with dignity. The lackey begs; the dignified deserve. The former solicits as a favor what the latter expects as his due. To be dignified means not to ask for what you deserve, nor to accept the undeserved. While the servile clamber about in the undergrowth of favoritism, the austere ascend by the staircase of their virtues or do not ascend at all. (*Amazonas* 1, no. 4 [Feb. 1, 1927]: 1)

In place of the decadent aristocratic elite that had ruled the region in so arbitrary a manner for so many years, *Amazonas* sought to form a "natural aristocracy" of truly worthy individuals—people who would reveal themselves to be so on the basis of individual merit and personal strength of character. The newspaper imagined an entire community of such autonomous, hard-working, dignified, ethical, male individuals. These were men who were to obey the same set of moral principles regardless of race or ancestry, who were to identify themselves with the same "common good" and "general interest" regardless of casta affiliation.[16]

If these "remade" individuals were to truly "seize the moment," however, if they were to take advantage of the unprecedented opportunity afforded them by the construction of the "Amazonas Highway," they would have to join forces with all other hard-working, disciplined, committed individuals. Only by acting with the strength that came from unity, argued *Amazonas*, could even these reborn/remade men be sure that their old enemies, the "caudillos," did not subvert the process of national integration, did not betray its promise of hope and regeneration.

It was in broaching this topic that *Amazonas* became more specific about where it expected to find such men. That is, in discussing the need for political organization, the paper departed from discussions of individual character and personal worth (discussions of the kind that characterized "The Superior Man" and "Dignity") and named the group whose members most closely approximated the image of the hard-working, principled, ethical man who would remake society in a new form.

In identifying who these "superior men" were, contributors to *Amazonas* did not attempt to create a new group that would appear alien to the local population. Rather, they worked with existing social distinctions, but gave them a transformed significance. It was the great divide between the casta española on the one hand, and the cholos, Indios, and runa on the other (see Chapter 2), that was preserved and reworked in naming the group that could remake society. Specifically, it was the disdain of elite groups for manual labor that was used as the basis for identifying the superior man. *Amazonas* inverted the terms of moral legitimacy associated with manual labor—making it into a virtue rather than a vice. On this basis, the paper attempted to erase distinctions between cholo, Indio, and runa, and to make common cause among all those who labored. For according to the newspaper, it was the region's *laborers* who exemplified the "superior man," who could make society over in new form:

Amazonas and Its Laborers

Because the highway from Amazonas to the coast holds out the promise of advancement and progress . . . the darkness and the misfortune [of the past] now have no reason to persist, [as thus we] approach the hour of redemption . . . for that rich section of Peruvian territory that until today [has been the] victim of its own disorganization and of the politics of competing factions. . . .

By good fortune we have arrived at the instant in which all the filth that . . . has the name of politics in our vocabulary, has been left behind in the sad memory of past hours and today we must comprehend . . . that [factional politics] did nothing for the general good and that the challenge of the present moment is the highway, the railway, navigation by water and navigation by air, and in short all such works that, confounding the selfish and the perverse, shout in exaltation to the four winds, "Well-being and progress." (*Amazonas* 1, no. 5 [Mar. 1, 1927]: 1)

As it had argued in other articles, here *Amazonas* asserted that the highway and the railway would redeem Amazonas, would deliver the department into a promised land of progress and advancement, would confound the selfish and the perverse, would end the hours of darkness and misfortune. But care had to be taken to ensure that the opportunity presented was not squandered. And it was specifically the region's laborers who had to join forces in order to guard against this possibility. The article continues:

As this occurs it is necessary to give guidance to the men who, through the sweat of their own brow, are going to put an end to the disgraces of the past, so that when the bell of collective happiness peals, the CLEVER do not come to eat the doughy bread of the SIMPLE and the sad hours that we should not even remember do not return once again.

The laborers of Amazonas, from the workshop, the countryside, and the mine, must organize themselves under the folds of the flag of the fatherland, by means of well-studied and proven regulations, but not in order to serve the interests of ill-intentioned caudillos, nor to engage in petty politics, nor to serve bastard interests, but in order to put themselves on a very high plane and from there contemplate only the interests of humanity and the fatherland. (Ibid.)

As did other articles in the paper, "Amazonas and Its Laborers" thus opposed the particular, self-serving interests of the region's caudillos with the general interest—of the region, of the fatherland, and of humanity. The article called upon all laborers to unite in order to serve these more general interests—which in turn would allow them to serve themselves. But how was this to be done?

> [In order to achieve] this we must establish a strong organization of mutual aid and assistance in Amazonas, not only with the goal of curing the sick and burying the dead, which is merely one small aspect of mutualism, but with the stronger and grander vision of sheltering and protecting one another mutually, having as our vindicating ideal a strong economic organization capable of establishing a stable and good future for everyone. . . .
>
> It is important, then, beginning today, that the airs of the coast of Peru begin to be felt in Amazonas, even if carried only in words, in order to lay the foundations of a robust social organism in which all the laborers of Amazonas can become involved, without any distinctions of class, not [strictly] urban laborers, nor peasants, nor miners, as it is important to keep in mind that the laboring family is one single family and that each time this family becomes divided by this or that cause, always unfounded and of little consequence, its exploiters can give [the laboring family] a little less bread and can require a bit more in the way of demands for its efforts and its sacrifice. (Ibid.)

The hard-working, laboring men of Amazonas were thus clearly those conceived of as the new men of principle—those called upon to oversee the process of national integration so as to bring progress to the region. They could succeed in this endeavor, however, only by overcoming the divisiveness and factionalism that had plagued the region for so long—a divisiveness that not only played directly into the hands of the elite by turning the "laboring family of Amazonas" against itself, but that was also the direct by-product of elite competition as members of the elite pursued their own self-serving "bastard interests." In order to prevent the caudillos from continuing to do this in the future, it was essential that all the members of the laboring family of Amazonas, without distinction, join together in a single organization able to defend the interests of all. The article ends on a note of exhortation:

> Children of the department of Amazonas, dreamers of your [own] greatness, visionaries of your future, we would like to see, as soon as possible, the resurgence of our beloved land and . . . we hope that this resurgence does not become food for ambition and depravity, something that can be avoided if we become custodians of a future to be won, an army of laborers correctly organized, that with tool in hand, sweat on the forehead, and optimism in the heart, are capable of casting out of [our] rich and exuberant zone all those who want to use ignorance . . . or political influence to make of [our region] a gold mine [to be] externally exploited.
>
> It appears that the supreme hour has arrived, [and] we imagine that this rich section of our [national] territory will be reborn like the phoenix of legend, because such is demanded by the children of our beloved native land, . . . who have gathered together in order to shout to the four winds their hope and their desire, applauding the patriots and the honorable ones and confounding those who, disguised as patriots, want [only] to perpetuate the traffic of eternal lies. (Ibid.)

This assertion of solidarity and the need for unity and organization to be established among those who occupied a similar "class" position acted as a powerful democratizing voice in regional affairs.[17] Never before had an attempt been made to make common cause on such a basis—to do away with the racial distinctions that had long divided the subaltern, and to unite the laboring poor as a whole (Indian and mestizo alike) against a landed elite that had manipulated their lives for so long, that had turned them against one another on the basis of casta affiliation.

EDUCATION

The task of steering the process of national integration in the proper direction thus fell to the region's hard-working, disciplined, responsible, laboring men— those who were willing to part with the decadent ways of the premodern past and to embrace the fatherland and the golden future it offered to all. This task, however, went far beyond simply organizing to protect the laboring family of Amazonas. It carried with it the heavy responsibility of preparing those unable to prepare themselves for participation in the national community (children), and of enlightening those unable to enlighten themselves (Indians). That is, overseeing the process of national integration implied a *cultural* revolution of sweeping proportions. For those who assumed the task were committing themselves to nothing less than making autonomous, rational, disciplined subjects out of the unshaped raw material offered them in human form.

"Education" was the cover term used in *Amazonas* to refer to the range of disciplinary processes and practices that had to be undertaken in order to make autonomous, independent, rational subjects out of the region's unformed and prerational Indians and children. The paper was very careful to refer to education as a special kind of labor—thus bringing this activity within the legitimate domain of the remade/reborn laboring multitude that was to bring the Chachapoyas region into the modern world. The importance the newspaper attributed to this form of labor, as well as its difficulty, would be almost impossible to exaggerate. Throughout the pages of *Amazonas*, education was characterized as the most heroic of endeavors—so much so that the liberation of the region was seen in large part as depending on its success. Teachers were depicted as shouldering a tremendous burden and responsibility, as sacrificing their youth, spirit, and intellect in a brave fight against virtually insuperable odds, all in order to do their part in freeing the region from the weight of the past.

The liberating potential of education at the most general level is conveyed by a front-page article from the paper.

The Great Labor of Education

For my Department, with sincerity and love.

Thought, willpower, feeling and action. The essential aspects of life

If we concern ourselves here with [education]—that labor par excellence—we cannot help but consider its value, weighing its undeniable importance in the march of progress . . . and the improvement of civilization; and if it is necessary to struggle in order to defend [education], we will face up to the struggle, confident that at each opportunity, we will have recourse to Science and to work, in a word to the assistance of the brains that think and the arms that truly labor.

And that labor, that select fruit of the ages, that inexhaustible source of perfection, is EDUCATION.

Education is thus the axis of the spiritual world, the lever of progress and civilization.

Nothing is more grandiose than the labor of guiding the generations on the path of the good; nothing is more worthy than molding the heart of infancy and preparing it to face the struggle and conquer in triumph; nothing is more glorious than to liberate the people from the infernal talons of ignorance and carry the clear light of civilization to the most remote and minuscule corner of the world; finally, nothing is more sublime than to complete the work of creation, giving soul and spirit to human material, in order to make it sovereign over itself. (*Amazonas* 1, no. 2 [Nov. 15, 1926]: 1)

The labor of education was thus sanctified by four distinct kinds of principles: natural, moral, rational, and spiritual. Education was inextricably linked to and helped make possible the forward march of civilization; it conformed to and promoted general moral/ethical principles of "the good" (which advanced along with civilization); it was supported by the rationality of science; and it even enabled the completion of the unfinished work of God's creation—by giving soul and spirit to those in whom these were lacking.

Having noted the transcendental importance of education, the article continued with a call to action despite, or precisely because of, the difficulty of the task ahead:

Thus noting what we are called upon to do we will not distract ourselves as we have until now, defeated, perhaps, by the greatness or the idealism of our own task, overwhelmed only with the thought that the heights we have to scale are rugged and immense. If until today we have slept, now we are awake and working; if until today we have faltered in our duties, we [now] attend to them; if until today we have been weak, slothful, and divided, we [now] are strong, active, and united.

We do the common good, we do everything possible in favor of Education because thus we will have fulfilled our human mission. (Ibid.)

It was not just any form of education, however, that could mold the region's preformed Indians and children into subjects useful to the nation. Only education that was modern, practical, and real was equal to the task at hand, for only such a form of education could free children from the artificial, sterile, and irrelevant environment imposed on them in the education of old. The article continued:

> We are taking care that our schools not be like old disciplinary prisons, dark houses of torture and boredom, forsaken cloisters lacking a single bench or book, without passion, without life, without real gardens that with their aromas and charms attract the children who, like butterflies or bees, make their cocoons or build their hives. We are taking care that instruction be practical, modern, real, objective, and that it cease with the barbarous routinism, the baneful and useless rules of memorization, the tedious theories, etc.; we are seeing to it that our children not be confined only to the narrow environment of the school, of the city; we are making sure that they get out to the . . . meadow, to the countryside and there breathe the pure air that will give them new life; we want them to run, jump, laugh, yell, and move; we want to be sure that [in the out-of-doors] our youngsters know the Divine Maker by his own work, by reality, by their own conscience, and thus can contemplate and admire the wise and grandiose marvel of Nature. (Ibid.)

Rarely was *Amazonas* more specific than in the article above about the content or method of "modern" education. The paper simply asserted that modern education would be immediate, concrete, and vital, that it would draw rather than force students into the classroom by awakening their natural tendencies and dormant curiosities. Once in the classroom, students who were there of their own free will could be shaped in the desired direction. So confident did the paper appear to be in the liberating potential of "things modern," and so convinced was it of the stultifying nature of traditional education, that the simple oppositions of natural to artificial, real to contrived, voluntary to imposed, were sufficient to justify the need for change.

The task of giving soul and spirit to those in whom it was lacking called for an ambitious form of education; similarly, such a delicate but important task could not be entrusted to just anyone. *Amazonas* made an impassioned appeal to all citizens—but especially to the region's youth—to rise to the occasion, to give of themselves in the noble effort of finishing the work of creation, of forming subjects useful to the nation. The same article concludes:

Therefore: YOUTH OF AMAZONAS! NOBLE YOUTH! TEACHERS (*maestros, maestras*)! FATHERS, MOTHERS: Think carefully about the great work that through the ages humanity has had and has still as the cornerstone of its ideals, and put your thoughts, work, action, if possible your life in the service of education; make it yours, work day and night in order to liberate and exalt the land that received us when we came to this world.

Above all else, it is our desire and it will be our practice to help and support the wave of action of the young people that value Education and work in favor of it: youth will be our glory because youth not only is hope but also is the vital energy force of life; but [only] youth that is aware and dynamic, youth that does not remain in the contemplation of an imaginary work, youth that does not live sleeping nor rest content with the perfection of its golden dreams. We will be with that practical, optimistic, and realistic youth, with that youth that thinks and produces and does what it says, that works and harvests, with that youth that walks smiling with the heavy load of life but that does not pause and reaches the dreamed-of goal of TRIUMPH. (Ibid., José Camus Chappa, Lima, Oct. 1926)

While education thus conceived was regarded as having tremendous liberating potential, it was particularly the education of the indigenous population that was seen as the most pressing task facing those who wished to liberate the region from the casta-controlled past. For Indians were regarded as almost hopelessly servile, backward, and superstitious—as totally lacking in individual autonomy and as barely conscious of the consequences of their acts. In short, Indians were seen as possessing little in the way of rationality—thus making their redemption an exceedingly difficult but highly noble endeavor for those truly committed to bringing the modern world to Amazonas. Much of the newspaper's crusading spirit toward and condescension concerning the region's indigenous population is captured in the following article:

The Education of the Indigenous

Throbbing at every moment in our hearts . . . is a vehemently held wish for progress: How do we . . . achieve it is the question that we pose to ourselves? . . . It would be difficult to present in global terms the different problems that we must overcome in order to realize our incessant desire [for progress] . . . but I will discuss one of its fundamental aspects . . . a pedestal upon which the rest is constructed, that relates to indigenous education. A

Nation or State is not composed solely of the mass of intellectuals . . .
but . . . assisting in integrating [the Nation] . . . are the people who live under the protection [of the Nation], and who need only to have spread in
their minds the intellectual nourishment that will redeem them from ignorance in order to be converted into useful elements of society. (*Amazonas* 1,
no. 4 [Feb. 1, 1927]: 3)

The goal of indigenous education was thus clear—to make the Indians into
"useful elements of society." But who would take it upon themselves to remake the Indian into useful form, and what specific characteristics would the
indigenous have to acquire in order to qualify as useful? The article continues:

It is the work of the present generation to see to it that this uncouth legion
of Indians acquires the understandings relevant to their existence, but it falls
especially upon the teachers, sponsored . . . by the State, to provide the instruction necessary to make of [the Indians] men conscious of their acts, with
defined personalities, capable of acting for themselves alone, without always
subordinating themselves to the powerful, who know how to claim their
rights, [who know] how to defend themselves as individuals, who learn from
their errors, and in the end possess the aptitudes [necessary] to be self-suffi-
cient, [thus] converting into reality the doctrines of protection and help that
occupy the thoughts of the true patriots of the present hour. (Ibid.)

In other words, it was the responsibility of teachers to finish God's work, to
make the indigenous population into autonomous subjects capable of principled behavior, conscious of the consequences of their acts, and in full exercise
of their individual rights. A special breed of highly moral and selfless teachers
was needed, however, to see this difficult task to a successful conclusion—
teachers capable of self-sacrifice in the interest of the greater national good:

In Amazonas, in order to be able to educate the Indian, apart from adequate
school buildings and teaching materials, we need teachers qualified for education, suitable people, consecrated especially to keep watch over their
pupils, without regrets for having sacrificed their intelligence, patience, and
will on the altar of good fortune, which they are called upon to provide to
these beings, so that while [the teachers] are at [the Indians'] side, they take
the place of their fathers, being as a consequence responsible for society according to their own conscience. . . . It is past time to subordinate personal

conveniences in favor of our younger brothers who live in a lamentable state of disgrace; the hour for demonstrations of kindness, protection, and favor toward this pleiades of humble men has sounded. (Ibid.)

Only teachers who were willing to take on the role of father or older brother in relation to the indigenous population—who would watch over their charges with the conscience and care that one gives to a close family member—could hope to redeem the Indian. What was needed was an extension of the bonds of family to embrace those who had until then been excluded from the fold of the fatherland.

It would take far more than just committed teachers to make the indigenous population into fully conscious beings useful to the nation. The collaboration of "society" was needed in order to overcome the major obstacle to succeeding in this noble effort—the *gamonal*, or local political boss:

> The campaign for the regeneration of the indigenous population will be seen to its completion, not only with the cooperation of the teachers but also with that of Society. . . . The Indian needs to reclaim his rights, to enjoy his [constitutional] guarantees, to feel the equality that until now has been a myth. No justification can be found for the *gamonal* to continue exploiting [the Indian's] labor for an insignificant salary, paid with the same product [the Indian] produces, [a salary] that does not serve to sustain him alone and even less to attend to his family; from there he is reduced to begging, [for] he has no alternative but robbery and assassination; and thus they end up in jail cells, they are punished for crimes committed unconsciously in which they participate as the agent of their patron and exploiter. (Ibid.)

The education of the indigenous was thus conceived of as being largely a political project. It consisted of freeing people who were depicted as "miserable, exploited creatures" from relations of servitude that prevented them from acting as autonomous individuals—relations that forced the indigenous to become powerless and impoverished pawns who acted on the orders of, and who were punished for committing the crimes of, those who exploited them.

The final aspect of the liberation of the indigenous population consisted of freeing them from the primitive rites and superstitions that condemned them to remain in a premodern state—what was referred to as the "religious problem" of the Indian:

More transcendental still, the object of intense preoccupation in these times, is the religious problem of the Indian. In some places in the sierra, although it seems an exaggeration to say so, the indigenous people have not progressed beyond totemism and animism, [while] in other regions they are found imbued with the most degrading superstition, with traditional beliefs deeply rooted in their spirit; most practice a cult made up of a variety of rites and fiestas that end up in intoxication, crime, etc. In said feasts the Indian sacrifices his [individual] goods in favor of the pomp of the event and the gluttony of the group . . . the teacher in the school must give to religious education a ground of morality; apart from [religious education in the school] the priests must carry out their mission without subjecting [the Indians] . . . to dogmas that they don't comprehend, [the priests] must polish the conscience of the herd to form beings of perfect morality . . . in short, they must try to imitate the work of the Divine Teacher, giving to religion a real, vital feeling. Perhaps the conception of death can be [used as] an incentive to moderate such vices and bad inclinations. (Ibid.)

As do so many other articles in *Amazonas*, this one also ends with an exhortation—to self-sacrifice and patriotism in the making of subjects useful to the nation: "Exalted spirits of renewal! Demonstrate the patriotism so often envisaged, do not lose heart before these short-lived obstacles. The Nation expects of you an assiduous effort for its prosperity" (ibid., Esteban Hidalgo y S., student of the Escuela Normal, Lima, Jan. 27, 1927).

Indigenous education is thus best conceived of as a broad-ranging project of cultural transformation in which economic, social, political, and "religious" elements were combined—a project whose successful implementation implicated most of society. While some (teachers) were called upon to give more of themselves than others in this endeavor, what was needed from all, according to *Amazonas*, was greater concern, greater care, greater involvement—so that society's "younger brothers" could become useful and proud members of the nation.

The education of mestizo and white children was seen in radically different terms than was the education of the indigenous population. Rather than forming men with defined personalities who were conscious of their acts, in full exercise of their rights as citizens, and free from their own superstitions as well as from the domination of the powerful, educating mestizo and white children implied a different set of disciplinary procedures and had different ends. For these children, education was seen as one element in a more general process of training in which unformed subjects were to internalize the forms of behavior and respect necessary to become disciplined, polite, respectful, responsible citizens.

According to *Amazonas*, urban children—mestizo and white alike—were at risk from forces far different from but no less dangerous than those faced by Indians. Forces of urban corruption could easily tempt unwary children down a slippery slope that left them unable to behave with moderation, restraint, and control, that left them totally lacking in self-discipline. Because of these ever-present dangers, virtually all aspects of children's behavior had to be carefully monitored and regulated—in order to mold them into the "democratized," responsible individuals of which the new social order was to be composed.

There was little in the daily life of children that did not come under the direct scrutiny of *Amazonas*. The following article typifies much of the paper's discourse about the temptations to which children were subject, and the forms of discipline necessary to shepherd them along the path of proper citizenship:

The Two Timetables
THE TIMETABLE OF THE BAD BOY

At 6 A.M.—He is sleeping.

At 7 A.M.—He continues sleeping.

At 8:30—He awakens, sits on his bed, yawns and, overcome with sloth, calls the servant and in a contemptuous tone orders him to serve breakfast.

At 9 A.M.—The bells of the public clock announce nine o'clock, at last he rises, does not wash his face, nor brush his teeth, he does not cut his fingernails, nor even shine his shoes.

At 9:15—He searches . . . through his shelf—that is always messy—for his schedule of classes in order to see which courses he has, finds it at last, but in the meantime has had to move all his books and notebooks and in the confusion he cannot find the school supplies that he needs; at this moment the bell of the clock rings—it is 9:30—And he has already missed the beginning of class.

At 9:30—He grabs whatever notebook [is handy], lights his delicious cigarette, and makes a dash for the schoolroom; and as a consequence during his flight he loses much of his tobacco.

At 9:45—He arrives at school, but the door is already closed, and faced with this situation he smiles with happiness, since he is left with no alternative but to go about directionless, roaming about the rustic, solitary and pestilent streets. . . .

At 10:00—If he is in school, he does not pay attention to the class; it appears that he gets bored with it, and thus he bothers his friends and as a consequence his teacher. If he is not in the classroom, this is the moment that he begins to meet with his famous gang, [and] they immediately begin to unleash a reciprocal interchange of ugly phrases. . . . Soon begins the accursed game of the "centavos" [gambling].

At 11:00 A.M.—If he is found at school, he only pretends to be attentive to the lesson of the teacher, and does no written work for lack of the necessary school supplies, since the only thing that accompanies him is a grimy notebook; as a consequence, he rests while his fellow students work. If he is not in school, he continues roaming his favorite streets.

At 11:30—The school bell rings—it is time to leave—and he is the first to get up [from his desk] but the last to line up; he goes through the streets jumping and skipping to the rhythm of an obscene vocabulary while throwing papers on the ground.

At 12:00 noon—He is still in the street, since he has paused to witness some sickening argument.

At 12:30—He arrives at home at last—lunch has already begun—he hurries to sit at the table, and without even having cleaned his hands he gobbles [his food], stuffing himself.

At 1:00 P.M.—He heads for his bedroom with the object of having a nice siesta, [but] instead kills time reading some vulgar magazine.

At 1:30—He leaves to go for a walk.

At 2:00 P.M.—He makes his way to school, without more supplies than a notebook and a deteriorated book.

At 2:15—He arrives at school late. . . . If the main door is found closed, he simply heads for the streets [so] familiar [to him].

At 3:00 P.M.—It is time for school recess, and he leaves his hiding place to meet his friends, to play, wallow, and scream his contentment, and carried away with his antics he mistakenly enters the classroom; the teacher reprimands him for his attitude and he laughs in reply, the laugh of insolence. If he is not in school he wanders about the streets without cease.

At 4:00 P.M.—The second school recess begins, and he plays rudely, mistreating and injuring his comrades. If he is found outside the schoolroom, he continues bathing himself in the turbulent waters of many vices, breathing in their infected and poisonous atmosphere.

At 5:00 P.M.— . . . If he didn't attend school, the instant he takes leave of his idle friends he immediately goes to his house to deceive his parents, telling them that he was helping out at school.

At 6:00 P.M.—He is in the street.

At 7:00 P.M.—He hurriedly sits down to eat, and gulps down his food, all the while having rotten teeth.

At 8:00 P.M.—It is the hour of his "appointment"—his depraved, sleep-walking friends are waiting for him, and in order to meet them he leaves the house without his parents' permission.

At 9:00 P.M.—Already at the side of his tramp companions . . . already on his way to the places of ruin, his tender lips already uttering what are, sadly, the celebrated words of Sardanópalo: "Eat, drink and be merry, all else is il-lusion."

At 10:00 P.M.—He begins to traverse the slippery slope of misfortune, singing, laughing, and crying like someone crazy.

At 10:30 P.M.—He is playing the favorite games of degenerates, losing the money that he secretly stole from his parents who spoiled him as a child, and who continue pampering him too much even now.

At 11:00 P.M.—The scandal begins—it is the tragic hour of fighting. The cursed game [of gambling] ends in a scene, and the bad boy is taken to jail.

At 12:00 P.M.—He is placed in a cell as gloomy and sad as his behavior, and there he sleeps together with the other criminals that carry with them the stigma of dishonor, [there] he sleeps the morbid, mournful sleep of the wretched.

Dearest children:

Do not follow this way of life, this repugnant timetable of the bad boy, if you do not wish to be what he is at present: the degenerate son who with his continuous bad deeds thrusts into the heart of his home the dagger of pain, the bad student in the school, the vile plaything of his own passions. Do not follow in the diseased footsteps of the bad boy, if you do not want to be what he will surely be in the future: the parasitic man who inspires pain, the bad father of the family, the wretched citizen of the fatherland, the heavy load for society, the useless and harmful being who will cry pathetically of his misfortune in his old age, for not having known to reform himself, for not having known to cure himself, for not having known that, when still a child, he had the remedy directly within his grasp. (*Amazonas* 1, no. 4 [Feb. 1, 1927]: 2)

What makes the boy in this article "bad" is that he exhibits behaviors, attitudes, and inclinations that all reflect a single underlying problem—a lack of control over his individual passions, emotions, and desires.[18] That is, the bad boy is depicted as totally lacking in self-discipline, as always seeking immediate gratification for whatever base instinct rules him from moment to moment. As a result, he is unable to live according to the general principles of fair play, honesty, and respect for himself and others expounded upon with such force in *Amazonas*. Rather, he mistreats and abuses everyone he encounters in his path—from his friends to his family. There can be no room for such an unprincipled person in the egalitarian world imagined in the pages of the paper. Indeed, every aspect of the bad boy's self-indulgent behavior reveals him to be precisely the opposite of what the paper asserts the region needs so badly—people who will serve a cause greater than the self, who will give of themselves for the betterment of all.

Each time the school appears in the article, it is presented as an alternative to the undisciplined, indulgent behavior of the bad boy. That is, implicit here is the notion that the schoolroom is the primary site where "proper" forms of behavior are internalized. Indeed, throughout the article, the dangers and temptations of "the street"—where free rein may be given to the passions—are consistently opposed to the safety and order of the schoolroom. And whenever the bad boy appears in the classroom, what makes his behavior bad is that he continues to resist the discipline that could do him so much good.

Immediately following the "Timetable of the Bad Boy," *Amazonas* presents the equivalent for the "good boy"—as a study in contrasts with the former's undisciplined, licentious behavior:

THE TIMETABLE OF THE GOOD BOY

At 6:00 A.M.—He wakes up and immediately rises from his bed, sincerely praises God, does his physical exercises, bathes himself, brushes his teeth, folds his nightclothes, and goes to his parents' room to wish them good morning.

At 7:00 A.M.—He writes out his school assignments and afterwards has breakfast.

At 8:00 A.M.—He is on his way to school, in the street, going always with an uplifted face and erect posture, courteously greeting the people he knows, never teasing the old people or the destitute, he doesn't spit on the ground, nor linger on the street corners, even less so in the entrance to the school.

At 8:30 A.M.—He enters the schoolroom with his head bared [without his hat], greets his teachers and fellow students, cleans his desk and places his school supplies in their place; he takes his proper place as soon as he hears the school bell ring.

At 9:00 A.M.—During the cleanliness review, his teacher presents him to the other students as a model of cleanliness, and he sings the school songs with enthusiasm.

At 9:15 A.M.—He devotes his attention to his classes, doesn't bother his friends, does his assignments with clarity and without plagiarizing from his friends.

At 10:00 A.M.—During school recess he plays with much animation and always by the rules; and later when recess ends he lines up immediately and returns to the classroom without bothering his fellow students. In the classroom he is always an active element, a valuable student; when he wants to ask his teacher a question he raises his finger first.

At 11:00 A.M.—He continues working.

At 11:30 A.M.—The school bell announces the hour of departure; as soon as he hears the bell he puts his school supplies in their place, falls in line, and files out correctly; in the street he does not pause to watch any fights. He always walks on the sidewalk.

At 12:00 noon—He arrives at home, greets his parents, puts his school supplies in their proper place, washes his hands and his mouth before and after lunch, chews well with his mouth closed, doesn't make noise with the silverware and plates, chats amiably with his family, and soon goes out for a walk in the street.

At 1:00 P.M.—He reviews his school assignments for the afternoon.

At 1:30 P.M.—He says good-bye to his parents and starts off for school; if by chance he encounters a beggar long the way, he is moved to give him part of his allowance and the other part he keeps to buy fruit or otherwise to deposit in the *Banco Infantil*.

At 2:00 P.M.—He arrives at school and greets his teachers and fellow students.

At 2:30 P.M.—He works with care during the afternoon.

At 3:00 P.M.—During recess he plays with enthusiasm, pays attention to the explanations of his teacher, loves his studies intensely, and wishes to be better every day.

At 4:00 P.M.—During his moment of relaxation [from school] he doesn't insult his friends, and doesn't scribble on the walls, doors, or windows; during class he is always the student with excellent ideas, the good-natured comrade, who doesn't envy the successes of his fellow students, does not grow vain with his own triumphs, nor is intimidated by defeat.

At 5:00 P.M.—He files out with all correctness to his house, puts his school supplies in their proper place and right away goes out for a walk.

At 6:00 P.M.—He is in the street with his friends.

At 7:00 P.M.—At dinner he observes the same rules as he did at lunch.

At 8:00 P.M.—With the prior permission of his parents he goes out for a stroll, and never joins bad boys, rather he prefers to go alone rather than be in bad company.

At 9:00 P.M.—He reads a good book or magazine, something serious and instructive.

At 10:00 P.M.—He prepares his school assignments for the following day.

At 10:30 P.M.—Satisfied with having completed his assignments, with having used the day well, he goes to bed to sleep a tranquil sleep, that type of sleep that is a mixture of sweetness and happiness, that only good boys sleep. In addition, the good boy: loves his parents, and his country and his fellow countrymen, is proud, is of honest and loyal spirit; never takes what belongs to another; doesn't slander anyone; doesn't mistreat animals; bathes from his head to his toes once a week and during the summer even more frequently; helps out at the cinemas and theaters when they present something moral and illustrative; and finally on festive occasions plays one or more "sports" in the playing field, since he enjoys them.

Dear children:

Follow this path of light of the good boy, if you wish to be what he is at present: the good son of the house; the model student at school, the boy of great and generous spirit; that commits himself to begin from the first step and rises by his own merit; who does not lose his courage before any obstacle; who considers it worthy of his greatest efforts to form himself in this manner, who carries within him beautiful ideals for which he lives; who serves some real need, who produces something, who leaves a memory of something. Follow in the brilliant footsteps of the good boy, if you want without any doubt to be what he is in the future: the honorable man who lives from his honorable work; who forges his personality in the crucible of pain; the good head of the household; the citizen who is useful to the fatherland; the happy old person who when he descends to the unknown and infinite world beyond the tomb, does so in a serene and tranquil manner, because he carries in his spirit the satisfaction of a job completed, the sweet satisfaction of leaving with his children a name to venerate and an example to imitate. (Ibid., Ricardo Feijóo Reina)

The "Timetable of the Good Boy" could not present more of a contrast with that of the bad boy, for the good boy is the antithesis of the bad boy in virtually every way. What makes him "good" is that he is firmly in control of his passions and emotions. Rather than give them free expression, he imposes his will upon them, and thus shows himself to be a disciplined young man. He is courteous, fair, kind, polite, organized, caring, and committed. From his hygienic personal habits to his table manners to his study habits to his behavior during moments of relaxation, he (literally) embodies and exemplifies the principles of fair play, ethical behavior, respect for himself and for others, and strength of character described so admiringly in the pages of *Amazonas*. This is the person of which the region is so much in need if it is to free itself from the weight of the past and remake itself in egalitarian form—the person who behaves according to moral and ethical principles applicable to all. This is the person who will rise according to his own merits, who will earn everything he acquires. This is the person who will make up the "natural aristocracy" of principled, dignified individuals of which the new social order is to be composed.

In this account, education again reveals itself to refer primarily to a set of disciplinary practices and techniques—to which "good boys" respond appropriately. That is, the notion that the schoolroom is primarily a site for internalizing "proper" forms of behavior is more than implicit in the timetable of the good boy. Virtually the entire day of the good boy is spent demonstrating his eagerness and ability to mold his behavior according to what is asked of him in the context of the school. Indeed, the "good boy" must routinize his activities according to a rigid and demanding temporal discipline if he is to become the kind of man of which the fatherland is so much in need.

Education thus referred to a wide range of disciplinary practices, most of which had little to do with learning literacy skills. Rather, within the domain of education was included practices as varied as lifting the veil of superstition from the minds of the indigenous, granting the indigenous the political protections they needed in order to defy those who exploited them, ensuring that the indigenous were not coerced into working for others and that they received fair price for their labor, instilling in children respect for the authority of teacher, parent, and country, and teaching children to walk on the sidewalk rather than in the street, not to spit on the ground, and not to gamble.

The particular aspects of this process of education emphasized in any given context differed according to the group being "educated." The process as a whole, however, was focused on "finishing the work of creation" by forming rational, principled, disciplined subjects who would be useful to the nation—subjects who would be equal before the law and in full exercise of their individual rights. One article from *Amazonas* expressed this democratizing, equalizing goal of education with unusual clarity and succinctness: "We are taking care that among our youngsters all be equal and that there not be rich nor poor, humble nor great" (*Amazonas* 1, no. 2 [Nov. 15, 1926]: 1). Another article expounded upon the same theme at somewhat greater length:

> Public or private education, when used in the service of preparing an elite or in the creation of a situation of future domination, is contrary to the moral life of Humanity. . . . True elites will emerge only through the equal cultivation [of education] in all young spirits. Pseudo-elites are formed through educational privilege rather than through natural ability, and must rely on force, on intrigue, and on tyranny in order to sustain themselves, in the process undermining all true social values of persistence and the progressive improvement of the human species. (*Amazonas* 4, no. 19 [May 1929]: 3)

THE WOMAN OF VIRTUE

The idealized vision of womanhood held up for public scrutiny in the pages of *Amazonas* differed profoundly from the rational, hard-working, principled individual into which men were to mold themselves if they were to free themselves of their oppressive casta overlords and become "useful elements to the nation." Above all else, the ideal image for women was a domestic one—it consistently located a woman in the home, as either mother, daughter, or sister, and denied her any productive role in the public sphere. The precise features that defined the "good" woman differed somewhat according to which of the various available domestic roles she was imagined as fulfilling. In general, however, "goodness" was defined in terms of emotive qualities that were depicted as being natural in women—selflessness, empathy, simplicity, and virtue. The good woman—whether as mother, daughter, or sister—was the one who lived to lighten the burden of others, the woman who felt the joys and sorrows of those close to her as if these were her own emotions, the woman who drew upon what was given to her as an endowment from nature to brighten the lives of those around her. In her youth she is innocence and purity. As a mother she sacrifices all to her children. In her declining years she silently bears all the sorrows and treasures, all the joys of a life selflessly given to others.[19]

Just as it was the nation that called upon men to refashion themselves in useful form, so, too, was it the new national community—to which people were to pledge themselves in creating an alternative to casta rule—that appealed to women to make themselves over in a new image.

The Fatherland Is in Search of a Girl

Aware, obedient, studious, sincere, graceful, of strong character, generous, and loyal.

A girl who is learning to think grand thoughts, to conceive noble visions, to treasure pure emotions, to do good deeds.

A girl who is helpful and loving to her brothers; always ready to do part of her mother's or father's work, who is clean in her habits, refined in her plays, good with the birds, animals, and plants, simple, natural, and true in all her life, the consolation and hope of her mother and father, the tender blessing of her home.

A girl who knows how to sympathize with others, who feels the pains and the joys of her friends and neighbors, who does everything she can to lighten the loads of those who suffer, who contributes all that she can to the general good, whose life is a ray of light.

A girl so good that badness flees from her like the night before the advancing day . . . so tender that everything in her overflows with love . . . so Christian that she always forgives . . . so strong that she always perseveres, so self-sacrificing that she always helps.

A girl who always aspires and hopes, a girl of beautiful spirit, who carries with her always a gleam from the Sky; whose life is a treasure of prophecies, a spring of riches and promises, a dawn of the glory that approaches.

The fatherland is always in search of such a girl, say it in a loud voice to the fatherland.

But, consider this, girl; You who read this, would you not like to be the girl sought after by your fatherland? Well then . . . in a soft voice I tell you:

You yourself can respond to your fatherland. You can come to be that girl that your fatherland is always in search of. (*Amazonas* 1, no. 4 [Feb. 1, 1927]: 2–3)

As the article makes clear, not just any girl would be worthy of inclusion in the new national community—based as it was on principles of morality, democracy, and the promotion of the general good. Only girls of exceptional moral purity, natural simplicity, and emotive empathy could truly be of service to the fatherland. For such girls could do much to help realize the morally based social order that was to be the foundation of national solidarity, progress, and prosperity. They could do so because, as the article puts it, their virtues would radiate outward, driving away badness like the night before the day, overcoming all obstacles in order to contribute to the general good. The fatherland would be proud to welcome such girls into its fold, for such girls were worthy representatives of the national community and all that it stood for.

It was thus the image of the young woman of virtue that was invoked to *represent* the nation. *Amazonas* drew upon an image of the mature woman of virtue, the mother, in constructing a narrative of *building* the nation—a narrative that drew upon woman's emotive qualities, her domestic location, and her child-rearing role to make of the "mother of virtue" a powerful force in world history. This image of mother as nation-builder is captured in the following article, located on the "Woman's and Children's Page" of the paper, and written by Josefina Saravia E.:[20]

What the Latin Woman Should Understand by Feminism

"*Let us first endeavor to fashion Mothers; so that afterward it will be easier to fashion Men.*"

It is both logical and imperative to devote the utmost attention to the education of women, residing as they do by natural law in the Home, [where reside] all feelings of virtue and interconnection, so that guided by the ideals of the home, women may learn how best to educate their sons, and how to understand human nature.

We all know that it is in infancy that the habits and feelings that guide the individual through his entire life are acquired; for this reason I believe that, in order to achieve an ideal society, it is the education of women that should be given the greatest priority, for it is She, called upon by her nature and by the conditions of her sex, to form and to fashion the human race. (*Amazonas* 1, no. 6 [Apr. 1927]: 3)

This first section of the article essentializes and universalizes Woman and the Home—both of which are presented as natural entities with invariant qualities. According to the author, since the universal Woman who resides in her natural domain is called upon by the conditions of her sex to form and fashion the "human race" (note the use of race in the singular, in place of the multiple races of the aristocratic order), it is essential that She be educated concerning how to properly mold and shape her sons (note as well the use of "the human race" to refer exclusively to males). What is at stake in this endeavor? Nothing less than the establishment of an "ideal society." As the article continues, the author makes it clear that the ideal society she envisions is one that takes a particular form—the *nation*, made up of free and equal citizens:

The child who was poorly educated during the first seven years [of his life] will as a general rule tend toward badness thereafter. . . . In contrast the child who was directed toward work and honor by the firm will of his mother, "will inevitably prosper and will give noble examples to his fellow citizens" [to emulate]. Examples of [the influence of] good mothers shine in the history of all countries, especially those of antiquity (Greece and Rome offer us a great many examples); we have the Spartan mother telling her son, her husband, or her brother, before they left for battle and as she gave them their shields: "Return with it [the shield], or on top of it," meaning to say with these words that they must conquer, and that she would rather see them dead than defeated! (Ibid.)

To the universal Mother and her essentialized domain of the Home, in this second section of the article the author adds an additional transhistorical entity—the Nation. The connection between Mother and Nation is explicit here, as it is the Mother who safeguards the interests of the nation by imparting to the men of Her domestic realm their duties to Her and to the Nation—which are depicted as being one and the same. Nationhood and motherhood thus mutually define and construct one another in the pages of *Amazonas*. That is, defending the ideals of the Nation defines an important part of proper motherhood, while mothers protect and help reproduce the Nation through the influence they wield within their natural domain of the home. Men are thus steered on the path of goodness, proper manhood, and loyalty to the Nation through the "early education" they receive at the hands of their mothers.

The role of good mothers in inculcating in their sons the values of nationhood was not limited to antiquity, but rather embraced all of history. As the article continues, the author refers to other exceptional mothers who played key roles in making nations via their influence on their sons:

> But it is not especially the woman-patriot to whom I wish to refer today, but rather the woman-model, who has existed at all times, it being my greatest desire that these rare examples multiply [in number]. It is mothers like that of Lincoln who, with unbreakable will, knew how to ignite the love of humanity in her young son, who was steadfast in the noble ambition of forging him in the crucible of virtue, who was able to make of him an honorable man, a great man. History tells us that when Lincoln was a young boy, his mother would sit him down near to her and read to him, at times about the history of the fatherland, at other times about the lives of great men, in this way ennobling the spirit of her son, so that when Lincoln was still very young and was visiting New Orleans, upon seeing a group of slaves he proclaimed to them: "When I have the chance to fight against this [slavery] I will fight, and I will fight vigorously," a promise that later became a noble reality. (Ibid.)

In other words, it was a Mother who, from within her natural domain of the Home, was instrumental in healing the one Nation that, above all others, symbolized the freedom and equality that was the rallying cry of *Amazonas*—the United States. But the role of the good Mother was not limited to healing the Nation that stood for freedom and equality. The author explains that another Mother of quality helped *give birth* to this Nation:

> History offers us no less interesting and noble an example of the mother-model in the mother of George Washington, a woman with a powerful will

to pursue the path of good, who knew to make of her son a true patriot . . .
a man of great honor and character. (Ibid.)

In these passages the connection between Mother and Nation is plain, as
the author continually asserts the existence of the timeless Mother—the one
"who has existed at all times"—who imparts to her sons the egalitarian and
democratic ideals upon which Nationhood is based. The Mother thus emerges
in these passages as the local embodiment of the Nation. That is, as reflected in
a number of passages quoted earlier in the chapter—and as has so often been
the case in projects of nation-building (Parker et al. 1992)—the nation is made
maternal, and motherhood is made national.[21] For it is through the Mother,
and the domestic realm over which she presides, that the Nation is made to
come to life in the hearts and minds of boys. This is the crucial educa-
tional/moral influence that a good mother could and should have on her sons.

As if to anticipate the objections of some of her readers, the author continues:

There will be no shortage of those who think that every individual who is
born predestined to be a great man will be so regardless of the circumstances
of his life, while others will remain unknown and of little consequence . . . but
I believe, I believe firmly, that the mother has the greatest part of the responsibility for giving to humanity a useful being (if she knows to truly educate her
son from the time he is in the cradle), or a useless and harmful creature (if
from the time he is little he is not cared for and no effort is made to root out
the bad inclinations and to develop in him the good ones). Naturally, for such
a difficult task, a woman needs a very special preparation; and I wish to insist
upon the importance of this matter with all the energy in my being. . . .

Therefore I believe that truly prosperous peoples will be those that are
wise enough to attend to the education of women, meaning by this the formation of their character, because only by forming good mothers will we be
able to fashion good peoples.

In addition to constructing a narrative of virtuous mothers building nations via the profound influence they exert on their sons, in articles such as
those discussed above *Amazonas* also introduced the notion that the home was
the key site for making boys into the proper kind of man. That is, the paper
imagined a discrete, autonomous domestic space as the locale within which

women of virtue and character would selflessly guide their sons on the path of good so that they could become elements useful to the nation.[22] Care of the home and of the young were not simply bequeathed to women by nature, asserted the paper; it was also entrusted to women by the nation. As a result, domestic space became national space; considerations of how the home was to be ordered and how children were to be raised became matters of national/public concern. For it could not be assumed that the ideals of nationhood could be properly communicated to future male citizens in just any kind of home environment, and by means of just any set of child-rearing practices. Mothers who wished to remain virtuous would therefore be sure to adjust their behavior accordingly.

Given this faith in the key role played by women and the home in the process of nation-building, it is not surprising that every issue of *Amazonas* included special sections—a "Woman's Column" and a "Children's Column"—devoted specifically to these topics. The "Woman's Column" went into considerable detail about how women were to order and maintain their domestic space (focusing on cleanliness and hygiene) if they wished it to be truly "proper"—if it was to be the environment most conducive to turning their sons into the right kinds of men. The column was particularly "helpful" in alerting mothers to the existence of hidden dangers within and around the home that threatened the integrity and order of the all-important domestic sphere. In this way, the paper proved that maintaining the home was anything but a simple task, and that *Amazonas* had an important part to play in "educating" mothers as to how it could best be done.

Some Useful Details for the Home

The good mother must know numerous details of domestic order to achieve the best result in the smooth functioning of the home.

There are things that seem insignificant but that can have a definite influence, favorable or adverse . . . and thus we are going to indicate some of the most frequent:

In the evenings, in cleaning out containers of gasoline, kerosene, or alcohol, there are people who bring a candle near to the container in order to see well. This constitutes a serious fire hazard. . . .

You should not add kerosene to a lantern that is already lit; it is necessary first to turn off the lantern, in order to avoid a fire. Many people have burned themselves, and have even burned down houses, due to this kind of negligence. . . .

In places like the department of Amazonas, where during certain times of the year both poisonous and edible mushrooms grow, it is necessary to be very careful, as poisonous mushrooms often result in death when eaten. . . .

In the rooms of sick children, you must be sure that the air is pure. In order to insure this it is necessary to prohibit people from entering the room or to limit entry to only a few, and to forbid animals from entering. The respiration of other people removes oxygen from the air that could otherwise be used by the one who is sick, and fills the air with carbonic gas, which is harmful. . . .

In places where the climate is hot and humid, many articles are damaged by the humidity and moisture. In some cases it is a good idea to put glass containers or crockery that contains quicklime in all wardrobes. It is a good idea to occasionally remove clothes from their wardrobes, place them in the sun, and turn them over repeatedly while passing a brush over the front and back of the clothing.

All the windows of a comfortable and clean house should be left a slight bit open. During the day it is a good idea to draw the curtains, so that the sunlight and air may enter. It is better to damage rugs and wall hangings than people . . . it is important not to forget that these are the most efficient and the cheapest ways to maintain health. (*Amazonas* 1, no. 6: 3)

The "Woman's Column" and the "Children's Column" of the paper both focused on educating mothers about the proper way to raise their children. Much of the paper's discourse focused on the importance of hygiene and health—on the care and maintenance of the bodies of future male citizens. The following article (from the "Woman's Column") captures much of the paper's discourse concerning the hidden dangers mothers needed to guard against if they wanted to provide their children with the proper kind of physical care—as well as the range of their own behaviors women needed to carefully monitor in order to be sure that they did not unwittingly interfere with the proper development of their sons:

What Mothers Should Never Do If They Wish To Preserve the
Health of Their Sons

Never clean your son's mouth when it is already clean.
Never make your son sleep in the bed of his parents.

Never ignore suppuration of vision in your son, as this can result in blind-
ness.

Never place grass or cobwebs on your son's navel as a method of healing.

Never allow dandruff to develop on the head of your son. . . .

Never give your son a pacifier.

Never kiss your son, or allow him to be kissed, on the mouth or on the
hands.

Never give your son a baby bottle unless necessary.

Never put the leftover milk from yesterday's bottle into today's bottle.

Never suckle your son each time he cries.

Never leave your son in dirty or wet diapers. (*Amazonas* 4, no. 19 [May
1929]: 3)

In other words, through their own ignorance, mothers could unknowingly
interfere with the proper development of their sons—by failing to provide
their sons with the kinds of physical, mental, and moral stimulation children
needed. Faced with this alarming possibility, *Amazonas* took upon itself the
task of training and educating women in the proper direction. The following
article typifies the paper's discourse on this dimension of being a "good
mother":

What Children Need

In addition to food, medicine, and hygiene, a child needs stories and toys.

The spirit of the infant is drawn to descriptions and explanations made in
an active voice. But it is important that the stories be simple, so as to exercise
the child's comprehension without tiring his mind. The stories should not
offend morality, nor be of such a nature that they disturb the imagination of
the child, especially during his sleep. If the stories have a basis of scientific or
moral instruction, they can be both interesting and useful at the same time,
with the result that when the moment arrives in primary school that a lesson
makes the child remember one of his stories, his attention and comprehension will be greater. The sleep of children has a major influence on their
lives. Although the child does not work he plays, and after playing he must
be forced to take a nap, and the nap will be a great restorer.

During sleep an active cellular renovation occurs. Those who work a
great deal and rest occasionally or never, with their minds or with their
hands, tempt death.

When the family goes visiting at night and takes the children, it is a good idea to be sure that as soon as they fall asleep, that they assume a horizontal position, that their shoes be removed, and that their clothes be loosened. When carrying them home it is necessary to cover them with a sheet or towel.

Dinner should be served to children much earlier than it is to adults. While the adults eat, the children should take a brief walk through the park or garden, and thereafter go to bed. (*Amazonas* 1, no. 6: 3)

Articles often employed pseudo-scientific language ("an active cellular renovation") in seeking authority for their claims, and not infrequently referred to the results of the latest scientific studies about "children" and "the home" conducted in the United States and Europe—acknowledged centers of expertise on "things modern."

Overall, the "home" constructed discursively in the pages of *Amazonas* was imagined to be a distinct, autonomous sphere of which mothers of virtue were to be the guardians. To be sure that dangerous influences and substances could not enter that might contaminate the environment so necessary to making boys into the right kinds of men, mothers were to monitor the external boundaries of the home. They were to maintain the internal order of the home as well, and within this more carefully bounded, ordered environment, mothers were to impose new forms of discipline on their sons—forms of discipline that would help turn their sons into the principled, patriotic, ethical individuals of which the region and the nation were so much in need if either was to remake itself in new form. That is, the processes of home-making and child-raising imagined in the paper reinforced individual and family boundaries even as they inculcated loyalty to the new communities of region and nation. According to the paper, the only legitimate sites of socialization in the new order were the home and the school (each being a variant of the other). Similarly, the only two legitimate roles/activities for adults in the new social order were living out the egalitarian ideals of the regional/national community or teaching others to do so.

The image of the timeless, universal mother was employed toward one additional end in the pages of *Amazonas*—a democratizing end. The selfless, transhistorical mother was depicted as prior to, as more fundamental than, and thus as overriding, all other possible differences or potential divisions among women:

The Mother

Señora:

There is a woman who has something of God in her due to the immensity of her love, and much that the angels have due to the inexhaustible diligence of her care; a woman that if she is old works with the vigor of youth; a woman that if she is ignorant, discovers with greater wisdom the secrets of life; . . . if she is educated accommodates herself to the simplicity of children, a woman who being poor is satisfied with what she loves, and being rich gives away her treasures with pleasure so as to not suffer in her heart the wound of ingratitude [from others]; a woman who being vigorous trembles at the cry of a child, and being weak is seen at times [demonstrating] the ferocity of a lion; a woman who while alive has a value we know not how to reckon, because once at her side all pain is forgotten; but after death we would give anything to look at her for a single instant, in order to receive from her a single embrace, to hear from her lips a single sound.

Do not ask me the name of this woman if you do not want your album drenched in tears, because I have known such a woman.

When you raise your children, read them this page, while they cover your forehead in kisses, and tell them that a humble traveler, in return for the sumptuous hospitality he received, has left for them a portrait of his mother. (*Amazonas* 1, no. 5 [Mar. 1, 1927]: 3)

Neither wealth nor social standing nor age nor education nor individual strength alters the essential nature of the woman of virtue—the woman who lives only to ease the burdens of others. Regardless of her station or situation in life, the woman of virtue overcomes the obstacles life places in her path in order to remain pure, selfless, and giving.[23]

Simply by virtue of asserting the existence of such general categories as "men," "women," and "children"—assertions that carried the unspoken but implicit claim that each was an internally undifferentiated category, to which applied a single set of identical concerns, interests, needs, and attentions—*Amazonas* interjected a powerful democratizing, homogenizing voice into local affairs. For it subtly erased distinctions of race and caste, ancestry and property ownership, that segregated the population into highly distinct and unequal social categories that did much to prescribe the life possibilities of those who occupied them. That is, *Amazonas* was erasing social distinctions that had encoded the highly unequal distribution of material wealth, social prestige, and political power upon which the entire system of aristocratic sovereignty was based. The paper was inviting, for example, women born into poverty of unwed mothers who were single heads of household and who were totally lacking in social position or claims to social respect to regard themselves as having the same interests and considerations as women of elite families who occupied the highest rungs of the social order (and vice versa). Similarly, it was encouraging mestizo boys, who were excluded from all important positions in public life, who had a very restricted set of life possibilities, and who were denigrated as having little social importance, to think of themselves as "being like" boys of the elite.

Furthermore, as an alternative to the presumption of automatic, inherited superiority made by all members of the elite as a result of the privileged station in life into which they were born, *Amazonas* presented a means of assessing the social worth of everyone according to universal standards based on "individual merit," which applied regardless of inherited social position. Backed by such an alternative system, those who sought to transform the region's social order were better able to question the elite's presumptions of superiority, and could make alternative claims for the kinds of behavior that were truly of value.

Nonelite members of society were aided considerably in their efforts to call into question the cultural logic and legitimacy of aristocratic sovereignty by the fact that the elite itself had been doing the same in political ritual and discourse for generations. That is, having publicly proclaimed the legitimacy of the principles of popular sovereignty for decades—to the point of claiming that the right to rule was contingent upon conformity to such principles—it was difficult for the elite to suddenly contradict itself and to assert that the kind of community imagined in the pages of *Amazonas* was somehow not legitimate. Neither, however, could the elite simply cease its violent, competitive, and aggressive behavior in favor of the "ethically based" forms of personhood and association called for by the paper. For in order to exercise positions of power, and to live according to the station in life to which all members of the elite aspired, it was necessary to engage in the kinds of "unethical" behavior discussed in previous chapters.

As a result, the regional elite was in the uncomfortable and quite vulnerable position of being unable to defend itself in ritual or discourse from the accusations and condemnations made by the social movement that coalesced around Ricardo Feijóo Reina and *Amazonas*.

It is difficult to estimate the precise number of people involved in Feijóo's movement, as he did not form an official political party until 1929, and the party's membership lists have not survived. In September 1934—by which time Feijóo had exercised the position of congressional representative for several years—Feijóo sent 6,000 membership cards to the departmental president of the "Independent Labor Party of Amazonas." Two months later, in November 1934, the departmental president of the party cabled Feijóo in Lima to request that an additional 2,000 membership cards be sent to Chachapoyas (Feijóo Reina 1935: 340, 341).

When it is remembered that the entire town of Chachapoyas had a population of only about 5,000 people at this time, it is clear from the 6,000–8,000 party members implied by the correspondence between Feijóo and the party's departmental president that the "Independent Labor Party of Amazonas" was a social movement of sweeping proportions. That is, Feijóo's call for democratization, moralization, and national integration struck a resounding chord among important segments of the local population.

7 Modernity as Emancipation II

The 'Alianza Popular Revolucionaria Americana'

> I spoke to them [peasant and mestizo "students" in the
> Popular University] in the following way: "How may great
> minds, how many deputies, senators, and doctors are there
> among you but who can never be so because you are from
> Quinjalca or Yambajalca or from whatever village and
> because you do not have a white face and a 'proper' last
> name. . . . Who among you can become officers in the
> military? . . . To become an officer you cannot be
> illegitimate. You must be white, tall, of good name and
> with blue eyes."
>
> *Victor Santillán Gutierrez, September 15, 1993,*
> *speaking of his organizing efforts among the peasantry of*
> *Amazonas in the early 1930s on behalf of the APRA*

In the latter half of 1929, fifteen to twenty adolescents began to meet in secret on Sundays at midnight in the cemetery of Chachapoyas. The vanguard of a new persecuted political party (the *Alianza Popular Revolucionaria Americana*, or APRA), they were deeply committed to transforming regional society so that equality and justice would obtain, so that the individual would be freed from relations of servitude with the more powerful.[1]

Great care had to be taken to arrive at the cemetery undetected by the gendarmes, who were constantly on watch for "suspicious nocturnal activities" as they patrolled the town armed with rifles. It was essential to pass along the quiet streets of Chachapoyas without being seen, as far as the town's eastern perimeter. Beyond this was a wooded ravine that led southward toward the cemetery. Several times the gendarmes spotted the young people as they attempted to reach the ravine, and gave chase while shooting their rifles. Although no one was killed or wounded, the fleeing Apristas were forced to seek refuge in the forested area that lay beyond the ravine in order to escape.[2]

The young Apristas met, in reverence, at the grave site of Victor Pizarro Rubio—ironically at one time the favorite son of the town's ruling Pizarro-Rubio casta. Victor was the son of Pablo M. Pizarro Farje and Rosa Rubio Linch, one of three couples who made up the core of the Pizarro-Rubio casta (see Chapter 1). The Pizarro-Rubio casta was unusually well-connected to the country's centers of power. Victor's father was the compadre of Peru's president/dictator, Augusto Leguía, the latter having played a key role in bringing the Pizarro-Rubio casta to power within the region (see Chapter 4) and in helping the casta remain in power thereafter. Because of the very close ties between the Pizarros and President Leguía, Victor's father had arranged for Victor to be awarded a scholarship to attend the Naval Academy in the nation's capital. Victor was further honored with an additional scholarship to continue his military studies at a naval institute in France.

The plan of the Pizarros was that Victor would return to Peru after finishing his military training, and would occupy an important post in the armed forces and/or the government—a position from which he could give great assistance to his family and casta. The Pizarro-Rubio casta, however, was to be sadly disappointed in Victor. Not only did he fail to live up to their expectations, but he betrayed virtually everything his family, class, and casta stood for by becoming a communist, and by helping to lead the fight against the entire casta order in Chachapoyas.

Like his fellow Chachapoyano Ricardo Feijóo Reina, Pizarro came to Lima in the 1910s and was transformed. The Lima of 1915 was in the throes of profound economic, social, and political change. Confronted by startling new ideologies—social, religious, and political—young Pizarro was intensely drawn to communism. Sent to France to continue his military studies, Pizarro "deserted" and went to the Soviet Union, where he lived for several years. In the aftermath of the Third World Congress of the Communist International he returned to Latin America in 1921, going to Uruguay, where he hoped to help expand the communist movement. Several years later he moved on to Peru with the same goal.

Pizarro's activities as a communist organizer came to an abrupt end, however, as a result of a bad beating he received at the hands of the Lima police during an anticommunist raid in 1927. Pizarro sustained severe damage to his kidneys due to the police attack, and soon thereafter was told that he had only a short time to live. At this point Pizarro decided to return to Chachapoyas, to live out his remaining days in his native land.

Upon his arrival in Chachapoyas, however, Pizarro found that his aristocratic family wished to have nothing to do with him. When they refused to take him in, he was reduced to living in a small shack on the outskirts of town, an outcast from the entire casta order. For the relatively brief period that he remained alive, Pizarro gave lectures on Marxism several times a week to whomever cared to listen. He was a big, heavy man and an impassioned speaker. His audience generally consisted of a small group of adolescents from the families of urban mestizo artisans, muleteers, petty shopkeepers, and cantina owners—people whose life possibilities had been severely circumscribed by the powerful casta families, and who were drawn to Pizarro's message of social critique and egalitarian change.

Pizarro did indeed die shortly after his return to Chachapoyas. Though the youths who risked their lives to gather at his grave site had been profoundly influenced by his lectures, it was not communism per se that captivated them or drew a significant part of the local population. Rather, it was the APRA— a political party of a more regional, Latin American nature—that attracted the townspeople in droves.[3]

It was at the grave site of Victor Pizarro that the founding members of the APRA committed themselves to one another and to the cause. Thereafter, the graveside meetings were used to discuss and settle matters of the utmost secrecy and importance to the party—matters that could not be broached in any other setting, where those not completely loyal to the cause might be listening.

One of the earliest actions taken by the original members of the APRA was to open a local branch of the *Universidad Popular Gonzalez Prada*, or Popular University, in Chachapoyas. The Popular University was originally established in Lima in 1921 by the APRA's founder—Victor Raúl Haya de la Torre—as part of his effort to forge links between the student movement and Lima's new but rapidly growing working class (Klaiber 1975; Stein 1980: 129–57). The university suffered growing repression by the government of Leguía after the exile of Haya de la Torre in 1923, culminating in the arrest of most of its important leaders in 1927 (Stein 1980: 143, 146). With the fall of Leguía in August 1930, however, the Popular University began to resurface. It was at this point that a university branch was established in Chachapoyas.[4]

The party's vanguard in Chachapoyas decided to develop the Popular University along two different fronts, one formal and the other informal. The formal teaching was to be offered at a meeting place in each of the town's four neighborhoods. The meeting places would be moved within their respective neighborhoods on an intermittent basis, in order to avoid detection by the police. These formal gatherings would provide an opportunity for a carefully screened group of people to gather to discuss issues of interest to the party and to the townspeople.[5]

The party's founders also decided to institute the Popular University—which was more commonly referred to as the *Universidad del Pueblo*, or the People's University—on a more informal basis. As one of the original Apristas put it, the People's University was to be *everywhere*—in the street, in people's homes, in chance meetings with people in the countryside, in casual discussions in bars. In short, the People's University was to be immediately "called in session" in any situation where it was possible to talk about the region's problems and potential solutions. In these more informal settings, the name of neither the party nor the university was to be invoked, for there were informers everywhere. But the issues of concern to the party could be promoted in these settings just the same. One of the early Aprista organizers described this aspect of the People's University in the following terms:[6]

We began the *Universidad del Pueblo* by talking with people in ordinary conversations, never mentioning the APRA, but talking about social problems, about poverty, about the lack of any connection between those who have something and those who have nothing: [Someone speaking to me casually at the market might say,] "Ay, I cannot afford to eat—rice is too expensive; I cannot afford to buy the things I need." [I would respond,] "I haven't bought rice today either. There is no rice to be found. How are we ever going to get rice if there is no road to Bagua, where all our rice comes from? How will we ever be able to afford the things we need if there is no road to the coast?" And from there we began to talk about these kinds of problems, and we organized among ourselves in the villages to bring people together so that we could build good roads. . . . We began in this way, person-to-person,

and we never let the darkness or the rain or the sun or *any* obstacle interfere
with our astonishing determination; but in politics you have to astonish people if you want to convince them that you are sincere. You have to astonish
them in the field of demonstration and in the field of action if you want
them to change the things that have shamed them in the past. You have to
convince them that you can be trusted, that you are a true friend.

The founding members of the APRA conceived of all of their organizing
efforts as being "educational" in nature—as falling under the rubric of informal gatherings of the People's University. The conception of education held by
the original Apristas, and the role of the People's University in relation to the
existing power structure, thus had a great deal in common with the notion
of education advanced in the pages of the newspaper *Amazonas* (see Chapter
6). That is, the Apristas conceived of education as a broad-ranging project of
cultural transformation that had the primarily political objective of undoing
the existing, highly stratified social order, and of forming rational, autonomous, principled subjects out of the region's men.[7] This view of the function of education and of the People's University informed virtually all the
"subjects" covered by the teachers of the university—from lessons on the history and geography of Peru to literacy training to general condemnations of
the existing state of affairs.

An extended critique of those who ruled the region was the theme most
consistently expounded upon in the People's University. In developing this
critique, the Apristas focused especially on attacking the cultural logic upon
which the aristocratic order was based—the cultural logic that was invoked
by members of the elite in attempting to justify their exalted position in local
society, their exactions of wealth and services from local producers, and their
insistence that the local population show them the proper forms of deferential
behavior at all times. In attacking the cultural logic of the aristocratic order,
the Apristas drew upon two alternative notions of legitimate cultural order—
one oriented toward the future (the modern nation-state) and the other oriented toward the past (the Inca empire)—and combined them in novel and
creative ways. The result was to forge a new cultural identity that acted as a
unifying force for those who had long been denied social worth and cultural
value—the same groups that the newspaper *Amazonas* argued made up the

"laboring family of Amazonas." These were the marginalized middle sectors of the towns, and the Indian peasants of the countryside—the two segments of the region's laboring poor.

The two sources of legitimate cultural order combined by the Apristas in constructing a new cultural identity for the laboring poor in large part reflected the two constituencies of which the "laboring family of Amazonas" was composed. One of these two alternative sources was to be found in the principles of popular sovereignty—principles of the kind that the newspaper *Amazonas* articulated with such frequency and force (see Chapter 6). That is, like the newspaper's editors, the region's Apristas seized upon notions of equality, justice, prosperity, and progress that had long been articulated in political ritual and discourse by the region's ruling castas, and used these notions to critique the aristocratic order as a whole. Notions of popular sovereignty—which projected a golden future for the region and its inhabitants—were particularly appealing to the marginalized middle sectors of the towns, the people who made up the vanguard of the party. At the same time, the Apristas also drew upon images of a golden age in the past, during the reign of the Inca, when "the people" had been united against their enemies, when a period of harmony had obtained, and when great things had been accomplished. Reference to the past greatness of the Inca was especially appealing to the rural peasantry.

In a kind of inversion of history, then, the Apristas drew upon both promises of a modern future and images of a golden past in order to turn the conventional cultural assertions of the elite upside down. According to the elite, their privileged position in society and their right to rule over their social inferiors was a birthright, derived from the traditional, hereditary caste position they occupied, inherited from their noble Spanish forebears. It was precisely this claim of hereditary superiority and caste-based privilege that came under attack by the Apristas. For the Apristas asserted that the Spanish had brought nothing of value to Peru, nothing but abuse, destruction, and decay—that they were, as the title of one book written about the casta families proclaimed, a "race of vipers" (*raza de víboras*).

Information derived from extensive interviews with surviving members of the Apristas reveals the ways in which teachers in the People's University elab-

orated a critique of the region's aristocratic families, and attempted to forge a
new cultural identity for the region's laboring poor—mestizo and Indian
alike:[8]

> We were forced to meet in secret . . . and so we were constantly on the look-
> out for [informal] opportunities to talk to others [about the ideas of the
> party]. Family celebrations were good for this: [Someone might say to me,]
> "Today is the birthday of the daughter of my *compadre*, let's have some coffee
> to celebrate . . . ," and from that point we began, we began to talk about
> what a family was, and what kinds of things families shared, all the while at-
> tacking the potentate, who refused to share *anything*, and from there we were
> able to get into everything—why we must all be united and why we have to
> defend our own situation. [I might say,] "All of us make up a single commu-
> nity, a single family. We served as the basis for the *Incanato* [the period of rule
> of the Inca empire], did we not? The *Incanato* built the great Inca Highway.
> The *Incanato* built huge fortresses. We could do so then because we were
> united. You were neither cholo nor white nor ugly; we were all united, and
> we want to continue being united; and none of this [from the elite,] "My
> ancestors came from Spain; we are all white; we speak properly, and dress
> properly." NO SEÑOR! I AM YOUR EQUAL! WE ARE ALL
> EQUAL! . . .
>
> [Criticizing the powerful] was our primary goal. . . . We would say to
> them [people at family gatherings like the one described above] that it was
> essential for the people (*el pueblo*) to learn to defend themselves. As an exam-
> ple, we explained that by building fortresses, the Inca had defended them-
> selves from attack by their enemies, and so we needed to understand that *our*
> enemies were those who had money, those who exploited us . . . we ex-
> plained that those who have always taken advantage of the people have been
> the upper class, the castas, the priests, and the *tinterillos* [shyster lawyers], who
> pretend to know a great deal but who know nothing . . . : [we would say to
> them,] "Why do they treat us like cholos, like Indios, like runa?" (Taped in-
> terview with Silvestre Rubio Goivin, muleteer, conducted on Mar. 20, 1983)

The Apristas thus seized upon notions of equality and justice derived from
the discourse of the modern nation-state and the principles of popular sovereignty, and grafted them onto a narrative of the accomplishments of the Inca
empire—evidence of which was clearly visible throughout the region in the

form of huge and impressive ruins. Great things had been possible during the reign of the Inca, the Apristas asserted, because the people were as one. They were not divided by insidious distinctions of any kind—not of race, ancestry, language, or culture—which denigrated some while celebrating others. When the Inca were supreme, the people were equal among themselves, said the APRA, and were united against their enemies. And so they must be again.

It mattered little that the Apristas' construction of a united Inca past was wholly fictional—that the Inca empire had actually been rent by extreme factionalism, largely (but not exclusively) due to resistance to imperial rule by the many "ethnic kingdoms" that were conquered in the course of Inca expansion (Larson 1988; Spalding 1984). Symptomatic of the divided state of the Inca empire were the ruined fortresses themselves. These huge ruins, which dotted the Chachapoyas landscape, were not even built by the Inca, but by a rival ethnic kingdom, the Sachapuyan, one of the many victims of Inca imperial expansion. The Sachapuyans fought fiercely to retain their independence, were conquered by the Inca with great difficulty during an extended campaign toward the middle of the fifteenth century (less than a century prior to the arrival of the Spanish), and thereafter continued to resist Inca domination (Aguilar Briceño 1963: 107–8; Collantes Pizarro 1969: 6–8). Indeed, so hated were the Inca by the Sachapuyans that, after the arrival of the conquistadors, the Sachapuyans sided with the Spanish in helping them defeat the Inca, rather than vice versa (Aguilar Briceño 1963: 109–11; Zubiate Zabarburú 1979).

The imposing ruins that the Apristas pointed to as a symbol of the unity and strength of the Inca thus represented precisely the opposite—the factionalized state of a weak empire. The struggles and divisions of the past, however, were made to disappear in the context of the exigencies of the present; a unified *Imperio Inca* was created out of the prehistoric past to stand as an example of what one possible future for the region might look like. Remote past and imminent future thus became mirror images of one another—and helped mutually construct one another—as the Apristas sought to remake history.

Teachers in the People's University thus took elements of a modern future yet to be won and a golden past tragically lost in order to fashion a convincing critique of the existing state of affairs. The critique focused on the stratified racial hierarchy of the aristocratic order, and the unequal distribution of wealth and power associated with this hierarchy. For it was this racially inscribed system of organization, argued the Apristas, that allowed the powerful to exploit the powerless, to insist that the latter continually demonstrate to the former the most demeaning forms of deferential behavior. It was this system of racially based inequality that prevented *el pueblo* from unifying among themselves, from becoming strong once more, from being able to do great things—as they had in the past.

In offering a challenge to this hegemonic racial structure, the Apristas attempted what might be called a strategy of "subversion from within." That is, rather than deny the existence of the racial categories of the aristocratic order per se, the teachers of the People's University sought to revalue and refashion the categories in such a way as to transform them from mechanisms of oppression into mechanisms of liberation—to turn them against those who had made such brutal use of them for so long. The Aprista critique thus preserved the category of *blanco* (white)—but equated it with "monied, immoral, oppressor" rather than with "aristocratic, Spanish-descended member of the nobility." At the same time, the Apristas collapsed cholo, Indio, and runa into a single category, *el pueblo* (the people)—but equated it with "poor, mistreated descendent of a great and noble civilization / true representative of the modern nation" rather than with "uncouth, semirational savage."

Within the Aprista's reworked system of social order, the "oppressors" remained within the racial classification of the aristocratic order, and thus were clearly associated with social division, hierarchy, and privilege—with characteristics that made it possible to depict them as premodern, nonegalitarian, and antinational. It was these characteristics and associations that justified the Apristas' assertion that those who claimed to occupy the most exalted position in the social order more properly belonged at its bottom. The "victims," on the other hand, were liberated completely from the aristocratic racial hierarchy—and all the negative and pejorative meanings associated with the categories they occupied within it. They were united under a single category derived from the egalitarian, inclusive discourse of the modern nation-state and popular sovereignty—one that stressed the strength, unity, and equality of this group, that qualified this group as preeminently national.[9]

The Apristas thus made common cause not only among the local groups that made up the "laboring family of Amazonas" (cholo, Indio, runa), but also with the nation-state and its democratizing discourse. That is, in their attempt to refashion and revalue the aristocratic racial hierarchy, the Apristas invoked a national form of authority and a national system of social classification. In so doing, however, they did not need to introduce a social category into local life that was foreign either to the laboring poor of the region or to the elite. Rather, the category *el pueblo* was one that had long been heard in public political ritual and in political discourse—and thus was one with which all social groups were already intimately familiar. Furthermore, the Apristas' assertion that el pueblo was a noble, moral, even sacred entity whose interests and needs took precedence over all others—that the people had to be served—was likewise not a notion that was foreign to local society. Ruling casta families had been saying precisely this in political ritual and discourse for decades—even as they made a public mockery of it (see Chapter 5). The Apristas thus seized hold of a category already publicly declared moral and legitimate by the state and the casta families alike—el pueblo—and made it their own. Furthermore, the Apristas used the casta families' consistent ridicule of the very notion of el pueblo—and of popular sovereignty in general—to delegitimate the elite, and to mobilize the local population under "the people's" banner.[10]

In so doing, the Apristas employed their remade and revalued system of social classification toward a novel end. Their division of the population into "blanco" (bad; monied; exploiter) and "el pueblo" (good; poor; victimized) had the important effect of excluding the white oppressors from membership not only in el pueblo, but also in the national community. That is, because the "oppressors" had betrayed the interests of el pueblo—which was tantamount to betraying the interests of the nation—they could easily be depicted as traitors to the national cause. In portraying the casta families in this light, the Apristas did nothing more than echo the language used by the elite for decades in all public political ritual and discourse—whenever members of the ruling casta sought to justify their position of dominance or to condemn those who opposed them (see Chapter 5).

The Aprista critique thus called for unity among cholos, Indios, and runa—among those who made up what the newspaper *Amazonas* called the "laboring family of Amazonas." Like the newspaper's editors, then, the Apristas attempted to forge relations of a more horizontal, "class" character to replace the vertical ties upon which casta organization was based. In this way, the Apristas attempted to construct what was not only an inner moral barrier between

themselves and the casta families, but also a boundary of more national proportions—between the larger Peruvian nation and the aristocratic order. It
was the elite families, argued the Apristas, who were responsible for the region's ills, and by implication for the nation's ills. For the families of the elite
had used their power and influence not only to exploit el pueblo, but also to
turn its members against one another:

> In addition [to the exploiters named above], we pointed out . . . that in the
> villages there was always the person who had 20 or 30 head of cattle [who
> had a bit more wealth than his fellows] . . . and when don Eloy Burga or
> some other *político* would appoint him governor . . . he would take on the
> airs of an important person, and would attempt to abuse his own people,
> forcing them to work or carry messages to the capital [Chachapoyas] without
> paying them anything, or to give them less money than they deserved for
> their animals. (Taped interview with Alberto Lopez Torrejón, carpenter,
> conducted on Apr. 12, 1986)

Teachers in the People's University explained to all who would listen that
they wanted to do away with the divisions among el pueblo created by the
elite so that the people could be strong again—that they wanted to bring to an
end the outrages to which everyone was subject at the hands of the region's
ruling casta families. As the teachers elaborated their critique of the casta order, they attempted to seize upon experiences of abuse and humiliation with
which all their listeners could identify—the insecurities of person and property
that were ongoing realities for virtually everyone:

> We would remind them of the abuses that had been forced upon them by the
> casta families—about the girls who had been raped, the money that had been
> stolen, and the humiliation that they had all endured: In those days the elite
> families all chose servants from among the *colono* [peon] families on their ha-
> ciendas, to cook and clean their [the elite families'] great homes, and to look
> after their children. Even boys in their teens had maids to look after them, to
> clean up for them, and also to bathe them! It was very common for boys of
> the elite to force themselves on their maids while they were being bathed.
> The poor girls could do nothing to defend themselves. When they became
> pregnant, the child was baptized, but not with the name of the father—for
> the casta families were determined to preserve the purity of their family

names. So the child was given the name of the prefect or the subprefect, and the girl was sent back to her family on the hacienda to raise the child.

We also spoke about the problem of justice. I would say to them [people at family gatherings; people engaged in casual conversations], "What can you do when they [the rich] steal your livestock and get away with it because they have money? What can you do when they use their money to buy justice when you protest [about the theft] to the judge, and you lose your court case after you have spent all your own money?"

We also reminded them about the way that they were not allowed to enter the homes of the rich by the front door nor to wait in the drawing room nor to sit on the furniture: We were forced to enter by the side door, and to wait [outside] where there was a dirt floor and to remain standing while we waited. You couldn't enter [the drawing room] because they said you were a cholo, a runa. [A member of the elite might say to a cholo or a runa,] "You are going to soil the chair if you sit in it!" And the chair was nothing but a wooden plank!

We also spoke about how the people had been abused in all the wars and battles that had been started by the castas. It was el pueblo, the Indios, who had been forced to fight in the wars, to die in the battles, while the blancos gave the orders, but always from a position of safety. (Taped interview with Carlosmagno Guevara Santillán, carpenter, conducted on Sept. 4, 1986)

In short, according to the teachers of the People's University, the aristo- cratic casta families had preyed upon and abused el pueblo in virtually every way imaginable. The castas had violated the sexual honor of el pueblo's women, had illegally seized the livestock of its men, had extorted the little currency el pueblo possessed, and had forced el pueblo's sons into battle to be killed and maimed. And as if these injustices were not enough, the casta families also insisted on the right to humiliate and denigrate el pueblo by treat- ing its members as beings of less social worth, less culture. The cholos, the Indios, the runa, were expected to behave in a manner befitting the inferior station in life they were said to occupy. That is, at all times they were expected to behave with subservience, deference, and "respect" for their superiors.

In addition to enumerating the abuses perpetrated on el pueblo by the casta families, the teachers of the People's University attacked claims by the mem- bers of the elite that descent from aristocratic Spaniards qualified them as a superior, hereditary elite entitled to rule over people they disparaged as their social inferiors—uncouth, barely civilized Indians. The Apristas did so by arguing that the conquistadors had been anything but noble, cultured, or elite. Rather, the Spanish had been brutal and rapacious men, willing to engage in the most barbarous forms of behavior imaginable in the course of their incessant quest for greater amounts of wealth. The heritage they had left Peru was the source of its problems, claimed the Apristas, not the source of its greatness. For the Spanish had destroyed the once-great Inca empire, and thereafter had turned brother against brother.

The Apristas thus sought to undermine the position of the elite by calling into question the historical vision the elite invoked in order to legitimate its claim to privileged status—by attacking the "origin myth" that established its members as an elite:

> Speaking of the Spanish Conquest, we said that the Spanish brought us nothing good. They kidnapped the Inca [Atahualpa, the ruler], used deceit to steal all of his wealth, and then murdered him. They destroyed the *Incanato* and all its great accomplishments, and they replaced it with the abuses and the greed of the conquistadors, the Jesuits, the priests, and others.
>
> The example I liked to use was of the priest of Quinjalca [a peasant village], who was allowed to divide the cemetery [of the village] into three parts—heaven, purgatory, and hell. Which part of the cemetery you buried the remains of your family members in depended on how much you were able to pay. A prayer to the dead? If you wanted to offer a prayer to the dead, . . . in which holy water was used . . . and [in which] the singers also wailed as they sung, then [the priest might say to the villagers,] "I am the representative of God and as [His] representative I can do this [the prayer to the dead] and so save the soul [of the deceased relative], so bring me three of your best bulls and I will choose one." One priest would have ten bulls, another 50, and still another 200! (Taped interview with Victor Santillán Gutierrez,[11] conducted on Aug. 10, 1990)

According to the Apristas, the casta families were anything but refined, cultured aristocrats whose ancestors had brought civilization to a benighted land. Rather, they and their predecessors were guilty of the worst kinds of outrage possible. They had come to power through deception and murder, had gone on to destroy a great civilization, and thereafter had divided, victimized, and abused the defenseless population of Indians in whatever way they could. In order to maintain themselves in their positions of power and privilege, members of the elite had subverted all the institutions that could have provided justice and protection to el pueblo. The elite had subverted the courts, the system of justice, the police, and even the Church. Its members went so far as to let their hunger for wealth put their own power at risk—by trading away security (in the form of the number of gendarmes adequate to protect them from their enemies) for profit:

> We criticized the Spanish severely, and we criticized as well the inheritance they left to those who had controlled the department ever since [the end of the colonial period]. . . . We reminded them [el pueblo] about the way the políticos stole the money of the government and el pueblo—by claiming that there were 40 gendarmes when there were really only, say, twelve, and then making one of their servants sign the [account] book [of the Gendarmery] as if the servant were the gendarme while the político pocketed the gendarme's salary. (Taped interview with Victor Santillán Gutierrez, conducted on June 10, 1991)

In contrast to a society built on abuses, outrages, and humiliations, the APRA proposed a society based on principles of equality, justice, individual independence, and the mutual respect of one person for another:

> These were the abuses we wanted to do away with. The APRA was for *equality*. And straight away [after critiquing the abuses of the elite] we would talk about the famous storming of the Bastille in France on the 14th of July and about the call for Human Rights. . . . We would tell them about how the Bastille fell, about how the people seized the Bastille, and we would explain that we must be just as united against the landowners. . . .
>
> For example, concerning the 28th of July—Independence Day—we asked for *whom* is this Independence Day? We spoke of what it means to be independent, to not have to be beholden to anyone, so that no one can dominate us, so that no one can command us. (Taped interview with Victor Santillán Gutierrez, conducted on July 30, 1990)

In this way the Apristas attempted to place Chachapoyas within a historical imaginary wholly different from the history of noble lineage asserted by the region's aristocratic families. The Apristas invited el pueblo to imagine itself as

centrally involved in a world-historical process whose importance and scope
went far beyond the parochial claims to nobility of the backward local elite. Indios, cholos, and runa—people who had long been denied social value of any
kind—were asked to think of themselves as important actors in a global process of the unfolding of democratic and equalitarian ideals. This was a movement whose glorious history stretched back at least as far as revolutionary
France in the West, and that encompassed ideals already uttered (in political
ritual and discourse) but yet to be made real in the recent history of Peru. El
pueblo could become a part of this history—could become a part of its *own*
history—if it so chose.

An Inca past construed as strong and unified was thus integrated with contemporary movements of democracy and equality to construct an alternative
origin myth for the region and its people, an alternative history to that authored by the aristocratic casta families. Continuity between remote Inca past
and modern present was asserted on the basis of what was claimed to be shared
democratic and equalitarian ideals. In this alternative history, the Spanish conquest of the Inca and the centuries of abuse that followed represented a kind of
Dark Age—a tragic but ultimately temporary interruption of a more fundamental history, a more vital social process, involving the progressive realization of principles of justice and equality. According to this alternative history,
neither the Spanish nor their heritage truly belonged in Peru. Both were ut-
terly foreign to what was essentially *of* the region and the nation—and thus
both had to be removed, exorcised, from local affairs.

Indeed, according to the Apristas, there was much that el pueblo would
have to do in order to help purge local life of the aristocratic heritage left by
the Spanish. If it was to rid itself of the pernicious influences of the casta families and become strong once more, those who made up el pueblo would have
to be prepared to confront those who oppressed them. They would have to be
prepared to fight in order to defend themselves. In order to convey this dimension of the APRA's vision to the region's laboring poor, teachers in the
People's University once again drew upon images of a strong Inca past:

> [I might say, addressing a group informally,] "Why do you submit to this hu-
> miliation of, '*Taitito, buenos días, buenas tardes*' [that is, addressing members of
> the elite with terms of deference and respect]? It is enough to say, '*Buenos*

días,' and nothing more, with your forehead held high [and not looking down at the ground, as cholos and runa were expected to do when addressing members of the elite]. The Inca always looked upward at the sun—the Indio, the most humble creature of all, always looked at the sun. It was for this reason that they built their fortresses on the tops of the mountains, so that from there they could gaze up at the sun; with their heads held high and toward the sky. Why do you do otherwise? . . . You are the equal of that man [a member of the elite]. You are all *closer* to God than he, for it is he who steals what belongs to you. On the other hand you are a humble man, a humble creature, so why this humiliation?" (Taped interview with Victor Castilla Pizarro,[12] conducted on Aug. 3, 1990)

Teachers of the People's University also commonly invoked the principles of popular sovereignty—specifically, notions of equality and justice—in appealing to el pueblo to resist the abuses of the powerful:

[I might say to people informally,] "Whenever the governor says to you, 'You must pay me, if not with money then with a chicken, a guinea pig, with a few eggs,' you must tell him, 'No, no, if you want my things you must pay for them.' If you do otherwise, it is a form of adulation. Never show adulation to anyone!" (Taped interview with Alberto Lopez Torrejón, conducted on Apr. 12, 1986)

Whether on the basis of a proud Inca past or a modern future still to be won, however, the most general exhortation of those who taught in the People's University was to stand up to injustice, to fight for what is right, so that the great and the humble would be treated in the same way:

[I might say to people informally,] "You must fight if you want justice, justice means everyone being on the same level, not on different levels; so that what is possible for the humble is the same as what is possible for the great." (Ibid.)

Teachers of the People's University did more, however, than just encourage el pueblo to refuse to engage in the kind of subservient behavior expected of them by members of the elite, and to expect to have to fight for justice. In addition, teachers also explained concrete strategies to "the people" that would help them to resist the demands of the region's políticos—those in Chachapoyas as well as in the rural districts. The APRA's strategy of resistance stressed above all else the strength that came from unity:

> The peasants, el pueblo, had very little power at that time. So we always tried to find ways to help them overcome this problem. In addition to those who ruled from the capital of the department [Chachapoyas], there was always the local boss in the village—the *compadre* of those in the capital, [who might say to a villager,] "You, go to Chachapoyas to deliver this message to the subprefect." [And I would say to the villagers,] "And you go? Does he come to your house to visit you, and ask you to go as a favor? Does he offer to pay you? You must be paid, and you must be free to refuse him. . . . And you must help one another resist. If [the governor] has a revolver and he threatens you, return with ten or twenty people together. In front of everyone, refuse him. Make it a communal cause. Together, you will overcome the ambition of this one person, the person whose ambition is *don dinero* ["Mr. Money"]. (Taped interview with Antonio Valdez Vasquez, muleteer, conducted on May 16, 1983)

The Apristas continually stressed unity as the most effective way of resisting the abuses of the local political bosses. As the passage above continues, we find the teacher of the People's University recommending this strategy as a way of resisting a different kind of abuse by a local boss:

> [And I would say to the villagers,] "If the governor tries to arrest you and take you prisoner for refusing his order, you must all unite, and twenty or thirty of you together should go to the governor and tell him, 'We are going to take you prisoner and we are going to burn down your house.' And you must burn down the house of the governor. But you can only do these things in common, when you are united. But each one alone and afraid, as you are now, never. We have to be united like our ancestors [the Inca] were in order to do tremendous things like this. Close by to us here are the great ruins, the *huacas* built by our ancestors. We must be united, as they were, in order to do great things like they did. (Ibid.)

The final element in the Apristas' plan for unifying the local population— for preventing each person from being "alone and afraid"—focused explicitly on the individual. That is, it focused on forming disciplined, proud, and autonomous subjects, each of whom would be capable of resisting oppression and speaking out against inequality. The Apristas believed that in order to do so, it was necessary to transform the consciousness of the regional population—to instill in them the independence of thought and the respect for justice upon which resistance was necessarily based. The best way to reach into the minds of the populace, believed the Apristas, was by instituting schooling and a program in literacy training among as much of the population as possible. The rationale behind this dimension of the APRA's vision is revealed by the teachers of the People's University:

All of these problems [of inequality, oppression, and servility] resulted from the ignorance of the people, and the lack of schools, where people learn to form their personalities and learn to defend their interests, to refuse to be humiliated. . . . We explained to el pueblo that the reason that [the elite] wanted us to remain ignorant was so that they could exploit us, so that we were not able to protest against this or that abuse. . . . [The elite] didn't want anyone to build new schools because they knew that schools produce leaders, and that when there is leadership then domination comes to an end automatically.

It was for this reason that we called our school *La Universidad del Pueblo* [the University of the People]—there we taught reading and writing. We brought with us loose pieces of paper and notebooks and we gave them to the students, and we told them that . . . in this notebook we would learn to write from "A" to "M": [A teacher in the *Universidad del Pueblo*, instructing a student, might say,] "Now you repeat [what I have written]; now in the other part [of the notebook] the other letters. Now let's do your name. The most important thing of all is for you to learn to write your name, because your name is *you*." And from there we would begin to talk about what it means to be a person, dragging the conscience of the student along behind. [A teacher would say,] "Well then, your name is Luis—write that." [And the student, eagerly responding to his teacher's request, might say,] "I know how to write now; I wrote my name on the wall [of my house]." And we would see his name, written on the wall of his house with a piece of charcoal from the fire. "Luis," or in that men always had two names, "José Luis." "José Luis Chasquirol." This is how he learned to write his name. . . . All of this was to form the personalities of these people. (Taped interview with Silvestre Rubio Goivin, muleteer, conducted on Mar. 22, 1983)

As implied in these passages, the Apristas conceived of their mission as going beyond simply protesting against abuse and organizing the local population to resist the casta families. In order to rid local society of all residual influences of the casta order, it was necessary to form rational, autonomous subjects out of the local population: people who were freed from feelings of inferiority and servility, who would not be in awe of the elite and its members' noble pretensions. Men who knew their own worth as individuals—who knew that they were the equals of any member of the elite—would be most capable of resisting their oppressors, would be able to fight for justice, would be able to stand up for their rights.

It was necessary, therefore, to free men's minds from the weight of the past, from the power and legitimacy of elite claims. Literacy and schooling were essential if this was to be accomplished, for it was by means of literacy that men could acquire the independence of thought necessary to question the assertions of the elite. To this day, the teachers of the People's University still speak with amazement about the success they had in transforming many people from weak, servile creatures into proud and strong individuals, who were able to confront the casta families with great determination. They describe this as a change in mentality, a change in orientation, a change that came from the schooling they received in the People's University:

> At this time . . . Amazonas was dominated by *la casta política* [the ruling casta families in Chachapoyas]. Each family had its own political bosses in the villages. The political boss of Conila [a peasant village] was *fulano de tal* [such-and-such a person], an Echaista. Another [competing] boss was a Rubista, and another, because he owned six cats [because he was slightly wealthier than his fellow villagers], a Burgista. The [ruling] political boss was generally the mayor, or the justice of the peace, or especially the governor. If he was a Rubista, he would tell other villagers, "You must become a Rubista." If he was asked why, he would say, "Because you must!"
>
> Each family had its own followers. . . . I used to ask people, "What is Rubismo? Why are you a Rubista?" They would respond, "Because I am a Rubista." "But *why*?" I would ask. "Because I *am*," they would reply, this time more stubbornly.
>
> The políticos had no dogma [no ideology]. Rubismo was nothing but being a follower of the Rubio family. If they [the elite families] had had dog-

mas, they could have established themselves and their principles, and could have had real influence.

But we [the Apristas] *did* have principles, which we taught in the *Universidad del Pueblo*. We attacked all those who took advantage of el pueblo—the political bosses, the priests, the tinterillos, the castas, everyone. And I had the satisfaction of seeing with my own eyes how we were able to prepare boys who spoke out directly against the políticos! Some left the APRA years later and became involved with the communists! Think of the social and political advance they made! Think of the enormous distance they traveled! (Taped interview with Nicolas Muñoz,[13] carpenter, conducted on Oct. 4, 1985)

By early 1930 there were secret cells of the APRA in virtually every district of all three provinces of Amazonas—six in Bongará, sixteen in Luya, and fifteen in Chachapoyas—with anywhere from one to eight members in each cell (see below). All were actively involved in promoting the People's University, and in increasing the ranks of the party. Cell leaders in the outlying districts of the department were uniformly "graduates" of the People's University in Chachapoyas. The following internal communiqué (dated February 8, 1930) is from a graduate of the Chachapoyas People's University who went on to become the secretary general of the party for the province of Bongará (this secretariat was located in the town of San Carlos). He writes to his former teacher in the Chachapoyas People's University, who was also the departmental secretary general of the APRA (this secretariat was located in Chachapoyas). The letter conveys something of the party's organizational efforts, its internal chain of command, and the relationship between the activities of provincial and departmental party representatives on the one hand, and those of the party's national headquarters in Lima on the other.[14]

After enumerating to the departmental secretary general the names of the party members in each of the province's six district-level cells, the provincial secretary general for Bongará reports:

As always, I continue moving forward, recruiting more adepts. . . . As soon as possible, I will make up a complete list of all party personnel, as well as of all comrades and sympathizers, and I will send it to you.

I have received a circular from the Secretariat of Organization in Lima, in which I have been ordered to establish the U.P.G.P. [the *Universidad Popular*

Gonzalez Prada] in Jumbilla [capital of Bongará province], as well as branches [of the university] in all of the districts. . . .

Until now I have received no communication from [the secretary general of] Luya [province], nor any APRA leaflets or newspapers from him. . . .

The Secretariat of Organization in Lima informs me that I have been sent the instructions necessary to start the university previously referred to. These instructions have yet to arrive.

Your student and comrade. ([APA1], Feb. 8, 1930)

The identities of those who made up the secret cells of the APRA in Bongará—and who were soon to initiate the People's University throughout the province, in town and countryside alike—reveal much about the kinds of people who were drawn into the vanguard of this movement of social transformation. Virtually all came from social backgrounds that would qualify them as cholos in the eyes of the elite. That is, they occupied a kind of intermediate racial/occupational stratum between the white, landed elite of Chachapoyas and the Indian peasants of the countryside. Though many owned small plots of land, none were peasants themselves. Rather, they made up a small rural "middle class" that as a whole was involved in a variety of economic activities—predominantly in agriculture, petty trade, civil service, artisanry, and transportation. Interestingly, they were literate as well—all had attended elementary school in Chachapoyas (at the *Centro Escolar de Varones* no. 131), and most had finished high school in Chachapoyas as well (at the Colegio Nacional San Juan de la Libertad). In other words, they were precisely the kinds of people to whom a critique of the casta order and a call for justice and democracy were most likely to appeal.[15]

As with the social movement that coalesced around Ricardo Feijóo Reina and the newspaper *Amazonas*, it is difficult to gauge the precise number of people who became involved in the APRA, and when they became so involved. It is clear, however, that Aprismo was an exceptionally widespread, unusually influential social movement from its earliest days—even more than Feijóo's Partido Laboral Independiente Amazonense. Indeed, many informants report that they gave visible support to Feijóo's party while they were clandestinely involved with the APRA, as the latter was outlawed while the former was not. One indication of the popularity of the APRA can be gleaned from the party's involvement in the presidential election of 1931—when it was (temporarily) not against the law to belong to the party. The departmental committee of the APRA for Amazonas claimed that 3,200 Apristas had voted in the election (*La Tribuna*, Nov. 2, 1931, p. 3). When it is kept in mind that illiterate peasants and women were still denied the franchise at this time, and that the entire population of Chachapoyas was only about 5,000 people, this figure clearly represents a social movement of major proportions.[16]

The Partido Laboral Independiente Amazonense and the APRA shared a great deal in terms of their vision of a transformed social order, and the role of the forces of modernity in effecting these changes. Both movements saw the department of Amazonas as a remote backwater where archaic forms of behavior and association lingered that had long since disappeared from the rest of the civilized world. Both movements also identified what was variously referred to as the "feudal" or "medieval" or "colonial" political structure as the most important obstacle to bringing the region into the modern world. The Partido Laboral and the APRA further concurred on the importance of bringing to an end the region's physical remoteness—by integrating it directly into national networks of communication, transportation, and education. And finally, the two movements agreed that effecting these changes depended critically on the ability to remake the region's poor, laboring men—to mold them into rational, autonomous, independent subjects who would carry within them the ideals of popular sovereignty.

In addition to lifting the weight of material oppression from the backs of el pueblo, then, the Partido Laboral and the APRA alike both sought to free people from the feelings of cultural inferiority and lack of worth from which they suffered within the hegemonic racial hierarchy of the casta order. This latter goal entailed constructing a new cultural identity for the people of the "laboring family of Amazonas." It depended on locating them within a historical trajectory that was independent of and more powerful than the historical vision of classical nobility asserted by the region's aristocratic families. Such an alternative historical trajectory for the laboring poor had to subsume the origin myth of the elite. It had to show that the classical world of nobility with which the elite families claimed kinship (in order to legitimate their status as elite) was anything but a fixed point of origin that could be invoked as representing something basic and essential about people in society. That is, an alternative historical imaginary for the laboring poor had to show that there was nothing natural or inevitable about the cultural assertions of the elite.

The more powerful vision of history and human nature asserted by the Partido Laboral and the APRA showed precisely this. It subsumed the historical vision of the elite because it showed classical nobility to be wholly artificial—to be a temporary and retrograde interruption of a historical and social process of global proportions. This was a process that was well under way (among the Inca) before the Spanish arrived to temporarily derail it—a historical and social process whose influence expanded in scope thereafter to engulf most of the globe (outside of Amazonas). The Partido Laboral and the APRA alike sought to apprise the laboring poor of this alternative history, to make them aware of the privileged position they occupied within this process of global transformation. They sought to do so by means of "education"—conceived of as a broad project of transformation in culture, consciousness, and politics.

It was in this sense that the local population looked toward what were seen as the "progressive forces of the modern world," located beyond the boundaries of Amazonas, for the region's salvation. It was in this sense as well that local society reached out to the state as its true friend and potential benefactor. For the central government, as the national representative of this global-historical process, was the most logical ally to help the laboring poor rid itself of the aristocratic elite. Indeed, all the government would have to do in order to bring this about would be to honor the principles of democracy, equality under the law, and individual rights and protections upon which it was founded as a republican state—principles whose legitimacy it had given voice to in political ritual and discourse for decades.

As we shall see presently, due to a series of reforms instituted by the central government in the early 1930s—which resulted in a profoundly different state presence in the region—it did indeed appear that the central government was finally disposed to make good on its long-standing promise to provide "the people" with the rights and protections upon which modern nationhood is based. Within a very short period of time, the coercive and extractive capabilities of the casta families evaporated, and at least some segments of the "laboring family of Amazonas" began to enjoy the kinds of privilege for which they had clamored in previous years. That is, for select portions of the region's laboring poor, local social relations increasingly appeared to resemble the democratic, equalitarian ideals expounded upon with such force by the Partido Laboral and the APRA.

In short, the formerly marginalized middle sectors of Chachapoyas no longer found themselves in a position where their life possibilities were so severely and obviously circumscribed by the elite. They no longer found themselves ridiculed and devalued, and forced to adopt demeaning and subservient forms of behavior when in the presence of the elite. Nor did the middle sectors find themselves excluded any longer from important social activities because of their "low" station in life. Instead, these very groups enjoyed new, expanded life possibilities. They acted and increasingly were treated as the equals of anyone. And they quickly seized hold of, reorganized, and actively began to determine the direction of the town's social and cultural life.

The formerly marginalized middle sectors of Chachapoyas—those who had led the fight for democratization and modernization—found that a new social and political space had opened up for them in the early 1930s. They found that they were empowered by the central government just as they sought alliance with the central government in order to be empowered.

8 The Disintegration of the Casta Order

The señoritas of the upper class, and all the members of
the upper class, were people who always looked down
their noses at the rest of us, but in a very short period of
time the moment arrived in which the high society of
Amazonas left [for Lima], and only a few [of the upper
class] remained. Most preferred to leave the region entirely
rather than mix with us. [They said to one another,] "We
must move to Lima, so we don't have to be among the
cholos, the Indios, the runa!" And from that point on the
[remaining] señoritas of the upper class began dancing
with me! Imagine that! We were all dancing together! And
only a few years prior there was none of that. And
afterward we [the Apristas] talked about how we had
changed the mentality of the people. It was as if we were
living in a different epoch!

Antonio Valdez Vasquez, muleteer and Aprista,
talking about the rapid changes in Chachapoyas society
during the early 1930s

Within the space of a few short years, the casta-based political order—with
its congerie of material, behavioral, and symbolic markers of privilege and
distinction—disintegrated in the Chachapoyas region. This chapter analyzes
the interacting set of national and local forces and relationships that initiated
this breakdown. It deals particularly with two interrelated processes: the emergence of a key transitional moment when those who had been involved in
the "movements of *democratización*" (see Chapters 6 and 7) rose up and seized
political power, and their subsequent attempts to convert the social order they
had formerly imagined into reality. In other words, a new political space was

opened and then quickly filled by those involved in the movements of democratización, resulting in profound changes in the organization of regional society.[1]

On August 22, 1930, army officer Luis M. Sanchez Cerro deposed President/Dictator Augusto Leguía in a military coup that brought Leguía's eleven years of rule to an end. Sanchez Cerro was from a humble background— a man of "the people"—rather than from the country's traditional ruling elite.[2] He had enormous popularity among and came to represent the hopes and aspirations of many of Peru's burgeoning lumpen proletariat and working class— the "masses" (Burga and Flores Galindo 1979: 186; Stein 1980: chs. 4–5). Indeed, 1930 was the point at which the masses, and the forces of populism, became decisive as independent forces in Peruvian politics for the first time— the point at which the traditional ruling elite was no longer so able to control the desires of the subaltern (Burga and Flores Galindo 1979: 150–91).[3]

At the fall of Leguía, the traditional elite was unable to rely on the institutions and mechanisms of rule that had served it so well in the past, because these institutions had been dismantled during the previous eleven years of Leguía's rule (referred to as the *oncenio*). While in power, Leguía had persecuted all the political parties of the elite—leading to their breakdown and disappearance from the national political scene—and had replaced them with a party structure of his own making (his was the "Democratic" party). He had also manipulated the electoral process so as to remove from office congressional representatives who were not faithful to his cause; as a result, most prefects and subprefects in the country's departments and provinces were also supporters of Leguía.[4] The Supreme Court and the lesser ranks of the judiciary nationwide (judges of the first and second instance), much of the staff of the national university, virtually all of the government bureaucracy (in Lima and in the provinces), and even the Archbishopry of Lima, were purged of anyone who was suspected of having lingering ties with or loyalty to those members of the country's traditional ruling elite who opposed Leguía (Basadre 1968–69, 13; Burga and Flores Galindo 1979: 125–42; Stein 1980: 41–48). The positions thus vacated were filled with the followers of Leguía.[5] After eleven years of relentless assault on its institutions of rule, the elite opposition had been effectively marginalized from the direct exercise of power in the sphere of public politics.[6]

When Leguía was deposed in the military coup of August 22, 1930, his successor, Sanchez Cerro, went about dismantling many of the political institutions created by Leguía (in particular, the president's political party) and purging the remaining institutions (the judiciary, the national university, and the government bureaucracy) of those loyal to the former president. The result was a significant power vacuum nationwide. Unable to draw on the political institutions of the pre-Leguía era—which had been dismantled during the oncenio—and confronted with the rise of "the masses" (Burga and Flores Galindo 1979: 150–206; Stein 1980: 49–82; Sulmont 1975), the country's traditional ruling class was not able to take a direct and decisive role in controlling the electoral process, as they had in the past.[7] Indeed, in the electoral contests of 1931, which decided upon a new president for Peru and a new Constituent Congress (which drafted a new constitution for the country), the main contending forces were two different *populist* figures who vied for the approval of the greatest number of "the people": Victor Raúl Haya de la Torre, founder and leader of the APRA political party, and Sanchez Cerro himself.[8]

The fall of Leguía in 1930 had immediate and extremely important repercussions within the Chachapoyas region. For the previous twenty years (since 1909; see Chapter 4), coalitions of the Pizarro-Rubio-Linch families had controlled most deputyships and senatorial posts for the region, the prefecture and subprefectures, most important judicial appointments, and the region's police forces—and thus were able to dominate departmental affairs as a whole (see Chapters 3 and 4). In the process, they systematically persecuted the leading families that made up the opposition—in particular the Echaiz, the Hurtado, and the Burga, but a host of other less-prominent families as well.

After such a long period of rule by a single power block, the state of the "opposition forces" in the Chachapoyas region paralleled the condition of the traditional political elite nationally. By the end of the oncenio, the leading families of the opposition in Chachapoyas were fragmented and dispersed. That is, despite their ongoing attempts to do so, the elite families of Chachapoyas who were made marginal during the extended period of rule by the Pizarro-Rubio-Linch coalitions ultimately failed to organize themselves into a viable new casta that could challenge the position of the region's power holders.

In large part, the ultimate failure of opposition forces to organize themselves into a viable challenger to the Pizarro-Rubio-Linch was the result of their two unsuccessful attempts to seize control of the department by force of arms—and the repression that came in the wake of these abortive uprisings. The first attempt came just prior to the presidential and congressional elections of May 1919. At this time, the Burga-Hurtado casta—which had been joined by the Echaiz family—found itself completely excluded from the *asambleas de mayores contribuyentes*, whose personnel was so crucial in deciding the outcome of electoral contests (see Chapter 3). Although the Echaiz-Burga-Hurtado casta subsequently organized its own asamblea (see Basadre 1980: 91), Congress refused to recognize its legality. Faced with certain loss when the voting results were tallied, the Echaiz-Burga-Hurtado forces mounted an assault on the prefecture and held it for a period of weeks, but were ultimately driven out by a combined force of Pizarro-Rubio-Linch clients and government troops (sent to Chachapoyas from the neighboring department of Cajamarca at the order of President Leguía).[9]

The second attempt to depose the ruling casta came in 1923–24, after Senator Pablo M. Pizarro had taken part in a failed national plot to overthrow Leguía (see Basadre 1968–69, 13: 112–27). When the president learned of Pizarro's involvement in the coup attempt, Pizarro made a hasty retreat from Lima to Chachapoyas, where he received word from the Ministry of Government that he was to surrender himself to the local authorities. He refused, and instead sought refuge at *Santa Cruz*, an estate his family owned near Chachapoyas.[10] With *Santa Cruz* as his base of operations, in early 1924 Pizarro attempted to lead a secessionist movement that would have established Amazonas as an independent political entity.

Taking advantage of these chaotic conditions, the Echaiz-Burga-Hurtado once again took control of the prefecture by force of arms, and again held it for approximately one month (in March 1924). When government troops arrived (from Cajamarca) to stamp out Pizarro's secessionist movement, however, the Echaiz-Burga-Hurtado casta was "evicted" from the prefecture. Thereafter, the troops delivered control of departmental affairs to the Rubio-Linch family, which had remained loyal to Leguía throughout all of Pizarro's "traitorous" activities despite its long-standing alliance with and ties of marriage to the Pizarro-Rubio casta.[11] The government troops lingered in Chachapoyas for a period of six months, scattering the forces of the Echaiz-Burga-

Hurtado, driving its leading members into flight and seclusion, and dismantling the casta for all intents and purposes. So favored was the Rubio-Linch casta by Leguía subsequently that the president appointed Arturo as Minister of the Navy in 1926, and as Minister of Government in 1928. With such strong backing from the country's leader, and with the forces of the Echaiz-Burga-Hurtado fragmented and dispersed, the Rubio-Linch faced no uprisings whatsoever from 1924 until the fall of Leguía in 1930.[12]

When Leguía's fall finally came, and the Rubio-Linch found itself without its national political patron, the ruling casta's enemies were anxious to strike. After so many years of persecution by the Rubio-Linch, however, the elite families of the opposition were weak and fragmented, their forces dispersed and lacking in unity. Informed of Leguía's demise via telegram by a political ally in Lima (see below), the Echaiz family was nonetheless quickly able to assemble an overwhelming group of armed followers, who attacked and took control of the prefecture in short order. Eleodoro Echaiz—one of five sons of Echaiz family patriarch José María Echaiz—was immediately installed as the new prefect. After a feeble and futile attempt by the Ministry of Government to appoint a prefect of its own choosing (see Chapter 1), Eleodoro Echaiz was declared the official prefect, and the central government left control of affairs in the hands of the region's new power holders.[13]

But who were the region's new power holders? What made it possible for the Echaiz family, fragmented and disorganized after Leguía's extended rule, to assemble on very short notice a large group of people who were sufficiently motivated to risk their lives in making an armed assault on the prefecture?

The Echaiz were successful in their bid for the prefecture because the family was able to draw on a non-casta-based political grouping—el pueblo—that had come into being by the late 1920s within the region. That is, it was the marginalized middle sectors of Chachapoyas who made up the vast majority of the armed group that the Echaiz led in taking the prefecture from the Rubio-Linch. Understanding the involvement of el pueblo in the "revolution" of August 1930 requires a consideration of the new forms of political alliance and contestation that emerged regionally (and nationally) toward the close of the oncenio.[14]

THE BREAKDOWN OF CASTA-BASED
POLITICAL GROUPINGS

As had occurred so often in the past, those who sought to challenge the region's power holders toward the end of the oncenio did so by means of the electoral process. In this case, the congressional and presidential elections of August 1929 provided the context for such a challenge. Early in 1929, well over a year prior to the fall of Leguía in the national capital and of the Rubio-Linch in Chachapoyas, Ricardo Feijóo Reina (publisher of *Amazonas*) declared his candidacy for the deputyship of Chachapoyas. In the process, he publicly opposed Arturo and Miguel Rubio-Linch, who had controlled the deputyships of Chachapoyas and Bongará provinces, respectively, for the previous twenty years. The Rubio-Linch candidates were almost certain to win again in the August elections, in light of the fact that they were the privileged clients of President Leguía.[15]

Feijóo spoke out against the Rubio-Linch family in extremely critical terms—branding its members as the worst kinds of tyrants and exploiters, who abused the local population without cease in order to satisfy their own lust for power and wealth (see Chapter 6). To have some chance of victory at the polls, however, Feijóo had to do more than this. It was also essential that he establish ties with at least some influential families in the Chachapoyas region.[16] And this is precisely what he did. By the time he announced his candidacy for the deputyship of Chachapoyas, it was known publicly that Feijóo had made a pact with the Echaiz, one of the Rubio-Linch's most important adversarial families. This pact in turn affiliated Feijóo with the Echaiz's affines and allies, the Hurtado and Burga families.[17]

Though this new alliance had superficial similarities to the broad coalition of white aristocratic families of Spanish descent that had made up the core and "second tier" of ruling castas in times past (see Chapters 2 and 3), it differed from casta organization in significant ways. For the broader environment within which the Feijóo-Echaiz pact was made in the late 1920s was qualitatively different from that of previous decades. The key difference involved the appearance of el pueblo on the national and local political scenes—and of a new breed of political leader who knew how to appeal to el pueblo.[18]

As explained in previous chapters, in 1926 a group of organic intellectuals who were deeply committed to the ideals of popular sovereignty began to emerge within the department of Amazonas. They worked tirelessly to bring new notions of legitimate social and political order to "the people" of Amazonas, and in the process helped bring el pueblo into being. Feijóo was among this group of organic intellectuals. Using his newspaper *Amazonas* as the mouthpiece for a transformed image of regional affairs, Feijóo had become the champion of a new kind of political constituency—the group that his newspaper called "the laboring family of Amazonas." That is, under the banner of democracy, equality, and a more open society—one stripped of the invidious distinctions of race and caste upon which the aristocratic order was based—Feijóo had mobilized on his behalf the marginalized middle sectors of the towns of Amazonas.

The new political community brought into being by the organic intellectuals of Amazonas was made up predominantly of carpenters, tailors, blacksmiths, saddlemakers, muleteers, breadmakers, petty merchants, small shopkeepers, cantina owners, and lower-level public employees—people who had long been denied social recognition of any kind within the cultural logic of aristocratic sovereignty. They were also people whose life possibilities had been severely circumscribed by the monopoly on power and privilege exercised by the regional elite. Feijóo and his fellow organizers were able to appeal to these marginalized people in large part because the transformed social order the middle sectors were asked to envision was one that promised to liberate them from both of these limitations.

On the one hand, the new society imagined within the movements of democratización was one in which restrictions of all kinds would be lifted from the backs of all individuals—one in which people would be free to pursue whatever life course they chose according to their inclinations and abilities, regardless of race, caste, or class. On the other hand, the social world being constructed in the minds of the middle class was one that inverted the symbolic valuation assigned to traditional elite and middle class. The middle class was asked to cast aside the denigrating image under which it labored within the cultural logic of aristocratic sovereignty—that of an ignorant, uncouth, racially impure group whose relegation to an inferior station in life required no explanation or justification. Rather than think of themselves as unworthy, and of the casta families as representing the elite, the middle sectors were invited to conceive of *themselves* as being the region's true elite. What made them an elite, however, was not race, or ancestry, or any other "accident of birth," but their moral and ethical superiority—they each exemplified the disciplined, hard-working, selfless individual of which the modern world was everywhere composed. As such, they were the vanguard of a movement of global proportions that boasted a deep history and was driven by evolutionary necessity. This was the movement that would "carry to the most remote corners of the national territory the renovating winds and the modern ideas of the current evolutionary epoch, in which the imperative of justice and humanity must triumph" (*Amazonas* 2, no. 15 [Mar.–Apr. 1928]: 1). That is, this movement consisted of the progressive realization, in time and through space, of the democratic and equalitarian ideals upon which modern life was based.

Though the Feijóo-Echaiz alliance included members of the traditional, landed elite (the Echaiz, the Hurtado, and the Burga), it differed from casta organization in fundamental ways. The alliance was predicated on a form of sovereignty (namely, the popular sovereignty of mass politics) that directly contradicted the aristocratic pretensions of the traditional elite. In terms of its social makeup, the alliance was overwhelmingly of middle-class origin. And the intellectual leader of this extensive middle-class group was a political/cultural broker who was himself of nonelite background.[19] Symptomatic of the importance of el pueblo in this alliance—and of the degree to which even the elite members of the alliance felt compelled to recast their image in the terms of popular sovereignty—was the following fact. Early in 1930, after having made its pact with Feijóo, the elite Echaiz family began to publish its own newspaper, called *Redemption* (*Redención*), which it used to articulate a bitter attack on aristocratic privilege—to promote the same egalitarian, democratic, popular ideals expressed by Feijóo in his newspaper.

The pact made between Feijóo and the Echaiz in 1929 thus created the possibility for new forms of political alliance and contestation within Chachapoyas. The potential challenge to the casta-based order represented by this new alliance was not immediately apparent. Indeed, the Rubio-Linch candidates triumphed over Feijóo in the elections of August 1929 by an overwhelming margin. But when President Leguía was driven from power in a military coup on August 22, 1930—precipitating a major crisis in the national political system—the threat posed by the emergence of el pueblo became obvious. For at this time, Feijóo, who was still an outcast from the casta order and therefore was living in Lima, immediately took two decisive steps: He wired his closest confidants in Chachapoyas to spread the word among his followers that the moment of their deliverance had arrived; they were to rise up against the Rubio-Linch, but under the leadership and guidance of their allies, the Echaiz. And he cabled members of the Echaiz, informed them of Leguía's demise, and told them to move on the prefecture. As Feijóo and the Echaiz had worked out in advance, Feijóo's numerous followers were at the disposal of the Echaiz in case of just such an eventuality.[20]

An elderly informant—one of the original Aprista organizers in Chachapoyas, who participated in this Echaiz-led assault on the Rubio-Linch-controlled prefecture—recalled the uprising in the following terms:

At the fall of Leguía, Ricardo Feijóo immediately sent a telegram from Lima [to the Echaiz], telling the Echaiz to take the prefecture. They had been waiting for the opportunity [to do so]. . . . Feijóo had many followers among el pueblo, and it was they who assisted the Echaiz [in the attack]. Many of us [the Apristas] joined in as well. The whole town was up in arms and the Rubio [Rubio-Linch] could not resist us. They [the Rubio-Linch] had to retreat into their house, and later escaped to *Boca Negra* [a hacienda of the Rubio family located near Chachapoyas]. . . .

Go look at the walls next to the door of Miguel Rubio's house. You can still see the bullet holes from the attack, when the Echaiz tried to break into his house and take him prisoner. . . .

The Echaiz led the attack, but without the help of Feijóo and his followers, and without us [the Apristas], they [the Echaiz] would *never* have succeeded. They were weak after so many years of rule by the Rubio [Rubio-Linch]. . . . It was really el pueblo that took the prefecture![21] (Taped interview with Victor Santillán Gutierrez, conducted on July 9, 1993)

The Echaiz were thus able to assemble a group of followers of overwhelming size to attack the prefecture and to seize control of the town, despite the fragmented state of their casta. They were able to do so because by the late 1920s, casta-based forms of organization and contestation were no longer the only available local options. Rather, new organizational forms, and new forms of contestation, had been made possible by the rise of el pueblo onto the national, and especially the local, political scenes—because a new political community had recently been called into existence through the efforts of Fei-jóo and his "fellow travelers."

As the armed assault on the prefecture attests, the democratized, moralized social order imagined discursively in the pages of the newspaper *Amazonas*—and also disseminated orally in the People's University—were extremely powerful motivating and unifying forces among the middle sectors of Amazonas. In fact, even before the uprising of August 1930, when all participants put their lives directly in danger, much of the population had become involved in the movements of democratización—and thus had already put their lives or their freedom at risk. For some, involvement consisted of contributing to the organizing efforts of the APRA and the People's University, and thus raising the consciousness of the region's laboring poor, and attempting to offer them some alternative to casta rule. For others, it meant contributing letters or even pieces of writing to the newspaper *Amazonas*—texts that, when disseminated publicly in the paper, helped reimagine the social world in which these people wished to live. For still others, it consisted of informing Feijóo of the abuses of ruling casta politicians—which Feijóo then published in his newspaper—thus making it possible for an emergent "public" to judge the actions of its leaders according to standards of justice and morality. And for a great many others, involvement meant simply not informing the authorities of the whereabouts or the identities of the principle participants—thus helping to create an environment in which these social imaginings were free to take shape in the minds of much of the populace.

Regardless of the specific ways in which people became involved in the movements of democratización, however, it is clear that the middle sectors played a major role in the creation of the imagined social order that was to be an alternative to casta organization. It is equally clear that, even prior to August 1930, a great many people were willing to risk a great deal in order to help bring about such a remade world.

When a moment of national political crisis finally came (in August 1930), and the ruling Rubio-Linch casta became vulnerable to attack, the Echaiz made no effort to mobilize a coalition of *elite* forces to strike at its old enemies, as it would have done in the past. Rather, symptomatic of the new state of affairs, in mounting its assault on the Rubio-Linch, the Echaiz drew upon an entirely new political constituency—el pueblo, the emergent middle class of the region. Likewise, when the Rubio-Linch forces attempted a "counter-revolution" the following year (in December 1931), they were themselves obliged to seek out a middle-class constituency—or rather, they attempted to attach themselves to what was in reality a popular revolt led by the APRA.[22] By 1930, el pueblo was a political force that could no longer be ignored.

Until it assisted the Echaiz in "storming the Bastille," the middle class had never played an organized role in such matters as a distinct group—one that perceived itself as having a common identity, a common set of interests, and a common group of enemies. For the middle class had not existed as such until a short time before this. Within a period of just a few years, then, el pueblo not only came into existence as a discrete entity, but also became involved in violent political activity. Thereafter, those who made up el pueblo found themselves in the unfamiliar position of being the core constituency for the region's new power holders.

THE "DEMOCRATIZACIÓN" OF PUBLIC CULTURE

The central involvement of el pueblo in the revolution of August 1930 and its emergence as the core constituency for the leaders of the Feijóo-Echaiz alliance had an immediate effect on virtually all aspects of public life. From this point onward, el pueblo became actively involved in the region's most vital social activities, began to occupy its key political positions, and assumed control over its most prestigious religious practices—areas that had been systematically denied to the middle sectors in the past. Furthermore, under the protection of its political patrons, el pueblo began to elaborate a range of new sociocultural forms—forms that strengthened the existence of el pueblo as a group, and that also celebrated the principles of equality and justice around which the middle sectors had mobilized as a political community.

The ascent of el pueblo into these multiple arenas of social, political, and religious life enabled people who had recently risked their lives to bring about a transformed social world to broadcast the legitimacy of the principles for which they had fought—and to do so in areas that until then had remained the exclusive preserve of the regional elite. The combined effect of these changes was twofold. First, they resulted in the emergence of a new kind of public culture in Chachapoyas—one in which the material, behavioral, and symbolic markers of hierarchy acted out on a daily basis in the reproduction of aristocratic sovereignty were replaced by the constant assertion and celebration of equality. Second, these changes created a situation in which the principles of popular sovereignty took on a transformed significance in public life. For the first time in the region's history, these principles came to define the standards to which individuals who occupied positions of "public trust" would actually be held accountable. This marked a radical change from the status of these principles during the period of casta rule—when they had acted as nothing more than empty phrases uttered mechanically in political ritual and discourse by elite groups who publicly flaunted their ability to disregard the most fundamental aspects of these principles.

POPULAR SOVEREIGNTY AND A REBORN ELITE

Elite families who had been systematically excluded from positions of power during the extended period of rule by the Pizarro-Rubio-Linch coalitions played a key role in undermining the aristocratic order. They did so largely because of their central involvement in the movements of democratización. There is much to suggest that these elite families participated in the movements out of pure expediency—that they wished for nothing more than to end the isolation and persecution they had suffered at the hands of the ruling casta. In the social context of the 1920s, however, the only available means for doing so was to join a social movement intent on dismantling the very aristocratic order in which these same elite families had formerly played such a prominent role. Indeed, once they joined the democratización movements, members of these elite families, whose backgrounds were thus "suspect," had to go to great lengths to prove that they were truly "reborn." That is, they were forced to distance themselves in all ways from the aristocratic privileges that they had so willingly exercised in the past. This was especially true of elite families who occupied positions of power in the new order. Thus, the only members of the old elite who exercised positions of authority after the revolution of August 1930 were among the most vocal and outspoken critics of the old order. As a result, there was no one left to preserve or protect traditional forms of privilege.

Even prior to the fall of the Rubio-Linch casta, then, elite families like the

Echaiz who sought to bring to an end their persecution by the ruling casta attempted to shed their elite image, and to recast themselves in populist form (in the case of the Echaiz family, via its newspaper, *Redención*). Upon taking power, not only the Echaiz, but all the elite members of the Feijóo-Echaiz alliance leadership, continued to present themselves as the sworn enemies of aristocratic privilege—as the champions of the people. Indeed, as the newspaper *Redención* was transformed from an organ of social criticism into the official mouthpiece of the central government in Amazonas (because its publishers, the Echaiz, controlled the prefecture), the Echaiz used the coincidence that the paper had begun publication the same year that the elite were overthrown (1930) to mark a kind of temporal/moral watershed in the history of regional affairs. Thus, below the title of issues of the paper from 1930 (after the month of August) is written, "Year One of the Redemption"; below the title of issues from 1931 is written, "Year Two of the Redemption"; and so on.[23]

The elite leaders of the new ruling alliance went to great lengths not only to celebrate the principles of popular sovereignty and nationhood in all political ritual, but also to include a prominent place for el pueblo in these celebrations—and to demonstrate their own unquestioned allegiance to the new order. Furthermore, in depicting these ritual events to "the public" (in the newspapers *Amazonas* and *Redención*), leaders sought constantly to remind el pueblo that those former members of the elite who occupied political office in the new regime did indeed represent the collective will of the people and the nation. That is, it was reinforced repeatedly in the public mind that the members of the elite Echaiz, Hurtado, and Burga families who exercised positions of power in the new order were truly committed to the public good and the general interest—principles for which members of el pueblo had so recently risked their lives in overthrowing the aristocratic Rubio-Linch casta and its allies.

In this regard, consider the following article depicting to the public at large the all-important ceremony in which Eleodoro Echaiz—who, although formerly a member of the elite, had nonetheless led the attack against the aristocratic Rubio-Linch—was sworn in as the new prefect:

Sr. Eleodoro Echaiz Sworn in as Prefect

... Sr. Eleodoro Echaiz, who had been exercising the position of prefect as the result of popular will, has also received the endorsement of the Council of Government to occupy this post. ...

With the object of swearing in the new prefect, Sr. Echaiz and a large number of his followers gathered at the People's Palace . . . [where] the judge of the first instance, having previously received the appropriate order from the Council of Government, administered the oath to Sr. Echaiz, and gave him the sash and staff that are the symbols of office, thus satisfying all constitutional requirements, making Sr. Echaiz the highest political official in the department.

The magistrate then said that in this case a right had been exercised that, through error, had fallen into disuse—that of choosing as the first political authority a native son, who understands the region's problems and is concerned about solving them. In so doing, said the judge, the government showed its wisdom. (*Redención* 1, no. 7 [Nov. 2, 1930]: 2)

In this way, *Redención* reminded its readers that Echaiz had been brought to power as the result of popular will, and also informed them that the central government had acknowledged the legitimacy of the people's choice—by appointing Echaiz as prefect. The interests of el pueblo and the state thus came together in the person of Eleodoro Echaiz. He was the legitimate ruler by public desire as well as by government decree. Indeed, the judge who administered the oath of office commended the government's "wisdom" in choosing a local man to direct departmental affairs, for such a man would involve himself in the region's problems and solutions in a way that no outsider could (the implicit comparison was with the recently ousted prefect—Sr. Távara, a Limeño hand-picked by leaders of the Rubio-Linch—whose abusiveness and lack of concern for anything other than his own self-aggrandizement el pueblo knew only too well). Thus the judge reinforced the idea that legitimate rule must be based on serving the public will and the common good—the very principles that had helped mobilize el pueblo as a political community—and that Echaiz was the man to defend such principles.

Public proclamations that local leaders represented the will of the people—and that they would defend the common good—had been commonly heard prior to the revolution of August 1930. During the period of casta rule, however, such proclamations were made in a social environment that belied their very content. For it was obvious to everyone that casta leaders served their own particular interests, that they represented no one's will but their own—least of all that of subaltern groups of cholos and Indios. After the beginning of the "redemption," however, the notion that leaders should serve the general good and obey the will of the people became a legitimate and valid expectation—one to which reborn members of the elite were especially anxious to demonstrate their obedience. For it was precisely the justice of such notions that had compelled the town's artisans and other independent laborers to take up arms against the aristocratic order. And it was only for this reason that a man who had formerly been a prominent member of the town's aristocratic elite—Eleodoro Echaiz—sat in the prefecture.

The manner in which the authors of *Redención* chose to represent the transformed state of affairs spoke clearly to the emergence of a new form of political legitimacy based on notions of popular sovereignty—and to the desire of reborn members of the elite to show their allegiance to such principles. In the article about Echaiz's induction ceremony, for example, the prefecture, which had formerly been called the Government Palace (*Palacio del Gobierno*), had been transformed into the People's Palace (*Palacio del Pueblo*). Indeed, as the article continued, the importance of el pueblo in the transformed political structure of the region, and the prominent place made for it in public political ritual, became increasingly obvious:

> Immediately thereafter el pueblo obliged Sr. Echaiz to take a walk around the main plaza, greeting him as he walked with continuous assurances of their support and solidarity.
>
> Sr. Abraham Cachay then presented Sr. Echaiz with the staff of office, which is a magnificent scepter of ivory engraved and fashioned by Sr. Cachay, who as everyone knows is an artist in works of this kind. (Ibid.)

Abraham Cachay was one of the town's leading carpenters and furniture-makers—thus his reputation as a master craftsman. He had also played a key combatant role in the revolution of August 1930. The ceremony inducting Echaiz into power as the region's new political leader, uniting the interests of people and state, thus culminated with one of Chachapoyas's most esteemed artisans, who had taken up arms against the old order, presenting Echaiz with a new staff of office that Cachay himself had fabricated.[24] Furthermore, this act took place in the town's main plaza, in the presence of el pueblo, whose members had assembled to watch the man they had helped bring to power take his legitimate place as the department's head.

The reborn elite leaders of the Feijóo-Echaiz alliance also employed the populist newspapers *Redención* and *Amazonas* to keep constantly in the public eye their critical attitude toward as well as their distance from the region's former power holders and all that they represented—to remind el pueblo that the elite leaders brought to power through the mobilization of the people were truly committed to the principles of popular sovereignty.[25] One of the key means of establishing this distance and credibility in the aftermath of the revolution of August 1930 consisted of a long, drawn-out spectacle in which the public servants of the new order—among whom were several reborn aristocratic families—investigated and exposed to el pueblo the graft, extortion, and theft perpetrated by the aristocratic Rubio-Linch casta during the once-nio. In so doing, the region's new leaders drew continuously on the notion of a common interest shared by the people and the nation alike, and publicly proclaimed themselves the defenders of this shared interest. In this way, they sought to place themselves squarely within the ranks of the people, and to prove beyond any doubt that the deposed casta had consistently betrayed the common good, thus disqualifying this "decadent elite" from inclusion in the new order. Deployment of the rhetoric of popular sovereignty by reborn elite families became a strategic means of effecting the public transformation so necessary to these families if they were to remain legitimate in the eyes of their constituency—if they were to separate themselves convincingly and effectively from the traditional elite in the public eye.[26]

Lending credibility to the entire investigation into the misdeeds of the Rubio-Linch was the fact that similar investigations were taking place all around the country—that all such investigations had national sanction. Shortly after taking office, President Sanchez Cerro—himself a populist figure who had a huge following among Peru's humble classes—established a National Tribunal of Sanction whose responsibility it was to look into precisely these kinds of abuse (Basadre 1968–69, 14: ch. 182). Thus, in self-righteously exposing to the public the crimes of the region's former rulers, members of the reborn elite could appear to be doing more than just attacking their old enemies. They could portray themselves as selflessly carrying out a sacred, patriotic mission—that of defending the fatherland and el pueblo alike.

Nicolas Hurtado, one of the leading members of the branch of the elite Hurtado family that was closely allied with the Echaiz, was appointed president of the *Junta Investigadora* (the Investigative Council) of the Departmental Tribunal of Sanction. Its other members, however, were drawn from Chacha-poyas's middle sectors—again reflecting el pueblo's new position of promi-nence.[27] One of the *Junta Investigadora's* first official acts consisted of providing Prefect Eleodoro Echaiz with a preliminary statement of the government monies misappropriated by members of the Rubio-Linch casta. Echaiz used the statement as the basis of a long letter denouncing the Rubio-Linch to the president of the National Tribunal of Sanction in Lima. The letter, sections of which are quoted below, was also reproduced on the front page of *Redención*. The letter reveals much about how the reborn elite leadership of the Feijóo-Echaiz alliance used the discursive space provided by the newspaper to rein-force the notion of a common good, to convey to el pueblo how committed its leaders were to the cause of the common good, and to reveal how funda-mentally the deposed casta had betrayed the cause of the people:

> In the Interests of Amazonas.
> Sr. President of the National Tribunal of Sanction:
> . . . It is without question that Amazonas, converted into a veritable fief of the Rubio Linch brothers for 21 years, is among those regions that has suffered most from the harshness and the moral prostitution of the tyranny of Leguismo. . . .
> In exercise of the right granted to me [by the Tribunal of Sanction] . . . I denounce Arturo and Miguel Rubio Linch, ex-deputies of Chachapoyas and Bongará, respectively. . . . The ex-representatives Rubio Linch, together with the ex-Inspector of Education Lucas Hilarión Rubio, have defrauded the government of 600,000 soles intended for the construction of the Amazonas highway . . . thus sacrificing the work, the enthusiasm, the hopes, and the future of an entire people to the base selfishness of an abject group of ex-ploiters.
> Those responsible must reveal where the money of the nation is to be found, for the responsibility falls upon them for the shameful disappearance of funds set aside by the State for public works between 1909 and 1930 . . . none of which was ever carried out. (*Redención* 1, no. 7 [Nov. 2, 1930]: 1)

The people and the nation did indeed have a common interest, asserted *Redención*, one that had been consistently betrayed by the Rubio-Linch casta for over twenty years. Motivated by "base selfishness," this "abject group of ex-ploiters" had made off with truly vast sums of money. Members of the Rubio-

Linch were guilty of more, however, than simple graft. Adding to the gravity of their crimes was the fact that, in managing the department as their personal fief, they had sacrificed the common good of region and nation for their own private gain.

Indeed, as Prefect Echaiz's open letter to the president of the National Tribunal of Sanction continued, it became clear that there was little that the Rubio-Linch had not been willing to do in order to enrich its members—including betray the most fundamental principles of community by preying on the misfortune of one's neighbors:

> Arturo Rubio Linch . . . should also be made to produce the . . . funds raised for the victims of the Chachapoyas earthquake, a quantity of 150,000 soles, contributed out of public concern, with the noble end of assisting the victims of that terrible catastrophe—a goal that was subverted completely by the maliciousness and cruelty of the aforementioned Rubio, who in his position as Minister of Government of the dictatorship of Leguía, was permitted the disgrace of playing politics with the tragedy of a people and the donations of the country and of foreign nations. (Ibid.)

The Rubio-Linch, Echaiz reveals, had prevented relief from reaching the innumerable victims of the great natural catastrophe that struck the town in May 1928—resulting in suffering and hardship still fresh in the minds of el pueblo. In addition, however, the deposed casta had betrayed the noble intentions of the Peruvian people, and people around the globe. People everywhere had been able to identify and empathize with the tragedy suffered by *el pueblo Chachapoyano*, and had selflessly given money to lessen their difficulties. To the great shame of region and nation alike, however, the Rubio-Linch casta had no such feelings of sympathy for its own people. Instead, it had undermined the offerings of support and solidarity offered by other peoples by stealing the money intended for the unfortunates of Chachapoyas. And as if these betrayals were not enough, the Rubio-Linch had also deceived the Peruvian government, who had entrusted the Rubio-Linch with the care of the monies—and thus with the care of the people.

Having defrauded the nation of its resources and the people of their future, and having betrayed the trust of the Peruvian people, the Peruvian government, and people around the globe, the Rubio-Linch had even been will-

ing to sacrifice the well-being of those pure of heart and innocent of all political intrigue—the region's children—in its lust for wealth:

> Lucas Hilarión Rubio, ex-inspector of education . . . during the dictatorship
> of Leguía, is guilty of stealing the funds destined for the construction of
> schoolhouses, desks, and schoolbooks, is guilty of having sold school sup-
> plies, is guilty of seizing arms belonging to the state, with the consent of ex-
> Prefect Távara, in order to maintain himself by force of arms, firing upon the
> people when necessary, and corrupting and cheating the teachers whose wel-
> fare was his responsibility.
>
> The aforementioned ex-inspector is guilty of having sacrificed the sacred
> interests of the children of Amazonas to his wretched aspirations, of having
> committed outrages against the culture of the collectivity. (Ibid.)

Again the Rubio family is seen to be guilty of having been willing to do
anything to satisfy its desire for wealth—of using armed force to intimidate
and corrupt, in the process betraying the most sacred of public concerns. Again
Redención opposes the common interests of the people of Amazonas—the
"culture of the collectivity"—to the "wretched aspirations" and "outrages"
of the decadent aristocratic elite. Again the reborn elite leaders of el pueblo
present themselves as the true defenders of the public trust.

What had the Rubio-Linch done with this money? Sr. Echaiz not only
raised the question of where the money was to be found, he also answered
this question. In so doing, he revealed to el pueblo the base corruption of the
Rubio-Linch casta—the shallow, self-serving, and self-aggrandizing ends to
which its members were willing to put monies destined for the common
good:

> As a result of [this graft], they have accumulated immense fortunes, [consist-
> ing of] some millions. This is demonstrated by the massive bank accounts
> they have in [Lima], the beautiful palaces they own on Avenida Arequipa, in
> the Plaza Bolognezi, in Avenida Alfonso Ugarte, in Barranco, and in other
> parts of [Lima], [by] the elegant Packard automobiles they drive valued at
> 150,000 soles each . . . and, overall, by the luxurious style of life they display
> to one and all. (Ibid.)

In the months that followed, the Departmental Tribunal of Sanction—and
its Investigative Council (*Junta Investigadora*)—reported in great detail on the

embezzlement perpetrated by members of the Rubio-Linch casta. The reports of the Investigative Council, sections of which were excerpted in *Redención*, provided detailed accounts of the various people responsible for stealing the "money of the nation," the unrealized purposes for which the revenues had been intended, and the dates the funds had been made available. A typical entry from a report is reproduced in the following table. By means of such "objective reporting," the reborn elite leaders of the Feijóo-Echaiz alliance succeeded in portraying an almost unbelievably malevolent image of the Rubio-Linch casta. For it became clear that the former ruling casta had defrauded the people and the nation, which were depicted as one and the same, out of tremendous sums of money intended for projects of immense benefit to the public at large—schools, hospitals, roads, police protection. Indeed, as portrayed in *Redención*, during the previous twenty years there was no trust so sacred that it had not been violated, no obligation so binding that it had not been disregarded, when it stood in the way of power or profit for the Rubio-Linch.

Chachapoyas, January 27, 1931
Sr. Prefect of the Department

Lucas H. Rubio

This man has made off with the following sums:

Reconstruction of Chachapoyas, Luya, and Bongará
[after the great earthquake of 1928]

October 30, 1929 . . .	Subvention for May and June	9,166.66 soles
December 31 . . .	Subvention for July and August	9,166.66
December 31 . . .	Subvention for Sept.–December	18,333.32
March 22, 1930 . . .	Subvention for January	4,583.33
April 30, 1930 . . .	Subvention for February	4,583.33
June 23, 1930 . . .	Subvention for March and April	9,166.66
August 20, 1930 . . .	Purchase of land for schools	3,300.00
August 6, 1928 . . .	For the Victims in Bongará	2,000.00
	TOTAL:	60,299.96 soles

Ex-Prefect Juan Antonio Távara

This public functionary . . . has made off with diverse sums [of money], by inflating the expenses of the [gendarme] garrisons as well as the number of gendarmes . . . as Lieutenant del Valle, the ex-jefe of the Gendarmes, has informed us. The following sums were given [by the government] to ex-functionary Távara:

August 3, 1929	For the Repair of the Hospital	416.64 soles
June 24, 1929	For the Garrison of Bagua	1,233.00
June 30, 1929	For the Garrison of Chachapoyas	2,564.00
July 30, 1929	For the Garrison of Bagua	1,233.00
July 30, 1929	For the Garrison of Chachapoyas	2,564.00
August 31, 1929	For the Garrison of Bagua	1,233.00
August 31, 1929	For the Garrison of Chachapoyas	2,564.00
Sept. 16, 1929	For the Purchase of a Horse	400.00
Sept. 30, 1929	For the Garrison of Chachapoyas	2,564.00
Oct. 30, 1929	For the Garrison of Bagua	2,466.00
Oct. 30, 1929	For the Garrison of Chachapoyas	2,564.00
Oct. 31, 1929	For the Purchase of a Large Drill, which has yet to be seen, which was to be used to repair roads and bridges that have never been repaired	1,978.00
Nov. 30, 1929	For the Garrison of Bagua	1,233.00
Nov. 30, 1929	For the Garrison of Chachapoyas	2,564.00
Dec. 31, 1929	For the Garrison of Bagua	1,233.00
Dec. 31, 1929	For the Garrison of Chachapoyas	2,564.00
Dec. 31, 1929	For the Hospital	833.36
Dec. 31, 1929	There appears a supposed expense for the personnel of the prefecture, in the name of AntonioT. Cueva, for the amount of 63.00 soles/month, from Jan. to August	472.00
Dec. 31, 1929	The same Sr. Távara charged 100.00 soles/month for . . . some suspicious purpose, from Jan. to June of 1930	600.00
Feb. 28, 1930	For the Garrison of Bagua	2,114.00
Feb. 28, 1930	For the Garrison of Chachapoyas	4,253.20
March 31, 1930	For the Garrison of Chachapoyas	2,126.60
March 31, 1930	For expenses of the *contingente de sangre* . . . which did not spend all the money allotted it	2,004.00
April, 1930	For the Garrison of Bagua	2,114.00
April, 1930	For the Garrison of Chachapoyas	2,126.60
May, 1930	For the Garrison of Bagua	1,057.00

May, 1930	For the Garrison of Chachapoyas	2,126.60
June 30, 1930	For the Garrison of Bagua	1,057.00
June 30, 1930	For the Garrison of Chachapoyas	2,126.60
July, 1930	For the Garrison of Bagua	1,057.00
July, 1930	For the Garrison of Chachapoyas	2,126.60
Aug. 24, 1930	For the transport of Engineer Augusto Reina Farje, whose own family provided him with pack animals, thus the prefecture spent nothing	5624.55
	Pasture for Pack Animals of the State:	
Feb.–July, 1930	Considering the months of February to July of the present year, the only months for which information is available, during which large sums were paid, when the animals were cared for by district governors free of charge	817.88
	SUM:	56,953.33 soles

Arturo and Miguel Rubio Linch

On Feb. 26, 1929 Arturo and Miguel Rubio . . . sent a memo to the Ministry of Fomento claiming 55,000.00 soles to rebuild and repair schools and other buildings in the three provinces [of the department] damaged or destroyed by the earthquake of May, 1928; 16,000.00 soles to restore electric light; 20,000.00 soles . . . for a public water system; 20,000.00 soles to complete construction on a public office building and 2,000.00 soles to build a public market in Jumbilla . . . for a total of 113,000.00 soles.

Such revelations were but further confirmation of what *Amazonas* and the People's University had been saying all along. The former ruling elite had indeed sacrificed the common good in order to serve its own private interests. It had done so on a scale, however, far beyond what anyone could have imagined.

Thus exposed, these behaviors served as a powerful symbol of the abuses of the past, in relationship to which those of the new order—elite and commoner alike—would be forced to measure their progress into the future. The "outrages" committed by the Rubio-Linch, displayed so prominently in the pages of *Redención* by a reborn elite leadership seeking to disassociate itself from its own past, thus served as a kind of morality lesson of what *not* to do—of how public wealth and public office were *not* to be used. By their very inappropriateness, these abuses helped define new legitimate forms of public behavior, legitimate ways of using public wealth. By attacking the old order so aggressively and self-righteously on the basis of its betrayal of the common good, the region's new power holders held themselves accountable for truly protecting and promoting the common good.

THE SOCIAL ASCENT OF EL PUEBLO

Members of el pueblo who had been centrally involved in the movements of democratización experienced greater recognition and legitimacy not only in ceremonial contexts and discursive spaces, but also in public life, where they were appointed to a variety of prominent positions. From these positions they were able to act upon and disseminate the equalitarian ideals around which el pueblo had coalesced as a political community, and to demonstrate the proper uses of public wealth and public office.

Key in this regard was el pueblo's new presence on the municipal council (of the province of Chachapoyas). For the first time in the region's history, the position of provincial mayor—head of the municipal council—was given to someone of relatively humble background. The first mayor appointed after the revolution of August 1930 was Victor M. Torres—a middle-sector merchant with no ties to the region's landed elite. In its prominently placed article about the new municipal council, *Redención* stated: "Sr. Victor Torres, worthy and hardworking merchant, has been chosen to preside over the members of the municipal council, all of whom are filled with good will to serve the interests of the people" (*Redención* 1, no. 7 [Nov. 2, 1930]: 2).

Indeed, the first "postrevolution" municipal council was filled with people who came from the formerly marginalized middle sectors, giving this group a degree of prominence, a kind of legitimacy, and a level of decision-making power it had never enjoyed in the past.[28] *Redención* lost no time in conveying to the reading public that the new municipal council was truly committed to the common good—that its members would make proper use of public wealth and public office. In the same article that introduced the new council members to el pueblo, the paper included the plans of each for what was called "local improvement." The new inspector of hygiene, for example, promised to take measures to improve the conditions of hygiene at the town slaughterhouse—a long-standing health problem due to the tendency for meat to sit unattended for several days before it was sold to the public. He promised as well to contact the departmental health officer (the *médico sanitario*) about obtaining the disinfectants necessary to conduct a general cleaning of the city in order to eliminate recurrent diseases. The inspector also informed the public that he would take more adequate measures to keep unwatched animals from wandering about the streets, as they defecated in the public water supply, creating further health problems. Other inspectors offered their own plans to improve local life. The council as a whole passed a resolution committing itself to a wide range of such projects, and announced its plans for change in a public notice that was posted in the "customary public places" throughout the province (in addition to being published in *Redención*). Most of the projects to which the council committed itself were carried out.[29]

In subsequent years, el pueblo continued to exercise a significant role in the municipal council. The fact that many of those appointed to the council were committed to the ideals of popular sovereignty undoubtedly had a major influence on their behavior as councilmen—and thus on the organization, regulation, and monitoring of many aspects of provincial life. In addition, however, as the newspaper article discussed above suggests, councilmen of the postrevolutionary period were held to new public standards—standards that the councilmen, as participants in the movements of democratización, had themselves helped to erect. For councilmen were able to legitimate occupying the positions they held only by demonstrating that they had "properly" used public office and public resources—that they had put into effect tangible improvements in local life. This represented a major change from the standards to which municipal councils of the casta period (whose members saw no need for explanations or justifications as to their use of public monies) had been subject. This change did not put an end to graft or the abuse of position, although both were greatly reduced in scale from this time onward. Rather, as of August 1930, it became necessary for the first time for councilmen to *conceal* their misappropriation of funds and their misuse of authority and to present themselves *publicly* as defenders of the common good—and to do so in a convincing manner. This need translated into tangible benefits for el pueblo, since councilmen who could not offer visible evidence of the benefits that devolved to the collectivity as a result of their tenure in office could not retain their positions of public trust.

Individuals sympathetic to the new order were also appointed to key positions in the police and the judiciary. For example, shortly after the revolution of August 1930, Abraham Cachay, the respected carpenter who had presented Prefect Eleodoro Echaiz with a new staff of office in Echaiz's induction ceremony as prefect, and who had played an important role as a combatant in the attack on the prefecture in August 1930, was appointed departmental head of the Gendarmery.[30] Cachay's appointment, and the policies he and his subalterns pursued thereafter, marked a key point of transition in the empowerment of the town's middle sectors, and in the breakdown of aristocratic sovereignty. Under Cachay's leadership, the "forces of order" ceased to be used to protect the interests of a small coterie of the elite and its many clients (and to demonstrate the ability of this group to dominate and shame members of the opposition). Rather, for the first time in the region's history, the means of force began to be employed to eliminate the arbitrary use of power by the elite, and to protect the life and property of el pueblo.

A number of factors contributed to this change. One was Cachay himself—an artisan who had been deeply involved in the movements of democratización from their earliest days, and who was sufficiently committed to the social transformation envisioned within the movements to take a leading role in the armed assault on the prefecture that overthrew the Rubio-Linch casta. Appointing as head of the Gendarmery a person with such well-known animosity toward aristocratic privilege was bound to result in significantly improved life circumstances for those who had been demeaned and misused under the old order. Cachay's policy of recruiting much of the rank-and-file of the Gendarmery from among the town's middle sectors—where his allies were the most dependable and his contacts the most secure—further strengthened the position of el pueblo.[31] For it placed "the people" as a whole in the position of safeguarding one another, where in the past they had been forced to act as individuals, each one seeking out a powerful elite ally to intercede on his behalf.

Cachay's appointment came at a time when the reborn elite leaders of the Feijóo-Echaiz alliance were at great pains to demonstrate their commitment to the ideals of equality, individual rights and protections, and impartial justice. Members of the new elite were extremely unlikely to call upon Cachay to use his constabulary to support assertions of aristocratic privilege in these circumstances. Rather, they were duty-bound to support all efforts to defend the new egalitarian order. Indeed, the very relinquishment of this key position, traditionally reserved for members of the elite, to a leading member of el pueblo was undoubtedly intended as a sign of good faith on the part of reborn elite leaders. That is, the decision of alliance leaders to let control of armed force rest with a man such as Cachay was an extremely effective way of demonstrating their compliance with and respect for the precepts of popular sovereignty—of making the formerly marginalized middle sectors *feel* empowered, as well as actually empowering them.

These factors combined to result in a significant improvement in the safety and security of those who made up el pueblo, and in a major change in their relationship with the forces of order. During the period of casta rule, the middle sectors rarely involved themselves with the gendarmes. When they did so, most often it was to protest police abuse rather than to seek out police assistance (see Chapters 3 and 4). Once it became clear that the gendarmes would no longer use their control of force to protect elite privilege—and that the police were to be led by one of "their own"—el pueblo felt free to call upon the gendarmes for protection or redress.

From this time forward, the middle sectors of Chachapoyas began to flood the gendarmes with requests to intercede on their behalf in a wide range of problems, forcing the gendarmes to devote considerable energy to responding to such appeals. The most commonly made request was that individual protections be extended to a person under threat by another. Unlike the appeals for garantías made during the casta period, however, these postrevolution appeals were not made by individuals temporarily without allies because the casta to which they belonged had been deposed. Rather, they came from el pueblo as a whole. Furthermore, again unlike past requests for garantías, these appeals were regularly heeded by the forces of order. An incident involving the request of a carpenter, Emilio Valdivia, that constitutional protections be extended to him and his family typifies the greater accessibility of the forces of order to the middle sectors, and the greater concern of the police for the needs of el pueblo.

Request for Individual Protections

Sr. Prefect of the Department:

Emilio Valdivia, of this locality, entered in the Electoral Register as No. 208107, with all respect reports to you the following: That my son-in law, Miguel Chota Trigoso, also of this locality, threatens me daily wherever he encounters me, and even comes to my house when I am not at home, where he insults and threatens my family. Last Wednesday he came to my house with a club in hand and threatened my family. As these continuous threats could at some point be acted upon or could provoke a situation that I, as a man, could not ignore, I write to you in demand of my garantías, so that the aforementioned Chota may be told to stop bothering and provoking me.[32] ([APA23], Apr. 14, 1931)

The difference between this *solicitud* and similar requests from the casta period was the response accorded it by the authorities. Prefect Echaiz immediately instructed the subprefect of Chachapoyas to look into the matter; he in turn ordered the chief (jefe) of the Gendarmery to investigate. Jefe Cachay dispatched a commission of men, including the second lieutenant in charge of the Chachapoyas Provincial Constabulary and two *soldados*, to interview Valdivia, the accused Chota, and anyone else they deemed necessary to determine the truth of the case at hand. After interviews had been carried out and the investigation had been completed, the gendarmes found that Chota had indeed been threatening Valdivia. They ordered him to desist immediately, or face imprisonment.[33]

In the casta period, the very fact that appeals for garantías were made indicated that those who petitioned were in positions of considerable weakness—that they lacked powerful allies who could intercede on their behalf, and that the legal system was their only recourse. These appeals were virtually never heeded, however; the hope of those who made them was that one day the ruling casta would change, at which point their requests could be acted on (see Chapters 3 and 4). The attention and care given to appeals for garantías after the rise of el pueblo was completely without precedent. Never before had the authorities been willing to invest such time or energy in investigating the problems of petitioners. In contrast to the conditions of the casta period, then, the responsiveness of the authorities to such requests after August 1930 indicated the *strength* of those who invoked the legal system. It signified that they did have powerful allies—allies who controlled the region's most important political positions, allies who could be counted on to listen carefully to requests for protection made by their core constituency.

Despite the changed environment in which the gendarmes operated in the early 1930s, and despite the fact that they were led by Abraham Cachay, there were still occasions on which members of the Gendarmery used their positions in an abusive manner. In these instances, the response of higher authorities—from Jefe Cachay to the subprefect to the prefect to the provincial judge—was unequivocal. Action taken against such gendarmes was swift and clear. They were generally removed from the Gendarmery and prosecuted for their crime.[34] This response to police abuse also represented a major change from the casta period, when casta leaders allowed the gendarmes considerable license in their relations with the local populace. For there was no other way at that time to maintain the loyalty of the police (see Chapters 3 and 4).

As the forces of order ceased to be used to protect and preserve elite privilege, the gendarmes ceased being regarded as a group of abusive, arbitrary men who preyed on the local population when it suited their purposes or those of their elite patrons. Rather, in that the gendarmes were called upon to safeguard el pueblo after the revolution of August 1930—and because much of the Gendarmery was drawn from among el pueblo—the animosity that had formerly characterized relations between the forces of order and the town's middle sectors dissipated. From this time forward, the gendarmes began to play a key role in preserving the sanctity of person and property around which el pueblo had mobilized as a political community. The fact that the gendarmes took on this role—and that they ceased to be used to defend aristocratic privilege—did much to create an environment in which new, more egalitarian forms of subjectivity and social relations could flourish.

Just as members of the municipal council became subject to new standards of proper behavior in their use of public office and public wealth, so, too, did the police become subject to new standards of conduct—according to which constitutional guarantees of person and property were rights to which el pueblo was entitled. In holding the forces of order to these new standards, alliance leaders may or may not have acted out of altruism or due to their commitment to the ideals of popular sovereignty. Regardless of their personal inclinations regarding such matters, however, the survival of those in power depended to a considerable degree on their ability to maintain el pueblo as a viable social entity.[35]

Middle-sector individuals also began to play an important role on the *Juntas de Pro-Desocupados*—a new entity established by the administration of President Sanchez Cerro to organize and oversee public-works projects. The central office of the junta in Lima funneled vast sums of money into the region in order to sponsor a variety of public works.[36] These monies were passed from the *Comisión Distribuidora de Fondos Pro-Desocupados* (part of the Ministry of Fomento) to the departmental junta in Chachapoyas, from there on to each of the three provincial-level juntas, which in turn sent the funds to the many district-level juntas in the countryside. Those serving on the departmental- and provincial-level juntas in particular came to wield considerable influence. Because they could decide which public-works projects would be carried out, junta members at these two levels of the administrative hierarchy played a major role in determining the development of the region's infrastructure.[37] Because they could contract out work projects to people of their own choosing, junta members had the opportunity to construct extensive clienteles. Because they were responsible for evaluating whether or not jobs had been satisfactorily completed, junta members determined the degree to which government monies were well spent. And because of their role in providing the central office in Lima with the financial accounting of their activities, junta members were able to defraud the state of huge sums of money.[38]

The behavior of junta members in all of these areas reflected the transformed conditions of the early 1930s—in which people committed to the ideals of popular sovereignty found themselves operating in conditions in which they were held accountable to conform to these principles. The very presence of representatives of el pueblo on the juntas—at all levels of the administrative hierarchy—represented its expanded role and increased importance in public life. The uses members of el pueblo made of their positions reflect their commitment to a transformed social order, as well as the conditions in which this commitment played itself out.

Membership on the juntas put middle-sector individuals in the position of being able to promote the development of roads, bridges, marketplaces, potable water systems, schoolhouses, and so on. All of these played an important role in el pueblo's vision of a transformed social order, in which the region's backwardness and isolation would be brought to an end—in which the region would be more fully integrated into modern, national life. Members of the junta appear to have taken to the construction of such projects with these goals in mind. They did indeed use their powers to construct extensive clienteles—but among the middle sectors of the towns rather than among the landed elite. They did so by awarding work contracts predominantly to skilled craftsmen and merchants.[39] These individuals in turn used the funds to employ a large number of artisans and laborers—people with the skills necessary to carry the projects through to a successful completion. (Prior to 1930, such projects had been undertaken by unpaid peasant laborers, under the guidance of the governors of their districts.) Juntas were also more thorough in evaluating work carried out under their auspices—junta inspectors carefully examined completed projects before monies were released to contractors. Thanks to the use of skilled laborers and thorough inspections, road and bridge repairs did not constantly have to be redone, as was the case under the previous regime. In addition, much of the misappropriation of funds carried out under casta rule—documented at length in *Redención*, and constituting politics as normal in the old order—came to an end. From 1930 onward, the greater accountability to the central office of the junta for the use of funds (accounting had to be provided on a monthly basis), the need to conceal any misappropriation of funds from the newly ascendant middle sectors, and the political capital to be gained by demonstrating to el pueblo the tangible benefits derived from occupying positions of public trust, combined to greatly lessen the incidence and scale of graft.

With representatives of el pueblo on the Juntas de Pro-Desocupados, operating in a transformed political environment, monies that had formerly been used to enrich casta leaders and to reproduce casta power were now available for public works. The "liberation" of these funds from casta control, and the distribution of these funds to members of el pueblo (in the form of work on infrastructure projects), allowed the region's new leaders to strengthen the position of their core constituency and to build stronger bonds of clientele among the middle sectors. It also allowed them to demonstrate their allegiance to the newly established standards of public accountability—according to which politicians were to serve the common good.[40]

By a decree of the Ministry of Education dated October 20, 1930, Leon M. Torres—a regular contributor of articles concerning youth and education to the newspaper *Amazonas*, and a graduate of Lima's training school for teachers (the *Escuela Normal*, or Normal School)—was appointed head of the Provincial Board of Education (*La Comisión Escolar de la Provincia de Chachapoyas*).[41] The head of this board had the important responsibility of organizing and overseeing pedagogical activities for all elementary-school teachers in the province. In consultation with the departmental superintendent of education, he was also charged with choosing who would teach in the many rural schools scattered about the countryside—as well as with reviewing the activities of and acting on complaints lodged against rural teachers by the communities to which these teachers were assigned.

Torres used his position to initiate a series of sweeping changes in the province's educational apparatus—changes that contributed in major ways to the dissemination of the populist principles around which el pueblo had mobilized as a political community. Torres immediately set about changing the teaching personnel of the region's schools. His goal was to replace the many unqualified individuals who, as clients of the Rubio-Linch casta, had been appointed to teach in the rural districts, with individuals who had some training and/or more of a genuine calling for their vocation. Virtually all of the new teachers Torres selected were drawn from "middle-sector" backgrounds, and/or had received training as teachers in Lima's Normal Schools.[42]

Assisted by Dr. José Sanchez Tirado—the new head of the national high school of Chachapoyas (El Colegio Nacional San Juan de la Libertad) and himself a regular contributor to the newspaper *Amazonas*—Torres also began to organize the teachers of the entire department into a union where common needs, concerns, and directions could be discussed. A directive from the Ministry of Education in May 1931 assisted the two men in their efforts. The ministry ordered that a series of *Conversatorios Pedagógicos*, or Pedagogical Discussions, was to be carried out in the capital of every province, among all school-teachers.[43] The Discussions—attendance at which was mandatory—were intended to familiarize teachers who lacked professional training with the latest advances in theories of education (the oficio from the superintendent of education mentions the "new discoveries in Experimental Psychology" and in "the basic science of Education").

As a graduate of Lima's Normal School, Torres was chosen to lead and organize the Discussions (for the province of Chachapoyas), which took place during June and July 1931.[44] In addition to expounding upon new developments in educational theory, Torres also seized the opportunity of having a large number of teachers assembled in Chachapoyas to further promote the idea of a teachers' union. By September 1931, he and Sanchez Tirado had succeeded in bringing the vast majority of the teachers of Amazonas into their union. An oficio was sent to the subprefect of Chachapoyas by Torres, elected secretary general of the "Departmental Union of the Teachers of Amazonas," upon the founding of the union:

Sr. Prefect of the Department:

I have the pleasure of informing you that on the 7th of the present month, all the primary-school teachers of this locality met in General Assembly and formed the Departmental Union of the Teachers of Amazonas, whose Executive Committee was elected by secret vote.

The teachers of Amazonas, always lovers of educational progress and of all works that contribute to the aggrandizement of the fatherland . . . like all the teachers of the nation have their eyes fixed steadfastly on a future of true democracy, one based on renovating ideals that contribute to the attainment of positive spiritual and moral advancement for the fatherland, for its teachers, and for its children.

The teachers of Amazonas . . . offer our modest contingent to our comrades in [the rest of] the republic, so that [together] we may form the . . . "Federation of Teachers of Peru," source of the light that will guide Peru toward the modern and more scientific educational, civic, and moral future that all great fatherlands demand of their children in general. ([APA32], *Sindicato Departmental de Maestros Amazonenses al Subprefecto*, Sept. 15, 1931)

Torres's position as head of the *Comisión Escolar*, his ability to enlist like-minded individuals into the ranks of the region's teachers, and his (and Sanchez Tirado's) organizing efforts put him and his fellows in the position of being able to implement the democratizing philosophy of education expounded upon with such force in the newspaper *Amazonas*. That is, the rapid ascent of el pueblo into the educational bureaucracy represented a key moment in the rise of the middle class. For it enabled people who had recently risked their lives to bring about a transformed social order to broadcast the legitimacy of the principles for which they had fought. It allowed them to establish the hegemony of a new cultural order—one based on notions of democracy, equality, individual rights, and individual merit. It put vocal and outspoken defenders of the principles of popular sovereignty in the position of being able to mold young minds and bodies in new directions—directions that undermined the exclusionary pretensions of the aristocratic elite.[45]

As evidence of the success of Torres and his fellow teachers in influencing the young people placed in their care—and in disseminating the principles of popular sovereignty among the local population—in 1932 the students of the National High School of Chachapoyas (El Colegio Nacional San Juan de la Libertad) took it upon themselves to publish their own newspaper. They called it *De Frente* ("Straight Ahead"), and used it to articulate the same populist principles found in *Amazonas* and *Redención*. In subsequent years, similar papers, published by schoolteachers, appeared in the capitals of the department's two other provinces.[46]

El pueblo thus succeeded in placing its patrons in the region's most important political posts in the aftermath of the revolution of August 1930. The formerly marginalized middle sectors also became actively involved in the town's most vital political and social activities—by means of their important presence on the municipal council, in education, and in the government bureaucracy. Furthermore, by late 1930 it was virtually certain that el pueblo would win national political representation as well. Once it became clear that the Feijóo-Echaiz alliance would succeed in maintaining control over the region, it was a foregone conclusion that Ricardo Feijóo Reina and his allies would be elected to the Constituent Congress in October 1931 (which did indeed come to pass). The Congress would write a new constitution for Peru, and members of el pueblo had every expectation that their representatives would help them achieve an expanded role in the life of the region and the nation (which also came to pass; see Basadre 1968–69, 14: ch. 188).

THE ELABORATION OF NOVEL SOCIOCULTURAL FORMS

In addition to achieving national political representation, and to becoming actively involved in regional politics, the formerly marginalized middle sectors began to organize among themselves to purge local life of the material, behavioral, and symbolic markers of privilege and inequality upon which the aristocratic order had been based. In order to do so, el pueblo began to lay claim to the very public spaces and social activities in which aristocratic sovereignty had been publicly enacted and reproduced on a daily basis. El pueblo "democratized" these public spaces and activities, and in the process created a new kind of public culture in Chachapoyas—one in which public displays of power by privileged and especially potent (male) members of the elite were replaced by peaceful and consensual interactions among a mass of (jurally) indistinguishable (male) citizens. That is, in the most general of terms, the middle class of Chachapoyas mobilized among itself in order to make into a concrete reality the social order imagined discursively in the pages of *Amazonas*.[47]

In the immediate aftermath of the revolution of August 1930, a series of "horizontal associations" (Wolf 1966) emerged in Chachapoyas—associations that expressed the newfound strength of the formerly marginalized middle sectors, and that did much to create the new kind of democratized public culture they so desired.[48] Interestingly, these organizations had much in common with, and in certain cases seem to have been modeled on, the egalitarian forms of association that the newspaper *Amazonas* had argued it was crucial to bring into being if the region's laborers were to free themselves from the influences of the casta-controlled past (see Chapter 6, "Amazonas and Its Laborers").

Among the earliest of the new organizations to form was one that was very similar to an institution first imagined publicly in the newspaper *Amazonas* several years prior—a society of self-help for the region's laborers (see Chapter 6). In 1927 *Amazonas* had appealed to the artisans and laborers of Amazonas, without distinction of any kind, to unite their forces in a single organization of mutual aid. Such an organization, said the paper, would bring to an end the divisions that had formerly plagued the "laboring family of Amazonas." For it would prevent the region's laborers from being manipulated by the elite caudillos, from being forced into serving the "bastard interests" of those who were in reality their enemies.

On September 25, 1930—just over a month after the Rubio-Linch casta had been swept from power by the general mobilization of el pueblo—such an organization was formed. It was called the "Fraternal Assembly of Artisans and Laborers of Amazonas." The letter sent by the president of the Fraternal Assembly to Prefect Eleodoro Echaiz upon the founding of the institution gives clear expression to the transformed political environment of late 1930—in which the formerly marginalized middle sectors were able to translate their recently established position of legitimacy into concrete changes in the organization of everyday life:[49]

> Sr. Eleodoro Echaiz, Prefect:
>
> I have the honor of informing you that the artisans and laborers of this locality, aware of your concern for the advancement, progress, and well-being of the country [the region], that for many years has been found in a deplorable state, under the control of the leaders of an insidious form of politics, and grateful for the rights and protections now extended to them, have met in public session to form the "Fraternal Assembly of Artisans and Laborers of Amazonas." We form this assembly with the goal of promoting our own affairs, and protecting our members in cases of sickness, death, and other similar circumstances. ([APA32], Sept. 25, 1930)

From its inception, the Fraternal Assembly placed itself within the trajectory of the region's recently begun democratic transformation—in the context of liberation from aristocratic rule, and the general extension of constitutional guarantees. The very terms in which the founders of the Fraternal Assembly chose to refer to themselves—"the artisans and laborers of this locality"—expressed their clear kinship with the social movement that coalesced around the newspaper *Amazonas*. For it was *Amazonas* that helped ennoble the region's laborers, that helped call them into existence as a distinct group with common interests and concerns.

The group's founders chose no features other than their occupations to distinguish members of the Fraternal Assembly. They remained without class or race (but not without gender). Here, too, founders of the Fraternal Assembly affirmed their connection to the movements of democratización of the late 1920s, for it was precisely the universalistic nature of the movements upon which their legitimacy was based. The new organization's statutes, however, reveal that hidden processes of inclusion and exclusion were at work in the formation of the Fraternal Assembly—and thus in the elaboration of a "democratized" social order to replace the aristocratic order of the elite.

The statutes of the Fraternal Assembly reveal it to have been a mutual-aid society whose members assisted one another in times of sickness, death, or other emergency, when the financial resources of any one member were inadequate to meet the need in question. The statutes put particular emphasis on funerals and sickness. The members of the Fraternal Assembly commit themselves to shoulder the cost of, and to organize all aspects of, the funerals of its deceased members, and to support each other's families during times of sickness, or when members are not able to sustain themselves for other reasons. In order to have the financial resources necessary to carry out these functions, the Fraternal Assembly collected dues of 1.50 soles per month (the equivalent of about one day's earnings for an artisan; see Nugent 1988: ch. 4) from its members.

The Fraternal Assembly of Artisans and Laborers of Amazonas was virtually the first organization of its kind in Chachapoyas—one that created horizontal links of solidarity among the region's (male) laborers. Although the membership list that originally accompanied the statutes has not survived, in the letter to Prefect Echaiz informing him of the founding of the Fraternal Assembly, the president makes reference to the organization's 208 members. Elderly artisan informants confirm that the assembly was very popular—that working men of all kinds joined in large numbers.[50]

The popularity of the Fraternal Assembly is not surprising considering that it freed laborers from having to rely strictly on their own individual resources in meeting difficulties and emergencies of various kinds—or more to the point, from having to offer political allegiance to a powerful patron in return for these much-needed resources. Once liberated from material dependence on local elite power holders, the region's artisans and laborers were also free to defy any lingering elite demands concerning deferential and subservient behavior. That is, by relying strictly on people who were "like themselves" for economic support during times of need, and thus establishing material autonomy from the region's aristocratic families, Chachapoyas's laboring men did more than just strengthen their identity as a group and establish strong horizontal ties of mutual assistance. They also helped create an environment in which one of the key elements that had drawn them together as a political community—their desire for independence from and equality with members of the elite—could not be compromised by residual vertical ties of material dependence. By means of the Fraternal Assembly, the laborers of the region helped construct the material foundations of an environment in which they could interact with the elite on an equal standing in public and private spaces—in which they could democratize their interactions with the elite.[51] The Fraternal Assembly thus helped clear a new political space in which the forms of individuality and social relations imagined discursively in the newspaper *Amazonas*—and articulated orally within the People's University—could become a more concrete reality.[52]

Despite its explicit disavowal of involvement in politics (see below), documentary evidence reveals that in addition to these mutual assistance functions, the Fraternal Assembly took on important functions that were informally political in nature. Its monthly meetings provided a forum in which decisions were made regarding virtually any issue raised by the membership. These included such matters as the abusive or disrespectful behavior of a governor or justice of the peace, the difficulty a member had in collecting a debt owed him for work performed, and even the physical security of the Fraternal Assembly's members.[53] Once a decision had been reached by the general membership, the executive council advised either the prefect or the subprefect of the problem, who in turn informed the appropriate party of its need to respond to the difficulty (see below).

The mandate written into the by-laws of the Fraternal Assembly—to mutually protect its members in whatever way possible—thus extended into the political sphere. Several examples will help illustrate this important aspect of its role. When carpenter and executive council member Roberto Lopez was attacked and beaten by a group of Rubio clients in January 1931, the Fraternal Assembly immediately appealed to its large membership to make inquiries regarding the whereabouts of the assailants so that they could be brought to justice—a request that bore fruit shortly thereafter. It turned out that the men who had attacked Lopez were hiding in a remote corner of an estate (*Condechaca*) owned by the Rubio family, located in the nearby rural district of Levanto. This was made known to Prefect Echaiz, and from there it was a relatively simple matter for Echaiz to have the governor of Levanto (assisted by two gendarmes provided by Jefe of the Gendarmery Abraham Cachay) apprehend the men, who were then jailed at the order of the judge of the first instance.[54] Similarly, when Fraternal Assembly member and saddlemaker Leoncio Quiñones y Jara was accused of murder, and was jailed on the strength of another man's testimony, the president of the Fraternal Assembly made inquiries to the prefect that shortly thereafter led to Quiñones's release (on bail, provided by funds from the treasury of the Fraternal Assembly).[55]

In this way, the Fraternal Assembly acted as an arm of surveillance and support beyond what the state bureaucracy was able to provide—one that attempted to safeguard the liberty and security of its members in ways that the region's new leaders were not always able to. The Fraternal Assembly thus acted as an extension of the state, working in cooperation with government bodies, in protecting the well-being of el pueblo.

Though the middle sectors had not been denied access to the judicial or political system in the past, aggrieved individuals could be sure of getting a hearing only when their elite political patron was in power. Legal recourse thus depended on personalistic ties of patronage and clientele, which underscored relations of dependency between members of the elite and their followers, and reinforced the hierarchical order upon which aristocratic sovereignty was based. Once the region's artisans and laborers were freed from having to rely on personalistic ties with powerful patrons, another important link in their dependence on the elite was severed. That is, never before had the town's laboring men as a whole been able to make demands upon the political system as an impersonal institution. Never before had the judicial system appeared as anything but a mechanism with which powerful individuals advanced their interests and those of their casta. Indeed, as argued in previous chapters (see Chapters 3 and 4), it was only by demonstrating their capacity to wield judicial power in precisely these self-serving terms that elite families could remain in power.

The ability of the region's laboring men to call upon the judicial and political authorities as the representatives of seemingly disinterested institutions beginning in 1930 did much to make the judicial system *seem* impartial—to make it appear as if "everyone" (townspeople in general, and those laborers in particular) was indeed equal under the law. In other words, by taking on functions that were more political in nature, the Fraternal Assembly helped strengthen the individual autonomy of those who made up the middle class, further contributing to the creation of a new kind of public culture in Chachapoyas—one in which the forms of remade personhood and social relations imagined in the newspaper *Amazonas* and in the People's University would not be compromised by lingering elite influence over the system of justice.

The overall effect of the Fraternal Assembly was thus much along the lines of what was originally envisioned for such an organization in the newspaper *Amazonas*. The assembly provided its members with unity, strength, and protection from the traditional landed elite, giving its members an option other than allying with one of the casta families to achieve personal security or to secure much-needed economic resources in times of crisis. Thus it helped undermine any material basis for the perpetuation of hierarchical relations, the foundation of the aristocratic order. In this way, the Fraternal Assembly helped create an environment in which the egalitarian forms of subjectivity and democratized forms of social relations around which el pueblo had mobilized as a political community could be given concrete expression.

The Fraternal Assembly did more, however, than just turn its gaze outward in order to monitor and control the activities of those who posed a threat to its members—thereby empowering and protecting the artisans and laborers it took under its care. The mutual-aid society also looked inward, carefully scrutinizing and evaluating the behavior of its members, in an attempt to introduce new forms of discipline and new standards of conduct among them. In the process, the Fraternal Assembly sought to make all its members subject to a single set of moral and ethical precepts. In this case, as in others already discussed, the kinds of discipline the Fraternal Assembly sought to impose, and the standards of behavior it sought to generalize, had been prefigured several years prior in the newspaper *Amazonas*—specifically, in the paper's discussions of the forms of subjectivity and the patterns of ethical conduct necessary if the region and its people were to make themselves over in modern form.

The Fraternal Assembly called upon its members to be disciplined, honest, restrained individuals whose behavior would never reflect negatively on the Fraternal Assembly. Indeed, written directly into the statutes was the warning that members who behaved in ways that brought shame upon or discredit to the Fraternal Assembly would be subject to dismissal. Dishonesty in business dealings was the most serious offense: members found guilty of anything less than honorable behavior in representing their profession to the public would be removed from the organization. In this way, the Fraternal Assembly sought to extend principles of fair play and ethical behavior into the realm of economic transactions—to ensure that the operation of the economy was not exempt from the principles of justice around which el pueblo had rallied as a political community. The organization itself represented a kind of tribunal for economic justice, as it vowed to act on complaints it received about its members.

Also included in the Fraternal Assembly's founding statutes was the requirement that members' comportment at all times be such that they were a credit to the institution. Should members fail to comply with this obligation, they would be removed from the Fraternal Assembly. Both in and out of the workshop, then, the Fraternal Assembly insisted that its members conform to new standards—standards of ethical, fair, and moral behavior that had much in common with those of the "superior man" imagined discursively in the pages of the newspaper *Amazonas* (see Chapter 6).

There was one important difference between the Fraternal Assembly of Artisans and Workers of Amazonas that was founded in 1930, and the similar organization imagined several years prior in *Amazonas*, namely, its social composition. For despite the inclusive language of the Fraternal Assembly's statutes, processes of exclusion, both gendered and class-based, were built into those statutes from the assembly's very inception. They did much to define and defend a particular kind of transformed public culture—one in which town-dwelling, adult, independent, working men, most of whom had a skilled trade, came to represent "the artisans and laborers of Amazonas."

The newspaper *Amazonas* had originally called for an organization that would unite *all* workers—from town and countryside alike—and thus had made an explicit appeal for unity between Indian peasant and mestizo artisan. The Fraternal Assembly of Artisans and Workers of Amazonas, however, was restricted entirely to the mestizo artisans of the towns. Perhaps the most important factor limiting the involvement of the rural peasantry was the monthly membership fee. The 1.50 soles per month that all Fraternal Assembly members were required to pay was not an insignificant sum even for town-based artisans, who were involved daily in monetary transactions, and who relied on cash purchases for subsistence. For rural peasants, however, the monthly fee was exorbitant. Most peasants relied almost entirely on subsistence production to provide their families with food during this period, and marketed very little of what they produced. As a result, most had relatively little disposable cash income (rural day labor, a rare practice in the early 1930s, was remunerated at the rate of 0.60 soles per day—well below the minimal cost of reproducing labor power; Nugent 1988: 235). An additional monthly cash outlay of 1.50 soles was therefore not even a consideration for most rural cultivators.

Regardless of the size of the monthly contribution, peasants would have purchased very little with such an expenditure. The Fraternal Assembly was in no position to offer peasants protection from abusive rural political authorities or landowners. Its influence was limited almost entirely to urban contexts. Nor could it free rural cultivators of the need to ally themselves with a more powerful patron in order to obtain much-needed economic resources or political favors. The Fraternal Assembly's focus on helping families shoulder the costs of funerals was similarly of little use to the peasantry, as rural networks of kin and community-based reciprocity in which all peasants were involved provided the social framework within which major life-cycle events such as funerals were carried out.[56]

In this way, the Fraternal Assembly constructed a clear class-based boundary that defined the outer limits of membership in the new organization— one that reinforced an old divide between town and countryside.

Equally important in structuring a distinct kind of democratized public culture within the towns, however, were the gender-based exclusions built into the Fraternal Assembly's founding statutes. As the organization's name implies, the Fraternal Assembly made no provisions whatsoever for female members—even though the town's nonelite sectors included a large number of working women who were breadmakers, livestock sellers, cantina operators, and seamstresses (full- and part-time). Despite this, the only kind of membership available to women was "inactive" membership—which women were granted automatically by virtue of being the wife or daughter or companion of an active male member of the assembly. This gender-based form of exclusion was a powerful means of reinforcing the images of domestic womanhood portrayed in the newspaper *Amazonas*. For just as the Fraternal Assembly of Artisans and Laborers was providing an organizational framework that empowered and defended male artisans, it was denying any such protection or empowerment to female artisans and laborers. Instead, only women located in the home were considered worthy of protection by the Fraternal Assembly.

A second form of horizontal association that emerged at this time, the "sport-culture club," also played an important role in actualizing the new notions of proper personhood and social behavior imagined discursively in the pages of *Amazonas*, and in transforming the nature of public culture. Sport-culture clubs, for young men and women alike, made their first appearance in the region in the months following the rise of the Echaiz-Feijóo alliance, largely due to the efforts of the new generation of teachers recruited by Leon M. Torres (see above).[57] The oficio sent to Prefect Eleodoro Echaiz at the founding of the club "Eleven Tigers," which fielded a soccer team of young men, is typical of the communiqués received by the prefecture describing this new form of organization. The fact that Echaiz is made an honorary member speaks clearly to the approval of such organizations by the region's new authorities:

> Sr. Prefect of the Department:
>
> I have the great pleasure of informing you that, in public session on the 8th of the present month, the sport club "Eleven Tigers" was formed. . . . At this meeting it was also unanimously agreed to designate you as an honorary member.
>
> In placing these matters before your consideration, allow me to emphasize that the mission of the institution over which I preside is cultural in nature, that we are concerned with local improvement and with the continual desire to awaken [in the populace] a love of sport, as well as to contribute to the dissemination of the good and wholesome ideals that devolve to the benefit of the collectivity, as the basis of a wholesome and ideological orientation toward the destiny of Amazonas, which will be nothing other than what its good children decide, guided by the norms of a proper understanding and an efficacious and moral effort on the part of all its sectors. ([APA32], Jan. 15, 1931)

The founding document of a second soccer club—the sport club "Sixth of June"—expresses many of the same ideals, and also makes explicit what remains implicit in the oficio above—the connection between these ideals and the nation:

> Sr. Prefect of the Department:
>
> I have the honor of informing you that in a meeting of the 1st of this month, the Sport Club "6 de Junio" has been constituted. . . .
>
> Given the patriotic goals which the club pursues, [that of] improving the

physical education of youth, we hope that we merit all the assistance that you, with your widely recognized patriotism, are known to lend to institutions of this kind. (Ibid., Apr. 8, 1931)

An oficio sent to the prefect by the founding members of the sport club "Eleven Friends" echoes many of the same sentiments:

Sr. Prefect of the Department:

I am pleased to inform your office . . . that today a group of young men of this locality, wishing to realize that noble end of promoting [the development of] physical culture, so necessary a factor to an integral education, has agreed to organize a sport club that has as its name: Sport Club "Eleven Friends." (Ibid., June 10, 1931)

In the early 1930s, between one and two dozen "sport-culture clubs" were formed among the young men and women of Chachapoyas. As suggested by the documents quoted above, all the clubs espoused their commitment to the ideals of progress, community, good intentions, moral behavior, and the prominent place of sport in training young bodies and minds in ways useful to the nation. In addition, in announcing the formation of the clubs to the prefect, club members consistently described themselves as "a group of young men" or as "youth," and nothing more. They are classless, raceless—totally unmarked. There are no distinctions of any kind to which they make explicit reference.[58]

The *Reglamentos Interiores* of the sport clubs, which were written for the internal use of their members rather than for the approval of the prefect, provide a window into the range of behaviors and activities that clubs took it upon themselves to monitor—and the forms of discipline to which club members voluntarily submitted. These regulations also provide considerable insight into how the clubs helped actualize new forms of democratized subjectivity and social relations of the kind imaged discursively in *Amazonas* and disseminated orally in the People's University. Finally, the regulations reveal the ways in which the democratized form of public culture that these new sociocultural forms helped bring into being was based on new processes of exclusion (especially of the rural peasantry)—processes implicated in the seemingly inclusive language of popular sovereignty itself:

Internal Statutes of the Athletic Club "Pro-Luya"

The Athletic Sport Club Pro-Luya is a social center of sport and culture . . . whose members enjoy and are subject to the obligations contained in these statutes. . . .

Part I. Concerning the Club

Art. 1. The Club is to be composed of at least 22 members, and however many additional members [are] decided.

Art. 2. Everyone who wishes to belong to the Club is obliged to pay an entrance fee of 20 centavos.

Art. 3. In order to be an active member one must be 21 years of age, and have an honorable job, profession, or form of employment.

Art. 4. The goal pursued by the Club is to achieve the highest level of [athletic] progress and refinement.

Part IV. Obligations of Members

Art. 19. Members must arrive for football matches well in advance of the beginning of the game, or else pay a fine of 20 centavos.

Art. 20. Athletic training will take place every Sunday at 2:00 P.M. Team members who arrive late, or who fail to arrive, will be fined 10 centavos.

Art. 21. Members have the following obligations:

a. They must pay a monthly fee of 10 centavos.

b. They must attend all [weekly] meetings of the Club.

c. For every infraction of the rules contained in these statutes, they must pay a fine of 10 centavos.

Part V. Penalties

Art. 22. Members who do not lend punctual assistance to the team captain, or who offer disrespectful words or acts to the captain, will definitely be removed from the Club.

Art. 23. During a football match, if a member is guilty of offering disrespectful words or acts to his teammates, or to players on other teams, he will be suspended from the Club temporarily. Continued infractions of this kind will result in his permanent removal from the Club.

Art. 24. Members will be removed from the Club for dishonesty in business, for bad conduct, for contagious disease,[59] or for whatever other cause casts aspersions or dishonor on the Club.

Part VI. Concerning Club Meetings

Art. 27. In opening meetings, the Club President will employ the following phrase: "In the name of God and the Fatherland, this meeting is opened." In closing meetings, the Club president will employ the following phrase: "In the name of God and the Fatherland, this meeting is closed."

Art. 30. It is absolutely forbidden, during meetings or outside the context of meetings, to discuss political matters, or any other matters that are outside the interests of the Club.

Part VII. General Dispositions

Art. 32. All members are required to buy a uniform, consisting of a white shirt with red stripes and with the letters CA on the left side and PL on the right side, and black pants with red stripes.

Art. 34. Under no circumstances will the Club take part in any matters related to politics.

Art. 37. The funds obtained by the club from its parties will be used to purchase sporting equipment. ([APA32], Feb. 12, 1932)

The sport clubs thus required of their members that they be a particular kind of social person—disciplined, moderate, fair, reasonable, and respectable, on the field and off of it. Members had to police their behavior carefully if they wished to remain associated with the club.

These clubs also attempted to discipline the bodies of the emergent middle class. Indeed, an important part of the statutes for all the clubs concerned training—an activity that was considered a serious part of the overall activities of the clubs. Athletic training for most clubs took place on Sunday afternoons. Members were expected to appear for practice on time, or else face a fine (usually of 10 centavos). Repeated instances of tardiness could lead to dismissal. Likewise with games. Team members who were to play on a given day were to arrive in advance of the game, or they would be fined (usually 20 centavos). In training as in games, club members who were disrespectful to other team members or the team captain were subject to suspension or expulsion. Punctuality and discipline were necessary characteristics for those who wished to be members of the team.

These sport clubs—in which a growing number of the region's young adults became involved—thus created new authority structures and social relations. As club members, all were held to a single set of rules, all had the same rights and obligations, regardless of family wealth or background. All were subject to a single set of behavioral standards, on and off of the field. Distinctions of race or ancestry—which had formerly created distinct sets of rules, opportunities, and liabilities for distinct groups—were made to disappear in the context of club membership. Such distinctions meant nothing as each club pursued its goal of athletic accomplishment. Rather, what counted within the context of these new organizational forms was the ability to discipline mind, behavior, and body, the ability to make a contribution to the team, the ability to demonstrate physical prowess and skills of athleticism—none of which depended on wealth or background. In this sense, the clubs were powerful democratizing agents indeed, for they erected new standards for achievement and individual recognition that operated independently of the distinctions of the aristocratic order.[60]

These sport-culture clubs also acted as the basis for new patterns of middle-class socializing. That is, each club began to host dance parties, with live music provided by local orchestras, to which much of the population was invited. These events represent the first large-scale, publicly legitimate social events that were both hosted by and oriented toward the town's middle sectors.

New kinds of distinction and exclusion, however, played a fundamental role in defining the new forms of subjectivity and social relation, and in structuring the more egalitarian public culture, implicated in the sport-culture clubs. Key in this regard were the ways in which the clubs contributed to the emergence of what might be called the nonpolitical, patriotic subject. All of the sport clubs emphasized the apolitical nature of the clubs—that in no circumstance would they involve themselves in any political matters whatsoever. This injunction extended to individual club members—who were expected to abstain from participation in politics as well—on pain of immediate and irrevocable dismissal from the club. The statutes of the sport-culture club "Kuelap"—a soccer club of young men formed in the town of Luya in 1932—expressed the matter in the following terms: "The members [of the club] are not to intervene in matters of a political nature.[61] They must exercise their civil liberties without compromising the club." While thus relinquishing their political rights, clubs commonly invoked what they called their "social rights." Again the sport-culture club "Kuelap" provides an apt example:

Sr. Prefect:

I have the great honor of informing you that yesterday the youth of this locale organized an association that has chosen the name "Sport-Culture Club 'Kuelap'." . . .

Said organization would not have been complete had the new entity not agreed to send a special note to the altruistic leader of our department, placing ourselves under his beneficent auspices, and invoking the social guarantees that the Constitution accords us whenever our purpose is to place ourselves on the path of physical, intellectual, and moral development. ([APA32], June 11, 1932)

Like all the sport-culture clubs, "Kuelap" described its goals in strictly apolitical terms:

The association called "Sport-Culture Club 'Kuelap'" is mutually cooperative in nature, and wishes to develop the brotherhood of its members. The society has as its goal the cultivation of sport in all its manifestations and will strive toward the moral and intellectual perfection of the collectivity. (Ibid.)

At the same time, the clubs were explicitly patriotic. Many include in their *Reglamento Interior* a statute such as: "In order to open meetings the president will employ the following: 'In the name of God and the Fatherland this meeting is declared open.' In order to close meetings the president will employ a like phrase" (ibid.).

In other words, the sport clubs constituted themselves as explicitly apolitical organizations that would avidly pursue the physical, mental, and spiritual "improvement" of their members, of their society, and of their nation. Members would discipline mind, body, and behavior faithfully and rigorously in order to become proper individuals. What they would *not* do, however, was threaten the forces of order. In this way, the clubs promoted what might be called *social* citizenship, and a socially democratized public culture, while they discouraged *political* citizenship.[62] Indeed, the distinction between the two is stated explicitly in the letter from Roberto Lopez A., the president of the sport-culture club "Kuelap," to the prefect, announcing the founding of the club (see above).[63]

Intellectual, moral, and physical development—all of which are depicted as noble and worthy ends—are thus clearly separated from the illegitimate activity of politics. Politics is constructed in such a way as to appear to be a threat to these laudatory forms of individual and social development. None of the writings of any of the clubs mentions "striving toward political perfection."

Rather, implicit is the idea that the recently democratized order embodies legitimate politics, while any challenge to the existing order is unfounded.

A second set of exclusions subtly defines the boundaries of el pueblo in such a way as to make it possible to equate "the people" in general with a particular people—members of the middle class and the elite (who commonly belonged to the clubs as well). The statutes were worded in such a way that peasants (and day-laborers) were automatically excluded (members had to be "honorably employed," buy an expensive uniform, pay dues, arrive without fail for practice). Despite the seemingly inclusive language employed by the clubs ("the youth of this locale," "a group of young men of this vicinity," etc.), those who were able to participate in the new democratized public culture of the era were restricted in clear terms, thus reproducing the long-standing divide between town and country, Indian and non-Indian.[64]

All these clubs fielded sports teams (soccer for the young men, volleyball for the young women) that began to play one another in public competitions that were attended by much of the local populace. These competitions became quite important affairs in the social life of the town. Young people aspired to be on winning teams, and to be recognized as strong players. Parents were able to take public pride in the athletic accomplishments of their children. Athletic competitions became public performances in which the new visibility and legitimacy of the middle sectors could be given clear expression. In addition, however, particular forms of individuality and social relations became embodied in these events. These were forms that publicly celebrated the principles of equality, discipline, and individual merit in relationship to which el pueblo had coalesced as a political community. They were also forms that affirmed el pueblo's commitment to the national community, and to the entire "educational" effort of forming useful citizens described in previous years in the newspaper *Amazonas*. The nation and the region thus mutually defined and constructed one another in these public performances, in which groups of young people competed to demonstrate which was best able to embody and to represent the new ideals upon which the remade social world was to be based.[65]

The president of the Peruvian Federation of Athleticism—the national affiliate of the International Amateur Athletic Association and the South American Confederation of Athleticism—made much of this explicit in the late

1930s, when he wrote to the departmental prefect to ask for his assistance in bringing the athletic activities of the region under the auspices of the Peruvian Federation of Athleticism:

> Sr. Prefect:
>
> . . . It will not have escaped your distinguished attention that amateur sport is the best way to develop young people of both sexes, because it draws upon movements that are natural to human beings, because of which all young people can engage in it, even those who are frail.
>
> To protect athleticism and to promote its development is thus to do good; and this is the labor in which we are involved, because it is our desire that the youth of today, men of tomorrow, learn how to struggle in order to succeed, but that they learn that this struggle must be noble, that it be the culmination of sustained effort. By means of sport we hope to carry out a double labor of education: to strive toward the physical perfection of the individual in the service of the collectivity, and to strive as well toward spiritual perfection, so necessary in men who must sustain a nation. ([APA31], Dec. 11, 1938)

TRANSFORMING THE RELIGIOUS SPHERE

Public culture was transformed not only by the empowerment of the formerly marginalized middle sectors, and the provision of the social and political space necessary to form organizations that would help actualize and express the legitimacy of el pueblo, but also by the democratización of Catholic religious practice.[66] During the period of casta rule, virtually all aspects of religious practice were structured to reproduce the distinctions of race and class upon which the aristocratic order was based. Indeed, there was a ranked hierarchy of prestige concerning religious spaces and activities that mapped directly onto the racial hierarchy of the aristocratic order. The region's most lavish and prestigious house of worship—the main cathedral of the Diocese of Chachapoyas—was open only to families of elite background. The elite used the cathedral for the celebration of a variety of religious and quasi-religious events—from weekly masses to important religious and political holidays. The fact that such celebrations were restricted to the aristocratic families—and that cholos and runa were virtually never in attendance—gave implicit religious sanction to the highly stratified social order. That is, such ongoing exclusionary practices lent an air of inevitability to a highly artificial social arrangement in which positions of power and prestige were reserved for individuals with the proper backgrounds.

The upper class also celebrated major life-cycle events—baptisms, engagements, marriages, etc.—in the cathedral. The rituals surrounding these events tended to be elaborate, during which members of the elite put on public display the wealth and power that was such an integral part of their social identity (see Chapter 2 for an example). When the town's more humble social elements wished to celebrate such turning points in the life cycle, on the other hand, they were restricted to Chachapoyas's smaller churches and chapels.[67] At every stage in the life course, then, the Catholic Church and public religious ritual were drawn upon to naturalize "private" social identity—to lend credence to distinctions of race, class, and gender upon which the entire aristocratic order was based.

Shortly after the revolution of August 1930, such restrictions concerning the use of Chachapoyas's main cathedral were eliminated. Monseñor Octavio Ortiz Arrieta, a Salesian of humble background who had been appointed bishop of the Diocese of Chachapoyas in 1920 (Pennati n.d.), played the decisive role in this regard.[68] Monseñor Ortiz had attempted to democratize access to the cathedral in the 1920s, but had been prevented from doing so by leading members of the ruling casta. After the rise of el pueblo in August 1930, however, there was little to stand in the way of his democratizing efforts.

From this time onward, use of the cathedral ceased being restricted to individuals of elite standing. Rather, people of all social classes and racial backgrounds began to celebrate major life-cycle events in the most prestigious of Chachapoyas's religious spaces, with the blessing of the bishop.[69] It is true that the cathedral continued to be used for the celebrations of important religious and political holidays. As attendance at these events was no longer restricted to the elite, however, the Catholic Church no longer had the same naturalizing function in relation to the aristocratic order. Rather, both the institution of the Church itself and the sacred space of the cathedral became sites within which the democratized social order around which el pueblo had mobilized as a political community could be made real. After 1930, the institutional and symbolic weight of the Church was increasingly put behind the legitimacy of an egalitarian rather than a stratified social order.[70]

A second change in religious practice introduced by Monseñor Ortiz centered on the patron saint of Chachapoyas. Until 1930, two completely distinct patron saints, and saint's day celebrations, were observed in Chachapoyas. Members of the elite recognized as the town's patron San Juan. The elite organized, sponsored, and participated in the celebration of San Juan de los Caballeros every year on June 24. After a mass in the cathedral spoken by the bishop, the procession honoring San Juan de los Caballeros left the cathedral and followed a roundabout route through the town. Leading the procession was a litter carried aloft by the mayordomo of the event and a group of his close associates.

The nonelite members of the town, on the other hand, recognized a different patron saint—San Juan de los Indios. The nonelite segments of the population organized, sponsored, and participated in the celebration of their saint yearly, also on June 24. The ritual honoring San Juan de los Indios began not at the main cathedral on the *Plaza de Armas*, but at one of the town's lesser churches (*Santa Ana*, located on one of the town's smaller *plazuelas*). The route followed by those who participated in this procession was entirely distinct from the route of the procession for the San Juan of the elite. Members of the elite did not participate in the procession honoring San Juan de los Indios.

The last year in which class-specific patron-saint celebrations took place in Chachapoyas was 1930. With the impetus of Monseñor Ortiz, beginning in 1931 Chachapoyas recognized a new patron saint and a new saint's day. As of August 15, 1931, all Chachapoyanos, regardless of social background, had the same *patrona*—the Virgen de Asunta.[71] In order to democratize the celebration of the town's patron saint's day, Monseñor Ortiz introduced a change in the sponsorship of the celebration. During the period of casta rule, a single wealthy individual had acted as sponsor for the entire celebration of San Juan. Under Monseñor Ortiz's system, whoever wished to do so offered a modest contribution to help pay for ritual events surrounding the celebration of the Virgen de Asunta. In this way, all members of the community could feel like they were directly involved in sponsoring the celebration of their patron saint.

The ascent of el pueblo into these multiple arenas of social, political, and religious life enabled people who had recently risked their lives to bring about a transformed social world to broadcast the legitimacy of the principles for which they had fought—and to do so in domains that until then had remained the exclusive preserve of the regional elite. The combined effect of these changes was twofold. First, they resulted in the emergence of a new kind of public culture in Chachapoyas—one in which the host of material, behavioral, and symbolic markers of hierarchy acted out on a daily basis in the reproduction of aristocratic sovereignty were replaced by the constant assertion and celebration of equality. Second, these changes created a situation in which the principles of popular sovereignty took on a transformed significance in public life. For the first time in the region's history, these principles came to define the standards to which individuals who occupied positions of "public trust" would actually be held accountable. This marked a radical change from the status of these principles during the period of casta rule—when they had been nothing more than empty phrases uttered mechanically in political ritual and discourse by elite groups, who publicly flaunted their ability to disregard the most fundamental aspects of these principles.

9 Conclusion

Modernity at the Edge of Empire

This book has grown out of efforts to understand why the process of building states and making national cultures described in much of the literature does not apply to the process by which the modern Peruvian nation-state took on a real presence in the Chachapoyas region.

In the case under consideration, state-building and nation-making were initiated from the *fringes* of the territorial state, by subaltern groups who had formerly been excluded from participation in the national community. Two key factors contributed to this development. First, although the social order was organized according to principles of aristocratic sovereignty, the ideological apparatus nonetheless espoused the legitimacy of popular sovereignty. Second, subaltern groups perceived popular sovereignty and modern nationhood (which were associated with equality, individual rights, private property, progress, and consensus) as representing powerful forces of liberation. The contradiction between aristocratic and popular sovereignty was rooted in the history of state-making in postcolonial Latin America. The perception that popular sovereignty and modern nationhood were emancipatory forces can only be understood in relation to the organization of everyday life during the period of aristocratic sovereignty.

Based on the material presented in the previous chapters, certain generalizations can be made concerning the countervailing forces—material and ideological—that characterized the operation of the aristocratic order and the state as a whole. At the turn of the twentieth century, the emerging Peruvian nation-state was rent by contradictions. Although founded as an independent state in the 1820s on liberal principles of democracy, citizenship, private property, and individual rights, the central government was not remotely able to make good on these arrangements even 100 years later. Although such principles were routinely invoked in political ritual and discourse, many parts of the country were organized according to principles diametrically opposed to these precepts of popular sovereignty.

Chachapoyas was one such region. Here, society was divided into highly unequal socioeconomic categories based on race, gender, property, and ancestry. The small handful of families that made up the "noble," landed elite claimed descent from Spanish forebears, and saw it as their exclusive, inherited right to rule the region free from the interference of the Indios and cholos, whose labor and product provided the elite with much of its wealth. Even social interaction with such people was kept to a minimum, and was structured in such a way as to require public deference and subservience from the subaltern.

The landed class, however, was far from internally unified. Rather, members of the elite saw themselves as having the inherited right to rule that *no one*—not even other members of the elite—could legitimately deny them. Furthermore, in order to exercise these rights, the elite did not hesitate to use violence. Those who interfered with the exercise of elite privilege therefore did so at their peril.

Because of peculiarities of the Peruvian political order, however, it was inevitable that each faction of the elite continually interfered with the others' ability to exercise positions of power. During this period, Peru was an internally fragmented polity. Unable to control its national territory directly, the central regime chose select elite groups in each region to act in its name, in the process denying the remainder of the elite access to political power. The result was endemic conflict, as elite-led factions struggled to control the local apparatus of state.

Competition for political office—with which came control over a variety of tribute-taking mechanisms—was especially intense in the Chachapoyas region. For landed families could not rely on their estates to provide them with wealth. Because of the poverty of agrarian pursuits, it was as if influential families were being thrust out of the agrarian world and into the public, political world, where all threatened to collide in their efforts to become the single privileged client of the state. Once in such a position, the ruling faction removed members of the opposition from public office, prosecuted them for supposed crimes, seized their goods, and did harm to their person and property. Because no one faction could control the political apparatus for any sustained period of time, however, members of *all* social classes and *all* elite-led factions suffered continual insecurity of person and property. For as each new faction rose to power, it persecuted its enemies in whatever way it could.

The ruling casta, then, used its powers of appointment and its control over armed force to persecute and harass members of the opposition in as systematic and comprehensive a manner as possible. Continuous persecution of the opposition was necessary because opposing castas refused to accept the position of the ruling group as legitimate. Rather, opposing castas saw their own aspirations as inherently more valid than the pretensions of those who controlled the prefecture, and thus constantly sought to take the place of the coalition in power. Only by engaging in consistent and coordinated persecution of opposing castas could the ruling casta fragment this hostile opposition sufficiently to make united action on the part of its enemies difficult or impossible. Only in this way could the ruling casta reproduce its position of regional dominance.

The ruling faction was also the official representative of the independent republic of Peru within the department of Amazonas—a republic founded on liberal Enlightenment principles of individual rights and protections, the sanctity of person and property, and equality under the law. As a result, although committed to making constant attacks upon the life and property of the opposition, the ruling faction was equally compelled to present itself in all political ritual, and in all political discourse, as the sole and true defender of state-endorsed principles of popular sovereignty. In these rhetorical and ritual spaces, the ruling elite elaborated a mythical social order that was the antithesis of factional politics and aristocratic hierarchy. In place of violence, insecurity, and privilege, everyday life was depicted as consensual and orderly, and individuals were portrayed as universally enjoying the protections of life, liberty, and property granted them by the Constitution. In ritual and discourse, unity and harmony prevailed, and distinctions of race, gender, and class—upon which the entire aristocratic order was based—ceased to exist. In place of such distinctions, the ruling faction asserted the existence of a mass of identical "citizens," all of whom were united behind the cause of promoting "progress" and "advancement."

The particular elite faction that controlled the apparatus of state was thus forced to offer public accounts of its deeds by invoking notions of equality, individual rights and protections, progress, and the "common good" that were in direct contradiction with its own actions—and that also provided a critical commentary on the cultural and material logic of aristocratic privilege itself. Aristocratic "sovereignty" could not be celebrated, or even acknowledged, in formal political spheres. Popular sovereignty had to be celebrated, on an ongoing basis, despite the fact that it had virtually no relation to any existing social reality. Indeed, there was a conspicuous silence about the very existence of the aristocratic order in all political ritual and discourse.

The ruling casta's ability to persecute the opposition in a systematic manner could not be sustained, however. Indeed, the period of strength and solidarity that characterized its initial phase of control was followed by a period of growing weakness, during which ruling casta members suffered many of the same violations of person and property as did members of the opposition. As contradictions inherent in casta rule made themselves manifest, political appointees from Lima who were not beholden to ruling casta leaders took on roles of growing importance in local affairs. Their presence made systematic and coordinated persecution of casta enemies increasingly difficult, as the Lima appointees broke the monopoly on political positions formerly enjoyed by the ruling casta and weakened its control over armed force. At the same time, members of the ruling casta began to struggle among themselves for access to key political positions and for control of tributary revenue, further undermining the effectiveness with which the ruling casta could persecute its enemies. In these transformed conditions, members of the opposition were able to unite against the ruling casta, and eventually to drive it from power. Just as the ruling casta was forced to demonstrate its ability to violate the "rights" of others in public in order to reproduce its position of dominance, the only means by which opposing castas could rise to power was by publicly violating the "rights" of members of the ruling casta. These conflictual dynamics of shame and countershame, violence and counterviolence, characterized the particular form of aristocratic sovereignty encountered in the Chachapoyas region.

Even as ruling faction and opposition alike were involved in a series of violent encounters with one another that served as public spectacles and statements about the ability of each to rule, rulers and ruled employed the central regime's discourse of popular sovereignty, progress, equal protection under the law, and the common good to represent their actions and those of their adverseries—if for different purposes (the ruling casta to legitimate, the opposition to delegitimate). The use of this discourse by *both* groups, however, blatantly contradicted the violent, personalistic, and competitive actions that characterized casta behavior in general. Despite this contradiction, however, neither group made any effort to conceal its violent behavior. To the contrary: the principles of aristocratic sovereignty required those who wished to occupy positions of rule to demonstrate their ability to dominate, shame, and impose their will on their adversaries.

Although casta groups routinely invoked the rhetoric of popular sovereignty in political ritual and discourse, it was clear to all that aristocratic sovereignty was the reigning social reality of the time. Conformity with the precepts of popular sovereignty never went beyond the limited domains of ritual and discourse, never had any concrete impact on the daily lives of the people of the region. Rather, these principles openly contradicted the aristocratic order throughout the period. Repeating such principles mechanically in ritual and discourse was thus in one sense a concession that the aristocratic elite made in order to maintain a relationship of mutual noninterference with the central government. Indeed, whenever the central regime attempted to go beyond these realms and impinge on elite privilege directly, it encountered outrage and fierce resistance.

In another sense, then, invoking the principles of popular sovereignty in ritual and discourse was anything but a concession to the central state. For what was important about ritual performances and discursive statements was not the egalitarian, consensual, selfless principles that figured so prominently within them, but rather which casta group was able to articulate these principles—which group was able to make ritual pronouncements that were in such blatant contradiction with the reality of the time.

The ruling casta's ability to represent its particular interest as the general interest, and to depict its abuse of power as rule by consensus, did much to transform the potentially subversive nature of the principles of popular sovereignty into a legitimating mechanism for the structure of aristocratic sovereignty. It did so not because the ruling casta hid its abuse of power from view, but because it did not. That is, the principles of aristocratic sovereignty required that rulers show their ability to dominate, shame, and impose their will upon those who would challenge their position. Making use of egalitarian rhetoric in political ritual and discourse to justify the persecution of their local enemies, and to ridicule their patrons in the national capital, accomplished precisely this for those in power.

The elite's active celebration of the principles of equality, citizenship, and individual rights in all political ritual and discourse, even as it ridiculed and violated these principles in everyday life, was ultimately its undoing. The vision of a world in which the material, behavioral, and symbolic distinctions of aristocratic sovereignty were made to disappear, in which violence and insecurity were eliminated, and in which individual rights and protections truly obtained for all, proved very powerful for people of all social classes. For it provided everyone with a vision of social justice and social order that could act as a radical alternative to the insecurities to which all were subject under casta rule. Only in the context of the massive dislocations in culture and economy experienced throughout Peru as a by-product of the late nineteenth-century crisis in global capitalism, however, did this vision of social justice become a powerful motivating force in local affairs. In the midst of the chaotic conditions that prevailed during this period, marginalized middle sectors of the local population coalesced into a "movement of democratization," and declared themselves the defenders of popular rule and the enemies of aristocratic privilege. In 1930, at a moment of crisis in the national political order, these marginalized groups rose up to challenge the elite in an armed confrontation and managed to seize control of regional affairs. Thereafter, these middle sectors made good on their earlier vows. They were instrumental in forming a new public culture in Chachapoyas based on the principles of popular sovereignty.

The success of the "revolution of 1930" was contingent upon a prior period of intense political mobilization among the mestizo artisans of the towns and the Indian peasants of the countryside. In the years leading up to the revolution, the democratización movement had attracted much of the local population to its cause. The movement's widespread appeal was (in part) a function of the new cultural order and moral universe to which it gave expression in public discourse—one that offered the subaltern a radical alternative to the demeaning and oppressive structure of casta rule.

Chachapoyas's marginalized middle sectors began to construct a new identity for themselves predominantly in the pages of a local newspaper—*Amazonas*. *Amazonas* asserted that the region *did* have a general interest, that its people *did* have common enemies, and that they *could* build an effective future. They could do so by rising up against the aristocratic families, whose incessant struggles for power had consistently undermined the common good. The paper asserted that Chachapoyas's ruling elite was anything but a noble caste descended from aristocratic forebears. Filling its pages with the litany of elite abuses with which the subaltern was intimately familiar, *Amazonas* argued that the elite was brutal and rapacious. Its members' ancestors had come to power centuries before (during the Conquest) through deception and murder, and thereafter had divided, victimized, and abused the defenseless population in whatever way possible—all in order to satisfy its insatiable hunger for power, privilege, and wealth.

Nor, the paper argued, were the region's mestizos and Indios the uncouth, semicivilized group they were depicted to be. Rather, they were the local embodiment of *el pueblo Peruano* (the Peruvian people). As such, they represented the region's only hope for salvation. It was el pueblo that was committed to the ideals of democracy, equality, and justice. It was *el pueblo Chachapoyano* who sought to end the abuses of its own aristocratic elite. In the absence of adequate protections by the state, however, el pueblo had been left to be mistreated by the elite families. Indeed, because these elite families had hung on so tenaciously to their positions of privilege, democracy and justice had yet to be established in Chachapoyas—and thus el pueblo Chachapoyano continued to be victimized by abuses from which other peoples had been liberated long before. Once rid of such coercive influences, el pueblo Chachapoyano would be free to realize its true potential, to make its unique contribution to the Peruvian nation. In the meantime, however, Chachapoyas was best understood as a remote backwater where prenational sentiments and archaic forms of behavior lingered that had long since disappeared from the rest of the civilized world.

The new cultural order imagined discursively within the movement of democratización thus directly contradicted the cultural logic of the aristocratic order—in particular, elite assertions of fundamental, inherent differences among distinct racial groups. The democratización movement undermined elite assertions of hereditary distinction by making common cause among those identified as belonging to inferior races (Indios, cholos, runa), and by combining them into a single, inclusive, nonracial category—el pueblo. El pueblo, taught the movement, was the region's only hope for salvation, for el pueblo represented the region's only progressive force for change.

In this way, the movement of democratización sought to place the region and its people in a historical imaginary independent of and more powerful than the aristocratic families' parochial claims to nobility. The explicitly *national* dimension to these efforts was crucial. El pueblo was a category derived in large part from the discourse of the nation-state, and thus the democratización movement invoked a national form of authority and a national system of social classification in challenging the aristocratic order. The authority and legitimacy of el pueblo, however, was not strictly national in character. By taking on the mantle of "the people," the marginalized middle sectors of Chachapoyas associated themselves with a movement that transcended national boundaries. They claimed to be a part of the rise of modernity—the movement of global proportions that had catapulted western Europe to preeminence worldwide, that had everywhere vanquished "backward," feudal elites, that had liberated the individual from *his* oppressors, and had ushered in an era of justice and prosperity.

The movement of democratización that swept through Chachapoyas in the 1920s and ultimately led to the overthrow of the landed elite exhibits several features worthy of comment. First, contrary to what is described in much of the literature on state-building and nation-making, modern, national culture did not come to Chachapoyas in the shape of an externally imposed set of cultural forms whose arbitrariness had to be naturalized by the institutions of the state. Rather, those involved in the movement embraced modern notions of time, space, and personhood without having been coerced or coopted, prior to the establishment of state institutions and their normalizing gaze. Indeed, the entire mobilization of the middle sectors occurred in the context of a broad cultural movement that opposed tradition to modernity—that branded the former as a backward, oppressive structure based on artificial and imposed distinctions that were used to justify brutality and greed. Modernity and nationhood were welcomed as powerful moral forces of emancipation—forces that would liberate the region from its oppressors, and would allow the true potential of the people at last to be realized.

In challenging the aristocratic order, then, the movement of democratización openly embraced "things modern" and "things national." In addition to doing away with exclusionary racial divisions, reconfiguring history, and reconceptualizing space, this challenge included accepting modern notions of discipline, order, hygiene, and morality. For these "personal" characteristics were seen as the antithesis of the violent and abusive behavior of the decadent aristocratic elite. In short, as an outgrowth of the movements of democratización, time and space were nationalized, and individuality was modernized.

Second, the new cultural identity and alternative moral universe authored from within the movement of democratización appeared to movement participants as anything but imposed, external, or arbitrary. Rather, these were to a significant degree created by the people themselves, and emerged in the form of a *recognition* on their part of the region's most essential and enduring characteristics. Indeed, these features were regarded as being eternal. Reflected in phenomena as diverse as the ancient architecture of the Inca and the personal proclivities of el pueblo, they were seen as integral to the region and its people.

National culture thus first emerged from within local society as something natural, eternal, and true—and as sufficiently motivating to the subaltern that, in order to make it a reality, they risked their lives in order to overthrow the elite in an armed confrontation. Thereafter, the formerly marginalized middle sectors took it upon themselves to actualize a new form of public culture based on popular sovereignty. It was only at this point that the modern nation-state began to take on a real presence in the Chachapoyas region—and that the state was able even to begin to implement the individualizing, homogenizing, naturalizing institutional practices discussed at length in the literature on making national cultures.

The process by which the nation-state took on a tangible presence in the Chachapoyas region thus inverts the scenario described in much of the literature on the formation of modern nation-states. Most recent literature on the subject has emerged out of the study of western Europe, or out of areas that were colonies (or near-colonies) of western European nation-states in the nineteenth and twentieth centuries. Relatively few recent works have focused on the study of Latin America.[1] The history of state formation, the class structures, the relationship of dominant classes to the state, and the attitude toward popular sovereignty of those who controlled the state apparatus were all profoundly different in western European countries (and their colonies) than in Latin America in general, and in Chachapoyas in particular. These differences, I believe, do much to explain why oppositional models of state-building and coercive understandings of making modern, national cultures are of limited use in understanding the history of state- and nation-building in postcolonial Latin America.[2]

European nation-states of the nineteenth and early twentieth centuries and their colonial domains existed in an imperial context that differed in fundamental ways from the position of Chachapoyas within the Peruvian polity. In the context of western Europe, the 1900s are commonly cited as the century of the nation-state—as the period during which centralized, bureaucratic states that had been hundreds of years in the making came under the control of solidary national communities based on the principles of popular sovereignty. The rise of capitalism is clearly fundamental to this process (Gellner 1983; Hobsbawm 1962, 1975; Nairn 1977; Tilley 1975). It was the triumphant bourgeoisie that, from its vantage point of state control, and based on its identification with the principles of modernity and nationhood, employed the classificatory, regulatory capacities of the state apparatus to monitor and oversee the gradual incorporation of select subaltern groups into the political community (Frader and Rose 1996; McClelland 1993; Rose 1992, 1993).[3] Ironically, the universalistic and inclusive discourse of the Enlightenment was used toward exclusionary ends in this process (Mehta 1990). This occurred because the bourgeoisie equated its own culture with human nature, and made full participation in the political community contingent (in part) upon the subaltern adopting "proper" and "respectable" attitudes, practices, and forms of behavior. The result of this process was to shape subjectivity in "modern" directions—and to produce a national citizenry and a more pliable labor force. In the process, differences of race and gender became essentialized and naturalized, and were used to reproduce bourgeois values as well as to exclude from the political community those who exhibited a nature that deviated from the culture of the bourgeoisie.

These developments in the metropole had significant repercussions in the more distant parts of empire. As Cooper and Stoler (1989) point out, the rise of the nation-state, citizenship, and the centrality of post-Enlightenment thought in general in defining legitimate forms of political association in western Europe created unique tensions in the colonies. For the coercive and exclusionary mechanisms and relationships upon which colonial rule was largely based blatantly contradicted the universalistic and voluntaristic discourses that defined legitimate political rule. Just as in the metropole, exclusionary practices were justified in the colonies by equating the culture of the metropolitan ruling elite with human nature, and by finding little of this human nature among "indigenous races and peoples" (thus the "civilizing mission" of the colonizers). Exclusionary practices in the colonies were in many ways more rigid than within the metropole (Cohn 1987; Kaplan 1995), and were organized more explicitly on the basis of race (Kelly 1995; Stoler 1989, 1992). In the colonies, the threat to metropolitan rule—and to bourgeois respectability—represented by the possible blurring of boundaries between colonized and colonizers (via social relationships and sexual liaisons) led to an extraordinary interest in the sexual and family lives of the colonized. This perceived threat also led to elaborate attempts on the part of colonizers to regulate these domains—to police racial divides, and at times to prohibit sexual unions. Indeed, the sexual morality and virtue of the colonized (and the colonizers) often became matters of "public" concern. Similar developments occurred within western European nation-states, if on a somewhat reduced scale.[4]

Peru and Chachapoyas could not represent more of a contrast with conditions in western Europe and its colonies. Chachapoyas was not colonized and controlled by a centralized European nation-state during the nineteenth and twentieth centuries. Nor did it lie within such a nation-state. For most of the nineteenth and early twentieth centuries, no centralized state existed in Peru whatsoever. Opinions as to precisely when Peru can be regarded as truly having become a territorial state differ from specialist to specialist.[5] Regardless of the specific date chosen, however, it is clear from the analysis presented in the chapters above that the state had very limited capacity to implement its central decisions, or to regulate/monitor the activities of its populace.

Not only was the Peruvian state poorly developed during the period in question, but no self-consciously modern bourgeois class committed to the principles of popular sovereignty arose to seize control of the apparatus of state. Rather, the "pseudo-state" that was Peru remained in the hands of shifting groups of regional elites who were strongly wedded to notions of aristocratic sovereignty. As a result, popular sovereignty did not become an ideological tool manipulated by elites. Nor did it become harnessed to the machinery of state as a means of molding a national citizenry and managing discontent among working classes (via limited extension of membership in the political community)—as it did in western Europe. Nor was modernity used as a boundary marker between primitive (subaltern) and civilized (elite)—or as a rationale for the domination of "inferior peoples and races" by a bourgeois, metropolitan elite (as it was in the European colonies).

To the contrary: in Chachapoyas, popular sovereignty was used as an explicitly anti-elite ideology—one that was seized upon by marginalized middle sectors to confront aristocratic privilege. It tended toward inclusion, not exclusion, of marginalized categories. In the hands of the subaltern, popular sovereignty was used to reconfigure racial boundaries from below. It did away with several derogatory racial categories completely (cholo, Indio, runa) by aggregating them into a single, nonracial category derived from the discourse of popular sovereignty—el pueblo. Furthermore, to the extent that formerly denigrated racial categories (Indio) continued to be recognized, the attitude toward them was one of inclusion. Only the racial category of the oppressors—blanco—became the object of hostility. By exorcizing the category "blanco" from the local scene, el pueblo did away with superordinate and subordinate racial categories altogether, defined itself in explicitly nonracial, national terms, and thus eliminated race as a means of social classification.

Unlike the situation that prevailed in western Europe and its colonies, then, in Chachapoyas race was not used in an exclusionary manner—for purposes of boundary maintenance, in order to mark clear and unequivocal lines between those who ruled and those who did not. Rather, because el pueblo was constituted by erasing/collapsing the boundaries between several formerly distinct subaltern racial categories, there was no interest in carefully policing racial divides, nor in prohibiting sexual liaisons. Nor did the sexual morality and virtue of the subaltern become matters of "public" concern, as they did in many European nation-states and their colonies.

In direct contrast with the behavior of European bourgeois classes, in Chachapoyas members of the aristocratic elite played no positive role in the implementation of popular sovereignty. Indeed, they were completely opposed to it. They did everything in their power to retain their traditional aristocratic privileges, to limit expressions of popular sovereignty to the domains of ritual and discourse, and to prevent popular sovereignty from moving directly into social life. Indeed, the elite went so far as to insist on the right to ridicule popular sovereignty—to counter all rhetorical and discursive expressions of equality and inclusion with public demonstrations of hierarchy and exclusion.

El pueblo's embrace of modernity and popular sovereignty must be understood in this light. El pueblo did indeed adopt modern notions of time, space, and personhood, did indeed adopt much of the discourse of self-discipline and control found among the European bourgeoisie—and reproduced (albeit in changed form and for different purposes) in the colonies under the institutional gaze of the colonial state apparatus. In so doing, however, el pueblo was not aping its own bourgeoisie. Nor was it being offered entrance into a political community on terms dictated by such a bourgeoisie. Rather, its members were opposing themselves to an indigenous aristocracy. And they embraced the principles of popular sovereignty voluntarily, as a way of differentiating themselves from this aristocracy in moral and ethical terms, in their efforts to divest this aristocratic elite of control of the state apparatus.

The Chachapoyan aristocratic elite therefore did not employ the classificatory, regulatory mechanisms of the state in order to monitor the gradual incorporation of the subaltern into the political community. Nor did this aristocratic elite employ the institutional gaze of state institutions to mold and shape subjectivity in "modern" directions—and thus produce a national citizenry and a malleable labor force. The elite did not do so because, first, its members did not themselves identify with notions of modern nationhood or personhood; and second, the government apparatus was poorly formed, and lacked the enforcement mechanisms in the absence of which the institutional gaze of the state has little effect (see Biolsi 1995; Corrigan and Sayer 1985; Verdery 1991).

The subaltern in Chachapoyas confronted an aristocratic elite that used its control over a weak state apparatus to reproduce traditional privilege. This meant that subaltern groups could realistically seize upon both modernity and a strong state as liberating forces. For modernity condemned traditional privilege and provided the subaltern with the vision of an alternative moral/ethical universe. And a strong state promised to safeguard and defend this alternative social order. The interest of the subaltern in implementing the institutions, values, practices, and other accouterments of modernity after it had seized control of state institutions must be understood in the same terms.

In other words, unlike the situation that prevailed in western Europe, an existing bourgeoisie already in control of state institutions did not use popular sovereignty as a way of managing the rise of subaltern groups. Rather, rising subaltern groups used popular sovereignty as a way of challenging an aristocratic elite, and in the process helped bring the modern state into being. Modernity and nation-state thus represented powerful forces of liberation that were spontaneously adopted from below rather than imposed from above.[6]

This is not to say, of course, that the image of society and personhood contained within the discourse of popular sovereignty corresponded to actual social conditions. As has been emphasized throughout the book, what people involved in the movement of democratización called "democracy" was anything but a process involving open and equal participation of all. Exclusion was an integral part of the movement. Democratización meant not only the empowerment of the urban, male middle class, but also the systematic exclusion of women and peasants from the more "open" society envisaged within the movement. Even though the transformations in local life effected by the movement were consistently cast in the universalistic language of the Enlightenment, these changes represented the interest and motivations of particular groups depicted as the interests and motivations of all groups. These and related processes of exclusion—built into the very process of state-building and nation-making—were to come to the fore in subsequent decades (see Nugent 1996).

The analysis presented above points to the dangers of attempting to generalize about processes of state-building and nation-making on the basis of the experiences of western European nation-states and their colonies. National cultures are not always constructed from above, by the imposition of a unitary and homogenous national essence on (what are assumed to be) subject populations with their own distinct, local cultures. Rather, in the making of national cultures, the "periphery" may reach toward the center to embrace the nation as much as (if not more than) the center reaches out to the periphery. Furthermore, in embracing the center, those in the peripheral locale do not necessarily abandon what is distinctively local (Hobsbawm 1990: 11; Sahlins 1989: 8-9). Local and national identifications may be interdependent and co-constitutive. The local and the national may call one another into being. Indeed, I would argue that state and nation are most solidary precisely when these conditions obtain.

The material from Chachapoyas shows that it is a mistake to assume that national cultures are best understood as elite projects at cultural homogenization. They do not necessarily imply an exclusive set of dominant meanings and essences that compete jealously with alternative subaltern meanings. They are not necessarily "totalizing" phenomena. Despite the apparent uniformity and homogeneity of national identifications, a single national identity may be embraced in quite distinct ways by different groups, for reasons that are regionally specific, historically variable, and grounded in local-level conflicts (cf. Hobsbawm 1990: 11).

It follows that the making of a national culture does not necessarily involve effecting a mystifying transformation on the artifical, arbitrary, and temporary, making it seem real, natural, and eternal. Rather, national cultures can emerge from within local/regional populations, as the result of being perceived as natural, true, and real. Thus state institutions and technologies of power that reorder space, rewrite history, and reconstruct subjectivity are not necessarily prior to the formation of a national culture. Instead, local populations' receptivity to state and nation may be important preconditions to such institutions and technologies ever becoming established in any given locale.

The widespread use of notions such as ideology, hegemony, habitus, and so on, in making sense of the rise of national cultures—conceived of as invented and arbitrary traditions—clearly indicates that analysts who employ these concepts regard those who hold national identities to be in bad faith—to be confused, mystified, the victims of a kind of hoax. As Benedict Anderson (1983: 6) has shown, however, what is important about communities in general is not that some are real and others are false, but the style in which they are imagined. I would add that it is equally important regarding national communities to ask who does and does not imagine the community to be national, in which forms, in which times and places, and why.[7]

The foregoing suggests that the boundary between "nation-state" and "society" is most easily drawn when the mission of the nation-state has failed, when its power has been forced into coercive form by those with whom it seeks interrelationship. To conceive of the nation-state as *only* coercive, however—to view its relations with society as strictly oppositional—is to privilege above all else one limited and contingent dimension of a relationship that is in reality much more dense and complex. This is reflected in the voluntary embrace by many people throughout the world of the reformulations of time, space, and personhood effected within nationalist imaginings, precisely because of their emancipatory appeal. It would be foolish to assert that these imaginings were *exclusively* liberating, even for those who embraced them so willingly. To ignore the empowering dimension of nationalist yearnings completely, however, is to disregard a long and distinguished genealogy in theoretical understandings of power—a genealogy that insists on understanding power as simultaneously enabling and disabling.[8] Moreover, it is to reify the nation, and to deny people any active, productive role in making and remaking their own lives.

Reference Matter

Notes

1. Chachapoyas is capital of the department of Amazonas in the northern sierra of Peru (see Map 1)

2. Television service became available to the people of Chachapoyas in the early 1980s. Despite the relatively hard times endured by many, most people either owned a black-and-white set themselves or knew someone who did. Shows that could be watched included *novelas* (soap operas) from Venezuela, local news, and at times programs from the national capital.

3. Not wishing to make informants uncomfortable during discussions, unless otherwise noted I did not take notes while they were speaking, or tape record our conversations. The group of informant statements quoted in the next section of the text were reconstructed from memory shortly after the discussions in question occurred.

4. All these are considered attributes of peasants. That Sanchez arrived in such a state and quickly amassed a fortune is therefore considered all the more remarkable. For a strikingly parallel case, see Edelman 1994.

5. "Merchants" are not an entirely cohesive, undifferentiated group. When using the term I am referring to the (approximately) twelve families who dominate the transport and sale of two kinds of goods: industrially produced and/or processed foodstuffs (for which they are the wholesale distributors; several merchants also have retail outlets for foodstuffs); and manufactured goods of many different kinds—both "necessities" (stoves, lamps, etc.) and "luxuries" (Seiko watches, fancy pens, etc.). In addition to these large-scale merchants, there are a number of smaller-scale and petty traders of various kinds, who are not seen by the local populace as belonging to the social category of "forastero."

6. The market vendors had formed a union in the early 1980s, and thus there was an organizational basis for their participation in the demonstration. This demonstration was but the continuation of a more general mobilization among the local populace

that had begun in the mid-1970s, the purpose of which had been to protest the neglect of the region by the central government, and to redress a whole series of long-standing regional problems—among which the provisioning of food figured prominently. A "neighborhood committee of struggle and faith" emerged in each of Chachapoyas's four neighborhoods at this time, and all four committees were joined together in an umbrella organization—the "Communal Representative Commission of Amazonas." These movements produced their own leaflets and handbills, but unlike the movements of the 1920s there was no newspaper that articulated their vision; by the 1970s the local newspaper was published by the Catholic Church. See Nugent 1994 for a full discussion of these matters.

7. The source of the extreme anti-Semitism manifest here is not clear, although undoubtedly the teachings of the Catholic Church regarding the "blood guilt" of the Jews for the "murder of Christ" was an important contributing factor.

8. This construction of the local community as a morally pure "folk" community threatened by impure foreigners has disturbing parallels with the anti-Semitism and racism of the German fascist movement of the 1930s (see Mosse 1975; Bauman 1989)—parallels made all the more disturbing by the explicit reference to Hitler. There are important differences between them, however. Limitations of space make it impossible to devote to this topic the attention it merits.

9. The following quotes come from *Amazonas*, a local newspaper that emerged in the mid-1920s as the mouthpiece for one of two political movements that helped overthrow the power of the landed elite. The editor of *Amazonas* actively solicited letters and even pieces of writing for the paper from the local populace, and people of all social classes responded. The paper thus became something of an open forum in which a transformed image of society was articulated. See Chapter 6 for a more developed analysis of the paper and its contents.

10. See Macartney 1934; Deutsch 1953; Deutsch and Foltz 1963; Bendix 1964; Tilly 1975, 1984; Abrams 1988; Corrigan and Sayer 1985; Cohen and Toland 1988; Migdal 1988; Gurr 1989; C. A. Smith 1990b; Bendix 1992.

11. "Primordial" in nature: Redfield 1955; Shils 1957; Geertz 1963; A. D. Smith 1986. Representing "rationally manipulated strategies": Cohen 1969; Gusfield 1973; Brass 1974, 1994; Barry 1978; Gourevitch 1979; Kasfir 1979; Bates 1982. Constituted by colonial and postcolonial forces of domination: Wallerstein 1967; Robinson 1974; Lemarchand 1982; Lustick 1980; A. D. Smith 1983; Laitin 1985; Stern 1987; C. A. Smith 1990a.

12. Recent examples of oppositional approaches to state-building in Latin America include C. Smith 1990a, 1990b; and Urban and Sherzer 1991. See Nugent 1994 for a discussion of these works.

13. Contested: Chatterjee 1989; Fox 1990a; Handler 1988; Marriot 1963; Verdery 1990. Constructed: Anderson 1983; Brow 1988; Herzfeld 1982; Lass 1988. Arbitrary:

Brass 1994; Llobera 1990; Fox 1990b; Oinas 1978; Salomone 1992; Hobsbawm and Ranger 1983.

14. Brow 1988; Chatterjee 1986; Lofgren 1989b; Williams 1990.

15. Cohn and Dirks 1988; Corrigan and Sayer 1987; Herzfeld 1987; Mitchell 1988. The same concepts are employed by those who analyze the emergence of counterhegemonic national ideologies that challenge the position of the dominant order. For example, see Chatterjee 1986, 1993; Evans 1992; and Urla 1993.

16. Implicit here is the notion that the institutions and agents of the state must oversee this process of imposition. There are two difficulties with such a view: first, it risks reifying "the state" (arbitrarily separating it from "society"); and second, it reproduces the idea that state-building is a process that begins from state centers and builds outward (for a critique of this position, see Nugent 1994; Sahlins 1989).

17. Cultural/linguistic characteristics: Anderson 1983; Bruckner 1978. Biological features: Dominguez 1986; Gilman 1991; Gilroy 1991. Some combination of the two: C. A. Smith 1990a; Williams 1989.

Benedict Anderson's original formulation (1983) of the rise of nationalism did not dwell on the problem of how states must naturalize what are in reality arbitrary and contingent national cultures—as so much work on the topic has since. Rather, Anderson focused on the way that the spread of vernacular languages via "print capitalism" resulted in the spontaneous emergence of print communities of predominantly national scope. Anderson writes somewhat more abstractly, if brilliantly, about why people would feel allegiance to or emotional connection with such communities—about why particular groups of people do and do not imagine the nation, in which times and places, and in which forms (see Fox 1990a: 7). In a later formulation (Anderson 1991: ch. 10), Anderson adopted a more "state-centered" interpretation in discussing the emergence of postcolonial states.

18. Though the commonality of those who make up the nation is usually based on notions of citizenship and popular sovereignty, this is not necessarily the case (see Kapferer 1988). The idea that the citizen represents the essence of the nation does not extend, of course, to minority populations. See Williams (1989; 1991) on the ways in which national cultures construct a contested boundary between the homogenous pure majority and heterogeneous minority populations. Vincent (1974) also discusses the ways in which specifically colonial societies commonly create an intermediate "ethnic" category between majority and minority populations.

19. See Anderson 1983; Corrigan and Sayer 1985; Hertz 1944; Herzfeld 1986; Rabinowitz 1994.

20. See Anderson 1991; Errington 1989; Frykman and Lofgren 1987; Vandergeest and Peluso 1995.

21. See Baram 1992; Dominguez 1989; Gable, Handler, and Lawson 1992; Trigger 1984; Wright 1985.

22. See Colls and Dodd 1986; Laitin 1992; Vandergeest 1993.

23. See Cohn and Dirks 1988; Corrigan and Sayer 1987; Derengil 1993; Dominguez 1989; Sayer 1992; Williams 1989.

24. See especially Dominguez 1989; Flores 1995; Fox 1990a; Lofgren 1995; Verdery 1990; Williams 1990.

25. In this regard, see the work of Sider (1986) on hegemony, as well as papers by Lagos (1993), Seligman (1993), and Gill (1993), and the various contributions to Joseph and Nugent 1994. The oppositional model of relations between "society" and "nation-state" is strangely at odds with the rich body of literature from anthropology and history alike, which, in the context of particular case studies, demonstrates a much more nuanced, sophisticated view. Most notable in this regard for Peru is the work of Florencia Mallon (1983b; 1995). For work from other parts of the world that adopts a similarly nuanced position, see Southall 1956; Fox 1971; Sabean 1984; Anderson 1983; and Sahlins 1989.

26. A subsequent volume will deal with the period 1935 to 1995, and the forces that led to modernity being perceived in negative, hostile terms. For a preliminary analysis of this phenomenon, see Nugent 1996.

27. In actuality, of course, there were positive and negative attitudes toward past and future expressed during this time period. The overwhelming emphasis, however, was as described in the text.

28. In stressing the more all-encompassing political fields within which changing beliefs emerge, I purposely move away from formulations that focus exclusively on local concerns—because of the implicit assumption that local social forms have a fixed and essential nature. Instead, the present analysis moves toward the broader contexts of power and history, which do much to produce changing community configurations within particular locales. An eloquent overview of this approach, including its genealogy, can be found in the work of William Roseberry (1989).

29. Burga and Flores Galindo 1979: 88–94; Caravedo 1979a; Cotler 1978: 119–84; Gorman 1979; Wilson 1982: 192; Yepes del Castillo 1980: 305–10.

30. On north coast plantation owners, see Klaren 1973; Gonzales 1985. On mine owners in the central sierra, see DeWind 1977; Mallon 1983b; Caravedo 1979a. On Lima industrialists and merchants, see Pike 1967: 168–86; Mallon 1983b: ch. 4.

31. On mine and hacienda owners from the northern sierra, see Deere 1990; Taylor 1986. On large estate owners in the central sierra, see Mallon 1983b: ch. 4; Manrique 1988. On wool merchants and hacendados from the southern highlands, see Basadre 1968–69, 10: 102–43; Cotler 1978; Flores Galindo 1977; Jacobsen 1993; Klaren 1988.

32. Favre 1965; Mallon 1983a; Taylor 1986. Important work on the nature of the Peruvian state in the second half of the nineteenth century is only just being completed (Mallon 1995; McEvoy 1995).

33. Cooper and Stoler (1989: 610–11) make a related point about the ways in

which the spread of Enlightenment notions of citizenship, consensus, and equality as the basis of legitimate political community during the nineteenth century created problems in European colonies, where rule was based on coercion and exclusion.

34. It was precisely the ability of estate-owning men who belonged to the racially pure casta española to manipulate the lives of women of their own social category, and of men and women alike among the mestizos and Indians, that made possible the reproduction of the "aristocratic" order through time.

35. Escalante Gonzalbo (1992) makes a related argument about "imaginary citizens" in his analysis of nineteenth-century Mexican politics.

36. The "races" of the Chachapoyas region were for the most part indistinguishable from one other in terms of phenotype.

37. The period in question runs from the end of the War of the Pacific (1883) until the early 1930s—when the state began to make its presence felt more directly within the region.

38. To clarify a possible point of confusion, the precepts of popular sovereignty were invoked in public political ritual, and in public and private political discourse, by members of the elite-led political faction temporarily in control of the local apparatus of state (see Chapter 5). Members of all social classes who were members of political factions temporarily out of power, and therefore under persecution by the ruling faction, employed the rhetoric of popular sovereignty in private discourse with state officials (see Chapter 3).

CHAPTER 2

1. Some of the products of the Marañon River canyon itself—coca, coffee, cacao, fruit, and opium—were integrated into markets farther west, but on a relatively minor scale.

2. The jungle department of Loreto was part of Amazonas from 1832, when Amazonas was created as a department (with Chachapoyas as its capital), until 1861. At this latter date, Loreto was established as a military province, with associated military industries to help control the Peruvian border with Brazil as well as to monitor foreign exploration.

3. An additional magnet was the artisanal hat-making industry, centered on the town of Moyobamba, which provided fine "straw" hats to several European countries at the end of the nineteenth century and the beginning of the twentieth. By the late nineteenth century, Italy, France, and Spain had established consular offices in Moyobamba to oversee the maritime export of their share of the trade, which was shipped to Europe via the Amazon River through Brazil and across the Atlantic. The hat trade collapsed along with the rubber trade in 1912, and subsequently the highlands of Cajamarca—to the west of Chachapoyas—became the site of hat manufacture, whereas

the straw (*bombonaje*) was shipped via mule train to Cajamarca by way of Chachapoyas (see Works 1984; Nugent 1988: 73–109).

4. Though economic influence was relatively minor, political connections with Iquitos were crucial in the consolidation of power by the Pizarro-Rubio casta after 1909. See Chapter 4.

5. For example, a number of young men from Chachapoyas who wished to be tailors, carpenters, and furniture-makers journeyed to Iquitos for their apprenticeships. When they returned as artisans, their contributions to architecture, dress, and the internal environment of the home reflected what they had learned from master artisans in Iquitos.

6. The Amazonian rubber boom collapsed in 1912, after which time Chachapoyas's ties with this region were considerably attenuated. Nonetheless, as late as the early 1920s, a number of Chachapoyas's landed families were in favor of joining an Amazonian movement for secession. On the Amazonian secession movement, see Karno 1973; and [OPS1].

7. Highland haciendas were focused more on raising livestock than on growing foodstuffs. Even so, herds were small, and production was not oriented toward commercial markets.

8. The National Constitution of 1920 provided a legal basis for peasant communities to establish communal tenure on lands they could demonstrate "rightfully" belonged to them. The number of communities that achieved this status grew considerably during the period of military rule from 1968 to 1980.

9. Chachapoyas also acted as a magnet for food products grown in Bagua (predominantly rice), in the valley of the Huayabamba River (now the province of Rodriguéz de Mendoza—predominantly cane liquor, fruit, wine, coffee, and brown sugar), and in the Marañon River canyon/valley (coca, coffee, fruit, and cacao).

10. Chachapoyas was distinguished from the rest of the Peruvian highlands by the fact that it did not experience any significant commercial expansion during the late nineteenth and early twentieth centuries. In southern Peru, the expansion of the wool market and the growth of roads and railroads precipitated a tremendous increase in the number of haciendas, and in the area of land they occupied. It also resulted in a sustained attack on the land holdings and institutions of peasant communities, and in a reconstitution and strengthening of colonial forms of domination (Collins 1988; Jacobsen 1993; Orlove 1977). In the central highlands, the growth of industrial mining at Cerro de Pasco, especially after the turn of the century, helped produce a permanent wage labor force out of former peasants, resulted in a general commercialization of the agrarian economy, and led to the privatization of much land formerly held under communal tenure by peasant communities (Mallon 1983b; Manrique 1988). And in the northern sierra, the commercial boom associated with the expansion of coastal, export-oriented, plantation agriculture created new markets for highland foodstuffs and labor. The results of this process included the emergence of novel forms of labor control

(the *enganche*; see Gonzales 1980; J. C. Scott 1976), fierce, violent competition among hacendados to control the new markets (Taylor 1986; Deere 1990), and a general monetization of the highland economy as a whole. The Chachapoyas region, however, experienced none of these radical changes. As a result, the agrarian economy remained largely under the control of the peasantry.

11. For a detailed consideration of the multiple forces that acted to limit the commercialization of foodstuffs in the Chachapoyas region, see Nugent 1988: 110–85.

12. This is reflected in the fact that most haciendas marketed little or none of the foodstuffs they produced. Some estates grew small quantities of sugarcane, from which they distilled cane liquor, most of which was sold in Chachapoyas (smaller quantities were sold throughout the region). Here as well, however, the small size of the urban market, the relatively undermonetized nature of the regional economy, and the large number of producers/sellers of cane liquor limited the opportunities for profit (see Nugent 1988: 110–85).

13. Features of the local ecology reinforced these tributary tendencies. In the region as a whole, there are very few large, continuous expanses of arable land—even along the region's major rivers (Aguilar Briceño 1963). Rather, arable land is distributed in relatively small patches throughout the region. As a result, it is difficult for any one person or family to build up a power base on the basis of their land holdings in one locale. Because of this more fragmented distribution of land, a power base was most effectively established by forming alliances with other individuals and families scattered throughout the regional space.

14. A review of hundreds of court cases, as well as thousands of pages of official and unofficial communiqués between political appointees, and between private individuals of all social classes and these appointees, revealed extremely few disputes regarding land (Mallon [1983b: ch. 2] and G. Smith [1989: ch. 2] both describe a similar situation in and around the Mantaro Valley region until circa 1870). Furthermore, those cases that did involve land disputes were rarely conflicts between hacendados and peasant communities, or between hacendados and individual peasant families. Rather, members of the same elite families most commonly disputed *one another* about claims to land. Siblings were almost invariably the disputants, and their conflicts focused on efforts to control the inheritance left them by their parents. Although the documentary record undoubtedly underrepresents the prevalence of interclass land disputes, it is clear that struggles over land played only a minor role in regional affairs.

15. The most onerous labor demands imposed on the peasantry involved public-works projects—for the most part, the maintenance of mule trails and bridges. District governors (and lieutenant governors) were responsible for the maintenance of this "infrastructure," and could call on the inhabitants of their districts (or subdistricts) to provide labor to carry out such maintenance. Much of the correspondence between governors, lieutenant governors, subprefects, and prefects concerns mobilizing labor for public works. Needless to say, peasants sought to avoid these impositions whenever

possible. The "legitimate" ability on the part of governors and lieutenant governors either to call on peasants to provide labor for public works or to forgive them this obligation gave these officials an important tool in recruiting clients and in punishing members of opposing coalitions.

16. In the town of Tarma, located on the eastern slope of the Andes but in central Peru, struggles were similarly focused on occupying political position (see Wilson 1990).

17. Such shamings did not necessarily focus only on other adult males. The "dependents" of such men—their wives, children, and clients in other social classes—were often the targets chosen in order to show the inability of a man to protect those who looked to him for protection.

18. See Bourdieu 1977 for a related discussion of distinct modes of domination, one of which is based on ongoing personalistic demonstrations of force. Foucault (1980) makes a similar argument in his discussion of different forms of sovereignty.

19. Despite the "piecemeal" manner in which good land is distributed, however, it is nonetheless easier to wrest a living from the land in Chachapoyas than in many other parts of the Andes. Though soils are not particularly rich, the region is blessed with more rainfall than many other parts of the Andes, and receives it distributed throughout more of the year (Nugent 1988: 185).

20. Hacendados liked to pass the planting and harvesting seasons on their estates, as in this way they were better able to control the fruits of the agrarian labor process.

21. Many of these families maintained complex genealogies complete with coats of arms that "proved" their elite status.

22. According to the population census of 1876, there were 870 whites in Chachapoyas (Peru 1878: 578). The casta española probably accounted for about half of the total number of people who claimed to be white.

23. This figure is based on a review of tax registers on landed property for a variety of years in the late nineteenth and early twentieth centuries.

24. According to elderly informants, when there was more work than the live-in domestic servants could perform, chola women were employed on a day-by-day basis to do extra ironing, clothes-washing, water-hauling, etc.

25. The casta española recognized *San Juan de los Caballeros* as their patron. Nonelite members of society revered *San Juan de los Indios*.

26. These proscriptions held even more strongly for the peasants of the countryside—the uncouth Indios who occasionally found themselves at the homes of the elite for the same reasons as did cholos.

27. Girls of the elite attended high school either at the *Colegio Nacional San Juan de la Libertad*—the national high school located in Chachapoyas—or, if possible, at an exclusive private high school in Lima.

28. The Colegio Nacional San Juan de la Libertad was not in operation from the

outbreak of the War of the Pacific in 1879 until 1906. During this period children of the middle sectors of Chachapoyas received no secondary education.

29. This generalization is based on two sources: informant interviews and life histories; and the marriage and baptismal registers of Chachapoyas.

30. Elite men often sought out sexual liaisons with women of the middle class, and left offspring that they neither acknowledged nor supported. Similarly, men of the middle class also had children by middle-class women with whom they never lived, and to whom they never offered any support. A large number of middle-sector households were therefore headed by women, who worked at a variety of occupations in order to make ends meet (most commonly as seamstresses, cooks, clothes-washers and ironers, thread-makers, weavers, and saddlebag-makers).

31. In Quechua, *taita* is a term of respect and deference generally reserved for older male relatives. It is often glossed as "father."

32. The goods most commonly transported into the Chachapoyas region were generally either light in weight and low in bulk (for example, fabric and matches) and/or conspicuous consumption goods for the elite (such as fine china and fancy wedding dresses). In addition to the people (many on state business) and the mail that moved into and through the region, the most important item transported through Chachapoyas from its jungle source in the east to artisan producers in the west was *bombonaje*—a form of straw that artisans in Cajamarca used to make hats (see note 3 above). The only local product exported out of the region (to the west) was cowhides, and these in small numbers.

33. "Sphere of influence" refers to the space within which a member of the elite had built up a sufficient number of clients (through distributing the "spoils" of landed wealth and/or political office) to be able to control the movement of goods and people with some security. "Spheres" did not have precise boundaries, and changed according to the political fortunes of members of the elite.

34. Morales (1989: 2) reports that until 1864, baptismal certificates divided the highland inhabitants of Peru into two groups: casta (of Spanish descent), and Indio (of aboriginal descent).

35. This upper echelon of the landed elite had not attained its high position by virtue of owning more land than other families. Estate ownership was necessary but not sufficient to enter into the realm of the region's true elite. Families who had a history of occupying high political office, and/or whose members attained high ranks in the national armed forces—and thus could count on extra-local resources and contacts—figured most prominently among the powerful families of the region.

36. The following analysis of marriage strategies is based on two sources: the marriage and baptismal register of Chachapoyas, maintained by the Catholic Church; and extensive genealogies collected from elderly members of the elite families in question.

37. The exception was the canyon/valley of the Marañon River, which was more

integrated into coastal markets than the rest of the region. Estates in this subregion produced coca, opium, cane liquor, tobacco, and coffee in small quantities for coastal markets. Even here, however, estates remained small and controlled little in the way of peasant labor. Furthermore, most families of the elite had access to land within the canyon.

38. Examples of casta cores formed out of multiple sibling marriages include the Hurtado-Rodriguéz casta (during the 1870s), the Burga-Hurtado casta (during the 1880s and 1890s), and the Pizarro-Rubio casta (during the 1870s and 1880s). More fragile casta cores were formed from single marital alliances—notably, the Santillán-Becerril (during the 1860s) and the Ocampo-Eguren (during the first decade of the twentieth century).

39. "Muleteer magnates" were individuals with a large number of peasant mule drivers as clients (see Nugent 1988: 73–109). Muleteer magnates and long-distance merchants actively sought out marriages with members of the landed elite, for without a strong local ally they would not be able to pursue their own affairs. As did most of the merchants who were the object of extreme animosity in the 1980s (see Chapter 1), a number of these merchant families came from the town of Celendín.

40. Marriage with first cousins was forbidden by the Catholic Church, a prohibition supported by the state's Civil Code of 1852. In practice, however, this formal rule was circumvented informally in a variety of ways. When the larger estates were preserved by marrying relatives with contiguous properties, the value of the property was maintained at a higher level, and could be used more effectively as collateral or security by individuals who sought to occupy the offices of departmental treasurer or treasurer of the *Sociedad de Beneficencia Pública* (the Public Beneficence Society) (I am indebted to Marc Edelman for suggesting to me this elite rationale for preserving the size of estates); in addition, such marriages kept a family's "sphere of influence" in any given locale from splintering.

41. With the death of the patriarch who arranged the marriages of his children according to these requirements—when his estate was divided among inheritors—there was little to hold the siblings and in-laws together (unless they managed to maintain control over the regional political apparatus). In that the offspring of the patriarch were usually adults with families of their own at the time of their father's death—and had already begun to arrange the marriages of their own children with the same strategic considerations in mind as had their father—once they had been freed from their father's control via inheritance they were apt to form alliances independently of one another. Indeed, because of marriage prohibitions with close relations, they were to a certain extent forced to look for new allies outside the sibling circle.

42. The following account of the wedding is based on a series of interviews with Señora Zoila Torrejón Monteza de Zubiate, who was thirteen years old at the time of the ceremony. Sra. Torrejón died in June 1993, at the age of 92. Interviews with her

were conducted at various times during my fieldwork (1983, 1985–86, and the summers of 1990, 1991, and 1992).

43. So skillful were the Eguren Hernandez sisters that they were entrusted with preparing the clothing for the Catholic Church's religious idols. It is said that they were provided with thread of gold and silver for such purposes.

44. The Torrejón home is described not only by Sra. Zoila Torrejón Monteza de Zubiate, but also in [AMC5]. Sections of the Torrejón home remained intact during the period of my fieldwork, although like most structures in the town, it had been badly damaged in the earthquake of 1928.

45. The second patio area of the Torrejón home was identical to the first in layout, but the rooms surrounding it were used for receiving the nonelite clients and friends of the Torrejón family (as well as for storage purposes).

46. I have been unable to discover why the fanfare was referred to as a "Diana."

47. The marinera is a dance of coastal Peru of Afro-Hispanic origins. While Stein (1980: 244 n. 8) asserts that it is performed by the urban and rural poor in coastal regions, in Chachapoyas the marinera has long been popular among the elite.

48. Pizarro alternated as senator (*senador propietario*) and substitute senator (*senador suplente*) during this period. The other senator in 1915 was Fernando Gazzani, who, like the other nonlocal senators of Amazonas during this period, was a *Limeño* (a native of Lima, the nation's capital) who had been given the position as a political favor. He never traveled to Amazonas, and played no role in local politics whatsoever.

49. Miguel was *diputado suplente* (substitute deputy) from 1911 to 1915—during which time a *Limeño* appointee formally occupied the position.

50. The official deputy—Oscar C. Barrós—had been granted his position as a political favor by the central regime; like Senator Gazzani, he never traveled to Amazonas, and played no role in local politics.

51. The powers of these appointees are outlined below.

52. Peru is divided into a nested hierarchy of administrative units, from department to province to district to subdistrict. The representatives of the executive branch of government assigned to each are, respectively, prefect, subprefect, governor, and lieutenant governor. The representatives of the judicial branch of government assigned to each unit are, respectively, district attorney, judge of the first instance, and justice of the peace (subdistricts have no judicial representatives of their own).

53. The departmental comptroller, or *tesorero fiscal*, was charged with overseeing the financial accounting for public offices.

54. I have been unable to determine who was subprefect of Bongará province in 1915. The following year the position was filled by Tomás Mesía, a high-ranking member of the Pizarro-Rubio casta, and related by marriage to both the Pizarros and the Rubios.

55. In 1893 the executive branch of government decided to make a single judicial

province out of the formerly separate judicial provinces of Luya and Bongará, and to appoint a single judge of the first instance, who would exercise jurisdiction over the new composite province. Its main motivation in doing so was that it was virtually impossible to find qualified judges who were willing to serve in Bongará—because of which untrained and unlettered justices of the peace were constantly forced to carry out the functions of the judge of the first instance.

56. This account is a verbatim quote taken from a taped interview. The account identifies 1913 as the year in which the confrontation took place. The president referred to, however—Colonel Oscar Benavides—did not take control of the presidency until February 1914, when he led a coup against elected president Billinghurst. Colonel Benavides initially had strained relations with the majority in both houses of Congress—which favored Augusto Leguía (president from 1908–12)—that Benavides had straightened out by mid-1914 (Basadre 1968–69, 12: 290, 303, 323). The confrontation between the Pizarro-Rubio and General Benavides thus probably took place in 1914 rather than 1913.

57. The *Compañía Nacional de Recaudación*, established by government decree in 1902, was originally responsible for the collection of consumption taxes on tobacco, sugar, matches, and other consumables; for the collection of a sales tax on fixed property; and for the collection of a production tax on the cultivation of opium (Basadre 1968–69, 11: 72–79, 89). In 1905 its powers were expanded to include the collection of taxes to support education (*rentas escolares*), a variety of departmental administrative costs (*rentas departamentales*), and also a production tax on the cultivation of coca (*mojonazgo de la coca*; Basadre 1968–69, 11: 190–91). In 1912 this *sociedad anónima* was replaced by another, the *Compañía Recaudadora de Impuestos*, whose duties and powers were much the same (ibid., 12: 266).

58. The judge of the first instance, however, was dependent on the prefect and subprefect to provide the armed force necessary to apprehend those he sought as suspects, witnesses, etc. Prefects and subprefects in turn were dependent on the cooperation of governors and lieutenant governors to do the actual work of apprehending the individuals concerned. At times, governors and lieutenant governors were assisted by the Gendarmery or the Guardia Civil when a particularly dangerous individual was sought.

59. The marriage also put the children of Luis Felipe and Robertina in the position of inheriting land and wealth from the two families that had come together at the marriage of Robertina's parents: the Torrejón Dávila (Robertina's father) and the Monteza Aguilar (Robertina's mother). Robertina's father, Luis Beltrán Torrejón Dávila, was a distant relative of Luis Felipe's mother, María Dolores Rojas Mesía, the Mesía family having intermarried extensively with the Dávila family.

60. Luis Beltrán Torrejón Dávila had also been prefect *accidental* of Amazonas in 1895, after the former prefect, Eloy Burga, had fled the region due to the impending

arrival of the Pizarro-Rubio forces, which had been brought to power as the result of civil war.

61. His engagement to Eva María came within just months of his arrival in Chachapoyas.

62. The series of prefects appointed from Lima in the 1895–1902 period—during which the Pizarro-Rubio casta also exercised regional hegemony—did not fare so well. All had serious difficulties with the ruling coalition due to their attempts to curb some of its excesses. Most complained bitterly about the opposition, threats, and attempts on their life that they endured. See below, Chapter 3.

63. In the early 1890s, when the Pizarro-Rubio casta had not yet established control over regional affairs, the Pizarro Rojas family married its 16-year-old daughter Carmen to 26-year-old merchant Miguel Ruiz Rodriguéz in an effort to expand its commercial links and possibilities.

64. I have been unable to find sufficient information regarding one other of the Pizarro Rojas children, Fortunato Pizarro Rojas, to be able to reconstruct the precise nature of the marriage strategy employed in arranging his marriage to María Aguilar. I have not been able to discover María's maternal last name, nor her precise relation with the elite Aguilar family (which Luis Felipe Pizarro Rojas joined by marrying Robertina Torrejón Monteza, whose mother was Josefa Monteza Aguilar).

65. After Toribio's death, Hortencia married Andres Collantes Rodriguéz, her second cousin.

66. Because this marriage occurred between relatives who were closer than the second-cousin limit proscribed by the Catholic Church, there is no record of it in the Church's marriage register.

67. The core of the Pizarro-Rubio casta consisted of three families: the Pizarro Rojas, the Pizarro Rubio, and the Rubio Linch. All three of these families pursued marriage strategies of the kind outlined in the text.

CHAPTER 3

1. It is difficult, and somewhat arbitrary, to define the precise number of castas in existence at any given point in time, as castas underwent a continual process of reconstitution and redefinition.

2. Both of these castas were formed by means of marital alliance between two prominent families, from which the name of the casta was derived—the Burga to the Hurtado and the Pizarro to the Rubio. In addition to this "major alliance," out of which the casta was born, each family was also intermarried with a number of other elite families, thus extending its network of alliances. These matters are discussed at length in the text below.

3. Specifically, the deaths of the Hurtado and Rodriguéz family patriarchs—each of whom had married a daughter to a son of the other in the 1850s in order to effect a strong alliance—left the children of the patriarchs with little about which to cooperate. As the six-year period of warfare (1879–85) undermined most existing political ties, the Hurtado allied with the Burga and the Rodriguéz with the Pizarro and the Rubio to form new, independent castas.

4. Whenever possible, reference is made to parallel developments in periods other than that used in the text for purposes of illustration.

5. The rise of the Pizarro-Rubio in 1895, and its subsequent domination of regional affairs until 1902, is described in the following *legajos* (document files): [APA6]; [APA10]; [APA63]; [APA61], 1893–96, 1898; [APA8]; [APA37].

6. The fall of the Rubio-Linch in 1930 and the rise of the Burga-Hurtado is described in the following legajos: [APA30]; [APA3]; [APA25]; [APA24]; [APA32]; [APA46]; [APA26]; [APA61], 1932; [APA33]; [APA58]. See Chapter 8 for a discussion of the unique historical developments surrounding the rise of the Burga-Hurtado in 1930.

7. See the developments of 1913 outlined in Chapter 4. The struggles between the Hurtado-Rodriguéz and the Santillán-Becerril and the ultimate victory of the former are described in the following legajos: [APA7], July 8, 1867 to 1878; [APA12]; [APA22]. Relevant information is also to be found in the pages of the official government newspaper, *El Registro de Amazonas, Publicación Oficial*, 1874.

8. The willingness of local castas to help a ruling regime in Lima remain in power by defeating opposition forces was not limited to containing opponents within the specific region controlled by the local casta. Rather, in times of political crisis, local casta leaders would go so far as to lead armed contingents into battle in regions wholly outside their own jurisdiction—as Prefect Manuel Hurtado offered to do for President Manuel Pardo during such a time of crisis in December 1872. (See [AGN1], Dec. 21, 1872. I am indebted to Carmen McEvoy for alerting me to the existence of this correspondence.)

9. The struggles between the Pizarro-Rubio and Justo Villacorta are detailed in the following legajos: [APA54]; and [APA6], June 14 and July 18, 1892.

10. The period of rule of the Burga-Hurtado is outlined in [APA60]; [APA6]; [APA10]; [APA14]; [APA36]; [APA61], 1893–96, 1898; [APA8].

11. As we will see, however, the distinction between seizing control by force and via elections is far from hard and fast, as ruling and out-of-power castas alike employed violence on a regular basis in their efforts to control the outcome of elections. In addition to the legajos mentioned in the notes immediately preceding this, for the elections of 1902, 1908, 1915, 1919, and 1924, see: [APA45], 1897–1904; [APA11], 1902; [APA17]; [APA5], 1915; [APA61], 1915; [APA51]; [APA9]; [APA15]. Sources for the remaining elections are listed in this and the following chapter.

12. As of 1896, a nine-person national election board, the *Junta Electoral Nacional*, appointed the members of departmental and provincial election committees (the *Junta Electoral Departamental* and the *Junta Electoral Provincial*, respectively). The provincial-level junta was supposed to call together all tax-paying literate males, 21 years of age or more, in a general assembly (an *asamblea de mayores contribuyentes*). From among these men, five were chosen at random to make up the body that was responsible for supervising identical *asambleas* and random-selection processes at the district level. The five *mayores contribuyentes* chosen for each province and district were in turn responsible for having a voting register made up for their respective jurisdictions (by appointing a *junta de registro electoral*, or voter registration board), and for making sure that the voting tables (the *mesas receptoras de sufragios*) were manned. The provincial junta also selected the *juntas escrutadoras*, or electoral review boards, for each province, which in turn selected juntas escrutadoras for each district (Basadre 1980: 53–58; Taylor 1986: 24).

13. Prior to 1896, voting was "indirect" and public. Land-owning, literate, adult males (age 21 or more) elected delegates from among their own number in public voting, in which each person signed his name to his ballot. The delegates thus chosen then cast their ballots in favor of congressional and presidential candidates (Basadre 1980). As of 1896, voting was made direct, but retained its public character. Until 1931, voting was restricted to land-owning, literate males (excluding peasants) who were either heads of households or were 21 years of age (ibid.).

14. Similar machinations often surrounded efforts to control the membership of the other bodies as well.

15. Voting took place in district capitals as well, but far fewer people voted there, and castas usually did not have the resources or manpower to contest the election in all districts.

16. Violence of this or related kinds was associated with the congressional elections of 1894 ([APA8], June 26, 1894), 1901 ([APA45], no. 206 [Apr. 9, 1901], decreto [Apr. 13, 1901]), 1907 ([APA13], decretos no. 101 [May 16, 1908], 108 [May 29, 1908]; [APA11], 1907, pp. 5–17), 1909 ([APA13], decreto no. 99 [Apr. 2, 1910]), 1913 (see Chapter 4), 1919 ([APA51], nos. 247 [Apr. 14], 249 [Apr. 25], 307 [May 22], 351 [June 7], 496 [Aug. 5]), and 1924 ([APA15], no. 249 [Dec. 11]), as well as the presidential elections of 1894 ([APA10], July 26 and Aug. 27, 1894), 1908 ([APA13], decretos no. 101 [May 16, 1908], 108 [May 29, 1908]), 1919 (Basadre 1980: 91; [APA51], nos. 247 [Apr. 24], 249 [Apr. 25], 307 [May 22], 351 [June 7], 496 [Aug. 5, 1919]), and 1924 (see text).

17. Attempts of this kind took place during the electoral campaigns of 1902 ([APA45], no. 33 [June 22, 1902]), 1907 ([APA11], pp. 5–17), 1909 ([APA13], decreto no. 116 [June 1, 1909]), and 1919 ([APA51], no. 249 [Apr. 25, 1919]).

18. Members of the opposition suffered persecution that was intended to exclude them from elections during the electoral campaigns of 1894 ([APA8], June 26, 1894;

[APA61], July 2, 1894), 1902 ([APA45], no. 34 [June 21, 1902]), 1908 ([APA13], no. 108 [May 29, 1908]), 1909 ([APA13], no. 144 [June 11, 1909]), and 1913 ([APA17], Apr. 30 and May 2, 1913).

19. Attempts on the lives of leading members of the opposition took place during the electoral campaigns of 1890 (interview, Mariano Rubio Pizarro, June 27, 1991), 1902 ([APA45], no. 33 [June 22, 1902]: The parties were none other than Pablo M. Pizarro and Eloy Burga; according to witnesses on the scene, each man attempted to murder the other, [APA11], 1902, nos. 94–97, Criminal Cases, June 1902), 1908 ([APA13], no. 108 [May 29, 1908]); 1909 ([APA13], no. 144 [June 11, 1909]), 1913 ([APA17], Apr. 30 and May 2, 1913), and 1924 (see text).

20. According to informants, the Pizarro forces also made an attempt on the life of opposing casta leader Eloy Burga at this time (interview, Victor Santillán Gutierrez, June 10, 1990).

21. *Dualidades* occurred in 1893 ([APA36], pp. 46–48, 53), 1894 ([APA34], May 16, 1894), and 1919 (Basadre 1980: 91). In addition to dualidades for congressional posts, out-of-power castas conducted dualidades to elect representatives to municipal government. Unlike the national congressional posts, however, there is some evidence that the municipal representatives actually met on a regular basis to protect the interests of their constituencies, leading to an entire system of what might be called "shadow government" (see [APA11], 1907, pp. 5–17).

22. Congress made such decisions until 1896, at which point a national election board assumed this role. In 1919, Congress was again granted the power (which it kept until 1930; Basadre 1980: esp. ch. 6); the department of Amazonas—of which Chachapoyas is the capital—was represented by two senators and three deputies (one for each of its three provinces).

23. The Supreme Court rather than the executive branch of government was charged with appointing provincial-level judges. In practice, however, the executive branch exercised a preponderant influence over such choices.

24. There were a number of factors that put the ruling casta's ability to dominate the region in constant question, most of which stemmed from the fact that the department's three deputies and two senators were not elected at the same time (one-third of each house of Congress came up for reelection every two years). Between elections, regional coalitions could change in composition and strength, possibly resulting in the election of a deputy who represented a coalition other than the ruling casta. Such an individual would appoint a subprefect and/or a provincial judge who advanced the interests of his casta, and conflict would then ensue. The majority in either house of Congress could change as well, with the result that either house could recognize as legitimate the election of candidates who represented castas other than the ruling casta. Again, conflict followed. Or relations between the president and Congress could sour (as they often did). In such cases, the president might attempt to appoint a new prefect and other local officials shortly before elections so that they could attempt

to push candidates who would be loyal to the president. The congressional majority, on the other hand, could refuse to recognize such candidates, and could accept only those who supported their position against the executive branch of government. A full discussion of these issues can be found in Chapter 4.

25. In addition to the *contribución personal*—imposed on male heads of household (intermittently through time according to changing national laws), taxes were assessed on local businesses (merchants, artisans, breadmakers, bar owners and market vendors), on the transport and sale of select local products (food staples, livestock, hides, and coffee), on rural and urban property, and on property sales (this list includes the tax-collection responsibilities of municipal government as well, whose members were likewise appointed by the ruling casta). The ruling casta also controlled appointments to the offices responsible for taxing "specialty" products—salt, tobacco, opium, liquors of various kinds, and *chancaca* (brown sugar).

26. Another way the ruling casta could recruit clients among the peasants and artisans was simply to leave them alone—to not subject them to the persecution and harassment to which so many others were subject, and to protect them from such harassment by their adversaries. Enjoying the "protection" of the coalition in power was sufficient in itself to enlist allies among the subaltern.

27. Although the ruling casta did indeed favor specific long-distance merchants with which it had formed alliances, this favoritism came at a price. The merchants in question were intermittently expected to provide the ruling casta with "loans" when the combination of locally derived and state-provided revenues was insufficient to meet the costs of local administration. Costs ran particularly high during periods of armed struggle with other castas, when the ruling casta was forced to put a larger number of men at arms than was normally the case (for examples, see [APA45], no. 111 [Nov. 23, 1899], in which the ruling casta procured a loan of 4,000 soles from local merchant Salomon Rodriguéz, which was used to help put down a major uprising; [APA 14], May 30, 1892, in which the prefecture obtained an interest-free loan of 1,700 soles from a local merchant; and [APA56], assorted issues, in which the prefecture obtained a series of loans from local merchant Remigio Ocampo in order to pay for costs of administration).

28. For instances in which the ruling casta used its power to favor merchants with which it was allied and to persecute merchants allied to other castas, see [APA61], Nov. 19, 1894; [APA8], Aug. 28, 1895; [APA45], no. 143 (Nov. 5, 1900); [APA51], nos. 220 (Apr. 11), 335 (June 10); [APA9], nos. 356 (July 7), 554 (July 17), 756 (Oct. 9).

29. New mercantile companies formed by members of ruling castas upon the ascent of their casta to power include: 1890–95—Luis Arce and Amadeo Burga ([APA14], Apr. 7, 1892); 1902–9—Felix Ocampo and Melquicidec Ruiz ([APA45], no. 47 [Nov. 22, 1902]); 1909–15—Mariano Feijóo and Miguel Saavedra ([APA17], Mar. 1, 1911); 1924–30—Moises Ampuero and Pedro Quiroz ([APA15], decreto no. 241 [Nov. 27, 1924]).

30. As taxes and permits were associated with the transport and sale of these products, the ability of governors and lieutenant governors to selectively assess taxes, issue permits, and fine those who neglected to pay taxes and who lacked the necessary paperwork, represented an additional source of income for these political appointees.

31. It is unclear the degree to which the sale of these goods within the zones of jurisdictions of governors and lieutenant governors was forced or voluntary. Indeed, the very distinction is problematic considering the nature of political power and the position of these functionaries during this period.

32. In addition to the innumerable cases referred to in the primary documents for the period as a whole (see especially the legajos in the following note), see also the many cases cited in the newspaper *Amazonas*; see as well Feijóo Reina 1934: 109–26; 1935: 459.

33. The number of requests for leaves of absence—specifically to pursue business dealings—is enormous. Examples from each of the periods identified at the beginning of the chapter can be found in the following legajos. For 1886–90: [APA54] and [APA50]. For 1890–95: [APA50]; [APA14]; [APA8]; [APA10]; [APA34]; [APA20]. For 1895–1902: [APA45], 1897–1904; [APA59], 1898. For 1902–9: [APA45], 1897–1904, 1907. For 1909–15: [APA13]; [APA59], 1913. For 1915–24: [APA55]; [APA51]; [APA9]; [APA64]; [APA15]. For 1924–30: [APA15] and [APA53].

34. This control over local tax revenues also allowed important members of the casta to line their own pockets, and to decide how much would be sent on to the central state. Incoming funds provided by the state to pay other employees and construct public works were similarly managed by the ruling casta according to its own needs.

35. [APA61], *Subprefecto del Cercado al Juez de 1ra Instancia*, Dec. 14, 1893, and Jan. 8, 1894.

36. When periods of political instability had passed, and the ruling casta was firmly in control of regional affairs, casta leaders reduced the number of gendarmes and members of the Guardia Civil actually at work in the region, but maintained the same number of police on the employment rolls. This practice allowed them to pocket the difference in salaries, and thus to further enrich themselves. This form of defrauding the central government was quite common in Peru at this time. The imaginary police were referred to as *altas supuestas*.

37. Former prefects, departmental treasurers, and provincial tax collectors were the most consistently prosecuted members of deposed castas. Examples include: for the War of the Pacific period, Pablo E. Santillán as prefect in 1881 and his cajero fiscal Lorenzo Risco ([APA68], Apr. 18, 1882; [APA8], Nov. 22, 23, and 29, 1893); for the 1885–90 period, Manuel S. Carbajal, treasurer of the Beneficencia Pública in 1886 ([APA45], no. 188 [Feb. 24, 1901]), and Manuel Trigoso, treasurer of the Beneficencia from 1886 to 1888 ([APA45], no. 109 [Aug. 19, 1900]); for the 1890–95 period, *apoderado fiscal* (provincial tax collector) Celso Eguren ([APA8], Aug. 8 and Nov. 23, 1893;

[APA61], Aug. 5, 1893), Prefect Alayza, and Subprefect Luis Arce ([APA45], Dec. 7, 1898, Jan. 17, 1899); for the 1895–1902 period, tesoreros fiscales Mariano Rubio and Mariano Albornoz (in 1895—the two were prosecuted by Tribunal Mayor de Cuentas in 1899, and were shielded from prosecution by their ruling casta; see [APA45], nos. 65 [May 22, 1899] and 178 [Feb. 23, 1901]); Tesorero Fiscal Benedicto Sotomayor (in 1899; [APA45], nos. 144 [Nov. 8, 1900], 173 [Jan. 17, 1901], 182 [Jan. 25, 1901]); for the 1902–9 period, Tesorero Fiscal Manuel R. Vargas ([APA9], no. 804 [Oct. 30]); for the long period of Pizarro-Rubio rule from 1909 to 1930, tesoreros fiscales Nicolas Tuesta and Juan M. Pizarro, and prefects Tomas Mesía and Cesar A. Gordillo (in 1921; [APA15], decreto no. 179 [Sept. 12]; see also the prosecutions discussed in Chapter 8).

38. A typical example was the case brought against rural priest Felipe S. Tuesta, a Burga-Hurtado client, by the Pizarro-Rubio forces for possession of contraband firearms. Tuesta was locked in jail for a period of over eight months, during which time the Pizarro-Rubio collected testimony, filed petitions, and built up a case against him. Tuesta's physical condition deteriorated considerably during this period, and he eventually had to be taken to the hospital. Although he was ultimately acquitted— when it was proven that all the evidence against him had been manufactured—the ruling casta had demonstrated to all, in a very forceful manner, their ability to dominate, shame, and abuse their enemies (see [APA19]).

39. Examples are numerous. For particularly graphic descriptions, see [APA14], Oct. 29, 1892; [APA11], no. 80 (July 22, 1902); and [APA13], decreto no. 23 (Jan. 19, 1910).

40. For Ocampo, see [APA63], Sept. 20, 1894. For Bonifaz, see [APA61], Dec. 30, 1895. The case of Manuel Arce is described in [APA45], no. 37 (July 12, 1902). The case of Mariano Eguren is described in [APA10], Sept. 6, 1894.

41. Obando was a landowner and merchant who was favored by the Burga-Hurtado, and who was able to expand his commercial activities for the time his patrons were in power as a result. Another landowner-merchant—Felix Ocampo, who was not a member of the ruling casta during this period—saw his store closed and locked by order of the prefecture ([APA61], Apr. 17, 1895).

42. [APA61], *Subprefecto del Cercado al Sr. Colonel Prefecto del Departamento*, July 22, 1893. By order of the judge of the first instance, and for reasons that remain unclear, Pizarro was released from prison on bail several days later (ibid., July 25, 1893), and, as often occurred with members of the elite who committed or attempted to commit egregious crimes, was never made accountable in the courts for his behavior.

43. In addition to oral accounts provided by Victor Santillán Gutierrez (from interviews conducted on July 30, Aug. 9, and Aug. 10, 1990, and June 26, 1991) and Mariano Rubio Pizarro (from interviews conducted on Aug. 10, 1990 and June 14, 1991), information relating to this uprising can be found in [APA30], Aug. 29, Sept. 2, and Sept. 27 (3 entries), 1930.

44. The activities of the Ingas are described in the following legajos: [APA25] (multiple entries); [APA30] (multiple entries); [APA3] (multiple entries).

45. This was a time-honored strategy for people in their position (see below in text). The Rubio-Linch succeeded in finding such allies outside of the region. By late 1931 it had struck an alliance with the leadership of the APRA political party in Lima, and together the two groups planned an uprising in Chachapoyas on December 5, 1931. Only the fact that the police were advised of the plot by informers prevented it from coming to fruition (see Chapter 8).

46. For example, see [APA13], decreto no. 99 (Apr. 2, 1910). I have not dealt with how a new regime in Lima overthrowing an older one affected the organization of a ruling casta. In such cases the powerful families that had cemented an alliance to gain control over the machinery of state suddenly found themselves with little about which to cooperate. Latent contradictions usually surfaced, and as often as not they ended up at one another's throats. Once more highly localized within the regional space, and facing severe persecution from the casta that had seized power, these families retrenched considerably, and later began to seek out new alliances, generally with other powerful families (thus, the women who were married into the family of the former political ally were for all intents and purposes "lost" to the family that had "given" them in marriage). Marriage alliances between "major" and "minor" landed families were subject to the same weakness. When the ruling casta lost its central support, it no longer had anything to offer its affinal allies. Actually, such ties became dangerous to the affines in question. As a result, they often took pains to disassociate themselves from their former patrons despite the bond of marriage. The same was true of merchants and muleteer magnates.

47. In addition to the oral testimony provided by Mariano Rubio Pizarro (interview, Aug. 10, 1990), information on the uprising and its defeat can be found in [APA54], Aug. 3 and 28, Sept. 24, 25, 26, and 30, 1886; and in most of the oficios in this legajo for the remainder of the year.

48. See [APA35].

49. For similar processes, see [APA13], decretos no. 108 (1909), 136 (1909), 99 (1910).

50. See [APA6]; [APA10]; [APA63]; [APA61], 1893–96, 1898; [APA8]; [APA37].

51. For example, see [APA13], decreto no. 99 (Apr. 2, 1910).

52. For example, see [APA54], Aug. 16, 1887; [APA45], Nov. 14, 1898; *Gobernador del distrito de Santa Rosa al Sr. Subprefecto*, July 8, 1906 [loose page, APA]; [APA47], June 18, 1919.

53. For example, see [APA63], Nov. 10, 1894, Feb. 7 and Apr. 4, 1895; see also oral testimony provided by Mariano Rubio Pizarro (interview, June 27, 1991).

54. In addition to the examples in this and the following chapter, see [APA13], decretos no. 95 (May 13, 1909), 17 (Jan. 17, 1910), 99 (Apr. 2, 1910); [APA17], Mar. 5, 1910; [APA9], no. 544 (July 14); [APA15], nos. 76 (Apr. 13, 1925), 119 (May 2, 1925).

55. At times these requests for protection were heeded—especially when the ruling casta wished to eliminate a coalition member who was becoming too troublesome or powerful.

56. Despite the efforts of core families to extend the geographic scope of their spheres of influence via marriage alliance, there were a limited number of "relatives" that senior family members could use for this purpose. The only kinship group with any kind of stability through time was an extended family consisting of a senior older couple (who managed the landed core of the family estate), their unmarried daughters (who joined the kin unit of their husbands upon marriage), their unmarried sons, and their married sons along with their spouses and children (until the death of the parents). Because casta organization and membership was subject to constant breakdown and reformulation, there was no larger kin unit with consistent or stable membership that could be drawn upon to recruit clients via marriage (compare Lewin 1987).

57. During some periods they were also to pursue and catch livestock thieves, and to send to the subprefect a list of all robberies committed in their jurisdictions every month ([APA35], no. 223 [Oct. 26]).

58. In theory, justices of the peace (a district-level position) were appointed by the provincial-level judge of the first instance in whose province their districts were located. In actuality, however, the provincial-level judge followed the recommendation of the district-level governor concerning these appointments when governors were "strong," but made appointments directly themselves during periods when "weak governors" were in office.

59. It was up to the governor to propose a slate of three individuals as candidates for lieutenant governor. The subprefect was then to choose one of these three, or to reject all of the candidates and insist that another slate be proposed. The governor's choice for lieutenant governor was always listed first on the slate. Thus, it is possible to reconstruct the degree to which the subprefect allowed the governor to choose the lieutenant governor.

60. It was not uncommon for these demonstrations of force to include various forms of physical abuse, from arbitrary imprisonment to beatings and denial of food while in jail to outright torture. The documentary record contains a large number of such cases. For a particularly graphic case involving torture, see [APA25], Dec. 13, 1930.

61. For example, see [APA14], Sept. 27, 1893; [APA63], Oct. 30, 1893; [APA10], Nov. 23 and 26, 1896; [APA13], decretos no. 30 (Mar. 2, 1909), 62 (Feb. 24, 1910); [APA15], nos. 119 (July 10, 1924), 122 (July 12, 1924), 150 (Aug. 18, 1924), 24 (Jan. 26, 1925), 73 (Apr. 3, 1925), 75 (Apr. 9, 1925).

62. This was especially true because the extraction of wealth in this region was based predominantly on tributary mechanisms, and was focused on a subsistence-oriented peasantry with little disposable wealth.

63. Such individuals usually waited until their new ally mounted an armed attack

on the ruling casta before committing themselves openly to the new alliance. There are many examples of such "betrayals" of family for political purposes. José María Echaiz, who married into the Pizarro family in the 1880s, had defected to the Burga-Hurtado camp by the early 1890s, by the late 1890s had realigned himself with the Pizarro-Rubio, and was a key figure in the May 1908 Pizarro-Rubio uprising against the Burga-Hurtado (see Chapter 4). By 1915, however, José María arranged to have his son marry a Hurtado, and in 1919 and 1924 was a central figure in major Burga-Hurtado uprisings against the Pizarro-Rubio. Echaiz helped lead the revolution of August 1930 against the Pizarro-Rubio (see Chapter 8). Felix Ocampo, who married into the Burga family in the early 1880s, sided with the Pizarro-Rubio against the Burga-Hurtado in the civil war of 1895, was marginalized by the Pizarro-Rubio in the 1895–1902 period, and subsequently helped the Burga-Hurtado contain the Pizarro-Rubio in the 1902–9 period. Javier Pizarro, son of Rosendo M. Pizarro, who married into the Echaiz family, was a combatant in the May 1908 Pizarro-Rubio uprising against the Burga-Hurtado. By 1919 Javier had realigned himself with the Burga-Hurtado, and was involved in an uprising against the Pizarro-Rubio.

64. Such benefits might include appointments to the aforementioned key political positions, monies provided by the central regime for public-works projects, appointment of family members to teaching or other posts in the government bureaucracy, relief from military conscription, licenses granting trade concessions or monopolies, awarding of work contracts, and tax relief.

65. The "law of justices of the peace" of December 1, 1901, gave these judges the right to charge one sol each from the accused and from the plaintiff in verbal disputes. Either the *síndico de rentas* (trustee of municipal income) or the *síndico de gastos* (trustee of municipal expenses), unpaid municipal appointees, was to check the account books related to charges from such cases twice a year ([APA11], nos. 83–84 [Aug. 23, 1902]). Needless to say, this law created the potential not only for conflict, but also for collusion between the judicial and municipal branches of government. It also made legal a practice that was undoubtedly already widespread among justices of the peace.

66. District appointees had terms of one year, which made it easy to replace strong with weak clients. Members of opposing castas also went to considerable lengths to discredit "strong" governors, and thus have them removed from office. Strong governors often found that charges of abuse of authority or misconduct had been brought against them. The prefect would inform a governor of the charges directly, and then it was up to the governor to answer the charges. This often initiated a "paper war," in which local citizens claimed that they did not enjoy the *garantías* to which they were entitled under the Constitution, while the governor claimed that his attackers were lying, were of the worst kind of people, were defaming the prefect, etc. Such a steady stream of complaints provided the prefect with an additional tool to use against a governor who did indeed go too far in abusing the local population. See [APA46], July 3, 1931.

67. Such individuals were not consulted about who was appointed to the positions of justice of the peace and lieutenant governor. Rather, the subprefect and prefect made these decisions independent of the governor, and simply informed him what they were. The independence of this "supporting cast" was a further safeguard against the governor developing a separate power base.

68. Weak clients would at times ally with a more powerful local family in order to be able to impose their will, in which case they in effect became the client of their new ally, and tended to disengage from the casta core. Because of this tendency to replace strong with weak appointees in the districts, members of the casta core often chose to reward "second-tier" members of the coalition (affines and their families) with other kinds of favor.

69. In such cases, the ruling casta often tried to absorb this potentially threatening manifestation of central power by marrying one of its daughters to the appointee.

70. There were two reasons why the central government felt it necessary to take such measures. On the one hand, to the extent that ruling casta members monopolized administrative and extractive positions, the central government was denied an important source of revenue. On the other hand, to the extent that the ruling casta continued to persecute and harass its enemies, it generated increasing hostility among much of the population. Such hostility was not conducive to the long-term stability of the central regime.

71. Contraband generally involved the movement and sale of *chancaca* (brown sugar), cane liquor, locally made wine, tobacco, straw hats, the raw material for straw hats, and salt by individuals who lacked the permits necessary to do so legally. The deterioration of the ruling casta's ability to control the movements of people and goods through space is a constant theme in the documentary record, particularly in communications from governors and lieutenant governors to subprefects and prefects. For particularly salient examples, see [APA9], no. 840 (Nov. 16, 1920); [APA45], Aug. 26, 1902; [APA15], nos. 129 (July 23, 1924), 25 (Jan. 26, 1925), 161 (Nov. 16, 1925). Contraband became more important after 1895, when the Indian head tax (the *contribución personal*) was abolished, and when the collection of taxes on the above-mentioned products became a much more important source of revenue for the ruling casta.

72. This concession was one of only two extended to exploit rubber trees during the entire period under investigation (see also [APA45], Sept. 5, 1903). Neither concession was ever worked. Indeed, although Burga prevented Muñoz from working his concession by force of arms, and then was granted the same concession himself, in 1904 he asked that the money he had paid for the concession be returned to him, because he was himself unable to work the concession. Burga's money was subsequently returned to him ([APA45], Jan. 8, 1904).

73. Further complicating the task of controlling the regional space effectively was the fact that a strong governor's network of clients—on which the ruling casta de-

pended in order to control the regional space effectively and which it had expanded and consolidated by virtue of the powers granted the governor by the prefect/sub-prefect—was also cut off when its patron governor was replaced by a weak client.

74. The documentary record contains many examples of officials refusing to vacate their posts, hand over the seal of office and files associated with their posts, etc. See [APA45], Jan. 17, 1898, Jan. 4, 1901, Feb. 17, 1903; [APA59], no. 137 (Mar. 3, 1913); [APA15], no. 155 (Oct. 31, 1925).

75. It was generally strong clients who resisted being relieved of their posts. Weak clients, on the other hand, often had to be forced into accepting such jobs to begin with, and were anxious to be rid of them at the end of their tenures in office.

76. See, for example, [APA61], June 15, 1898; numerous cases of desacato are also listed in [APA45].

77. A clear example is seen in the increase of cases of "contempt of authority" suffered by appointees of the Burga-Hurtado casta once the civil war of 1894–95—which eventually drove them from power—began (see [APA63], various entries, July 12, 1894 to July 19, 1895).

78. This case was complicated by the fact that although Pizarro had been stripped of his position as senator of Amazonas, a number of the appointees of his casta remained in their posts: the Burga-Hurtado and Echaiz forces who temporarily controlled the prefecture lacked the strength to force their replacement.

79. Notable examples include [APA13], decretos no. 136 (June 27, 1908), 144 (June 10, 1909); [APA59], Apr. 29, 1913.

80. For purposes of clarity, I have presented coalition organization as undergoing a cycle of centralization and decentralization. In actuality, the processes in question were not always so regular in character. Rather, tendencies in both directions often took place simultaneously in different parts of the regional space, or reversed themselves. This irregularity only made the ability to enjoy one's individual rights and protections, and to move people and goods through the regional space, even less dependable.

81. During periods of extended rule by a single casta, usually one favored individual increasingly dominated long-distance exchange, becoming more involved in it as the tenure of his patron endured.

82. The subprefect of each province issued passports (*pasaportes*) to those who traveled from place to place within the department, making this process of monitoring more effective, for those in transit had to show the passports to the authorities of the towns through which they traveled. A passport included the name, birthplace, age, and profession of its owner, the purpose of his travels, and a physical description (including hair and skin color, the presence or absence of beard and mustache, the kind of eyebrows, forehead, mouth, nose, eyes, lips, and any other distinguishing characteristics). Needless to say, the subprefect could issue a passport or not, as he chose. Members of the ruling coalition were generally given them freely. Although the

archive of the prefecture of Amazonas contains a large pile of these decaying passports, I have not been able to determine the degree to which their use was a general practice.

CHAPTER 4

1. Most notably: Salomon Rodriguéz, brother-in-law of Pablo M. Pizarro Farje, was comptroller of Amazonas in 1907; Pablo M. Pizarro was head of one of the two police forces in town in 1904; and Salvador M. Pizarro Alvis was justice of the peace of Lámud in 1907, then was launched into the position of interim judge of the first instance of Luya-Bongará when the regular judge went missing (see below).

2. The following account is based on a combination of documentary sources and interview data. In addition to the documents cited in the text, interview data was provided by Carlos Echaiz (Aug. 13, 1990), Máximo Rodriguéz Culqui (July 6, 1990), Mariano Rubio Pizarro (June 27, 1991), Victor Santillán Gutierrez (July 13, 1993), and Celso Torrejón (July 14, 1990).

3. For the Bongará revolt, see [APA13], decreto no. 102 (May 17, 1908).

4. After the changes in election procedure introduced by the electoral law of 1895, a national electoral board (the *Junta Electoral Nacional*) with no connection to local politics was empowered to choose the composition of local electoral review committees—or to decide which local electoral review committee would be recognized. This national board thus played the key role in deciding the outcome of elections.

5. I have been unable to discover how Leguía and Pizarro became so closely tied to one another.

6. Miguel A. Rojas Mesía was even with President Leguía during the failed coup attempt of May 29, 1909, when the forces of Leguía's main political opponent—Nicolas de Piérola—broke into and seized control of the presidential palace in Lima, and attempted (but failed) to force Leguía to sign a proclamation of resignation. After Leguía refused to sign, his captors paraded him down a prominent thoroughfare in the center of Lima (the *Jirón de la Unión*). During this moment of crisis, Leguía's minister of government, Miguel A. Rojas Mesía, was at his side (Basadre 1968–69, 12: 60).

7. Pedro L. Traverso, departmental adjutant to the *Segunda Comandancia del Norte* (the headquarters for which was in Trujillo; the Segunda Comandancia was one of a small number of *comandancias* into which the country as a whole was divided) as well as departmental military judge, could not be described as a client of the ruling alliance. He was, however, an ally, and he could be counted on to hand down rulings in the alliance's favor (because of which the Burga-Hurtado/Ocampo alliance attempted to convert civil or criminal cases into military proceedings when so doing afforded them the opportunity to strike at their casta enemies).

8. In doing so, Leguía undoubtedly consulted with his new minister of govern-

ment, Miguel A. Rojas Mesía, whose sister, María Dolores, was married to Juan M. Pizarro Farje.

9. For an example concerning Amazonas, see Basadre 1968–69, 11: 61.

10. The appointments were made in early January, but the Pázaras, Mayor de Guardias Mancilla, and Comandante Leon did not arrive until early February.

11. Even earlier, the Burga-Hurtado/Ocampo alliance had interpreted the rise of Leguía as creating conditions in which local allies of the new president might make an attempt to seize power. Leguía assumed office on September 24, 1908 (Basadre 1968–69, 11: 168). Apparently expecting an assault on or near that date, Prefect Manuel Hurtado began to concentrate arms and ammunition in the departmental capital of Chachapoyas, calling in weaponry that was scattered among several of the Guardia Civil's outlying commissaries ([APA13], decreto no. 174 [Sept. 14, 1908]).

12. Lieutenant of the Guardia Civil Daniel del Risco (from a local family) resigned on February 1 ([APA13], decreto no. 7 [1909]); head of the *Comisario del Aychayacu* (the provincial unit of the Gendarmery for Bongará province) Melquisidec Ruiz (also from a local family) resigned on February 18 (ibid., decreto no. 20 [Feb. 18, 1909]); the adjutant of the Segunda Comandancia del Norte and highest-ranking military judge of the department Pedro L. Traverso (whose tenure began in October 1905) resigned on February 25 (ibid., decreto no. 23 [Feb. 25, 1909]). A number of other low-level appointees resigned during this period as well.

13. For example, Teobaldo Vivanco, inspector of the Guardia Civil, arrived March 2 ([APA13], decreto no. 31 [Mar. 2, 1909]); Subinspector of the Guardia Civil Rafael V. Durand arrived on February 13 (ibid., decreto no. 86 [May 7, 1909]).

14. Alferez V. Castro y Merino, head of the Guardia Civil commissary at Bagua, was murdered on February 17 ([APA13], decreto no. 19 [Feb. 17, 1909]).

15. See Chapter 2 for an analysis of the marriage strategies of all the Pizarro Rojas children.

16. In December 1913, having successfully fended off an attempt by the Burga-Hurtado casta to seize regional control earlier in the year, Prefect Juan M. Pizarro followed the same procedure—taking it upon himself to appoint new district governors.

17. After the elections were over, Rubio was replaced by Alejandro Anduaga, a powerful hacendado and member of the ruling elite, who had been closely tied to the Pizarro-Rubio for years.

18. Control of these routes had also played a central role in determining the outcome of the Wars of Independence in northern Peru (Aguilar Briceño 1963) and of national political conflicts (for example, the large-scale rebellion of Coronel Viscarra in the latter half of 1899; see [APA45], nos. 91–111, 1899, and nos. 1–41, 1900), and in determining whether the forces behind failed national insurrections had a route of escape to Peru's jungle regions and away from those in control of the government.

19. Enemy casta leader Eloy Burga and his brother Amadeo had married two Hurtado-Eguren sisters, who were daughters of Manuel Hurtado (prefect of Amazonas

during the Pizarro-Rubio's failed election uprising of 1908). The Burga-Hurtado thus had an unusually strong presence in Levanto, and it was essential to take extra care in order to control the district during the elections.

20. Similar considerations obtained in appointing governors to certain key districts in Luya province. Although no important mule trails passed through Luya, the Burga and Ocampo both owned estates in the district of Lonya Chico (Burga's property was *Utcubamba*, while Ocampo's was *Cococbó*). In this key district, the Pizarro-Rubio appointed as governor José del Carmen Tuesta, whose abuses of the population are detailed in the long quote from Juan Mendoza below.

21. Comandante of the Gendarmery Pantoja was almost entirely inactive during this period.

22. Dr. Leonardo del Mazo took up his post as judge of the first instance of Luya and Bongará on January 13, 1908 ([APA13], decreto no. 151 [Aug. 3, 1908]).

23. [APA13], decreto no. 94 (May 13, 1909). The victim was Manuel Malaver, who was scribe (*amanuense*) of the subprefecture of Luya. He resigned on May 3 in an attempt to escape the wrath of the Pizarro-Rubio (ibid., decreto no. 81 [May 3, 1909]).

24. Major Vargas was jailed by the victorious Pizarro-Rubio forces nonetheless, and was replaced with an officer of their choosing. Only a series of appeals from the military commander of the North (whose headquarters was in Trujillo) managed to extricate him ([APA13], decreto no. 279 [Aug. 27, 1909]).

25. Del Mazo was in such a hurry to quit the region that he left a number of court cases pending, and left a number of people who had been imprisoned under the most questionable of circumstances stranded in jail with no legal authority on hand to continue with their cases. The prefect remained deaf to their plight despite receiving appeals for justice (see [APA13], decreto no. 104 [May 24, 1909]).

26. Wealthy landowner and member of the elite Amadeo Torrejón was president of the *Junta Electoral Departamental*, or Departmental Registration Board, of Amazonas ([APA13], decreto no. 57, *Torrejón al Subprefecto del Cercado*, Apr. 5, 1909). Bardales was forced to delay the meeting of the contribuyentes first until April 5, and then a second time until April 14, because a number of the contribuyentes designated by the National Election Board were in the countryside, and had not been able to return to Chachapoyas by the first two dates set for the meetings (March 30 and April 5). This was undoubtedly due to the unusually heavy rains that occur at this time of year, and the difficulty of travel over the dirt trails of the Chachapoyas region.

27. Wealthy members of the elite who had been forced to go into hiding temporarily due to casta struggles—as Eloy Burga had in this case—generally had the resources and the connections to avoid capture outside the department of Amazonas.

28. Months later, the Pizarro-Rubio casta was still using its control over the judicial system within the region to harass Burga. On December 9, 1909, the judge of Luya-Bongará sent a communiqué to the prefect of the neighboring department of

San Martín asking for his help in apprehending Burga. In addition to an explication of the crime for which Burga was being sought, the communiqué contained a detailed physical description of him.

29. Pablo M. Pizarro was elected (substitute) senator of Amazonas at this time, and like his casta allies enjoyed the privilege of running unopposed.

30. At this point, the prefect was Sr. G. Grimaldos.

31. [APA13], decreto no. 99 (Apr. 2, 1910). It is revealing that Sr. Ocampo found it necessary to leave the regional space entirely in order to disseminate his version of events as a public discourse.

32. [APA13], decreto no. 108 (June 2, 1909). Pázara responded identically to the plea he received from the Chachapoyas jail in late May from hacendado José Isaac Puerta, jailed on the flimsiest of pretexts by Luya-Bongará judge Leonardo del Mazo in early May. Sr. Puerta had been forced to languish in prison thereafter because del Mazo, in his haste to flee from the wrath of Javier M. Pizarro, left Sr. Puerta's case unresolved (see note 25 above). Because the judge of Chachapoyas province, José A. Urteaga, also absented himself from the region during this period (also to be out of harm's way), there was no one to accept the appeal to bring Sr. Puerta's case to a close. Puerta wrote to the prefect: "As an insult, rather than present himself in the robes of a magistrate, Dr. del Mazo should be dressed in the chains that convicts . . . are forced to wear" ([APA13], decreto no. 104 [May 24, 1909]). Prefect Pázara refused to take action on the matter, however, because he felt that the way that Sr. Puerta's protest was worded was offensive to the dignity of the authorities.

33. Anduaga was married to Cristina Astequier Pizarro, whose mother was Josefa M. Pizarro Farje, sister of casta leaders Pablo M. and Juan M. Pizarro Farje.

34. [APA45], nos. 57 (Apr. 15, 1903), 82 (Nov. 8, 1903); [APA17], June 18, 1904, and Oct. 3, 1906. Anduaga continued his abuse of Burga-Hurtado clients during periods of political turmoil in later years; see [APA51], no. 146 (Mar. 14, 1919); [APA15], no. 224 (Oct. 29, 1924).

35. In that all males between the ages of 21 and 60 were eligible for the draft, it is difficult to know what "unjust" refers to here—other than the fact that it was generally only peasant and mestizo males who were actually conscripted into the armed forces.

36. Other examples of the Pizarro-Rubio casta using its control over the judicial system and its monopoly over the machinery of state to persecute clients of the deposed alliance—both during and after its rise to power—include the plea of "Indian" Juan Chavez, resident of the pueblo of Magdalena, asking that his constitutional rights be protected, protesting the abuses of the parish priest in March 1909 ([APA13], decreto no. 30 [Mar. 2, 1909]); the protest of Marcelina Arévalo, mestiza resident of the town of Chachapoyas, claiming that Subprefect Rubio had kidnapped her and held her in jail for fifteen days during June 1909 (ibid., decreto no. 123 [June 16, 1909]); the appeal of Dolores Tafur de Vega, mestiza resident of Lámud, asking that the constitu-

tional rights of her husband Teófilo be protected in light of the abuse he was forced to suffer as a prisoner in the Lámud jail at the hands of Subprefect Gustavo A. Rubio (ibid., decreto no. 23 [Jan. 19, 1910]); and the request of Lucia F. vda. de Saavedra, appealing for protection of her constitutional guarantees in light of the threats she had received from several men who, knowing that her husband was dead and that she was alone, were using her small farm as if it were their own ([APA17], Mar. 5, 1910).

37. The documentary record contains an enormous number of protests from peasants and peasant communities concerning abusive governors, lieutenant governors, and justices of the peace.

38. The matter was ultimately decided by Congress on August 19, 1912 (Basadre 1968–69, 12: 207–23).

39. The ruling casta focused its energies on controlling the prefecture, subprefectures, and various district governorships of the department, for in this way it could manufacture the electoral result it desired. To this end, members of the ruling casta attempted to intimidate Billinghurst's appointees into deserting their posts and quitting the region. The strategy worked fairly well. Between January and May 1913, there were several such "desertions." Each time, however, the executive branch in Lima immediately assigned a new individual to replace the one driven out of the region, confounding the efforts of the ruling casta. The Pizarro-Rubio did succeed, however, in placing one of its clients—Nestor Alvaro Santillán—in the subprefecture of Chachapoyas province by early February when the subprefect appointed from Lima, Sr. Olivera, was forced to take over the prefecture due to the hasty departure of Prefect García Rosell. Alvaro immediately began to attempt to replace pro-Billinghurst governors with clients of the Pizarro-Rubio casta. The latter, however, aware that the prefect and the subprefect were divided on this issue, found various pretexts on which to resist the orders of the subprefect (for example, see [APA59], Feb. 27 and Mar. 1, 3, 7, and 10, 1913).

40. *Mayor de Guardias Wenceslao Roca al Sr. Subprefecto del Cercado*, May 7, 1913 (loose page, APA).

41. It was undoubtedly by means of such widely distributed and discussed edicts that people throughout the region, of all social classes, learned of the discourse of garantías (constitutional rights and protections), which they used in private communiqués with authorities in an attempt to defend themselves during periods when they were isolated and relatively defenseless, decades before anything like general literacy or schooling had been achieved (see Chapter 5).

42. The relevant documents include: [APA59], Apr. 19, 22, 28, 29 (two documents), and 30 (two documents), 1913; [APA17], Apr. 30 and May 2, 1913.

43. Torrejón's role had been restricted to signing and circulating a document inciting the villagers of these pueblos to revolt against the Pizarro-Rubio.

44. David Torres Aguirre, a career politician from Lima who had never set foot in Amazonas, was given the post of regular senator.

45. Torrejón's loyalty to the Burga-Hurtado was based in part on a series of affinal ties established between the Torrejón and the Hurtado families over the course of several generations. It was partly on the strength of these ties that Prefect Manuel Hurtado chose Torrejón as comandante of the Gendarmery in 1890 ([APA60], Dec. 4, 1891).

46. Luis's decision to accept the offer of marriage alliance from the Pizarro-Rubio was undoubtedly related to the fact that, with his former political patrons (the Burga-Hurtado) forced out of their position of dominance in 1909, and defeated in 1913, the aging *militar* found himself without a protector for himself or his family just as he was becoming less able to look after things himself. His concern turned out to be well founded. He died shortly before the wedding took place.

CHAPTER 5

1. The assassination attempt on President Pardo was part of a broader attempt to seize control of the central political apparatus in a number of departments in northern Peru—among them San Martín (an uprising timed to coincide with the assassination attempt was put down after much fighting), Amazonas, and Cajamarca. (Reference to these three revolts is made in [APA7], Aug. 28 and 29, Sept. 1, 2, 4, 5, 8, 9, and 12, and Oct. 10, 1874.) In his personal correspondence with President Pardo, Prefect Manuel Hurtado made direct reference to the uprising in San Martín ([AGN1], Sept. 19, 1874). For reasons that are not clear, Hurtado does not directly refer to the fighting in Chachapoyas in his personal letters to the president (although Hurtado alludes indirectly to local difficulties in his letter of Sept. 19). He does refer in his correspondence to the fighting in Cajamarca, which continued in the months following the assassination attempt ([AGN1], Jan. 23, 1875). I would like to thank Carmen McEvoy for bringing these documents to my attention.

2. Chachapoyas, Sept. 3, 1974, in [APA56], 3, no. 2 (Sept. 14, 1874). The principles of popular sovereignty were also made known to the general populace in speeches by ruling casta leaders given during political rituals commemorating national holidays (fiestas patrias and others) and major public-works projects (bridge and road construction), as suggested by the newspaper article quoted here.

3. In a personal letter to President Pardo, Prefect Manuel Hurtado explains that arrangements have been made to hold a special religious service in the town's main cathedral on Sunday, September 13, to give thanks that the president survived the assassination attempt. In describing those who will participate in the service, Prefect Hurtado does not employ the kind of inclusive rhetoric that characterizes the newspaper article quoted in the text. Rather, in this private communiqué, Hurtado explains that public officials, as well as "all the friends" of the president, are to participate ([AGN1], Sept. 10, 1874).

4. Santillán's casta had staged a similar uprising in 1872, when it had first been driven from power (see [APA7], Dec. 2, 4, 5, 10, 11, 15, 18, 26, 1872; Jan. 2, 10, 27, 1873; Feb. 12, 1873; Mar. 8, 1873; see also the personal correspondence between Manuel Hurtado, prefect of Amazonas, and Manuel Pardo, president of Peru, especially [AGN1], Dec. 7 and 14, 1872, and Jan. 4, 1873.

5. Relevant information on the persecution of the Santillán-Becerril by the Hurtado-Rodriguéz can be found in [APA7]: see especially the entries for the years 1872–77.

6. For a case in which the ability to control troop movements over the bridge became an important consideration, see Chapter 2.

7. All of these developments are discussed in *Memoria Administrativa, que el Prefecto del departamento de Amazonas, Coronel Don José Alayza, presenta al Sr. Director del Gobierno,* 1893 (part of [APA36]); [APA61], Oct. 23 and Nov. 13, 1893; [APA10], Dec. 2, 1893.

8. [APA14], Aug. 21, 1893; [APA61], Aug. 5 and 24, 1893; [APA63], Aug. 7 and 8, 1893.

9. The marginalization of the Pizarro-Rubio began in August 1890, when Manuel Hurtado became prefect of Amazonas. From his vantage point as prefect, Hurtado was gradually able to ensure that his casta would prevail over its enemies. Particularly important in this regard were the machinations that led to Pablo M. Pizarro being sacked as head of the Guardia Civil in July 1891 ([APA10], Oct. 28, 1891; [APA60], Apr. 2 and Dec. 4, 1891).

10. See *Memoria Administrativa, que el Prefecto del departamento de Amazonas, Coronel Don José Alayza, presenta al Sr. Director del Gobierno,* 1893 (part of [APA36]).

11. Unlike many other social contexts described in the literature, the obligatory use of the discourse of popular sovereignty had no direct limiting, constraining, or structuring effect on consciousness or action (for example, see Comaroff and Comaroff 1991; Corrigan and Sayer 1981, 1985).

12. For reasons that are beyond the scope of the present work, the bridge was ultimately built at Balzas.

13. See [APA10], Sept. 23, 1895.

14. See Gupta 1995 for a fascinating discussion of the discursive construction of the state in a radically different social context.

15. The uprising is described in [APA61], Feb. 11, 12, 14, 17, 20, 21, and 26, 1898, and Mar. 2, 3, 7 (2 documents), 13, and 19, 1898.

16. The archival record is filled with virtually identical orders. Often governors depicted themselves as having attempted to capture such delinquents despite the dangers posed, but having been prevented from doing so by the heavily armed nature of the men in question, and the fact that the delinquents had taken refuge within the estate of a high-ranking member of an opposing casta.

17. The population of the entire district of La Jalca in 1876 was 1,187. Of these, 267 people were below the age of 10, and 34 were above the age of 65 (Peru 1878).

The figure of 886 was derived by subtracting these very young and very old people from the district total.

In the text I refer only to labor involved in transporting the stones. I lack the information necessary to estimate how much labor was involved in what was undoubtedly the much more labor-intensive task of obtaining and shaping the stones.

18. [APA61], *Circular a los Gobernadores de los distritos de Olleros, Molinopampa, Levanto, Chiliquín, y Quinjalca,* Apr. 20, 1898. Those who hauled salt for the state were paid a daily wage out of the departmental treasury, but one far below what was considered "just compensation" for this task—because of which there was much resistance to performing it ([APA9], no. 770 [Oct. 15, 1920]).

19. See also [APA61], *Subprefecto al Gobernador de San Miguel,* June 14 and 20, 1898.

20. There are many such communiqués. The following are representative examples drawn from the periods of casta control outlined at the beginning of Chapter 3. For 1890–95, see [APA60], Apr. 10, 1891. For 1895–1902, see [APA61], June 10, 1898. For 1902–7, see [APA45], no. 55 (Feb. 20, 1903). For 1909–15, see [APA13], no. 103 (Apr. 7, 1910). For 1915–24, see [APA9], no. 651 (Aug. 18, 1920); [APA15], no. 137 (Sept. 3, 1924).

21. For example, see [APA51], no. 475 (July 23, 1919); [APA9], nos. 539 (July 12, 1920) and 563 (July 20, 1920). Even hacendados might be compelled to provide "public" services of this kind—particularly for the repair of roads that ran through their properties. At such times hacendados were also appealed to in the language of patriotism and the common good in legitimating the demand for services (see [APA61], *Subprefecto del Cercado al Ciudadano Pedro Tejada,* June 20, 1898).

22. The "Rules" also included restrictions concerning gambling (where it could and could not take place, and at what hours of the day and night) and cockfighting (underaged children were not allowed to attend, and cockfighting itself was allowed only in licensed establishments).

23. [APA63], *Circular a los Gobernadores de la Provincia,* June 15, 1895. See Chapter 4 for another example of this kind of edict, with almost identical wording.

24. The role of public education in making known to the general populace the principles of popular sovereignty is difficult to evaluate. Prior to the 1930s, teachers were trained either poorly or not at all, having been assigned their posts by casta leaders as a form of patronage, in order to expand the webs by which the ruling casta controlled the regional space. The national Ministry of Education had little input into the content of teaching materials in isolated departments like Amazonas, and no control over the quality of teaching itself.

25. For example, see [APA61], Apr. 25 and Aug. 31, 1894; [APA63], July 26, 1894.

26. Indeed, although it is impossible to resolve such a question definitively, there is much evidence to suggest that many people believed precisely the opposite: the violent actions, interpersonal confrontations, and instances of individual humiliation that characterized political life during this period; the fact that public demonstrations of the

ability to violate the principles of popular sovereignty were the only means by which a casta could rise to or remain in a position of power; the position of aristocratic sovereignty as the basis of organization for everyday social interaction; and the use of notions of equality, citizenship, progress, and patriotism by members of ruling castas to justify the worst kinds of abuse and forms of extortion.

CHAPTER 6

1. Overviews are provided by Morner 1985; Pike 1967; and Thorp and Bertram 1978.

2. Particularly important in this regard was the process by which the state increasingly monopolized control over armed force.

3. The regime of Nicolas de Piérola (1895–1900) marks the beginning of these centralizing efforts (see Basadre 1968–69, 10: 128; Mallon 1983b: ch. 4).

4. Most of Leguía's "modernizing" efforts were debt-financed, the loans coming from North American investors. Indeed, the 1920s was a period during which U.S. investment in Peru increased dramatically (see Pike 1967: 228–29; Caravedo 1977: 69–79).

5. During the 1920s, revolts broke out in Cajamarca (Gitlitz 1979; Taylor 1986; one of Chachapoyas's castas was involved in this movement), Iquitos (Basadre 1968–69, 13: 92; several of Chachapoyas's castas considered joining this movement; Chachapoyas's ruling casta helped the central government stamp it out); in Chachapoyas itself (briefly), and in the southern highlands in Puno (Collins 1988) and Cuzco (Rénique 1991). In the 1930s, additional regional movements developed in Trujillo, Cajamarca, Arequipa, and Cuzco, to name only the most important (Genaro Matos 1968; Klaren 1973; Caravedo 1979b; Rénique 1979; Taylor 1986; Slater 1989). Some regional elites rebelled because they resented the attempts of the central government to curb their privileges.

6. Ricardo Feijóo Reina was born in 1905, in Chachapoyas, to Lizardo Feijóo and Alejandrina Reina. He attended elementary school in Chachapoyas at the Centro Escolar de Varones no. 131, and secondary school at the Colegio Nacional San Juan de la Frontera (also in Chachapoyas), distinguishing himself as a student at both. In 1916 he was awarded a prize by the Ministry of Education for an essay on Garcilazo de la Vega. After finishing secondary school, he moved to Lima and entered the Escuela Normal, or teachers training school, where he was the valedictorian of his class. In 1924 he entered the Faculty of Letters at the Universidad Mayor de San Marcos in Lima, graduating in 1924, and continuing his studies in the doctoral program of that faculty. In 1931 he graduated with a law degree from the Faculty of Law of the same university.

7. For overviews of regional associations in Peru, see Jongkind 1974; Lloyd 1980; Lobo 1982; Mangin 1959; and Skeldon 1976.

8. By 1930 still another newspaper, *Redemption* (*Redención*), had appeared, enunciating many of the same principles (see Chapter 8).

9. Correspondence between Feijóo and the departmental president of the party implies 6,000–8,000 party members. For a discussion of the validity of these numbers, and the scope of the movement, see the text below.

10. Feijóo's staff consisted largely of the sons and daughters of landed families who were not members of the ruling casta, and who had taken flight to Lima in order to seek out new possibilities. Most became students either at the National University of San Marcos, or at the "Normal Schools" in Lima where teachers were trained.

11. See, for example, *Amazonas* 1, no. 6 (Apr. 1927): 1.

12. One of the most common themes in the newspaper (and one that is largely true to life) is the way that the casta families have squandered the resources and opportunities made available by the national government to assist in the region's "progress." Here is a case, then, in which different social groups have different orientations toward what was earlier called the "annihilation of regional space." Casta leaders were interested in this process only to the extent that it made available to them resources that would help strengthen their positions within the region. *El pueblo*, on the other hand, was obsessed with the problem for its own sake. For this group, the annihilation of regional space was a potentially *liberating* force.

13. Students of *indigenismo* will recognize a number of familiar themes in the following pages. Classic works of *indigenismo* from Peru include those contained in Aquezolo Castro 1976, and the work of Valcarcel (for example, 1925a, 1926b). Works from Mexico include Aguirre Beltran 1976; Caso 1971; Gamio 1960; and Vasconcelos 1925. For analytic treatments of *indigenismo* in Peru, see Chevalier 1970; Deustua 1984; Marzal 1981; and Rénique 1991. For works dealing with the Mexican context, see especially Brading 1985. Tamayo Herrera 1980 attempts a comparative analysis of *indigenismo* in Mexico and Peru.

14. The glorification of youth can be seen in virtually all issues of *Amazonas*.

15. This article is borrowed from the writings of José Ingenieros, a leader of the Latin American university reform movement that began in Buenos Aires, Argentina in 1918. The student radicals of Argentina had a profound effect on their Peruvian counterparts—among whom was Ricardo Feijóo Reina (see Walter 1963 and Portantiero 1978 for overviews of the university reform movement).

16. Another dimension of the moral discourse on the "man of principle" advanced by the paper consisted of an attack on alcohol consumption. A more developed consideration of this topic is beyond the scope of the present work.

17. It should be clear that I am not using "class" in a technical, analytic sense, but rather to refer to the broad similarity in working conditions faced by those whom the article identifies as belonging to the "laboring family of Amazonas."

18. It is interesting that in the first several lines of the article, it is revealed that the

bad boy has a servant who serves him his breakfast. It was predominantly families of the elite who had servants in Chachapoyas during this period.

19. *Amazonas* recognizes no roles for adult women other than mother and prostitute. Women of virtue are consistently located in relation to domestic space, and domestic relationships—as explored in the text below.

20. Either a "Women's and Children's Page" or, more commonly, a separate "Women's Column" and "Children's Column" were regular features of *Amazonas*. I have been unable to identify Josefina Saravia E., the author of the article quoted in the text.

21. The feminization of the nation was extended to the region as well. See "Beloved Native Land" (*Amazonas* 1, no. 2 [Nov. 15, 1926]: 1), quoted above.

22. Here we see a further elaboration of "education" as a metaphor for a range of disciplinary practices whose goal is to form particular subjectivities (note as well how the author of the article uses the terms "woman" and "mother" interchangeably).

23. In addition to the discourse on the "woman of virtue" discussed above, the newspaper included a number of articles on motherhood. In these articles, individual men wrote to the paper expressing their most intimate feelings of love for their mothers. These articles may have acted to project a common, inner subjectivity shared by "the people" in general. Interestingly, these articles were "confessional" in nature, rather than exhortative (as were the articles discussed above in the text), and thus represented a distinct "subject position."

CHAPTER 7

1. The "cells" of the APRA (Popular American Revolutionary Alliance) that met in secret in Chachapoyas at this time were segregated by gender. The following account is based on interviews with the few surviving members of the original Apristas—all of whom are male.

2. Other Apristas, however, were not so fortunate—a number were killed as they attempted to evade the police, both in Chachapoyas and in the region's smaller towns and villages. Virtually all of my elderly informants who were Apristas in their youth recall the names of those who were killed, as well as the specific locations and circumstances of their deaths.

3. Standard reference works on the APRA include Bourricaud 1966; Haya de la Torre 1973, 1977; Klaren 1973; and Sanchez 1934. To date, relatively little work has been done on the early organizing efforts, by means of which the party extended its influence into the highland provinces (however, see Vega-Centeno Bocangel 1991).

4. Informants say they had received the order to establish the Popular University in Chachapoyas from the party headquarters in Lima. For an overview of the university's activities in Lima, see Klaiber 1975.

5. The teachers came predominantly from among the original founders of the party in Chachapoyas.

6. The following quote is taken from a taped interview with "Carlos A. Mestanza Chota," carpenter, conducted on September 12, 1986 (at the request of "Sr. Mestanza," I have used a pseudonym to conceal his identity).

7. The surviving original Apristas of Chachapoyas (all male, as noted above) were largely silent on issues related to the oppression of women—despite their recognition that rape was one of the most common crimes committed in the region. When asked specifically about whether they spoke out about the rights of women, informants rather uncomfortably replied that whenever they used the terms *hombre* or *el pueblo*, they intended them to apply to men and women alike.

8. During an extended period of fieldwork in Chachapoyas (from December 1982 until November 1983, and from January 1985 until December 1986), and during shorter visits thereafter (during the summers of 1990, 1991, 1992, and 1993), I had the opportunity to speak at length with a number of the founding members of the APRA about their participation in the Popular University—as well as about the organizing activities of the party in general. The following account is based on information provided by these individuals. No written documentation has survived concerning the Popular University's activities in Chachapoyas, as it was necessary for teachers to burn all evidence of their membership in the APRA due to the persecution the party suffered at the hands of the central government.

9. The category *el pueblo* did not deny the existence of cholos or Indios. It simply sidestepped the thorny issue of the racial character of the groups by uniting them in a broader category that was not explicitly racial.

10. That is, the Apristas seized upon what had been the "public transcript" (J. C. Scott 1990) of the regional social order, and used the fact that it had been declared publicly legitimate to undermine the authority of the ruling elite—whose behavior generated a "hidden transcript" that could not be represented in political ritual or discourse.

11. Sr. Santillán was jailed several times in the 1930s and 1940s for his involvement with the APRA.

12. Due to his involvement in Aprista activities in Chachapoyas in the early 1930s, Sr. Castilla spent several years as a young man in *El Fronton*, a prison located on an island off the coast, just outside Lima.

13. In 1934 Sr. Muñoz was forced to flee Chachapoyas for Iquitos, where he lived for several years, in order to avoid further persecution as an Aprista.

14. For background information on the organizational structure of the APRA, see Stein 1980: 159–61.

15. All the members of the cells were men (see notes 1 and 7).

16. The 3,200 voters claimed by the APRA in the election of 1931 is obviously an

exaggerated figure. Even so, it is still clear that the APRA had become a major force by the time the election of 1931 took place.

CHAPTER 8

1. It should be emphasized at the outset that what was referred to as "democracy" involved anything but the open and equal participation of all in the political process. Rather, important processes of exclusion were an integral part of the movement. As explained below, democratización meant not only the empowerment of the urban male middle class, but also the systematic exclusion of women and peasants from the more "open" society envisaged within the movement. Though the transformations in local life effected by the movement were consistently cast in the universalistic language of the Enlightenment, these changes in fact represented the interests and motivations of particular groups. In order to emphasize this, I have chosen to retain the folk term *democratización* rather than replace it with the English "democratization."

2. Stein (1980: 115–18) reports that the traditional aristocracy of the country was never comfortable with Sanchez Cerro, even though its leaders ultimately backed him in his bid for the presidency. They considered him to be a cholo and an "upstart caudillo," and found his dark skin and his "crude" behavior offensive.

3. A spontaneous uprising of the masses had been decisive in the presidential election of 1912, but thereafter the elite had managed to reassert its control over the electoral system (see Basadre 1968–69, 12: 208–16).

4. Leguía began this process of purging in 1919, when he assumed control of the country via a coup, dissolved Congress, and called elections for an entirely new Congress in which only candidates loyal to him were allowed to participate. He also returned the country to its pre-1896 method of deciding the outcome of subsequent congressional elections. According to this method, in cases where an election was disputed, the ruling majority in Congress—which was pro-Leguía because of the 1919 manipulations—decided who would be recognized as the winner. Needless to say, these changes allowed Leguía to retain a very loyal Congress (Basadre 1968–69, 13: 29–32).

5. It has been widely noted that Leguía encouraged sycophantic behavior on the part of those who surrounded him.

6. Leguía introduced a series of reforms in tributary policy that did much to transform regional elites from "patrimonial" lords who controlled tax collection directly into "prebendal" representatives of the government bureaucracy who were beholden to the state for their positions (Wolf 1966). These changes in tributary policy seriously undermined the autonomy and independent decision-making power of regional elites. For example, *Juntas Departamentales*, which had previously controlled much in the way of departmental tax revenues, were dissolved under Leguía. Similarly, provincial mu-

nicipal councils came to be named directly by the Ministry of Government. At the same time, Leguía's administration poured a tremendous amount of money into regional arenas such as Chachapoyas—in order to fund infrastructural projects (predominantly roads). As the representatives of the central government within their respective regional arenas, local elites controlled the actual use and distribution of these funds.

As a result of these changes, elite groups did not need to look to the peasantry for most of the revenues that would sustain the privileged station in life to which they aspired. As a result, extractive pressures on the peasantry eased somewhat. Further, because local elites were beholden to the central government for revenue, they needed to demonstrate continued loyalty to Leguía.

7. Symptomatic of the importance of the emergence of the "masses" at this time was the creation of what Basadre (1968–69, 14: 136–38) has called Peru's first true political party—the APRA. It was the first in the sense that no party before had had a permanent bureaucracy of national scope, and it was the first party to articulate a program based on social and economic questions, rather than on administrative problems or abstract principles of law.

8. The country's traditional elite succeeded in defending its interests during the decade immediately following the oncenio, but nothing more (Basadre 1968–69, 14: 8). Basadre (ibid.: 7) describes the decade of military rule following the oncenio as one of three forms of military rule that have characterized Peru. This particular form emerges in contexts where there is a political vacuum, and where traditional political groupings are impotent when confronting dangers faced by the nation (in this case, Aprismo and communism). The dominant classes welcome military intervention in these circumstances as a way of limiting or forestalling their own loss of power and privilege, and of limiting the gains of subaltern groups.

9. See [APA51], nos. 249 (Apr. 25, 1919), 253 (Apr. 29, 1919), 307 (May 22, 1919), 324 (May 30, 1919), 340 (June 6, 1919), and 351 (June 7, 1919); Basadre (1980: 91) also mentions that violence surrounded the electoral process in Chachapoyas prior to the elections of May 1919.

10. *Santa Cruz* was located in an inaccessible section of the valley of the Sonche River, just to the east of the village of Huancas (to the east of Chachapoyas).

11. Pizarro's wife was Rosa Rubio Linch, sister of congressional representatives Miguel and Arturo Rubio Linch.

12. Symptomatic of the way that Leguía persecuted and marginalized all who were not completely and unquestionably loyal to him—resulting in a vacuum when he fell from power—was his treatment not just of Pablo M. Pizarro, but of the entire Pizarro family in the aftermath of Pablo's debacle of 1923. From that point onward, the Pizarro family as a whole disappeared from all public positions in the Chachapoyas region. They have no public presence whatsoever after 1923.

13. As early as 1931, these families had begun to follow a time-honored pattern of alliance formation in the region—that of cementing their ties via marriage. On

July 11, 1931, Samuel Echaiz Ocampo—one of five sons of Echaiz family patriarch José María Echaiz—was married to Blanca Feijóo Hurtado (Ricardo Feijóo Reina's first cousin, Ricardo being the illegitimate son of Blanca's uncle). Several years later, on May 25, 1936, another son of patriarch José María Echaiz, namely José María Echaiz Ocampo, was married to Aida Burga Tejada, daughter of Burga family patriarch Buenaventura Burga Hurtado (by his second wife, Manuela Tejada). Further cementing the ties among these families was the marriage of Clementina Echaiz Ocampo, a daughter of patriarch José María Echaiz, to Victor Burga Hurtado, son of Burga patriarch Buenaventura Burga Hurtado (by his first wife, Carolina Hurtado Eguren). The latter marriage occurred in the early 1930s as well.

14. "Revolution" is the word used by virtually all informants in discussing the movement of August 1930. This includes elderly members of formerly elite, landed families, as well as members of the movements of democratization involved in the "revolution."

15. Arturo Rubio Linch was deputy of Chachapoyas from 1909 to 1930. His brother Miguel was substitute deputy of Bongará from 1909 to 1912 (during which time Limeño Aurelio Sousa was the figurehead deputy), and was regular deputy from 1912 until 1930 (Echegaray 1966).

16. Such an alliance was necessary for two reasons. First, only members of the elite voted at this time, so the backing of at least some of them was needed for a chance at electoral success. Second, leading families of the elite maintained caches of arms, without which Feijóo could not even consider making a violent assault on the ruling casta.

17. Although the Echaiz family had begun the century closely tied to the Pizarros—to whom it was related affinally—to the point of being involved in armed uprisings against the Burga-Hurtado family in 1908, its members were subsequently eased out of important positions within the Pizarro-Rubio casta as a function of the internal contradictions of casta rule (see Chapters 3 and 4). By 1913 the Echaiz had switched sides completely, and had joined the Burga-Hurtado in an armed uprising against the Pizarro-Rubio (which failed; see Chapter 4). By 1915 the Echaiz had deepened its commitment to the Hurtado family by intermarrying with it. The Echaiz and the Hurtado families remained close allies thereafter.

18. My discussion here obviously owes much to Eric Wolf's groundbreaking analysis of the role of political brokers in the formation of the Mexican state (Wolf 1956).

19. Feijóo was the illegitimate son of a man of the landed class and a chola who managed to rise to prominence because the national political environment allowed him to use his considerable intellectual gifts in a way that would not have been possible in previous decades.

20. The pact that Feijóo made with the Echaiz in 1929 was well known in Chachapoyas, and was often referred to by elderly informants. Much of the more detailed information upon which this section is based is derived from interviews with Carlos Echaiz conducted during the summers of 1990 and 1991.

21. The rather truncated nature of this account—concerning an event of fundamental importance in the history of the region—leads me to suspect that the APRA's role may have been more limited than the interviewee implies.

22. In the presidential elections of October 1931, in which the Apristas claimed massive fraud, Sanchez Cerro defeated APRA leader Haya de la Torre. Within Chachapoyas, APRA congressional candidates were likewise defeated. In response, the APRA organized an armed uprising for December 5, 1931—just days before Sanchez Cerro was to take power in the national capital. Revolts were planned for Trujillo, Lambayeque, Chachapoyas, and Cajamarca (see Basadre 1968–69, 14: 174, for reference to the Cajamarca revolt). The uprising in Chachapoyas was to be led by Lucas H. Rubio. It was avoided, however, when several former gendarmes, who were among those approached as possible participants, betrayed the plans to the prefect (see [APA1], *Luis Cachay, F. Torrejón, y Francisco Poquionia al Sr. Prefecto del Departamento*, Dec. 4, 1931).

23. This practice parallels closely that of the *Convention Nationale* of revolutionary France, which in 1793 abandoned the Christian calender (used for centuries prior) and adopted a new calender, starting with Year One (as of September 22, 1792, when the Republic was first proclaimed). In this way the Convention marked a decisive end to the ancien régime and the beginning of the Republic.

24. Cachay had also been appointed departmental head of the Gendarmery, another reason for his participation in the induction ceremony (see below).

25. Symptomatic of the new legitimacy of the principles of popular sovereignty was the fact that the name of the newspaper *Amazonas* was changed to *La Voz del Pueblo* (The Voice of the People) in 1931.

26. It was of course also necessary that these reborn elite families *behave* in ways that reinforced their claims of having undergone a transformation.

27. Middle-sector members of the junta included Gabriel Baella (a local merchant/muleteer), Pedro Quiroz (another merchant/muleteer), and Adolfo Angulo (a carpenter).

28. Other members of the first postrevolution municipal council were: Miguel Chumbe Tejada, a metalworker by trade, and a sympathizer of Feijóo's *Partido Laboral Independiente Amazonense*; Juan H. Alva Torres, a tailor and, like Miguel Chumbe Tejada, a man with strong sympathies for Feijóo and his Partido Laboral; Baltazar Cáceres, also a tailor, who was likewise deeply involved in the movement of democratización; and Antonio Cachay (brother of Abraham Cachay), a carpenter, who finished his secondary education in the 1930s in Chachapoyas, attended the Normal School that opened in the town in the 1930s, and subsequently became a teacher.

29. The plans of the various members of the municipal council for "local improvement" are outlined in *Redención* (1, no. 7 [Nov. 2, 1930]: 2–3). Information on the completion of their projects is to be found in the *Archivo de la Municipalidad de la Provincia de Chachapoyas* (AMC). Documents in the archive are grouped by year, each group being wrapped in paper and tied with a string.

30. [APA25], Sept. 6, 1930. Cachay had spent some time in the army earlier in his life, during which time he had achieved the rank of second lieutenant. After the revolution of 1930, Cachay taught physical education to boys in the high school in Chachapoyas (the Colegio Nacional San Juan de la Libertad). He was well known for instilling a sense of discipline in his students.

31. According to Victor Santillán Gutierrez, Antonio Valdez Vasquez, Victor Castilla Pizarro, and Máximo Rodriguéz Culqui. In addition to alerting me to this strategy of Cachay, these men (the last of whom was a gendarme himself) reviewed membership lists of the Gendarmery from the early 1930s (from September 1930 onward), which I had obtained from the Archive of the Prefecture of Amazonas (APA), and identified the backgrounds of the individuals listed therein.

32. It is very likely that Valdivia was a member of the Fraternal Assembly of Artisans and Laborers of Amazonas, the new mutual-aid society formed in the aftermath of the revolution of August 1930. If so, this may explain part of the responsiveness of the gendarmes (see below).

33. [APA32], Apr. 14 and May 4, 5, 6, and 7, 1931. A great many similar appeals for protection, with the same kind of responsiveness on the part of the authorities, can be found in [APA23], 1932, 1933; and [APA28].

34. There are relatively few cases of police abuse in the early 1930s within the town of Chachapoyas (for examples, see [APA25], Oct. 28, 1930; [APA32], May 2, 1931; [APA61], Aug. 11, 1932). Supporting the entire changed relationship between el pueblo and the gendarmes was the fact that the leaders of the Feijóo-Echaiz alliance— in their zeal to show their respect for the new order—also appointed individuals sympathetic to el pueblo to provincial judgeships. The most important of these positions was the judge of the first instance of Chachapoyas. After several interim appointments, this post was filled on July 11, 1931, by Dr. José Sanchez Tirado, a regular contributor to the newspaper *Amazonas* and an important intellectual force in the democratización movement ([APA24], July 11, 1931).

35. For examples of firm action taken against gendarmes who violated the rights of middle-sector individuals, see [APA25], Nov. 3, 1930; [APA32], May 6, 1931; [APA61], Aug. 14, 1932.

36. See [APA52], 1937 (pp. 47–48, which have figures for the period 1932–37).

37. Particular project proposals—along with detailed budgets—were made by provincial-level juntas. They had to be approved by the central office of the junta in Lima.

38. Junta members did not do financial accounting themselves. They did, however, choose the individuals who did the accounting work—thus presenting the opportunity for much collusion and graft.

39. These generalizations are based on a review of [APA52], 1931–37; and of [APA38], 1931–37.

40. The Juntas de Pro-Desocupados helped empower the formerly marginalized

middle sectors in one additional way. The monies made available to the juntas for public-works projects came from the Ministry of Fomento, and were dispersed to the juntas by the *Caja de Depósitos y Consignaciones*. The caja, however, did not have the means to actually deliver the funds to the departmental junta in Chachapoyas. As a result, the caja relied on merchant houses with stores located in the northern coastal city of Chiclayo and the highland city of Cajamarca to deliver the funds to Chachapoyas (the merchant house of *Hilbek, Kuntze i Cía* was the most commonly relied upon). The merchant houses in turn relied on any one of several long-distance merchants from the town of Celendín (see Map 1)—who had operated on a small scale in Chachapoyas for some time, and who had been involved in the movements of democratización—to carry the funds to Chachapoyas. In other words, as the central government began to establish a stronger presence in the region—and in a way that helped empower el pueblo—it helped reinforce the viability of and became directly tied to a sector of long-distance merchant exchange.

41. See [APA32], Mar. 2, 1931. Torres was also appointed head of Chachapoyas's elementary school for boys (*Escuela de Varones* no. 131). The departmental superintendent of the office of primary education, Torres's superior, was H. N. Revoredo, a member of the elite, and a close friend of the Burga family (one of the three elite families who made up the elite component of the new ruling alliance).

42. This discussion is based on conversations with Victor Santillán Gutierrez, one of the original APRA organizers in Chachapoyas, during the summers of 1990-93.

43. [APA32], *Inspector de Enseñanza al Subprefecto del Cercado*, May 4, 1931.

44. The documents in question are to be found in [APA32], *Comisión Escolar de Chachapoyas al Subprefecto*, June 4, June 9, and July 30, 1931.

45. As of 1935, the position of the region's teachers in inculcating the ideals of popular sovereignty in their students was reinforced by the establishment of a teachers' training school (*Escuela Normal*) in Chachapoyas itself. The Normal School drew students from among the town's middle sectors. Upon graduation, they were given teaching posts in the department's rural districts.

46. *Taringuicho* ("The Dancer" [derived from Quechua]) was the paper that appeared in Jumbilla, while *Brecha* ("The Breach") appeared in Lámud.

47. It was clear soon after the storming of the prefecture by el pueblo that the Apristas were to be the "poor cousins" in the arrangement. They were awarded virtually no public posts despite their participation in the uprising, and in the elections of the following year (October 1931), Feijóo's followers backed Sanchez Cerro rather than Haya de la Torre, leader of the APRA. Furthermore, none of the APRA candidates who ran for seats in the Constituent Congress were successful. As a result of their marginalization, the APRA organized a rebellion for December 5, 1931—which was disclosed to authorities in Chachapoyas on December 4, and was therefore averted (see note 22 above).

48. In addition to those discussed in the text, other horizontal associations that

began to emerge at this time included rotating credit associations and a chamber of commerce.

49. The "Fraternal Assembly of Artisans and Workers of Amazonas" was modeled on the "Fraternal Confederation of Mutual Aid"—a mutual-aid society that appeared in Chachapoyas in 1920 among the town's artisans (see [APA17], July 18, 1920; and *Libro Copiador de Oficios a la Prefectura i demas autoridades del Departamento*, Sept. 1, 1920). The "Fraternal Confederation" was introduced into the area by a carpenter who had spent time in the jungle city of Iquitos, where he had become familiar with mutual-aid societies. The society was very short-lived, enduring for only a space of months.

50. The statutes reinforced gender inequality and nuclear family forms; wives, children, and other dependents of male members were automatically "inactive" members. No allowance was made for women to be full, active members. This is especially significant considering that a large number of women—married and unmarried—worked at least part-time as seamstresses, breadmakers, cantina operators, and livestock sellers.

51. As noted at the beginning of the chapter, these changes did not in reality represent democracy and equality (understood as universal principles that apply equally to all). Rather, they represented the empowerment of a particular social sector that was cast in universalistic language.

52. The Apristas also helped form a series of rotating credit associations among the populace in the 1930s—also with the goal of freeing those of more humble backgrounds from having to rely on rich patrons for money in times of economic necessity.

53. For examples, see [APA61], Mar. 21, Apr. 7, and Apr. 14, 1932.

54. [APA32], Jan. 15 and 26, 1931; [APA28], Feb. 12, 1931. While the towns of Amazonas were effectively purged of the deposed casta's influence in the aftermath of the revolution of August 1930, the same cannot be said of the countryside. Struggles between clients of the Rubio-Linch casta and the representatives of the Feijóo-Echaiz alliance continued until 1933, when another crisis in the national political order resulted in the downfall of the Echaiz. From August 1930 until 1933, then, clients of the Rubio-Linch continued to cause difficulties for the ruling alliance in the countryside, and made occasional forays into the towns as well.

55. See [APA32], July 20, 1931.

56. In addition to paying monthly dues, candidates for membership had to be at least 19 years of age, have an occupation recognized as "honorable," and be admitted by the majority vote of the members. The latter two of these requirements would have further restricted the entry of peasants into the assembly, for they were not considered to be honorably employed—and thus they were unlikely to have been accepted by majority vote of the members.

57. Informants report that athletic teams and competitions were organized for the first time in the 1920s, but only within the limited context of public school—appar-

ently under the stimulus of President Leguía's Ministry of Education. Outside of school, however, elite children and young adults refused to associate with their social inferiors.

58. An oficio to the prefect from a group of young women who wished to form a sport club reveals a similar concern with promoting the disciplinary practices necessary for a proper training of the body ([APA32], June 2, 1931): "I have the honor of informing you that the members of the Club 'Natividad Lopez,' in a special meeting, unanimously agreed to designate you honorary member and protector. We greatly appreciate the honor you do us by accepting, and hope that we merit the assistance necessary to make of our athletic activities a true path of education, so that they can make up an integral part of our culture." Natividad Lopez (Torrejón) was a nun, elementary-school teacher, and member of the upper class of Chachapoyas, who is still remembered for her tireless efforts in educating the more humble social elements of Chachapoyas.

59. None of the other sport-culture clubs expressed a concern with infectious disease in their statutes. The appearance of such a concern here was undoubtedly related to the emergence of a more general discourse about the virtues of domestic womanhood and individual self-discipline that was current at the time (see Chapter 6).

60. This extended even to forms of dress. Club requirements that all purchase the same uniform, which was to be used at all times during practice as well as for games, meant that on the playing field all were dressed alike regardless of background. Upper- and middle-class youths commonly played on the same sports teams, and thus the point about new authority structures having emerged after the revolution of August 1930 refers specifically to these groups.

61. The prohibition in question refers to membership in the outlawed political party, the APRA.

62. This was true even though the franchise was extended to middle-sector groups as of the presidential and congressional elections of 1931 (see Chapter 6).

63. As noted in Chapter 7, the ancient ruins of the Chachapoyas region came to symbolize the essential and timeless unity of the region and its people—a unity that had been destroyed by the Spanish Conquest and its aftermath. This concern with essential unity in the emergence of el pueblo can be seen reflected in the name of this sport-culture club. *Kuelap* is a huge ruined fortress with enormous stone walls (of up to 20 meters in height) located a day's walk above the town of Tingo.

64. Although sport clubs were segregated by gender, young women were not prohibited from participating in this new avenue for achieving social recognition. Unfortunately, no regulations for the women's sport clubs have survived, and thus it has been impossible to compare their organization with that of the men's clubs.

65. Several other forms of horizontal association emerged at this time that also expressed and helped actualize the newfound strength and public legitimacy of the town's middle sectors. Among the most important of these were neighborhood associations.

Neighborhood associations took upon themselves the responsibility for a number of tasks and activities, the most important of which was the physical upkeep of their neighborhoods. Membership in the associations was not mandatory, but informants report that the vast majority of people in each of Chachapoyas's four neighborhoods joined. Each association member was expected to contribute labor intermittently in order to help maintain the streets, sidewalks, and watercourses of the neighborhood.

66. I have been unable to find written documentation to confirm what informants related to me concerning the precise years in which the key changes in religous practice described in the text occurred. These changes will be familiar to students of Latin American society.

67. The occasional exceptions to this pattern prove the rule. On those rare occasions when cholos or Indios were able to use the main cathedral for baptisms, marriages, etc., it was only because a powerful patron within the ruling casta had interceded on their behalf as a special favor.

68. Ortiz was himself a man of humble background (he had been a carpenter before entering the Catholic Church), who as a Salesian was part of the democratizing movement within the Church that began circa 1900 (see Klaiber 1992).

69. The only restrictions on use of the cathedral that remained after 1930 concerned the ability of interested parties to pay the fees necessary to host the desired ceremony (baptism, marriage, etc.). Peasants were least able to pay such sums, and thus informal processes of exclusion continued to limit their use of the cathedral.

70. In stark contrast to the practices of his predecessors, Monseñor Ortiz began visiting families of humble background in their homes, and ministering to their needs. Furthermore, he did so even prior to the revolution of August 1930. His willingness to disregard distinctions of race and class in the performance of his religious duties further contributed to the breakdown of the aristocratic order.

71. The Virgen de Asunta had appeared in Ecuador in the early 1800s, where a sacred litter was built in her honor. The litter was brought to Chachapoyas from Ecuador shortly thereafter by a member of the Chachapoyas elite—Julian Monteza. Sr. Monteza originally kept the litter in his home, but by the mid-1800s the litter had come to be housed in a small chapel in Chachapoyas built in honor of the Virgin. During the nineteenth and early twentieth centuries, it was predominantly members of Chachapoyas's humble social classes that sought out her aid and comfort. After 1930 the Virgin was elevated to the status of the town's new patrona.

CHAPTER 9

1. Prominent exceptions include C. A. Smith 1990a, 1990b;, Urban and Sherzer 1991; and Joseph and Nugent 1994. Smith conceives of building a national community as an elite project, and frames her discussion of the failure of an elite nation-building

project in nineteenth-century Guatemala in relation to the need to impose an alien notion of the nation from above on culturally alien (in this case, Indian) groups. Urban and Sherzer take an approach very similar to Smith's (see Nugent 1994 for a discussion of these works). The volume by Joseph and Nugent, which focuses on Mexico (and which appeared after the present manuscript was written), presents a much more nuanced and sophisticated understanding of the complex processes that have given rise to modern nation-states.

2. I am referring specifically here to nineteenth- and early twentieth-century Latin America (see below). With the passing of the twentieth century, state structures have become increasingly centralized and solidary, and ruling groups have openly embraced the rhetoric of popular sovereignty. In the context of the crisis in and reorganization of global capitalism that began in the early 1970s (Harvey 1989; Mandel 1975), these developments set the stage for dynamics of a more coercive/oppositional nature.

3. In earlier centuries, of course, the European bourgeoisie had struggled with an aristocratic nobility to control the apparatus of state—a position of dominance from which the bourgeoisie went on to form cultures of national scope. Even for this earlier period, however, the parallel with the Chachapoyas case is quite limited. It would be highly inaccurate and misleading to equate the diverse marginal social groups that came together under the banner of el pueblo—artisans, muleteers, petty merchants, peasants, and public employees—with the increasingly affluent and powerful European bourgeoisie during the rise of capitalism.

4. See the various contributions to Frader and Rose 1996. I do not mean to imply, of course, that all aspects of building nation-states were coercive either in western European countries or in their colonies and ex-colonies. Indeed, I suspect that processes similar to those described for Chachapoyas played a role in the making of modern nation-states in general. I do assert, however, that differences between Chachapoyas and these "European" contexts in class structure, degree of state centralization, and relationship of ruling classes to modernity represent important points of contrast that need to be emphasized in understanding the nature of building the nation-state in these respective regions. These points are developed in the text below.

5. Jorge Basadre, Peru's foremost historian, identifies the administration of Nicolas de Piérola (1895–1900) as the time when the formerly fragmented polity of Peru coalesced into a more cohesive state (Basadre 1968–69, 10: 127–28). Julio Cotler, another highly esteemed social scientist, refers to the early 1930s as inaugurating the beginning of the Peruvian state (a date supported by the present study).

6. Social movements and ideologies based on popular sovereignty were sweeping through much of Latin America during this period, pointing to the generality of the processes described for Chachapoyas. Examples for select countries include the following. For Brazil, see Weffort 1970. For Mexico, see Córdova 1973 and Cornelius 1973. For Argentina, see Fayt 1967 and Murmis and Portantiero 1971. For Chile, see Drake 1978. For Central America, see Acuña Ortega 1993 and Acuña Ortega and

Molina Jiménez 1991. For more general works that consider Latin America as a whole, see Graham 1990, Hale 1986, and Johnson 1958.

7. For a related point, see Fox 1990a: 7.

8. Abrams 1988; Foucault 1980; Giddins 1981–85; Mitchell 1991. This understanding of power is hardly original with writers of the last two decades. Perhaps the classic statement of the simultaneously enabling/disabling character of power is Hegel's discussion of the master-slave dialectic (1967: 228–40).

Bibliography

PRIMARY SOURCES

Archivo General de la Nación, Lima

[AGN1]: *Manuel Hurtado al Excelentísimo Señor Manuel Pardo.*

Archivo de la Municipalidad de la Provincia de Chachapoyas, Chachapoyas

[AMC1]: *Amazonas* [newspaper]. 1926–31.
[AMC2]: *Contribución Industrial, Provincia del Cercado de Chachapoyas.* 1919.
[AMC3]: *Contribuciones Rurales, Provincia del Cercado.* 1920. *Actuación de Matrículas de la Contribución Rural.*
[AMC4]: *Contribuciones Rústicas, Provincias del Cercado, Luya y Bongará.* 1919.
[AMC5]: *Contribuciones Urbanas, Provincia del Cercado.* 1919. *Actuación de Matrículas de la Contribución Urbana.*
[AMC6]: *La Ortiga* [newspaper; assorted issues]. 1913.
[AMC7]: *Predios Urbanos, Provincia del Cercado de Chachapoyas.* 1920.
[AMC8]: *Registro Electoral, Provincias del Cercado, Luya y Bongará.* 1920, 1924.
[AMC9]: *La Voz del Pueblo* [newspaper; assorted issues]. 1931, 1932, 1933.

Archivo Prefectural de Amazonas, Chachapoyas

[APA1]: APRA [containing documents relating to and correspondence concerning the activities of the APRA, 1930–35].
[APA2]: *Beneficencia de Chachapoyas.* 1890–93.
[APA3]: *Caja de Depósitos y Consignaciones del Departamento de Amazonas.* 1930.
[APA4]: *Compañía Nacional de Recaudación.* 1908.
[APA5]: *Compañía Recaudadora de Impuestos.* 1913, 1915.

[APA6]: *Comunicación Dirigida a los Ministerios*. 1891–96.

[APA7]: *Copiador de Comunicaciones Dirijidas a los Juzgados de la Primera Instancia del Cercado y Luya*. 1867 (from July 8), 1868, 1869, 1870, 1871, 1872, 1873, 1874, 1875, 1876, 1877, and 1878.

[APA8]: *Copiador de Oficios a Diferentes Autoridades [de la Subprefectura del Cercado]*. 1893, 1894, 1895.

[APA9]: *Copiador de Oficios [de la Subprefectura del Cercado] a la Prefectura del Departamento de Amazonas*. 1920.

[APA10]: *Copias Simples [de comunicaciones de la Subprefectura del Cercado a la Prefectura]*. 1891–99.

[APA11]: *Corte Superior de Loreto, Amazonas y Cajamarca al Prefecto de Amazonas*. 1901–2, 1907.

[APA12]: *Cuaderno de Comunicaciones [de la Prefectura] Con el Juez de Primera Instancia de Esta Provincia y Ajente Fiscal del Departamento*. 1865, 1866.

[APA13]: *Decretos (Prefectura)*. 1908–10.

[APA14]: *Decretos y Informes de la Prefectura de Amazonas*. 1892–93.

[APA15]: *Decretos y Resoluciones de la Prefectura del Departamento de Amazonas*. 1924.

[APA16]: *Decretos y Resoluciones de la Subprefectura de Luya*. 1924.

[APA17]: *Diversos Años del 1849 al 1924. Varias Reparticiones Administrativas*.

[APA18]: *Haciendas, [Sus] Propietarios i Producciones*. 1889.

[APA19]: *Juicio seguido contra el Presbítero don Felipe S. Tuesta por el delite de ocultación de armas, Zona Militar de Amazonas, No. de Orden 55*. 1909.

[APA20]: *Juzgados de Primera Instancia*. 1896, 1897.

[APA21]: *Juzgados de Primera Instancia de Chachapoyas a la Prefectura*. 1920.

[APA22]: *Juzgados de Primera Instancia de las Tres Provincias, y Jueces de Pas de las Mismas*. 1879, 1880.

[APA23]: *Legajo, Comunicaciones de la Subprefectura del Cercado a la Prefectura*. 1931, 1932, 1933.

[APA24]: *Un Legajo de Oficios de la Corte Superior de Cajamarca*. 1931.

[APA25]: *Un Legajo de Oficios de las Gobernaciones del Departamento*. 1930.

[APA26]: *Un Legajo de Oficios de la Subprefectura de Luya [a la Prefectura]*. 1931.

[APA27]: *Un Legajo de Oficios de la Tesorería Fiscal*. 1930.

[APA28]: *Un Legajo de Oficios del Juzgado de la Primera Instancia del Cercado de Chachapoyas*. 1931, 1932, 1933.

[APA29]: *Legajo de Oficios del Juzgado de Primera Instancia*. 1935.

[APA30]: *Un Legajo de Oficios del Juzgado de Primera Instancia de la Provincia del Cercado*. 1930.

[APA31]: *Legajo de Oficios Varios*. 1938.

[APA32]: *Un Legajo de Oficios Varios—Dentro del Departamento*. 1930, 1931, 1932.

[APA33]: *Legajo de Solicitudes. Correspondiente al año 1933*.

[APA34]: *Libro Copiador de Comunicaciones Dirijidas Por Esta Prefectura a los Gobernadores de los Distritos de las Provincias y Prefecturas de toda la República*. 1894.

[APA35]: *Libro Copiador de las Comunicaciones de la Subprefectura con la Prefectura del Departamento*. January 1–December 29, 1857.

[APA36]: *Libro Copiador de las Comunicaciones Dirigidas a las Direcciones de Gobierno, Policía y Obras Públicas*. 1893.

[APA37]: *Libro Copiador de Licencias Expedidas Por Este Despacho [la Subprefectura del Cercado]*. 1898, 1899, 1900.

[APA38]: *Libro de Caja, Junta de Pro-Desocupados de Amazonas*. Consecutive years, 1931–37.

[APA39]: *Libro de la Corte Superior de Cajamarca y Juzgados de Primera Instancia de Amazonas*. 1894.

[APA40]: *Matrícula de Contribuciones del Departamento de Amazonas. Rectificada Para 1912*. Lima: Imprenta del Estado.

[APA41]: *Matrícula de Contribuyentes. Quinquenio de 1918–22. Departamento de Amazonas. Provincia de Luya*. Lima: Imprenta del Estado.

[APA42]: *Matrícula de Contribuyentes (Rectificacion). Departamento de Amazonas. Provincias de Bongorá [sic], Chachapoyas y Luya*. 1906.

[APA43]: *Memoria Administrativa, que el Prefecto del departamento de Amazonas, Don Eloy Burga, presenta al Sr. Director del Gobierno*. 1894.

[APA44]: *Memoria de su Presidente Señor José Gabriel Baella, Junta de Pro-Desocupados, Chachapoyas*. May 1934.

[APA45]: *Mesa de Partes, Prefectura del Departamento de Amazonas 1897–1904, 1907*.

[APA46]: *Oficios, Gobernadores al Prefecto*. 1931.

[APA47]: *Oficios a la Prefectura de los Diferentes Gobernadores*. 1919.

[APA48]: *Oficios de las Diversas Autoridades del Departamento*. 1929.

[APA49]: *Oficios del Juzgado del Cercado*. 1934.

[APA50]: *Oficios de Varios Gobernadores*. 1890.

[APA51]: *Oficios Dirijidos [Por la Subprefectura del Cercado] a la Prefectura y Demas Autoridades del Departamento*. March 12–October 31, 1919.

[APA52]: *Oficios i Otros Documentos de la Junta Departamental Pro-Desocupoados de Amazonas*. Consecutive years, 1931–37.

[APA53]: *Oficios Recibidos de las Gobernaciones del Departamento, 1927, 1929*.

[APA54]: *Oficios Recibidos de Varios Gobernadores*. 1886, 1887.

[APA55]: *Prefecto al Subprefecto [del Cercado] y Correspondencias de Varios Gobernadores*. 1919.

[APA56]: *El Registro de Amazonas. Publicación Oficial* [weekly newspaper; assorted issues]. July 4–December 19, 1874.

[APA57]: *El Registro Oficial del Departamento de Amazonas* [newspaper; assorted issues]. 1910.

[APA58]: *Resoluciones de la Prefectura.* August 9, 1933–April 30, 1934.

[APA59]: *Subprefecto de Chachapoyas al Prefecto.* 1898, 1913.

[APA60]: *Subprefecto del Cercado al Prefecto del Departamento de Amazonas.* 1891.

[APA61]: *Subprefectura del Cercado al Prefecto,* 1893, 1894, 1895, 1896, 1898, 1915, 1932.

[APA62]: *Subprefectura [del Cercado] a la Prefectura.* April 1913.

[APA63]: *Subprefectura del Cercado de Chachapoyas. Libro Copiador de Oficios a Diferentes Autoridades.* 1893–95.

[APA64]: *Subprefectura del Cercado de Chachapoyas.* Second semester, 1920.

[APA65]: *Subprefectura de Luya al Prefecto.* 1893.

[APA66]: *Tesorería Fiscal a la Prefectura del Departamento de Amazonas.* 1913.

[APA67]: *Tesorería Fiscal de Amazonas.* 1908.

[APA68]: *Juzgados.* 1881–82.

Other Primary Sources

[OPS1]: *Colección de Artículos.* 1922. *"Colección de artículos sobre el movimiento revolucionario del 5 de Agosto de 1921." El Oriente* [newspaper]. Apr. 1, 1922 [no publisher listed].

[OPS2]: *Redención* [newspaper; assorted issues]. 1930–31.

[OPS3]: *Registro de Bautismos.* 1870–1935. Main Cathedral, Chachapoyas.

[OPS4]: *Registro de Matrimonios.* 1870–1935. Main Cathedral, Chachapoyas.

SECONDARY SOURCES

Abrams, Philip. 1988. "Notes on the Difficulty of Studying the State." *Journal of Historical Sociology* 1: 58–89.

Acuña Ortega, Victor Hugo. 1993. "Clases subalternas y movimientos sociales en Centroamerica (1870–1930)." In V. H. Acuña Ortega, ed., *Las repúblicas agroexportadoras (1870–1945).* Madrid: Ediciones Siruela.

Acuña Ortega, Victor Hugo, and Iván Molina Jiménez. 1991. *Historia económica y social de Costa Rica (1750–1950).* San José: Porvenir.

Aguilar Briceño, Luis A. 1963. "Mi Departamento Amazonas." *Estudio Monográfico.* Lima: Imprenta DPPGC.

Aguirre Beltran, Gonzalo. 1976. *Obra polémica.* Mexico: Instituto Nacional de Antropología e Historia.

Alexander, Robert J. 1974. *Aprismo; The Ideas and Doctrines of Victor Raul Haya de la Torre.* Kent, Ohio: Kent State University Press.

Anderson, Benedict. 1983. *Imagined Communities: Reflections on the Origin and Spread of Nationalism.* London: Verso.

———. 1991. "Census, Map, Museum." Chapter 10 of *Imagined Communities:*

Reflections on the Origin and Spread of Nationalism. Rev. ed. London: Verso.

Aquezolo Castro, Manuel. 1976. *La polémica del indigenismo.* Lima: Mosca Azul Editores.

Ayarza, Victor R. 1921. *Reseña histórica del senado del Peru.* Lima: Imprenta Torres Aguirre.

Baram, A. 1992. "Territorial Nationalism in the Middle East." *Middle Eastern Studies* 26 (4): 425–48.

Barry, Brian. 1978. "Ethnicity and the State." In D. J. R. Bruckner, ed., *Politics and Language: Spanish and English in the United States.* Chicago: University of Chicago Press.

Basadre, Jorge. 1968–69. *Historia de la República del Perú, 1822–1933.* 6th ed. 17 vols. Lima: Editorial Universitaria.

———. 1980. *Elecciones y centralismo en el Perú.* Lima: Centro de Investigación de la Universidad del Pacífico.

Bates, Robert. 1982. "Modernization, Ethnic Competition, and the Rationality of Politics in Contemporary Africa." In Donald Rothchild and Victor A. Olorunsola, eds., *State Versus Ethnic Claims: African Policy Dilemmas,* 152–71. Boulder, Colo.: Westview Press.

Bauman, Zygmunt. 1989. *Modernity and the Holocaust.* Ithaca, N.Y.: Cornell University Press.

Bendix, Regina. 1992. "National Sentiment in the Enactment and Discourse of Swiss Political Ritual." *American Ethnologist* 19 (4): 768–90.

Bendix, Reinhard. 1964. *Nation-Building and Citizenship.* New York: Wiley.

Biolsi, Thomas. 1995. "The Birth of the Reservation: Making the Modern Individual Among the Lakota." *American Ethnologist* 22 (2): 28–53.

Blanchard, Peter. 1982. *The Origins of the Peruvian Labor Movement, 1883–1919.* Pittsburgh: University of Pittsburgh Press.

Blok, Anton. 1975. *The Mafia of a Sicilian Village, 1860–1960: A Study of Violent Peasant Entrepreneurs.* New York: Harper & Row.

Bonilla, Heraclio, Pierre Chaunu, Tulio Halperin, Pierre Vilar, Karen Spalding, and E. J. Hobsbawm. 1972. *La Independencia en el Perú.* Lima: Instituto de Estudios Peruanos (IEP).

Borneman, John. 1993. "Uniting the German Nation: Law, Narrative, and Historicity." *American Ethnologist* 20 (2): 288–311.

Bourdieu, Pierre. 1977. *Outline of a Theory of Practice.* Cambridge: Cambridge University Press.

Bourricaud, Francois. 1966. *Ideología y Desarrollo. El caso del partido Aprista Peruana.* Mexico: El Colegio de México.

Brading, David. 1985. *The Origins of Mexican Nationalism.* Cambridge: Centre of Latin American Studies.

Brass, Paul. 1974. *Language, Religion and Politics in North India*. Cambridge: Cambridge University Press.

―――. 1994. *Ethnicity and Nationalism: Theory and Comparison*. Newbury Park, Calif.: Sage Publications.

Brow, James. 1988. "In Pursuit of Hegemony: Representations of Authority and Justice in a Sri Lankan Village." *American Ethnologist* 15 (2): 311–27.

Brown, Michael, and Eduardo Fernandez. 1991. *War of Shadows: The Struggle for Utopia in the Peruvian Amazon*. Berkeley: University of California Press.

Bruckner, D. J. R., ed. 1978. *Politics and Language: Spanish and English in the United States*. Chicago: University of Chicago Press.

Brush, Stephen. 1977. *Mountain, Field, and Family: The Economy and Human Ecology of an Andean Valley*. Philadelphia: University of Pennsylvania Press.

Burga, Manuel, and Alberto Flores Galindo. 1979. *Apogeo y Crisis de la República Aristocrática*. Lima: IEP.

Caravedo, Baltazar. 1977. *Clases, lucha política, y gobierno en el Perú, 1919–1930*. Lima: Ediciones Retama.

―――. 1979a. *Burguesía e industria en el Perú*. Lima: IEP.

―――. 1979b. "Poder central y decentralización. Peru, 1931." *Apuntes* 5 (9): 111–29.

―――. 1983. *El problema del descentralismo*. Lima: Centro de Investigación de la Universidad del Pacífico.

Caso, Alfonso. 1971. *La comunidad indígena*. Mexico: Secretaría de Educación Pública.

Chatterjee, Partha. 1986. *Nationalist Thought and the Colonial World: A Derivative Discourse?* London: Zed Books.

―――. 1989. "Colonialism, Nationalism, and Colonized Women: The Contest in India." *American Ethnologist* 16 (4): 622–33.

―――. 1993. *The Nation and Its Fragments: Colonial and Postcolonial Histories*. Princeton: Princeton University Press.

Chevalier, Francois. 1970. "Official Indigenismo in Peru in 1920: Origins, Significance, and Socioeconomic Scope." In Magnus Morner, ed., *Race and Class in Latin America*, 184–96. New York: Columbia University Press.

Cohen, Abner. 1969. *Custom and Politics in Urban Africa*. Berkeley: University of California Press.

Cohen, Ronald, and Judith D. Toland, eds. 1988. *State Formation and Political Legitimacy*. New Brunswick, N.J.: Transaction Books.

Cohn, Bernard S. 1987. "The Census, Social Structure, and Objectification in South Asia." In Bernard S. Cohn, ed., *An Anthropologist Among the Historians and Other Essays*, 224–54. Delhi: Oxford University Press.

Cohn, Bernard S., and Nicholas B. Dirks. 1988. "Beyond the Fringe: The Nation State, Colonialism, and the Technologies of Power." *Journal of Historical Sociology* 1 (2): 224–29.

Collantes Pizarro, Gustavo. 1969. *Datos Históricos del Departamento de Amazonas.* Chiclayo, Peru: Imprente "El Arte."

Collier, David, and Ruth Berins Collier. 1991. *Shaping the Political Arena: Critical Junctures, the Labor Movement, and Regime Dynamics in Latin America.* Princeton: Princeton University Press.

Collins, Jane L. 1988. *Unseasonal Migrations: Rural Labor Scarcity in Peru.* Princeton: Princeton University Press.

Colls, Robert, and Philip Dodd, eds. 1986. *Englishness: Politics and Culture, 1880-1920.* Beckenham: Croom Helm.

Comaroff, John, and Jean Comaroff. 1991. *Of Revelation and Revolution: Christianity, Colonialism, and Consciousness in South Africa.* Vol. 1. Chicago: University of Chicago Press.

Cooper, Frederick, and Ann L. Stoler. 1989. "Tensions of Empire: Colonial Control and Visions of Rule." *American Ethnologist* 16 (4): 609–21.

Córdova, Arnaldo. 1973. *La ideología de la Revolución Mexicana: La formación del nuevo régimen.* Mexico: Ediciones Era.

Cornejo Koster, Enrique. 1941. "Crónica del movimiento estudiantil peruano." In Juan Carlos Portantiero, ed., *Estudiantes y Política en América Latina: El proceso de la reforma universitaria (1918–1938),* 232–66. México: Siglo XXI.

Cornelius, Wayne. 1973. "Nation Building, Participation, and Distribution: The Politics of Social Reform Under Cárdenas." In Gabriel A. Almond, Scott L. Flanagan, and Robert J. Mundt, eds., *Crisis, Choice, and Change: Historical Studies of Political Development,* 392–498. Boston: Little, Brown.

Corrigan, Philip, and Derek Sayer. 1981. "How the Law Rules." In Bob Fryer, Alan Hunt, Doreen McBarnet, and Bert Moorhouse, eds., *Law, State, and Society.* Beckenham: Croom Helm.

———. 1985. *The Great Arch: English State Formation As Cultural Revolution.* Oxford: Basil Blackwell.

———. 1987. "From 'The Body Politic' to 'The National Interest': English State Formation in Comparative and Historical Perspective." Paper presented to the Mellon Symposium on Historical Anthropology, California Institute of Technology, Pasadena, California.

Cotler, Julio. 1978. *Clases, estado y nación en el Perú.* Lima: IEP.

Deere, Carmen Diana. 1990. *Household and Class Relations: Peasants and Landlords in Northern Peru.* Berkeley: University of California Press.

Denich, Bette. 1994. "Dismembering Yugoslavia: Nationalist Ideologies and the Symbolic Revival of Genocide." *American Ethnologist* 21 (2): 367–90.

Derengil, Selim. 1993. "The Invention of Tradition as Public Image in the Late

Ottoman Empire, 1808–1908." *Comparative Studies in Society and History* 35 (1): 3–29.

Deustua, José. 1984. *Intelectuales, indigenismo, y descentralismo en el Perú, 1897–1931*. Cusco: Centro de Estudios Rurales Andinos "Bartolome de las Casas."

Deutsch, Karl. 1953. *Nationalism and Social Communication: An Inquiry Into the Foundations of Nationalism*. Cambridge: Technology Press of MIT.

Deutsch, Karl, and W. Foltz, eds. 1963. *Nation-Building*. New York: Atherton Press.

DeWind, Adrian. 1977. "Peasants Become Miners: The Evolution of Industrial Mining in Peru." Ph.D. diss., Columbia University, New York, N.Y.

Dominguez, Virginia R. 1986. *White By Definition: Social Classification in Creole Louisiana*. New Brunswick, N.J.: Rutgers University Press.

———. 1989. *People as Subject, People as Object: Selfhood and Peoplehood in Contemporary Israel*. Madison: University of Wisconsin Press.

Douglas, Mary. 1966. *Purity and Danger: An Analysis of Concepts of Pollution and Taboo*. London: Routledge and Kegan Paul.

Drake, Paul. 1978. *Socialism and Populism in Chile, 1932–52*. Urbana: University of Illinois Press.

Echegaray, I. R. 1966. *La cámara de diputados y las constituyentes del Perú*. Lima: Imprenta del Ministerio de Hacienda y Comercio.

Edelman, Marc. 1994. "Landlords and the Devil: Class, Ethnic, and Gender Dimensions of Central American Peasant Narratives." *Cultural Anthropology* 9 (1): 58–93.

Errington, S. 1989. "Fragile Traditions and Contested Meanings." *Public Culture* 1 (2): 49–65.

Escalante Gonzalbo, Fernando. 1992. *Ciudadanos imaginarios: Memorial de los afanes y desventuras de la virtud y apología del vicio triunfante en la República Mexicana, tratado de moral pública*. Mexico City: El Colegio de México.

Evans, Kristi S. 1992. "The Argument of Images: Historical Representation in Solidarity Underground Postage, 1891–87." *American Ethnologist* 19 (4): 749–67.

Favre, Henri. 1965. *La evolución de la situación de las haciendas en la región de Huancavelica, Perú*. Lima: IEP.

Fayt, Carlos S. 1967. *La naturaleza del Peronismo*. Buenos Aires: Viracocha.

Feijóo Reina, Ricardo. 1934. *Cuestiones constitucionales*. Lima: Imprenta "La Confianza."

———. 1935. *Departamento de Amazonas: Labor Parlamentaria*. Lima: Imprenta "La Confianza."

Flores, Richard R. 1995. "Private Visions, Public Culture: The Making of the Alamo." *Cultural Anthropology* 10 (1): 99–115.

Flores-Galindo, Alberto. 1977. *Arequipa y el Sur Andina: Siglos XVII–XX*. Lima: Horizonte.

Foucault, Michel. 1980. *Power/Knowledge*. Ed. Colin Gordon. New York: Pantheon.

Fox, Richard G. 1971. *Kin, Clan, Raja and Rule: State-Hinterland Relations in Preindustrial India*. Berkeley: University of California Press.

———. 1990a. "Introduction." In Fox 1990c, 1–14.

———. 1990b. "Hindu Nationalism in the Making, or the Rise of the Hindian." In Fox 1990c, 63–80.

———, ed. 1990c. *Nationalist Ideologies and the Production of National Cultures*. American Ethnological Society Monograph Series, no. 2. Washington, D.C.: American Anthropological Association.

Frader, Laura, and Sonya O. Rose., eds. 1996. *Gender and the Reconstruction of European Working Class History*. Ithaca, N.Y.: Cornell University Press.

Frykman, Jonas, and Orvar Lofgren. 1987. *Culture Builders: A Historical Anthropology of Middle-Class Life*. Translated by Alan Crozier. New Brunswick, N.J.: Rutgers University Press.

Gable, Eric, Richard Handler, and Anna Lawson. 1992. "On the Uses of Relativism: Fact, Conjecture, and Black and White Histories at Colonial Williamsburg." *American Ethnologist* 19 (4): 791–805.

Gamio, Manuel. 1960. *Forjando patria*. Mexico City: Editorial Porrúa.

Geertz, Clifford. 1963. "The Integrative Revolution: Primordial Sentiments and Civil Politics in the New States." In Clifford Geertz, ed., *Old Societies and New States*. 105–57. Glencoe, Ill.: Free Press.

Gellner, Ernest. 1983. *Nations and Nationalism*. Ithaca, N.Y.: Cornell University Press.

Genaro Matos, Teniente Coronel (R.). 1968. *Operaciones irregulares al norte de Cajamarca: Chota, Cutervo, Santa Cruz, 1924–25 a 1927*. Lima: Imprenta del Ministerio de Guerra.

Giddens, Anthony. 1981–85. *A Contemporary Critique of Historical Materialism*. 2 vols. Berkeley: University of California Press.

Gill, Leslie. 1993. "'Proper Women' and City Pleasures: Gender, Class, and Contested Meanings in La Paz." *American Ethnologist* 20 (1): 72–88.

Gilman, Sander. 1991. *The Jew's Body*. New York: Routledge.

Gilroy, Paul. 1991. *There Ain't No Black in the Union Jack: The Cultural Politics of Race and Nation*. Chicago: University of Chicago Press.

Gitlitz, John. 1979. "Conflictos políticos en la sierra norte del Perú: La montonera Benel contra Leguía, 1924." *Estudios Andinos (Lima)* 9 (16): 127–38.

Gonzales, Michael J. 1980. "Capitalist Agriculture and Labour Contracting in Northern Peru, 1880–1905." *Journal of Latin American Studies* 12: 291–315.

———. 1985. *Plantation Agriculture and Social Control in Northern Peru, 1875–1933*. Austin: University of Texas Press.

Gootenberg, Paul. 1989. *Between Silver and Guano: Commercial Policy and the State in Post-Independence Peru.* Princeton: Princeton University Press.

Gorman, Stephen. 1979. "The State, Elite and Export in Nineteenth-Century Peru." *Journal of Interamerican Studies and World Affairs* 21: 395–418.

Gourevitch, Peter. 1979. "The Reemergence of 'Peripheral Nationalisms': Some Comparative Speculations on the Spatial Distribution of Political Leadership and Economic Growth." *Comparative Studies in Society and History* 21: 295–314.

Graham, Richard, ed. 1990. *The Idea of Race in Latin America, 1870–1940.* Austin: University of Texas Press.

Gramsci, Antonio. 1971. *Selections from the Prison Notebooks.* New York: International Publishers.

Gupta, Akhil. 1995. "Blurred Boundaries: the Discourse of Corruption, the Culture of Politics, and the Imagined State." *American Ethnologist* 22 (2): 375–402.

Gurr, Ted Robert. 1989. "War, Revolution, and the Growth of the Coercive State." In James A. Caporaso, ed., *The Elusive State: International and Comparative Perspectives*, 49–68. Newbury Park, Calif.: Sage.

Gusfield, Joseph. 1973. "The Social Construction of Tradition: An Interactionist View of Social Change." In D. Legge, ed., *Traditional Attitudes and Modern Styles in Political Leadership*, 83–104. Melbourne: Angus & Robertson.

Hale, Charles A. 1986. "Political and Social Ideas in Latin America, 1870–1930." In Leslie Bethell, ed., *The Cambridge History of Latin America*, vol. 14 (c. 1870–1930), 367–441. Cambridge: Cambridge University Press.

Handler, Richard. 1988. *Nationalism and the Politics of Culture in Quebec.* Madison: University of Wisconsin Press.

Haraway, Donna. 1989. *Primate Visions: Gender, Race, and Nature in the World of Modern Science.* New York: Routledge.

Harvey, David. 1989. *The Condition of Post-Modernity.* Cambridge: Basil Blackwell.

Haya de la Torre, Victor Raúl. 1977. *Obras Completas.* 7 vols. Lima: J. Mejía Baca Editores.

Hegel, G. W. F. 1967. *The Phenomenology of Mind.* Translated by J. B. Baillie. New York: Harper & Row.

Hertz, Frederick. 1944. *Nationality in History and Politics: A Psychology and Sociology of National Sentiment and Nationalism.* New York: Oxford University Press.

Herzfeld, Michael. 1982. *Ours Once More: Folklore, Ideology, and the Making of Modern Greece.* Austin: University of Texas Press.

———. 1986. "Of Definitions and Boundaries: The Status of Culture in the Culture of the State." In P. P. Chock and J. R. Wyman, eds., *Discourse and the Social Life of Meaning*, 75–94. Washington, D.C.: Smithsonian Institute Press.

———. 1987. *Anthropology Through the Looking Glass: Critical Ethnography in the Margins of Europe*. Cambridge: Cambridge University Press.

Hobsbawm, Eric J. 1962. *The Age of Revolution, 1789–1848*. New York: New American Library.

———. 1975. *The Age of Capital, 1848–1875*. New York: Scribner.

———. 1990. *Nations and Nationalism Since 1780: Programme, Myth, Reality*. Cambridge: Cambridge University Press.

Hobsbawm, Eric, and Terence Ranger, eds. 1983. *The Invention of Tradition*. Cambridge: Cambridge University Press.

Ingenieros, José, and Victor Raul Haya de la Torre. 1928. *Teoría y táctica de la acción renovadora antimperialista de la juventud en América latina*. Buenos Aires: Editorial Claridad.

Jacobsen, Nils. 1988. "Free Trade, Regional Elites and the Internal Market in Southern Peru, 1895–1932." In Joseph L. Love and Nils Jacobsen, eds., *Guiding the Invisible Hand*, 145–76. New York: Praeger.

———. 1993. *Mirages of Transition: The Peruvian Altiplano, 1780–1930*. Berkeley: University of California Press.

Johnson, John J. 1958. *Political Change in Latin America: The Emergence of the Middle Sectors*. Stanford: Stanford University Press.

Jongkind, Fred. 1974. "A Reappraisal of the Role of the Regional Associations of Lima, Peru." *Comparative Studies in Society and History* 16: 471–82.

Joseph, Gilbert M., and Daniel Nugent, eds. 1994. *Everyday Forms of State Formation: Revolution and the Negotiation of Rule in Modern Mexico*. Durham, N.C.: Duke University Press.

Kapferer, Bruce. 1988. *Legends of People, Myths of State: Violence, Intolerance, and Political Culture in Sri Lanka and Australia*. Washington, D.C.: Smithsonian Institute Press.

Kaplan, Martha. 1995. "Panopticon in Poona: An Essay on Foucault and Colonialism." *Cultural Anthropology* 10 (1): 85–98.

Karno, Howard L. 1973. "Julio César Arana, Frontier Cacique in Peru." In Robert Kern, ed., *The Caciques: Oligarchical Politics and the System of Caciquismo in the Luso-Hispanic World*, 89–98. Albuquerque: University of New Mexico Press.

Kasfir, Nelson. 1979. "Explaining Ethnic Political Participation." *World Politics* 31: 365–88.

Kelly, John D. 1995. "Threats to Difference in Colonial Fiji." *Cultural Anthropology* 10 (1): 64–84.

Klaiber, Jeffrey L. 1975. "The Popular Universities and the Origins of Aprismo, 1921–1924." *Hispanic American Historical Review* 55 (4): 693–715.

————. 1992. *The Catholic Church in Peru, 1821–1985: A Social History.* Washington, D.C.: Catholic University of America Press.

Klaren, Peter F. 1973. "Modernization, Dislocation and Aprismo." Institute of Latin American Studies, Latin American Monographs, no. 32. Austin: University of Texas Press.

————. 1988. "The Origins of Modern Peru, 1880–1930." In Leslie Bethell, ed., *The Cambridge History of Latin America*, vol. 5 (1870–1930), 587–640. Cambridge: Cambridge University Press.

Lagos, Maria L. 1993. "'We Have to Learn to Ask': Hegemony, Diverse Experiences, and Antagonistic Meanings in Bolivia." *American Ethnologist* 20 (1): 52–71.

Laitin, David D. 1985. "Hegemony and Religious Conflict: British Imperial Control and Political Cleavages in Yorubaland." In Peter Evans, Dietrich Rueschemeyer, and Theda Skocpol, eds., *Bringing the State Back In*, 285–316. Cambridge: Cambridge University Press.

————. 1992. *Language Repertoires and State Construction in Africa.* Cambridge: Cambridge University Press.

Laitin, David D., and Said S. Samatar. 1987. *Somalia: Nation in Search of a State.* Boulder, Colo.: Westview Press.

Larson, Brooke. 1988. *Colonialism and Agrarian Transformation in Bolivia: Cochabamba, 1550–1900.* Princeton: Princeton University Press.

Lass, A. 1988. "Romantic Documents and Political Monuments: The Meaning-Fulfillment of History in Nineteenth-Century Czech Nationalism." *American Ethnologist* 15 (3): 456–71.

Lemarchand, René. 1982. "The State and Society in Africa." In Donald Rothchild and Victor A. Olorunsola, eds., *State Versus Ethnic Claims: African Policy Dilemmas*, 44–66. Boulder, Colo.: Westview Press.

Lewin, Linda. 1987. *Politics and Parentela in Paraíba: A Case Study of Family-Based Oligarchy in Brazil.* Princeton: Princeton University Press.

Llobera, J. R. 1990. "Catalan National Identity: The Dialectics of Past and Present." *Critique of Anthropology* 19 (2–3): 11–38.

Lloyd, Peter. 1980. *The 'Young Towns' of Lima: Aspects of Urbanization in Peru.* Cambridge: Cambridge University Press.

Lobo, Susan. 1982. *A House of My Own: Social Organization in the Squatter Settlements of Lima, Peru.* Tucson: University of Arizona Press.

Lofgren, Orvar. 1989a. "Anthropologizing America." *American Ethnologist* 16 (2): 366–74.

————. 1989b. "The Nationalization of Culture." *Ethnologia Europaea* 19 (1): 5–24.

————. 1995. "Being a Good Swede: National Identity as a Cultural Background." In Jane Schneider and Rayna Rapp, eds., *Articulating Hidden His-*

tories: Exploring the Influence of Eric R. Wolf, 262–74. Berkeley: University of California Press.

Lomnitz-Adler, Claudio. 1992. *Exits from the Labyrinth: Culture and Ideology in the Mexican National Space*. Berkeley: University of California Press.

Lustick, Ian. 1980. *Arabs in the Jewish State: A Study in the Control of a Minority Population*. Austin: University of Texas Press.

Macartney, C. A. 1934. *National States and National Minorities*. London: Oxford University Press.

McClelland, Keith. 1993. "Rational and Responsible Men: Gender, the Working Class, and Citizenship in Britain, 1850–1867." Paper presented at the Annual Meeting of the Social Science History Association, Baltimore, Md., Nov. 4–7.

McEvoy, Carmen. 1995. "La utopia republicana: Política Peruana, 1871–1919." Ph.D. diss., Department of History, University of California at San Diego.

Mallon, Florencia. 1983a. "Murder in the Andes: Patrons, Clients and the Impact of Foreign Capital, 1860–1922." *Radical History Review* 27: 79–98.

———. 1983b. *The Defense of Community in Peru's Central Highlands*. Princeton: Princeton University Press.

———. 1995. *Peasant and Nation: The Making of Postcolonial Mexico and Peru*. Berkeley: University of California Press.

Mandel, Ernest. 1975. *Late Capitalism*. London: Verso.

Mangin, William. 1959. "The Role of Regional Associations in the Adaptation of the Rural Population of Peru." *Sociologus* 9: 23–35.

Manrique, Nelson. 1988. *Yawar Mayu: Sociedades terratenientes serranas, 1879–1910*. Lima: DESCO (Centro de Estudios y Promoción del Desarrollo).

Marriot, M. 1963. "Cultural Policy in the New States." In Clifford Geertz, ed., *Old Societies and New States: The Quest for Modernity in Asia and Africa*, 27–56. Glencoe, Ill.: Free Press.

Marzal, Manuel María. 1981. *Historia de la antropología indigenista: Mexico y Peru*. Lima: Pontificia Universidad Católica del Perú.

Mayer, Enrique. 1985. "Production Zones." In S. Masuda, I. Shimada, and C. Morris, eds., *Andean Ecology and Civilization: An Interdisciplinary Perspective on Andean Ecological Complementarity*, 45–84. Tokyo: University of Tokyo Press.

Mehta, Uday. 1990. "Liberal Strategies of Exclusion." *Politics and Society* 18: 427–54.

Migdal, Joel. 1988. *Strong Societies and Weak States: State-Society Relations and State Capabilities in the Third World*. Princeton: Princeton University Press.

Miller, Rory. 1982. "The Coastal Elite and Peruvian Politics, 1895–1919." *Journal of Latin American Studies* 14: 97–120.

————. 1987. "Introduction." In Rory Miller, ed., *Region and Class in Modern Peruvian History*, 7–20. Institute of Latin American Studies Monograph, no. 14. Liverpool: University of Liverpool.

Ministerio de Hacienda y Comercia [MHC]. 1942. *Censo nacional de población de 1940, Tomos III, IX*. Lima: Dirección Nacional de Estadística, República del Perú.

Mitchell, Timothy. 1988. *Colonizing Egypt*. Cambridge: Cambridge University Press.

————. 1991. "The Limits of the State: Beyond Statist Approaches and Their Critics." *American Political Science Review* 85: 77–96.

Morales, Edmundo. 1989. *Cocaine: White Gold Rush in Peru*. Tucson: University of Arizona Press.

Morner, Magnus. 1985. *The Andean Past: Land, Societies, and Conflicts*. New York: Columbia University Press.

Mosse, George. 1985. *Nationalism and Sexuality*. Madison: University of Wisconsin Press.

Murmis, Miguel, and Juan Carlos Portantiero. 1971. *Estudios sobre los orígenes del Peronismo*. Vol. 1. Buenos Aires: Siglo XXI.

Murra, John. 1972. "El 'control vertical' de un máximo de pisos ecológicas en la economía de las sociedades andinas." In Iñigo Ortiz de Zuñiga, ed., *Visita de la provincia de León de Huánuco en 1562*, 2: 429–76. Huánuco, Peru: Hermilio Valdizán.

Nairn, Tom. 1977. *The Break-up of Britain: Crisis and Neo-Functionalism*. London: New Left Books.

Nettl, J. P. 1968. "The State as a Conceptual Variable." *World Politics* 20: 559–92.

Nugent, David. 1988. "The Mercantile Transformation of Provincial Urban Life: Labor, Value and Time in the Northern Peruvian Sierra." Ph.D. diss., Anthropology Department, Columbia University, New York, N.Y.

————. 1991. "Control of Space, Stability of Time: The State as Arbiter of Surplus Flows." In Alice Littlefield and Hill Gates, eds., *Marxist Approaches in Economic Anthropology*, 161–85. Society for Economic Anthropology, Monographs in Economic Anthropology, no. 9. Lanham, Md.: University Press of America.

————. 1994. "Building the State, Making the Nation: The Bases and Limits of State Centralization in 'Modern' Peru." *American Anthropologist* 96 (2): 333–69.

————. 1995a. "Structuring the Consciousness of Resistance: State Power, Regional Conflict and Political Culture in Contemporary Peru." In Jane Schneider and Rayna Rapp, eds., *Articulating Hidden Histories: Essays on the Influence of Eric R. Wolf*, 207–27. Berkeley: University of California Press.

————. 1995b. "Artisanal Cooperation, Forms of Labor, and the Global Economy: Chachapoyas, 1930s to the 1990s." *Journal of Historical Sociology* 8 (1): 36–58.

———. 1996. "From Devil Pacts to Drug Deals: Commerce, Unnatural Accumulation and Moral Community in Modern Peru." *American Ethnologist* 23 (2): 258–90.

O'Brien, Jay, and William Roseberry, eds. 1991. *Golden Ages, Dark Ages: Imagining the Past in Anthropology and History.* Berkeley: University of California Press.

Oinas, Felix J., ed. 1978. *Folklore, Nationalism, and Politics.* Columbus, Ohio: Slavica Press.

Orlove, Benjamin. 1974. "Reciprocidad, desigualdad, y dominación." In Giorgio Alberti and Enrique Mayer, eds., *Reciprocidad e intercambio en los Andes peruanos,* 290–321. Lima: IEP.

———. 1977. *Alpacas, Sheep, and Men: The Wool Export Economy and Regional Society in Southern Peru.* New York: Academic Press.

———. 1993. "Putting Race in Its Place: Order in Colonial and Postcolonial Peruvian Geography." *Social Research* 60 (2): 301–36.

Parker, Andrew, Mary Russo, Doris Summer, and Patricia Yaeger, eds. 1992. *Nationalisms and Sexualities.* New York: Routledge.

Parker, David S. 1992. "White-Collar Lima, 1910–1929: Commercial Employees and the Rise of the Peruvian Middle Class." *Hispanic American Historical Review* 72 (1): 47–72.

Paz Soldan, Carlos Enrique. 1919. *De la inquietud a la revolución: Diez años de rebeldías universitarias (1909–1919).* Lima: Biblioteca de "La Reforma Médica."

Pennati, Eugenio. N.d. *Monseñor Octavio Ortiz Arrieta S.D.B. Obispo de Chachapoyas: Serie 'Vida Salesiana.'* Lima: Editorial Salesiana.

Peru, Dirección de Estadística. 1878. *Resumen del censo general de habitantes del Perú hecho en 1876.* Lima: Imprenta del Estado.

Pike, Frederick B. 1967. *The Modern History of Peru.* London: Weidenfeld and Nicholson.

Portantiero, Juan Carlos. 1978. *Estudiantes y política en América Latina: El proceso de la reforma universitaria (1918–1938).* Mexico City: Siglo XXI.

Rabinowitz, Dan. 1994. "To Sell or Not to Sell? Theory Versus Practice, Public Versus Private, and the Failure of Liberalism: The Case of Israel and Its Palestinian Citizens." *American Ethnologist* 21 (4): 827–44.

Redfield, Rolbert. 1955. *The Little Community.* Stockholm: Almquist & Wiksells Boktrycker.

Rénique, José Luis. 1979. *El movimiento descentralista Arequipeño y la crisis del '30.* Lima: Taller de Estudios Políticos, Universidad Católica del Perú.

———. 1991. *Los sueños de la sierra: Cusco en el siglo XX.* Lima: CEPES (Centro Peruano de Estudios Sociales).

Robinson, Francis. 1974. *Separatism Among Indian Muslims*. Cambridge: Cambridge University Press.

Rose, Sonya O. 1992. *Limited Livelihoods: Gender and Class in Nineteenth-Century England*. Berkeley: University of California Press.

———. 1993. "Respectable Men, Disorderly Others: The Language of Gender and the Lancashire Weavers' Strike of 1878 in Britain." *Gender and History* 5 (3): 382–97.

Roseberry, William. 1989. *Anthropologies and Histories*. New Brunswick, N.J.: Rutgers University Press.

Sabean, David. 1984. *Power in the Blood: Popular Culture and Village Discourse in Early Modern Europe*. Cambridge: Cambridge University Press.

Sahlins, Peter. 1989. *Boundaries: The Making of France and Spain in the Pyrenees*. Berkeley: University of California Press.

Salomone, F. A. 1992. "Playing at Nationalism: Nigeria, A Nation of 'Ringers'." *Geneva-Africa* 30 (1): 55–76.

Sanchez, Luis Alberto. 1934. *Haya de la Torre o el político*. Santiago, Chile: Biblioteca América.

Sarfatti Larson, Magali, and Arlene Eisen Bergman. 1969. *Social Stratification in Peru*. Berkeley: Institute of International Studies, University of California.

Sayer, Derek. 1992. "A Notable Administration: English State Formation and the Rise of Capitalism." *American Journal of Sociology* 97 (5): 1382–1415.

Schneider, Peter, Jand Schneider, and Edward Hansen. 1974. "Modernization and Development: The Role of Regional Elites and Noncorporate Groups in the European Mediterranean." *Comparative Studies in Society and History* 14: 328–50.

Scott, C. D. 1976. "Peasants, Proletarianization and the Articulation of Modes of Production: The Case of Sugar-Cane Cutters in Northern Peru, 1940–1969." *Journal of Peasant Studies* 3: 321–41.

Scott, James C. 1990. *Domination and the Arts of Resistance: Hidden Transcripts*. New Haven, Conn.: Yale University Press.

Seligman, Linda J. 1993. "The Burden of Visions Amidst Reform: Peasant Relations to Law in the Peruvian Andes." *American Ethnologist* 20 (1): 25–51.

Shils, Edward. 1957. "Primordial, Personal, Sacred and Civil Ties." *British Journal of Sociology* 8: 130–45.

Sider, Gerald. 1986. *Culture and Class in Anthropology and History: A Newfoundland Example*. New York: Cambridge University Press.

Skeldon, Ronald. 1976. "Regional Associations and Population Migration in Peru: An Interpretation." *Urban Anthropology* 5: 233–52.

Slater, David. 1989. *Territory and State Power in Latin America*. New York: St. Martin's Press.

Slotkin, Richard. 1985. *The Fatal Environment: The Myth of the Frontier in the Age of Industrialization, 1800–1890*. New York: Atheneum.

Smith, Anthony D. 1983. *State and Nation in the Third World*. New York: St. Martin's Press.

———. 1986. *The Ethnic Origins of Nations*. Oxford: Basil Blackwell.

Smith, Carol A. 1990a. "Failed Nationalist Movements in Nineteenth-Century Guatemala: A Parable for the Third World." In Fox 1990c, 148–77.

———. 1990b. "Introduction: Social Relations in Guatemala over Time and Space." In Carol A. Smith, ed., *Guatemalan Indians and the State: 1540–1988*, 1–30. Austin: University of Texas Press.

Smith, Gavin. 1989. *Livelihood and Resistance: Peasants and the Politics of Land in Peru*. Berkeley: University of California Press.

Southall, Aidan W. 1956. *Alur Society*. Cambridge: W. Heffner and Sons.

Spalding, Karen. 1975. "Hacienda-Village Relations in Andean Society to 1830." *Latin American Perspectives* 2: 107–22.

———. 1984. *Huarochiri: An Andean Society Under Inca and Spanish Rule*. Stanford: Stanford University Press.

Stein, Steve. 1980. *Populism in Peru: The Emergence of the Masses and the Politics of Social Control*. Madison: University of Wisconsin Press.

———. 1986. "Popular Culture and Politics in Early Twentieth-Century Lima." *New World* 1 (2): 65–91.

Stern, Steve J., ed. 1987. *Resistance, Rebellion, and Consciousness in the Andean Peasant World: Eighteenth to Twentieth Centuries*. Madison: University of Wisconsin Press.

Stocking, George. 1987. *Victorian Anthropology*. New York: Free Press.

Stoler, Ann L. 1989. "Making Empire Respectable: The Politics of Race and Sexual Morality in Twentieth-Century Colonial Cultures." *American Ethnologist* 16 (4): 634–60.

———. 1992. "Sexual Affronts and Racial Frontiers: European Identities and the Cultural Politics of Exclusion in Colonial Southeast Asia." *Comparative Studies in Society and History* 34 (3): 514–51.

Sulmont, Denis. 1975. *El movimiento obrero en el Perú, 1900–1956*. Lima: Pontificia Universidad Católica del Perú, Fondo Editorial.

Tamayo Herrera, José. 1980. *Historia del indigenismo cuzqueño, siglos xvi–xx*. Lima: Instituto Nacional de Cultura.

Taylor, Lewis. 1986. "Bandits and Politics in Peru: Landlord and Peasant Violence in Hualgayoc, 1900–1930." Centre of Latin American Studies. Cambridge Latin American Miniatures, no. 2. Cambridge: Cambridge University.

———. 1990. "Los orígenes del bandolerismo en Hualgayoc, 1870–1900." In Carlos Aguirre and Charles Walker, eds., *Bandoleros, abigeos y montoneros:*

Criminalidad y violencia en el Perú, siglos XVIII–XX, 213–45. Lima: Instituto de Apoyo Agrario/Pasado & Presente.

Thorp, Rosemary, and Geoffrey Bertram. 1978. *Peru, 1890–1977: Growth and Policy in an Open Economy.* New York: Columbia University Press.

Tilly, Charles. 1975. *The Formation of National States in Western Europe.* Princeton: Princeton University Press.

———. 1984. *Big Structures, Large Processes, Huge Comparisons.* New York: Russell Sage Foundation.

Trigger, Bruce G. 1984. "Alternative Archaeologies: Nationalist, Colonialist, Imperialist." *Man,* n.s. 19 (1): 355–70.

Urban, Greg, and Joel Sherzer. 1991. *Nation-States and Indians in Latin America.* Austin: University of Texas Press.

Urla, Jacqueline. 1993. "Cultural Politics in an Age of Statistics: Numbers, Nations, and the Making of Basque Identity." *American Ethnologist* 20 (4): 818–43.

Valcarcel, Luis E. 1925a. *Del Ayllu al imperio Inca.* Lima: Editorial Garcilaso.

———. 1925b. *De la vida Incaika, algunas captaciones del espíritu que la animó.* Lima: Editorial Garcilaso.

Vandergeest, Peter. 1993. "Constructing Thailand: Regulation, Everyday Resistance, and Citizenship." *Comparative Studies in Society and History* 35 (1): 133–58.

Vandergeest, Peter, and Nancy Lee Peluso. 1995. "Territorialization and State Power in Thailand." *Theory and Society* 24: 385–426

Vasconcelos, José. 1925. *La raza cósmica, misión de la raza iberoamericana.* Paris: Agencia Mundial de Librería.

Vega-Centeno Bocangel, Imelda. 1991. *Aprismo popular: Cultura, religion y política.* Lima: Tarea.

Verdery, Katherine. 1990. "The Production and Defense of 'The Romanian Nation'." In Fox 1990c, 81–111.

———. 1991. "Theorizing Socialism: A Prologue to the 'Transition'." In *Representations of Europe: Transforming State, Society, and Identity. American Ethnologist* 18 (3): 419–39, special issue.

Vincent, Joan. 1974. "The Structuring of Ethnicity." *Human Organization* 33: 375–79.

Wallerstein, Immanuel. 1967. "Class, Tribe and Party in West African Politics." In Seymour M. Lipset and Stein Rokkan, eds., *Party Systems and Voter Alignments.* 497–518. New York: Free Press.

Walter, Richard J. 1963. *Student Politics in Argentina: The University Reform Movement and Its Effects, 1918–1964.* New York: Basic Books.

Weffort, Francisco. 1970. "El populismo en la política brasileña." In Celso Furtado et al., *Brasíl hoy,* 54–84. Mexico City: Siglo XXI.

Weinstein, Barbara. 1983. *The Amazon Rubber Boom, 1850–1920*. Stanford: Stanford University Press.

Williams, Brackette F. 1989. "A Class Act: Anthropology and the Race to Nation Across Ethnic Terrain." *Annual Review of Anthropology* 18: 401–44.

———. 1990. "Nationalism, Traditionalism, and the Problem of Cultural Inauthenticity." In Fox 1990c, 112–29.

———. 1991. *Stains on My Name, War in My Veins*. Durham, N.C.: Duke University Press.

Wilson, Fiona. 1982. "Property and Ideology: A Regional Oligarchy in the Central Andes in the Nineteenth Century." In David Lehman, ed., *Ecology and Exchange in the Andes*, 191–210. Cambridge: Cambridge University Press.

———. 1990. "Ethnicity and Race: Discussion of a Contested Domain in Latin American Thought." In Agnete Weis Bentzon, ed., *The Language of Development Studies*. Copenhagen: New Social Science Monographs.

Wolf, Eric R. 1956. "Aspects of Group Relations in a Complex Society: Mexico." *American Anthropologist* 58: 1065–78.

———. 1966. *Peasants*. Englewood Cliffs, N.J.: Prentice-Hall.

———. 1968. *Peasant Wars of the Twentieth Century*. New York: Harper & Row.

———. 1982. *Europe and the People Without History*. Berkeley: University of California Press.

Wolf, Eric R., and Edward Hansen. 1967. "Caudillo Politics: A Structural Analysis." *Comparative Studies in Society and History* 9: 168–79.

Works, Martha Adrienne Teresa. 1984. "Agricultural Change Among the Alto Mayo Aguaruna, Eastern Peru: The Effects on Culture and Environment." Ph.D. diss., Department of Geography, Louisiana State University, Baton Rouge.

Wright, Patrick. 1985. *On Living in an Old Country: The National Past in Contemporary Britain*. London: Verso.

Yepes del Castillo, Ernesto. 1980. "Los inicios de la expansión mercantil capitalista en el Perú (1890–1930)." In Juan Mejía Baca, ed., *Historia del Perú*, 7: 305–403. Lima: Librería-Editorial J. Mejía Baca.

Zapata Cesti, Victor A. 1949. *Historia de la policía del Perú*. Lima: Dirección General de la Guardia Civil y Policía.

Zubiate Zabarburú, Alejandro. 1979. *Apuntes sobre la fundación de la ciudad de San Juan de la Frontera [Chachapoyas]*. Lima: n.p.

Index

In this index an "f" after a number indicates a separate reference on the next page, and an "ff" indicates separate references on the next two pages. A continuous discussion over two or more pages is indicated by a span of page numbers, e.g., "57–59." *Passim* is used for a cluster of references in close but not consecutive sequence.

124, 164, 259, 264, 292; and the economy, 27–28, 34–35, 332ff, 336; workers on a, 66, 98, 126, 185, 242–43; Amazonas compared to a, 183–84

Hat trade, 331–32, 335, 349

Haya de la Torre, Víctor Raúl, 234, 258, 366, 368

Hernandez, Alberto, 43

Highway, Amazonas, 191–94, 201, 272

Higos Urco, battle of, 23

Hohagen, Engineer, 151–54. *See also* Bridge across the Marañon

Home, description of, 35–36, 43–47 *passim*, 337; as a place for women, 219, 221–26, 228, 296, 361

Huayapa, Anselmo, 88–92

Humiliation, of enemies, 30–33, 73–79, 84, 107, 143, 148, 157f, 172, 174, 181, 280, 311–13, 358; of officials, 96–100; of subaltern groups, 184, 236, 242–49 *passim*, 255; of dependents, 334. *See also* Persecution of the opposition

Hurtado Cubas, Rosa Victoria, 136

Hurtado family, 30, 39, 113, 135, 258–63 *passim*, 268, 271, 340, 356, 365

Hurtado, Lizardo, 132, 135

Hurtado, Manuel, 54, 98, 106–11 *passim*, 135, 340, 352, 356f

Hurtado, Nicolas, 271

Hurtado Eguren, Carolina, 365

Hurtado Eguren family, 114, 352

Hurtado-Rodriguéz casta, 58, 61, 145–50 *passim*, 336, 340, 357

Hygiene, 212–18 *passim*, 225–28, 279, 316

Incas, 236–39 *passim*, 244, 246ff, 254, 316, 370

Independence, Wars of, 23, 352

Indian head tax, *see under* Tax

Indios (Indians), 19, 162, 165–68, 252, 303, 334f, 354, 371; dominated by white elite, 13, 15, 30, 36–38, 42, 57, 238, 243f, 256, 269, 309, 331; envisioned by *Amazonas*, 186–87, 212, 237, 295, 314; education of, 205–11, 219; as part of *el pueblo*, 185, 201, 204, 240f, 246, 313ff, 319, 362. *See also Runa*

Indigenismo, 360n

Inga brothers, 77–79, 346

Inheritance, 41, 55–56, 333, 336, 338

Iquitos, 24–25

Judge of the first instance (*juez de la primera instancia*), 48–52 *passim*, 76, 89–92 *passim*, 101, 155, 161, 187, 257, 267, 292, 337f, 345, 347; appointment of, 68–69, 105, 108, 367; Leonardo del Mazo as, 115–16, 353; Salvador M. Pizarro Alvis as, 48, 116–18, 120, 122, 351

Junta Investigadora (Investigative Council), 271–72, 274–75

Juntas de Pro-Desocupados, 284–85, 367. *See also* Public-works projects

Juntas de registro electoral (voter registration boards), 61–62, 105, 341

Junta Electoral Nacional, see National Election Board

Juntas escrutadoras, see Electoral review boards

Justice of the peace, 63–70 *passim*, 77–78, 95, 102, 250, 292, 337f, 347ff, 351, 355; appointment of, 50, 82–83, 86, 92, 121–22, 125, 347, 349; duties of, 51–52, 83, 161f, 338

"Kuelap" (sport club), 301–2, 370

"Laboring family of Amazonas," 202–5, 237, 240–41, 253–54, 262, 289, 360

LaTorre, Gaspar, 79

Leguía, Augusto, 108ff, 128ff, 139, 183, 273, 338, 351f; *oncenio* of, 17, 177–78, 234, 257–61 *passim*, 271, 359, 363–64, 370; fall from power, 16–17, 60–61, 73ff, 235, 257–64 *passim*; failed 1924 coup against, 59, 62, 259; and Pablo M. Pizarro, 63, 108, 351, 364. *See also under* Coup

Leon, Comandante, 352n

Lieutenant governor, 70, 95, 121–26 *passim*, 130, 168, 187, 333–38 *passim*, 355; appointment of, 50, 82–83, 86, 89, 121–22, 125, 347, 349; duties of, 51–52, 83, 161f, 333, 337f, 344

Lopez, Noe, 63–67 *passim*

Library of Congress Cataloging-in-Publication Data

Nugent, David
Modernity at the edge of empire : state, individual, and nation in the northern Peruvian Andes,
1885–1935 / David Nugent.
    p.   cm.
Includes bibliographical references and index.
ISBN 0-8047-2782-1 (cl : alk. paper). — ISBN 0-8047-2958-1 (pb : alk. paper)
1. National state—Case studies.   2. Nationalism—Peru—Chachapoyas (Province)—History—Case
studies.   3. Chachapoyas (Peru : Province)—Social conditions—Case studies.   4. Chachapoyas
(Peru : Province)—Politics and government—Case studies.
I. Title.
JC311.N838   1997
320.985'46—dc21   96-49742
CIP

(∞) This book is printed on acid-free paper.

Printed in Great Britain
by Amazon